Global Financial Markets at the
Turn of the Century

Series in International Business and Economics
Series Editor: Khosrow Fatemi

Titles include:

Related Elsevier Science Journals—Sample copy available on request

Global Financial Markets at the Turn of the Century

Edited by

Ilhan Meric
Rider University

and

Gulser Meric
Rowan University

2001
PERGAMON
An imprint of Elsevier Science

Amsterdam - London - New York - Oxford - Paris - Shannon - Tokyo

ELSEVIER SCIENCE Ltd
The Boulevard, Langford Lane
Kidlington, Oxford OX5 1GB, UK

First edition 2001

Library of Congress Cataloging in Publication Data
Global financial markets at the turn of the century/edited by Ilhan Meric and Gulser Meric.
    p. cm. – (Series in international business and economics)
    Includes bibliographical references and index.
    ISBN 0-08-043798-2 (alk. paper)
    1. Financial institutions. 2. Finance. I. Meric, Ilhan. II. Meric, Gulser. III. Series.
HG173.G635 2001
332–dc21   00-065448

British Library Cataloguing in Publication Data
Global financial markets at the turn of the century
    1. Financial institutions 2. Finance
    I. Meric, Ilhan II. Meric, Gulser
    332
ISBN 0-08-043798-2

Typeset by The Midlands Book Typesetting Company, United Kingdom.

♾ The paper used in this publication meets the requirements of ANSI/NISO Z39.48-1992 (Permanence of Paper).
Printed in The Netherlands.

Contents

Contributors

Alan Alford, KPMG-ECS, USA
Lakshman Alles, Curtin University of Technology, Western Australia
Parviz Asheghian, California State University–San Bernardino, USA
Alejandra Cabello, Universidad Nacional Autónoma de México, Mexico
Chun-Hao Chang, Florida International University, USA
Rosita P. Chang, University of Hawaii, USA
Andreas Christofi, Monmouth University, USA
Benjamin H. Eichhorn, Rider University, USA
S.G.M. Fifield, University of Dundee, UK
André Fourçans, ESSEC, France
Dilip K. Ghosh, Rutgers-the State University of New Jersey, USA
Jean-Pierre Gueyie, Université de Quebec à Montreal, Canada
Iftekhar Hasan, New Jersey Institute of Technology, USA
Tanweer Hasan, Roosevelt University, USA
Kurt R. Jesswein, Murray State University, USA
Halil Kiymaz, University of Houston–Clear Lake, USA
Ramakrishnan S. Koundinya, Bernard M. Baruch College, USA
Ricardo P.C. Leal, Federal University of Rio de Janeiro, Brazil
François M. Longin, ESSEC, France
A.A. Lonie, University of Dundee, UK
Roswell Mathis, New Jersey Institute of Technology, USA
Gulser Meric, Rowan University, USA
Ilhan Meric, Rider University, USA
Abraham Mulugetta, Ithaca College, USA
Yuko Mulugetta, Cornell University, USA
Kasume Nishiyama, Prebon Yamane (USA Inc.), USA
Chee K. Ng, Fairleigh Dickinson University, USA
Edgar Ortiz, Universidad Nacional Autónoma de Mexico, Mexico
Theresa E. Pactwa, Florida International University, USA
Andreas Pericli, Federal Home Loan Mortgage Corporation, USA

D.M. Power, University of Dundee, UK
Arun J. Prakash, Florida International University, USA
Vanitha Ragunathan, University of Queensland, Australia
Mitchell Ratner, Rider University, USA
Scheherazade S. Rehman, George Washington University, USA
Tulin Sener, State University of New York, USA
C.D. Sinclair, University of Dundee, UK
Michael A. Sullivan, Office of the Comptroller of the Currency, USA
M.T. Vaziri, California State University–San Bernardino, USA
Radu Vranceanu, ESSEC, France
Carol N. Welsh, Rowan University, USA
M. Raquibuz Zaman, Ithaca College, USA

Part I

Introduction

1

Global Financial Markets at the Turn of the Century

ILHAN MERIC and GULSER MERIC

The origins of the modern global financial markets lie in the international operations of the British banks, often with family connections at the top level, that once financed the trade of the British empire (see O'Brien, 1996). In the eighteenth century, families like the Rothschilds managed banks with international operations across Europe. In the nineteenth century, banks controlled by the Morgan family extended their operations to the Western hemisphere.

The world's financial markets showed a strong globalization trend in the twentieth century. With the removal of barriers to cross-border flow of capital in many countries, financial markets became truly global during the last two decades of the twentieth century (see Gultekin et al., 1989 and Henry, 2000). A truly global financial market allows investors to benefit from international diversification by making it possible for them to invest in different countries' securities and enables firms to raise funds from all parts of the world. During the 1980s and early 1990s, the volume of global equity transactions rose over 1000 per cent and the value of global bonds outstanding rose over 500 per cent (see Lee et al., 1997).

Although the globalization of the world's financial markets has contributed significantly to the welfare of nations, the history of global finance is also replete with many crises. There have been 158 episodes of currency crisis and 54 episodes of banking crisis between 1975 and 1997 (see Christoffersen and Errunza, 2000). The global stock market crash of October 1987 and the emerging markets crisis of 1997–1998 have demonstrated that the world's national financial markets are closely linked to one another (see

Roll, 1988 and Stiglitz, 1999). This book contains four studies that provide empirical evidence on the effects of several important worldwide financial crises (Chapters 8, 14, 15, and 21).

The research papers included in the book are presented as separate chapters and they study various important current issues in the world's financial markets. Part II contains four chapters (2 through 5) that study several important European issues. The problem of fiscal coordination in the European Union (EU) is discussed in Chapter 2. André Fourçans and Radu Vranceanu argue that, although EU members may have many things in common, they are still different in many respects, particularly in terms of their economic interests and customs. They conclude that, since spending from a centralized (federal) budget requires uniform spending rules, it is neither enforceable nor politically sustainable.

The introduction of a common currency in the European union, the euro, on January 1 1999 was one of the most important international monetary developments since the collapse of the Bretton Woods era. In Chapter 3, Scheherazade S. Rehman provides an in-depth analysis of the impact of the euro on international banks in terms of the euro changeover costs.

In Chapter 4, with Benjamin H. Eichhorn and Carol N. Welsh, we study the effects of integration on the financial characteristics of manufacturing firms in Germany, France, and the UK. We find that, although these three countries are members of the EU and they have integrated economies and financial markets, their manufacturing firms have significantly different financial characteristics.

In Chapter 5, with Alan Alford, we search for variance change breakpoints in the way assets are priced in European capital markets. We find that the events that cause variance change are primarily domestic events, not pan-European events. We conclude that domestic factors cannot be ignored when pricing assets even when markets are integrated.

Part III contains five chapters (6 through 10) that study several important issues related to Asian financial markets. Chapter 6 deals with the lead/lag relationship and volatility interactions across five major Asian stock markets. Andreas Christofi, Andreas Pericli and Kasume Nishiyama estimate the joint distribution of stock returns in Hong Kong, Japan, Singapore, South Korea, and Taiwan as a Vector Autoregression (VAR) with innovations following an Exponential GARCH process. Their methodology detects the existence of asymmetric transmission of volatility innovations across the five stock markets. Negative innovations in a market increase volatility in another market considerably more than positive innovations.

In Chapter 7, Lakshman Alles, Rosita P. Chang and Ramakrishnan S. Koundinya study the importance of the country and industry factors on debt-financing decisions by firms in Japan, Korea, Malaysia, Taiwan, and Thailand. The country factor is found to be highly significant while the industry results are mixed. The impact of the country factor is found to be strong in the more developed countries such as Japan, Korea, and Taiwan, but not in Malaysia and Thailand.

The causes and implications of the 1997 collapse of the financial markets in East Asia are discussed in Chapter 8. M. Raquibuz Zaman concludes that corporate restructuring is needed in the region to restore economic health and that the old network-based business relationships must yield to more open (transparent) and competitive interactions between the enterprises.

The relative financial performances of US and Pacific-Rim industries are compared in Chapter 9. Parviz Asheghian and M.T. Vaziri determine that there are no significant differences between US and Pacific-Rim industries in terms of the return on equity, return on sales, asset turnover, and equity margin ratios. However, return on assets ratio in US industries is higher than it is in Pacific-Rim industries. It implies that US industries are more efficient in terms of asset utilization compared with Pacific-Rim industries.

In Chapter 10, Chee K. Ng compares the returns and variances of the closed-end country funds of Indonesia, Malaysia, the Philippines, Singapore, and Thailand with the strategy of investing in the stock markets of these countries. He concludes that US investors should prefer investing in the stock markets of the ASEAN-5 countries.

In Part IV, there are five chapters (11 through 15) that study several important issues related to US and Latin American financial markets. Alan Alford and Vanitha Ragunathan document empirical evidence for the influence of US monetary policy on world stock returns in Chapter 11. They find that the world market portfolio yields, on average, over 110 basis points in excess of the one-month Eurodollar rate when US monetary policy is expansionary, but over 78 basis points less when US monetary policy is contractionary.

The asset management, financing strategy, managerial efficiency and performance of multinational banks operating in the United States are studied in Chapter 12. Iftekhar Hasan, Tanweer Hasan and Roswell Mathis III find empirical evidence that the subsidiaries of foreign multinational banks in the United States have weaker performance compared with their US counterparts largely due to credit problems, lack of diversification in lending, and management inefficiency.

In Chapter 13, using a sample of seven Latin American stock markets, Arun J. Prakash, Theresa E. Pactwa, Chun-Hao Chang and Michael A. Sullivan find that the incorporation of skewness into an investor's portfolio decision causes a major change in the construction of the optimal portfolio. They present empirical evidence that indicates that investors trade expected return of the portfolio for skewness.

Chapter 14 studies the financial reforms and financial liberalization measures implemented in Mexico after the 1994 financial crisis. Alejandra Cabello concludes that, although the Mexican market has a good potential for stable long-term growth and high returns, foreign institutional and individual investors are investing in Mexico with a short-term vision.

In Chapter 15, with Ricardo P.C. Leal and Mitchell Ratner, we study the co-movements of the US, Argentinian, Brazilian, Chilean, and Mexican stock markets during the 1997–1998 emerging markets crisis. We find that the US stock market had significant contemporaneous influence on the movements of the four Latin stock markets during the crisis.

In Part V, there are five chapters (16 through 20) that deal with several important emerging markets issues. Chapter 16 studies the factors that influence equity returns from emerging stock markets. S.G.M. Fifield, C.D. Sinclair, A.A. Lonie and D.M. Power demonstrate that emerging markets offer global fund managers excellent opportunities for increasing portfolio returns, while simultaneously reducing portfolio risk. They find that the choice of industries or individual securities is likely to have less influence on the performance of the portfolio than the selection of the right countries in which to invest.

In Chapter 17, Tulin Sener finds that global portfolios outperform domestic portfolios and that including emerging markets would improve the performance of global portfolios. She argues that choosing assets in terms of their compound returns will underestimate the assets which benefit most from diversification. She suggests that country selection based on the creditworthiness criterion may not be an appropriate strategy.

Chapter 18 studies the effects of analyst recommendations published in weekly *Para* [Money] magazine on stock prices in the

Istanbul Stock Exchange. Halil Kiymaz's empirical findings suggest that there are statistically significant abnormal returns around the publication date.

Chapter 19 deals with banking, economic development, and integration issues in emerging markets. Edgar Ortiz and Jean-Pierre Gueyie emphasize the role of banks in economic development and in achieving integration. They explain the benefits of economic integration and the risks of financial integration and globalization. They conclude that emerging markets should promote economic development, taking full advantage of the benefits brought about by economic integration, and that it is important for these countries to strengthen their banking system.

Bank risk management practices in emerging markets are studied in Chapter 20. Kurt R. Jesswein discusses the recent advances in risk measurement and management techniques in banks and explains how these techniques can be used in emerging markets. He concludes that emerging countries that nurture and pursue risk management efforts within their economies will see their financial markets stabilize and strengthen.

Part VI contains two chapters (21 and 22) that deal with international currency markets. In Chapter 21, Abraham Mulugetta, Yuko Mulugetta and Dilip Ghosh study the impact of currency depreciation on the performance of international funds. They compare the 1994 Mexican crisis and the 1997 South-east Asian emerging markets crisis. They find remarkably similar patterns of performance for international funds during both crises.

François M. Longin studies extreme movements in foreign exchange markets in Chapter 22. Risk management is concerned with catastrophic events such as stock market crashes and foreign exchange crises. The VaR (Value at Risk) models consider 'normal' market conditions and they are completed by stress testing studies focusing on catastrophic events. François M. Longin proposes a rigorous new method based on extreme value theory to define catastrophe scenarios used in stress testing methods.

References

CHRISTOFFERSEN, P. and ERRUNZA, V. (2000) Towards a global financial architecture: Capital mobility and risk management issues, *Emerging Markets Review*, Vol. 1, No. 1, pp. 3–20.

GULTEKIN, M. N., GULTEKIN, N. B. and PENATI, A. (1989) Capital controls and international capital market segmentation: The evidence from the Japanese and American stock markets, *Journal of Finance*, Vol. 44, No. 4, pp. 849–870.

HENRY, P. B. (2000) Stock market liberalization, economic reform and emerging market equity prices, *Journal of Finance*, Vol. 55, No. 2, 529–564.

LEE, C. F., FINNERTY, J. E. and NORTON, E. A (1997) *Foundations of Financial Management*, West Publishing Company, New York.

O'BRIEN, T. J. (1996) *Global Financial Management*, John Wiley and Sons Inc., New York.

ROLL, R. (1988) The international crash of October 1987, *Financial Analysts Journal*, Vol. 44, No. 5, pp. 19–35.

STIGLITZ, J. E. (1999) Reforming the global economic architecture: Lessons from recent crises, *Journal of Finance*, Vol. 54, No. 4, pp. 1508–1521.

Part II
European Markets

2

European Monetary Union: The Case for Fiscal Coordination

ANDRÉ FOURÇANS and RADU VRANCEANU

Introduction

The establishment of European Economic and Monetary Union (EMU) on January 1 1999 created an entirely new situation in economic history. A group of eleven developed nations decided then to transfer monetary policy into the hands of a supranational institution, the European Central Bank (ECB).

Member states which joined EMU gave up monetary policy and lost the ability to adjust exchange rates between currencies. It is of course true that the previous European Monetary System had already restricted the use of monetary policy. However, significant margins of fluctuation between currencies persisted and the crises that occurred in 1992 and 1993 demonstrated that, where there are sustained disparities between the economic fundamentals, monetary adjustments provided the necessary economic correction.

Governments of the countries belonging to EMU maintain, however, fiscal autonomy. But fiscal flexibility is restricted by the Stability and Growth Pact (1997), implying budget deficits in line with the convergence criteria of the Maastricht Treaty (1992). According to the former document, member states of the monetary union are unconditionally required to avoid 'excessive deficits'[1].

No doubts, in EMU the use and role of fiscal policy will change. Insofar as the aim of monetary policy conducted by the European Central Bank is to ensure price stability, and, given that intra-Community exchange rates no longer exist, fiscal policy will assume a new role in terms of economic stability. It will have to be relied upon as a stabilizing factor in the event of a slowdown in growth or employment in one country or region (the so-called asymmetric shocks). This role will be all the more crucial since wage flexibility and workers' mobility do not appear to be important enough to bring about on their own the necessary adjustments in the event of economic recession or social crisis. Moreover, the value of the euro on the foreign exchange markets also depends, and will continue to depend, probably to a large extent, on the fiscal and taxation policies pursued by the Member States, and on the consolidated outcome at Union level.

Finally, with the deepening of the single market caused by the single currency and keener competition between firms belonging to the Euro member states, taxation policy can be expected to come under severe pressure to prevent both unwarranted economic distortions which might arise from tax differentials and undue losses in tax revenue for some member states.

For these reasons, the economic and structural policies pursued by the Euro member states through fiscal policy and taxation policy will be set against a general economic and environmental background significantly different from the previous one. And the role of fiscal policy itself will be greatly affected.

The chapter is organized as follows. The next section presents the main challenges of fiscal policy in an integrated Europe and analyzes the recent institutional advances. Following this, a simple model is used to analyze the economic coordination issue. The conclusion and policy implications are then presented.

EMU: Fiscal Policy in Practice

Objectives of Fiscal Policy

One of the traditional roles of fiscal policy is to try to regulate the economic cycle. Its main instruments are the variation in budget balances and volumes, arrangements for funding public deficits and reducing or increasing statutory charges. However, with a view to ensuring the stability of the single currency, the Economic and Monetary Union rules not only prohibit monetary funding of public deficits but also, through the Stability and Growth Pact, constrain the use of fiscal deficit as a means of regulating the economic cycle (Von Hagen and Eichengreen, 1996). By prohibiting any overrun of more than three per cent in the budget deficit, which might be subject to a fine (except in the event of an exceptional slowdown in the economy), the Pact denies governments the possibility of running up the deficit (see the Appendix to this chapter for details of the Pact). Yet, it is true that once medium-term budget equilibrium has been achieved, as suggested in the Pact, the margin of three per cent of GDP is far from negligible. But it does first require a solution to the current deficit problems facing most of the Euro member states, and this will take some time[2].

Consequently, although national fiscal policy remains in the hands of national governments, they lose part of their freedom and traditional fiscal recovery policies have to be reduced in scope. Fiscal policy will has to be geared to new goals, in particular to restructuring public expenditure to prioritize policies which will have the greatest effect on growth, if these can be determined. A targeted spending policy may hopefully replace one of uncontrolled and massive injection of public investment.

It is also necessary to examine the extent to which it is useful to coordinate national fiscal policies at European Union level and/or, without their being contradictory, the need for an increase in the European Union budget, and hence its role in ensuring short-term economic stability. These are sensitive issues from both the economic and political point of view and must take a number of factors into account.

Firstly, the coordination of national fiscal policies need not result in these policies being virtually identical. National specificities of all kinds will persist and will entail political and economic choices that may be different. Fiscal structures may continue to differ without this involving any non-compliance with the public deficit limits. These considerations of subsidiarity must never be forgotten as they are crucial to acceptance of the Union and its proper functioning.

Secondly, with regard to the possible transfer to Union level of certain items charged to the national budgets, with the relevant funding, an extremely cautious approach is required because of the national economic and political consequences.

Finally, coordination of fiscal policies is desirable in economic terms to treat spillover effects and the policy mix.

Spillover Effects and the Policy Mix

A primary objective of fiscal coordination is to tackle the problem of spillover effects between different countries within the union. These effects could be exacerbated by the monetary integration, a situation that might prompt some countries to pursue policies which are less than ideal for the Union as a whole.

When considering the direct interaction between the union members, any fiscal stimulus in one or several countries leads, at least in the Keynesian short-run, to: (1) an increase in imports of this or those countries, and therefore an increase in exports from other countries; (2) an increase in the euro-zone interest rate. The degree of importance of these effects depends on the size as well as on the budgetary expansion of the country or countries under consideration.

We know from the Mundell-Fleming analysis that the short-run efficiency of fiscal policy is higher on a fixed exchange rate system than on a flexible exchange rate regime. Yet the leakages from the increase in imports resulting from the higher economic integration diminishes the efficiency of fiscal policy. The increase in aggregate demand in the expanding country(ies) raises production – except if all the increase translates into import 'leakages'. The export push of other countries also raises production in these countries. Yet the higher interest rate slows down investment and consumption in the euro-zone as a whole. All in all it is a priori difficult to evaluate the net impact of a fiscal expansion on each country and on the single currency zone. Econometric analyses suggest that the net effect may be limited. The question is now to know to what extent the single currency, and the deepening of economic integration that will follow, will affect this impact.

As far as the interactions between the Union and the rest of the world are concerned, the external equilibrium will also depend upon the policy mix. If capital mobility between the Union and the rest of the world is significant, fiscal stimulus and resulting increase in interest rates in one country would appreciate the euro, and entail undesirable consequences on the euro-zone balance of payments. Here too it will be difficult to avoid coordination.

The impact of fiscal policy would also depend upon the actual budget deficit and the indebtness levels – even more so within the EMU. An increase of these values has a higher influence on the interest rate risk premium the higher their levels are. And conversely, mutatis mutandis. Here too, some coordination of fiscal policy would be useful to treat this 'externality' effect.

Another factor to take into consideration is the impact of fiscal policy on economic growth composition and on the capital stock (European Commission, 1997). The increase in the interest rate and the appreciation of the euro exchange rate negatively influence investments and the capital stock. And from there, long-term growth and employment.

Fiscal coordination would also be useful to treat the policy-mix problem between a centralized monetary policy conducted by the European Central Bank (ECB) and decentralized fiscal policies conducted by each member state. These policies interact. Monetary policy depends, in a way, on the budgetary situation of Euroland. And the budgetary situation is also influenced by monetary policy. Exchanges and coordination between these two policies would therefore be welcomed to ensure the right policy mix, without jeopardizing the independence of the ECB and its price stability objective. And, at the same time, to ensure the domestic objective of high non-inflationary growth as the external balance of payments objective.

Even though fine-tuning should be excluded, in some cases it would be critical to closely coordinate fiscal and monetary policies: inflationary situations, strong growth slowdowns, asymmetric shocks, etc.

Finally, it will be required that the EMU members speak with one voice in international summits and negotiations. For that to happen, they will need, at least, to agree on their fiscal policies.

How to Manage Fiscal Policy

The various solutions that we shall consider here attempt to provide a response to the challenge posed by the single currency. The aim is to reconcile as far as possible a European monetary policy pursued by a European Central Bank independent from the political authorities with fiscal and tax policies which are still, broadly speaking, national policies.

Fiscal Policy: the Status Quo – the Non-Cooperative Setting

This solution is advocated by some countries on grounds of the sovereignty argument. Often, such a claim is based on the ignorance of the economic linkage between economies within a monetary union. Indeed, fiscal policy has more than domestic effects; when a government decides to modify its domestic spending, income and other structural aggregates in the partner countries change too. That is why, from an economic perspective, a (sovereign) government which chooses freely its own spending level is not really independent, insofar as it is obliged to take into consideration how its partners would react to its own policies. Unfortunately, sometimes the status-quo discourse only masquerades a strong temptation for opportunistic behaviour, wherein a country targets the non-cooperative outcome hoping that all the rest behave cooperatively.

It would be difficult to secure political support for such a strategy. It would jeopardize to some extent consolidation of the single market and runs counter to the spirit of solidarity which underpins European integration. There is no need to dwell on the fact that it would also inevitably give rise to political tension between the member states.

A Unified Community Budget?

Elementary microeconomics shows that cooperative solutions are better than non-cooperative ones. A move towards a federal-style Community budget with a farther-reaching stabilizing and redistributive function would, theoretically, be the best way of achieving economic objectives and of dealing with the various short-term economic situations that the member states might have to face[3]. However, such an institution is not likely to emerge for political considerations, at least in the short term and even in the medium term.

It will probably be necessary to give the Union budget a greater role – once the single market has attained the more advanced stage of integration that will inevitably come with the single currency – so as to better ensure sustainable and lasting growth and employment. From this perspective, the Union budget would act as a factor for stability in regional and/or national economies. This could be put on a more or less automatic basis by adjusting national contributions to the European budget where economic trends differ from a specified Community average, on the lines of the federal system in the United States.

One might also envisage a more systematic transfer of more national fiscal resources to the Community budget (the MacDougall report mentioned a figure of between five and seven per cent of GDP. Somewhere between three and five per cent of GDP would probably be adequate) in order to set up a stabilization fund to support member states that suffer an exceptional slowdown in their economies. Some public expenditure common to the euro-zone and the Union in general (relating to infrastructure, the environment, and defence) could be transferred to European level. It must be stressed that if this objective were adopted, it would be part of a long-term approach and not a short-term proposal.

Limits to Deficits

In the absence of a federal-style procedure, the cooperative outcome might be approximated by enforcing mandatory bounds on deficits. The main difficulty stems from the lack of information and experience necessary to correctly assess these targets for each country.

For an upper limit, the pragmatic solution was to establish a uniform target adjusted only to the output size (three per cent of GDP). Several important factors, like savings behaviour, age structure, social security systems, etc. were neglected.

Under certain circumstances (not very realistic, but also possible) countries may engage in a different battle, where the bad non-cooperative outcome implies inadequate public spending and income.

In order to understand better these points, more formalism is helpful. The following model aims to introduce in a simple way the main challenges of coordination of fiscal policies in a monetary-integrated Europe. Early work in this field was carried out by Bryson (1994) and Artus (1995), but using different versions of the model at hand. We bring into the picture only the basic links between two hypothetical countries, with identical economic structure.

EMU: Fiscal Policy in Theory

Main Assumptions

The Elementary Macroeconomic Model

We consider two identical countries (1 and 2) under a monetary union agreement. (The assumption of symmetry will vastly simplify the calculus while not altering the main insights.)

The basic equations are two IS relationships, one for each country, plus a joint LM relationship:

$$\begin{cases} y_1 = \alpha(G_1 - bi + sy_2) \\ y_2 = \alpha(G_2 - bi + sy_1) \\ m = k(y_1 + y_2) - li \end{cases} \tag{1}$$

where $y_{1,2}$ represents output, $G_{1,2}$ public spending, b the sensitivity of investment to the common interest rate i, s the import sensitivity to income and α a Keynesian multiplier; m is the exogenous stock of money, while k and l are the two standard sensitivities of the demand for money with respect to income and interest rates.

The solution of this elementary model is:

$$\begin{cases} y_1 = \zeta(l + \alpha bk)\, G_1 + \zeta\alpha(ls - bk)\, G_2 + \zeta(\alpha sb + b)\, m \\[2mm] y_2 = \zeta(l + \alpha bk)\, G_2 + \zeta\alpha(ls - bk)\, G_1 + \zeta(\alpha sb + b)\, m \qquad (2) \\[2mm] i = [\alpha k(G_1 + G_2) - (1 - s\alpha)\, m]\, [l(1 - \alpha s) + 2\alpha bk]^{-1} \end{cases}$$

where: $\zeta = \alpha[l(1 - \alpha^2 s^2) + 2\alpha bk + 2\alpha^2 sbk]^{-1}$

Neglecting all the constant terms, the simplified expressions for output in the two countries are:

$$\begin{cases} y_1 = \mu_1 G_1 + \mu_2 G_2 \\[2mm] y_2 = \mu_1 G_2 + \mu_2 G_1 \end{cases} \qquad (3)$$

with: $\mu_1 > 0$, $\mu_1 + \mu_2 > 0$, $\mu_2 \lessgtr 0$.

Note that the sign of $\mu_2 =$ sign of $(ls - bk)$, that is the cross-effect of a change in the spending level of one country on the income of the other one may be *positive* or *negative*. The intuition behind this is straightforward: increasing spending in one country raises aggregate demand, income and thus imports from the second country, which has a first positive effect on the second country's output. But the simultaneous increase in the (common) interest rate may harm investment in the second country, leading to an adverse cross-country crowding-out effect.

Two countries with a high import propensity might well be characterized by a positive μ_2. To the contrary, if investment is highly responsible to increases in the interest rate, the μ_2 parameter might be negative: in this case, a cross-country crowding-out effect is responsible for the decrease in output.

As will be made clearer later on, this indeterminacy may entail a serious policy difficulty.

It is important to remark that when applied to sovereign states, most models of this kind suggest that the cross-border macroeconomic effects of fiscal policies are small, as the trade effect and the interest rate effect tend to offset each other (Oudiz and Sachs, 1984; Eichengreen 1993). Yet, in the framework of the EMU, no a priori evaluation of the relative importance of the two effects can be assessed. The completion of the single market and the removal of trade barriers may strengthen the positive import-driven effect; the removal of capital controls and the elimination of the exchange risk given the single currency would strengthen the adverse cross-border crowding-out effect. As compared with the sovereign countries' case, the latter effect may be enhanced, given that in the monetary union a single interest rate on different governments' bonds of equivalent maturity should prevail (if neglecting the default risk).

The Objective Function of Governments

In keeping with traditional literature, output fluctuations are costly, and government would like to minimize them. Thus, they will run out higher public spending in periods where output falls below the normal level and reduce spending in the reverse situation.

There is obviously a political cost of running deficits, as people feel that they charge the future generations with the debt burden. More important, as mentioned by Von Hagen and Eichengreen (1996), high deficits entailing high debt levels would destabilize the euro, insofar as the European Central Bank may be tempted to bail out spendthrift governments (despite formal interdiction by the Maastricht Treaty).

To take these assumptions into consideration, an elementary loss function for country $k = (0,1)$ may be written:

$$L_k = (\bar{y} - y_k)^2 + \theta_k G_k \text{ with } \theta_k > 0 \tag{4}$$

where y stands for normal output and where public spending G_k is a proxy for deficits (introducing taxes proportional to income would not modify the main results).

The analysis below develops the symmetric case wherein the two governments have identical priorities, i.e. $\theta_1 = \theta_2 = \theta$.

The Non-Cooperative Setting

The government in one country minimizes the loss function given its beliefs about the other government spending choice; in the Nash equilibrium these beliefs are realized: each government undertakes the spending level expected by the other one, denoted G_1^e and G_2^e.

The two reaction functions are:

$$G_1^* = \arg\min_{G_1} L_1(G_1, G_2^e) = \frac{1}{2\mu_1^2}(2\mu_1\bar{y} - 2\mu_1\mu_2 G_2^e - \theta) \tag{5}$$

$$G_2^* = \arg \min_{G_2} L_2(G_2, G_1^e) = \frac{1}{2\mu_1^2}(2\mu_1\bar{y} - 2\mu_1\mu_2 G_1^e - \theta) \tag{6}$$

In equilibrium $G_1^* = G_1^e$ and $G_2^* = G_2^e$. The solution comes out:

$$G_1^N = G_2^N = \frac{\bar{y}}{(\mu_1+\mu_2)} - \frac{\theta}{2\mu_1(\mu_1+\mu_2)}, \tag{7}$$

implying:

$$y_1^N = y_2^N = y - \frac{\theta}{2\mu_1} \tag{8}$$

As normal output cannot be reached without a positive spending (equation 3), and as spending itself entails some costs proportional to θ, the equilibrium output will be lower than the normal output.

One may evaluate the total loss function for the optimal values:

$$LN = L_1(G_1^N, G_2^N) + L_2(G_1^N, G_2^N) = \frac{\theta[(\mu_2-\mu_1)\theta + 4\mu_1^2\bar{y}]}{2\mu_1^2(\mu_1+\mu_2)} \tag{9}$$

The Cooperative Setting

In the cooperative situation, the two governments agree on the amount of public spending so as to minimize the total loss. From an institutional point of view, this case would occur if a federal government took over the spending function of the national governments. Such an institution would require deep political integration, insofar as public spending involves expenses in politically-sensitive fields such as education, healthcare, defence and social security.

The decision problem implies:

$$\min_{G_1, G_2} \sum_{k=1,2} \{L_k = (\bar{y} - y_k)^2 + \theta G_k\} \tag{10}$$

with the solution:

$$G_1^C = G_2^C = \frac{y}{(\mu_1+\mu_2)} - \frac{1}{2}\frac{\theta}{(\mu_1+\mu_2)^2} \tag{11}$$

which leads to the equilibrium output:

$$y_1^C = y_2^C = \bar{y} - \frac{1}{2}\frac{\theta}{(\mu_1+\mu_2)} \tag{12}$$

In keeping with conventional microeconomic analysis, the cooperative setting entails a smaller loss for the agents than the non-cooperative case. The loss function evaluated for the optimal spending levels is:

$$LC = L_1(G_1^C, G_2^C) + L_2(G_1^C, G_2^C) = \frac{\theta[4\bar{y}(\mu_2 - \mu_1) - \theta]}{2(\mu_1 + \mu_2)^2}$$

Then, the difference $LN - LC = \frac{1}{2}\left[\frac{\mu_2}{\mu_1(\mu_1 + \mu_2)}\right]^2 > 0$

Output in the cooperative case may be higher or lower than in the non-cooperative case, depending on the sign of the parameter μ_2:

$$\sum y_k^C = \sum y_k^N + \frac{\theta}{\mu_1(\mu_1 + \mu_2)} \tag{13}$$

If the propensity to import (s) is very high, μ_2 would be positive: the cooperative outcome may imply a larger output. But if the sensitivity of output with respect to the interest rate is high, the cooperative output may be lower than the non-cooperative one.

The deficit may also be higher or lower:

$$\sum G_k^C = \sum G_k^N + \frac{\theta\mu_2}{\mu_1(\mu_1 + \mu_2)^2} \tag{14}$$

Note that if governments do not care about deficits, the cooperative solution is identical to the non-cooperative one, whatever μ_2. The same equivalence holds when $\mu_2 = 0$ (that is the positive global aggregate effect is strictly compensated by the adverse interest rate effect).

For the time being, the role of μ_2 is rather instrumental to our analysis. In the following it is argued that it matters a lot from a policy point of view.

Decentralized Budgetary Policies

In the case of decentralized budgetary policies (absence of federal government) the cooperative equilibrium may be reached if an omniscient supranational authority assigns the correct (cooperative) deficit targets to the countries participating in the single market. Needless to say, a lack of information problem may arise, given that the limits to be imposed would have to be specific to each country. In a simple model like the one presented here, the limits are the same for the two countries. But when differences in structural characteristics or priorities are taken into consideration, the limits would diverge. In the absence of perfect information about these parameters and relationships, perfect targets cannot be devised. The only pragmatic solution available is to seek large approximations for the optimal targets.

Of course, a government which thinks that its partners will respect the targets has a strong incentive to deviate. Only a credible punishment may deter it.

The model sheds some light on the way the limits on spending and deficits should be enforced.

The Case of $\mu_2 < 0$: High Interest Sensitivity of Investment

In this case the non-cooperative outcome would entail too high a deficit (despite higher output). The situation is depicted in Figure 2.1. Point **N** corresponds to the non-cooperative equilibrium, to be found at the intersection of the two reaction functions, equations (5) and (6). We also represented two iso-loss curves, passing through **N**. Iso-loss curves placed closer to the vertical axis

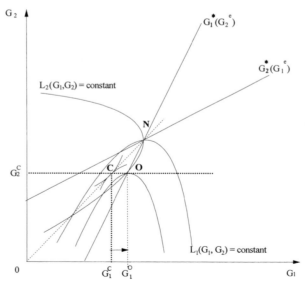

FIGURE 2.1: *The case of $\mu_2 < 0$*

correspond to lower losses for country 2; iso-loss curves placed closer to the horizontal axis correspond to lower losses for country 1. Point **C** is the cooperative equilibrium (the respective iso-loss curves are tangent). The figure shows that, in order to achieve the cooperative outcome, spending should be bounded upward.

In view of this analysis, the maximum three per cent deficit of GDP stated by the Stability and Growth Pact could be interpreted as a pragmatic response of the European Union to the issue of upper limits on deficits, in order to prevent non-cooperative outcomes once countries are deeply integrated.

Imagine now that the government of country 1 believes that the government of country 2 will stick to this target. It expects therefore a gain from shifting spending G_1^C to the higher level G_1^O. To prevent this action, a sanction would apply to opportunistic governments. The fine must be high enough to prevent any discretionary behaviour, i.e. it should be larger than the gain to be obtained through any unilateral deviation.

The Stability and Growth Pact provides this type of sanction, insofar as any government exceeding the three per cent of GDP target would pay a significant fine (except in deep recessions). An 'honest' government would have no reason to oppose it, on grounds of the sovereignty argument, insofar as it can only benefit from a measure which ensures the cooperative behaviour of its partners.

The Case of $\mu_2 > 0$: High Import Propensity

As already mentioned, this case would occur if the cross crowding-out effect is weaker than the import-driven output revival. The situation described above would be reversed: in the non-cooperative case deficits and output would be too low.

With unreliable estimations μ_2, one may not rule out the possibility that countries engage in a race towards inadequate spending levels. In such a case, downward limits on spending may be justified. Minimum spending levels on education, social security and so on can in this view be considered. The non-fulfilment of this minimum would also have to be punished: a country which expects the others to respect the downward limit would otherwise gain by unilaterally reducing its own spending.

Needless to say, if this downward limit on spending is theoretically defensible, the likelihood of its being politically acceptable is very low.

Conclusions

The idea that in the EMU fiscal coordination would be better than non-cooperation is more than trivial, and only few euro-sceptics would question it. Also, there is nothing very original in explaining that good coordination would be achieved through a centralized (federal) budget. The truth is that nowadays the latter is not politically sustainable. While the nations participating in the European Union have many things in common, they are still very different in many respects, particularly in their economic interests and customs. Spending from a centralized budget requires uniform spending rules which could not be enforced today.

The pragmatic choice of decentralized spending with safeguards such as legal limits and penalties for deviants seems to be the only solution if one intends to push forward the European integration process. Yet, an obstacle remains: the lack of relevant information about the economic structure of the European Union. As a practical device, upper limits on deficits would prevent the non-cooperative outcome if public spending in various countries provides strategic complements ($\mu_2 < 0$); to the contrary, floor limits must be assessed too, in order to prevent the non-cooperative outcome if public spending in various countries provides strategic substitutes ($\mu_2 > 0$).

Appendix: Details of the Stability and Growth Pact

The 'reference value' for budget deficits is at three per cent of GDP; but this is 'to be seen as an upper limit in normal circumstances'. National budgetary policies should 'create room for manoeuvre in adapting to exceptional and cyclical disturbances', while avoiding excessive deficits. Hence the medium-term budgetary objective is to be 'close to balance or surplus': effectively a balanced budget over the economic cycle.

Strategy

The Pact can be seen as a 'twin-track strategy', providing:

- a 'preventive, early-warning system' for identifying and correcting budgetary slippages before they breach the three per cent threshold; and
- a 'dissuasive set of rules' to deter Member States from incurring, or failing to correct, an excessive deficit.

Deadlines

- The European Economic and Finance Council (Ecofin) has three months following the submission of budget figures by a Member State to decide whether an 'excessive deficit' existed.
- If Ecofin decided after another four months that no effective action had been taken by the Member State in question, it could make the recommendation public.
- Failing action by the offending country within one month, Ecofin could then issue a notice for the Member State to take deficit-reduction measures.
- If within another two months no satisfactory measures had been taken, Ecofin would, 'as a rule', decide to impose sanctions.
- The total time between the reporting date for budgetary figures and any decision to impose sanctions would have to be less than ten months.

Penalties

The possible sanctions take the form of frozen deposits that can be transformed into fines. The non-interest-bearing deposits consist of two elements: a fixed sum equal to 0.2 per cent of GDP; and a supplement equal to 0.1 per cent of GDP for every percentage point by which the budget deficit exceeded the three per cent reference level.

The provisions would, however, be subject to two qualifications: there would be an upper limit of 0.5 per cent of GDP; and if the excessive deficit were due to non-compliance with the government debt criterion (60 per cent of GDP), only the fixed sum would be due.

If the deficit persisted two years later:

- the deposit would become a fine, and be paid automatically into the Community Budget;
- a new non-interest-bearing deposit would have to be made.

Possible Derogations

Derogations from this procedure are possible if an excessive budget deficit is the result of 'exceptional and temporary' circumstances, in particular 'in the case of significant negative annual real growth':

- As a rule, an economic downturn will be considered exceptional only if there is 'an annual fall of real GDP of at least two per cent'.

- A Member State will also be able to request that a fall of real GDP between 0.75% and 2% be considered exceptional in the light of 'the abruptness of the downturn'.

References

ARTUS, P. (1995) *La Politique budgétaire en union monétaire et les critères de Maastricht*, Document de travail de la CDC, No. 16/T.

BRYSON, J. H. (1994) Fiscal policy coordination and flexibility under European monetary union: Implications for macroeconomic stabilization, *Journal of Policy Modelling*, Vol. 16, No. 6, pp. 541–557.

EICHENGREEN, B. (1993) European monetary unification, *Journal of Economic Literature*, Vol 31. pp. 1321–1357.

EUROPEAN COMMISSION (1997) Economic Policy in EMU, *Economic Papers*, part B, section II–8, No. 125, November.

MACDOUGALL, D. (1977) *Report of the study group on the role of public finance in European integration*, Chaired by Sir Donald MacDougall, Economic and Finance Series, No. A13, Commission of the European Community, Brussels, April.

MASSON, P. R. (1996) Fiscal dimensions of EMU, *Economic Journal*, Vol. 106, pp. 996–1004.

OUDIZ, G. and SACHS, J. D. (1984) Macroeconomic policy coordination among the industrial economies, *Brookings Papers on Economic Activity*, Vol. 1, pp. 1–64.

SALA-I-MARTIN, X. and SACHS, J. (1992) Fiscal federalism and optimal currency areas: evidence for Europe from the United States, in CANZONIERI, M.B., GRILLI, V. and MASSON, P.R. (eds.) *Establishing a Central Bank: Issues in Europe and Lessons from the US*, Cambridge University Press, Cambridge, pp. 195–219.

VON HAGEN, J. and EICHENGREEN, B. (1996) Federalism, fiscal restraints and European monetary union, *American Economic Review*, Vol. 86, No. 2, pp. 134–138.

Notes

1. A state has an 'excessive deficit' when it is so declared by the European Council upon a report by the European Commission and a judgement by the Monetary Committee. See the details of the Pact in the Appendix to this chapter.
2. As mentioned by Masson (1996), historical evidence suggests that "average deficits should be no more than 1% to rule out deficits in excess of 3% except very rarely". The same author emphasizes the consistency of the balanced budget proposal in this context.
3. The MacDougall Report (1977) advocates strongly in favour of this policy. While its recommendations were never passed through, Sala-i-Martin and Sachs (1992) emphasize in a theoretical paper its continuous relevance.

3

Euro Changeover Costs for International Banks

SCHEHERAZADE S. REHMAN

Introduction

In February 1992, the heads of state of 12 nations (the European Council) signed the Treaty on the European Union (EU), also known as the Maastricht Treaty, which came into force on November 1 1993[1]. The Treaty[2], among others, represented a benchmark in the evolution of global investment and trade activities as by 1999 it called for the creation of European Economic and Monetary Union (EMU) with a single currency – the euro – a common European Central Bank (ECB) and common monetary policies. The euro was introduced on a non-cash basis on January 1, 1999 and is to replace the national currencies of those EU nations that are EMU members by July 2002.

The introduction of the euro on January 1, 1999 was one of the most important international monetary developments since the collapse of the Bretton Woods era. Within a few days of its introduction it caused unprecedented changes in the world's financial markets that have had far-reaching implications for international banks and non-bank financial institutions as they are affected by foreign exchange, capital markets and investment and trade patterns. The nature and magnitude of these changes, however, are far from clear.

It is the objective of this chapter to provide an analysis of the impact of the introduction of the euro on international financial market participants in general and international banks in particular in terms of the euro changeover costs incurred.

The Potential Global Role of the Euro

The long-term aspects of EMU and its euro on the rest of the world largely depends on the answers to two related questions. Firstly, will the euro over time challenge the US dollar as the world's main reserve, trade and investment currency? Secondly, will the EMU project make the global monetary system more or less stable?

The euro joined the ranks of major international currencies in 1999. But it is still unclear to what extent and how rapidly it will develop into a major global reserve, investment and trade currency. Even less clear is its impact on the established global role of the US dollar. While it is clear that the euro plays an important role in the international financial markets, claims that it will eventually supersede the role of the US dollar in global financial and trade transactions are unrealistic. If it remains stable the euro will capture the EMU member states' currency share, including that of the previous ecu[3] while surpassing the current investment and trade role of the Deutschmark. Over time, the euro could capture the market shares of other European currencies as well. Table 3.1 shows the daily foreign exchange turnovers of the major currencies in 1995 and 1998 and Table 3.2 shows the global financial market and trade shares of selected currencies.

The ability of the euro to challenge the global role of the US dollar as the major international currency will depend on the economic performance of the EMU member states, the European Central Bank's ability to ensure price stability in the face of asymmetric economic shocks, the EMU governments' ability to maintain socially acceptable levels of employment, and on EMU's credibility as perceived by financial markets. Of the 15 EU nations to date, 11 have meet the Maastricht convergence criteria[4] with the United Kingdom, Finland and Denmark choosing not to participate and Greece not qualifying. Table 3.3 shows the real GDP growth and inflation rates for Euroland between 1996 and 1999 and Table 3.4 shows the labour market developments in the euro area.

Given the importance, yet fickle nature, of global foreign exchange and capital markets with an approximate daily turnover of over US$1.4 trillion and US$8 trillion respectively, the euro has to be carefully managed. Prior to the introduction of the non-cash euro in 1999, and currently, the European Central Bank (ECB) and national governments have gone to extraordinary lengths to convince the global financial markets of their commitment to the euro through the introduction of appropriate political, monetary and economic policy measures. Perhaps the biggest problem for Euroland is the

TABLE 3.1: *Foreign Exchange Markets and the Euro (daily averages in billions of US dollars)*

	Turnover[1] in 1995			Turnover[1] in 1998		
	Total	vs. US dollar	vs. EMU currencies[2]	Total	vs. US dollar	vs. EMU currencies[2]
US dollar	1313.4	–	*201.1*[3]	1741.0	–	*125.1*[3]
Euro currencies[2]	869.8	551.4	106.1	968.4	709.1	62.4
Deutschmark	583.8	364.9	51.7	602.7	413.1	17.1
French franc	127.2	72.5	10.9	102.6	82.6	5.6
ECU	36.2	25.2	28.2	22.7		
Japanese yen	371.4	329.9	407.2	363.3		
Pound sterling	139.7	102.8	211.9	159.4		
Swiss franc	116.3	85.7	138.8	108.7		
Total	1571.8	1313.4	1981.6	1741.0		

Source: Central Bank Survey of Foreign Exchange and Derivatives market Activity (1995, 1998); BIS 69th Annual Report, p.117.

Note: Estimates shown in italics.

1 Average daily turnover, net of local inter-dealer double-counting. The table reports the turnover in which a given currency appears on one side of a transaction; consequently, each transaction is counted twice. To take this into account, the total (which also includes other and unallocated currencies) is divided by two.

2 In the survey, decompositions are available only for the Deutschmark, French franc, pound sterling, ECU and the sum of all other EMS currencies. In order to estimate turnover for EMU currencies, the sum of other EMS currencies is broken down using figures on local currency trading based on the methodology used in Table V.5 of the 67th Annual Report.

3 Before the start of EMU, foreign exchange transactions between prospective members' currencies were sometimes carried out using the US dollar as a vehicle. As a result, an estimation of the current importance of the euro, the dollar and the yen based on the subtraction of intra-EMU turnover in 1998 leads to an overestimation of importance for the euro, an underestimation for the yen and a correct estimation for the dollar.

weakened euro despite good macroeconomic performance. The euro opened on January 1 1999 at US$1.1775 and closed on January 29, 2001 at US$0.9232, showing a 21.6% drop in value over the 16-month euro's life span. During 1999, the euro depreciated against all major currencies, 17%, 22% and 11% against the US$, yen, and pound sterling, respectively, and has never recovered to its opening value. Since the beginning of 2000, the euro has continued to drop against the dollar, yen and pound sterling respectively. Among others, a major factor contributing to the euro's decline has been the relative strength of the real economy and inflation prospects of US economy against the rest of the world. In conjunction, the US Federal Reserve's series of interest rate hikes in 2000 has not aided the euro's value. It is anathema to ECB officials as they see the signs of recovery in the Euroland economies during 2000 being dismissed by the foreign exchange market as it defies economic logic and

TABLE 3.2: *Selected currency shares in global financial markets and trade (%)*

	US$	DM	All EU[1]	EURO CURRENCIES	YEN
Official foreign exchange[2]	64.1	15.9	21.2	n.a.	7.5
(of which developing countries)	(63.5)	(15.6)	(21.9)		(8.3)
Foreign holdings of bank deposits[2]	47.5	18.4	42.5	n.a.	4.2
Net issuance of international debt security markets (1999)	43.0	n.a.	n.a.	48.0	−1.0
Developing countries[1] debt[2]	50.0	n.a.	16.1	n.a.	18.0
Denomination of world exports (1992)	47.6	15.3	33.5	n.a.	4.8
Foreign exchange market turnover[2]	37.9	15.5	32.0	n.a.	12.4
Gross issuance of international bond and note markets (1999)	43.0	n.a.	n.a.	39.0	7.0
All international private assets[3]	4.1	10.6	6.4	n.a.	1.8
(excluding intra-EU holdings)	(50)	(n.a.)	(10)		(18)

Source: 1996, 1997 and 2000 IMF and 1996, 2000 BIS data.

[1]   Including intra-EU holdings. This considerably overstates the EU position (and thus, understates US dollar and yen position)

[2]   1995

[3]   Includes only Deutschmark, Pound sterling and French franc.

seems insistent on being short in the euro. (See Table 3.5 for a history of ecu/euro exchange rates movements.) Until recently, the markets have assumed a 'wait-and-see' attitude. But as the introduction of the euro on a cash basis in 2002 draws closer, bankers, investors and traders are becoming nervous and are scrambling to produce new 'euro strategies'.

TABLE 3.3: *Real GDP growth and HICP[1] inflation in euroland (annual percentage changes)*

	BE	DE	ES	FR	IE	IT	LU	NL	AT	PT	FI	Total
REAL GDP												
1996	–	–	–	–	–	–	–	–	–	–	–	1.3
1997	–	–	–	–	–	–	–	–	–	–	–	2.3
1998	2.7	2.2	4.0	3.2	8.9	1.5	5.0	3.7	2.9	3.8	5.0	2.8
1999	2.3	1.5	3.7	2.7	9.4	1.4	5.0	3.5	2.2	2.9	3.5	2.3
HICP												
1995	–	–	–	–	–	–	–	–	–	–	–	2.5
1996	–	–	–	–	–	–	–	–	–	–	–	2.2
1997	0.9	0.6	1.8	0.7	2.1	2.0	1.0	1.8	0.8	2.2	1.4	1.6
1998	1.1	0.6	2.2	0.6	2.5	1.7	1.0	2.0	0.5	2.2	1.3	1.1
1999	–	–	–	–	–	–	–	–	–	–	–	2.0
Feb 2000	–	–	–	–	–	–	–	–	–	–	–	

Sources: Eurostat, national estimates, ECB *Annual Report* 1999 p. 29, and ECB *Monthly Bulletin*, April 2000, p. 32.

[1]   Harmonized Index of Consumer Prices.

the transition dual currency period alone the euro changeover costs to the banking sector could be as high as ecu 18–22.5 billion (US$22.8–28.35 billion).

Several large EU banks had also estimated initial changeover expenses. According to Barclays Bank, it would cost US$200 million. The Deutsche Bank identified 3500 separate steps which it would have to take to adjust its operations, costing US$175 million. The Bayerische Vereinsbank planned to spend US$98 million, the ING Group US$117 million, Postipankki US$32.6 million and the Credi-tanstalt US$93.5 million on the transition process. Private research groups consider these amounts to be very conservative and predict that the actual cost is twice as high. Recently, some banks have revised their estimates. For example, both Barclays Bank and the Deutsche Bank concluded that their previous estimates were widely off the mark and that the cost of revamping the information technology infrastructures alone could reach well over US$350 million each.

Studies conducted by the consulting group BMS Bossard[8] suggest that during the transition dual currency period with the non-cash euro (1999–2002) each of the major banks would have to invest up to US$750 million. Once the final single currency period begins in 2002, they may have to invest approximately US$500 million each in addition (BMS Bossard, 1996).

Costs by Functions and Products

During the transition dual currency period (cost in the range US$22.8–28.35 billion) and with the beginning of the final euro dual currency adjustment period (cost in the range US$15.2–18.9 billion), it is expected that over 50 per cent of these costs will be generated by information systems/technology changes with the remaining expenses associated with finance and treasury depart-ments, accounting and fiscal matters, legal departments, commer-cial aspects and marketing departments, and personnel/staff retraining. Other costs will be incurred by securities quotations, fixed income trading, valuation methods, arbitrage models, etc.

One of the most comprehensive and detailed reports on the euro's specific changeover costs to the European banking sector was conducted by the Banking Federation of the European Union in its 1995 survey (op. cit.). It surveyed more than 100 banks in 14 coun-tries. Not surprisingly, the Federation concluded that adopting the euro would be an 'unprecedented challenge' to the banking industry. Table 3.6 provides a summary overview of the results of the

TABLE 3.6: *Cost of transition to the euro by product and functions (% of total cost)*

Function	Product									
	Notes and coin	Automatic Teller Machine	Cards and services	Payment systems	Foreign exchange dealing & treasury management	Loans	Deposits	Capital markets	Other	Total cost
Information technology	4%	3%	7%	15%	6%	5%	4%	5%	5%	54%
Marketing & PR	1%	1%	1%	6%	1%	2%	2%	0%	1%	15%
Legal	0%	0%	0%	1%	1%	0%	0%	1%	1%	4%
Audit and security	2%	0%	0%	0%	0%	0%	0%	1%	0%	3%
Accounting & management	0%	0%	0%	1%	1%	0%	1%	0%	0%	3%
Staff training	1%	1%	1%	2%	1%	1%	1%	1%	1%	10%
Stationery	1%	0%	0%	2%	0%	1%	2%	0%	0%	6%
External reporting	0%	0%	0%	0%	0%	1%	0%	0%	0%	0%
Other	3%	1%	0%	0%	0%	0%	0%	0%	0%	5%
Total cost	12%	6%	9%	27%	10%	10%	10%	8%	8%	100%

Source: Counting the Cost of EMU, *Balance Sheet*, Vol. 5, No. 3, Autumn 1996, p. 13.

survey by product and function costs as a percentage of the total operational and of the total changeover costs.

Tables 3.7 and 3.8 illustrate the estimated euro changeover costs by bank function and bank product as a percentage of the total euro changeover costs.

The costs for foreign exchange, information systems/technology and payment systems are discussed in more detail below.

Foreign Exchange Costs

The EMU and its euro have eliminated foreign exchange (FX) trading in 11 member states' currencies, which has resulted in a large income loss to EU banks. It also decreased treasury income and cut earnings from cross-border payments channeled through correspondent banking relationships. Studies have found that, on the average, a large European bank earns about 12.5 per cent of its total revenue from FX operations.[9] Over 60 per cent of these

TABLE 3.7: *Transition costs by bank function during the dual and single currency periods*

Bank Functions	% of Total euro changeover costs [Total $25.3 billion]	Dual currency period ($ billion) [Total $12.6 billion]	Single currency period ($ billion)
Information technology	54%	$13.662	$6.804
Marketing and PR	15%	$ 3.795	$1.890
Legal	4%	$ 1.012	$0.504
Audit and security	3%	$ 0.759	$0.378
Accounting & management	3%	$ 0.759	$0.378
Personnel training	10%	$ 2.530	$1.260
Stationery/printing	6%	$ 1.518	$0.756
Other	5%	$ 1.265	$0.630

TABLE 3.8: *Transition costs by bank product during the dual and single currency periods*

Bank Products	% of Total euro changeover costs [Total $25.3 billion]	Dual currency period ($ billion) [Total $12.6 billion]	Single currency period ($ billion)
Notes & coins	12%	$3.036	$1.512
ATMs	6%	$1.518	$0.756
Cards and services	9%	$2.277	$1.134
Payment systems	27%	$6.831	$3.402
Foreign exchange & treasury management	10%	$2.530	$1.260
Loans	10%	$2.530	$1.260
Deposits	10%	$2.530	$1.260
Capital markets	8%	$2.024	$1.008
Other	8%	$2.024	$1.008

revenues are presently accounted for by European currencies, therefore, with the introduction of the euro, European banks have experienced a reduction of approximately 60 per cent of their FX revenues.[10] Such FX trading losses are estimated to be approximately ten per cent of net revenues derived from FX trading, which amounts to about a one per cent loss of total bank revenues.

Estimated FX revenue losses by non-EU banks operating in Europe do not vary much from those of their EU counterparts. On the average, US banks obtain about 13–16 per cent of their total revenue from European operations. Just as in the case of their EU counterparts, approximately 10–13 per cent of this revenue is accounted for by FX-related transactions. The introduction of the euro has generated losses amounting to approximately 60 per cent of FX-related revenue, which is approximately one per cent of the total net European income generated by these banks. Table 3.9 provides estimated 1997 euro changeover losses incurred by three major US banks.

Information Systems/Technology Costs

Prior to 1999, besides the hugely anticipated 'Y2K' software problem, domestic financial institutions had been concerned about the ability of software companies to speedily create programs that included dual currency and accounting systems. Non-financial institutions also faced the challenge of revamping their information systems. As mentioned before, information systems/technology costs, for EU and non-EU banks alike, are estimated at over 50 per cent of total euro changeover costs. This means that approximately US$25.5 billion is being spent by European banks on information systems/technology changes during the current dual currency transition (January 1 1999–December 31 2001) and an anticipated US$17 billion during the final euro dual currency adjustment

TABLE 3.9: *1997 Estimated euro changeover losses of three major US banks ($ in millions)*

	Citibank	Chase Manhattan	Bank of America
Consolidated net income (1997)	$3600	$3710	$3200
Net income from EU operations	$522	$538	$464
Net income originating from FX dealings from EU operations	$60	$62	$53
FX income loss due to the Euro	$36	$37	$32
FX income loss due to the Euro as a percentage of total net income	1%	1%	1%

Source: 1997 Annual Reports.

period (January 1 2002–July 1 2002). Most information systems/ technology costs are generated by money transmission (60%), loans and deposits (20%), and FX, treasury management and capital market (20%) operations. Moreover, initially the most immediate problems were faced by the wholesale banking sector, which started using the euro on January 1 1999. At that time, the costs of holding two sets of currencies at cash points increased.

However, currently, other concerns are pressing. For example, the costs of resizing cash machines (ATMs) and tills for the new euro notes, reprinting brochures and printing separate cheque-books for the euro accounts, as well as the training of staff, are yet to be fully estimated. According to a survey by the British Bankers Association and the Association of Payment Clearing Services (1995), the cost of changing ATMs in the UK will be approximately US$3300 per ATM. With 22,000 ATMs in the UK, the total costs is approximately US$73 million. This represents approximately four per cent of overall bank operating costs. The study also reported that the costs of adjusting bank card systems in 1995 was approximately US$177 million, representing approximately 12 per cent of total bank operating costs.

Payment System Costs

Most of the studies concerning the euro's impact on banks have concluded that the major effects relate to the euro's payment system and to the costs of sustaining it. One such study estimated (Montgomery) the payment system costs for UK banks to reach about US$3.3 billion (in systems and networking revamping) or about 27–30 per cent of the total estimated changeover costs. But estimates for individual banks vary widely from US$125–190 million for large banks to about US$7.5 million for smaller banks. It should be noted that the study was based on the assumption that the UK would be joining EMU and that there would be a 'Big Bang' approach to the euro (i.e., it would be introduced overnight with no dual currency transition period). But because there is currently a dual currency transition period (1999–2001), these estimates have since been doubled; thus, approximately US$6.6 billion will be required to revamp systems and networks, with costs ranging from US$250–380 million for large banks to approximately US$15 million for smaller banks. These estimates were confirmed by the previously cited 1995 study by the Banking Federation of the European Union.

Other Costs

The financial sectors are concerned about a variety of problems occurring during the transition stage because they may not be able to resolve them as they tend to be on the public side. For example, domestic financial institutions are concerned about policies governing debt conversion. EMU required all new government debt to be issued in the euro beginning January 1 1999. However, the conversion of existing debt between 1999 and 2002 is under the jurisdiction of individual nations. Initially, the German government had not yet decided what to do with its stock of outstanding government bonds which expired after 1999, while the French had announced that they would convert theirs to euros during the first year of EMU. The Germans had hesitated because they not only feared that euro-denominated debt could be more expensive to service but were also concerned that German investors could shun such debt when given a choice of Deutschmark, Swiss franc or even US dollar denominated debt. Consequently, German banks had pressured their government to follow the French lead. They feared that if Paris created a pool of liquidity in the euro before Frankfurt, this could give the French financial markets a competitive edge. However, even today, member states are at different stages of euro debt conversion for their existing stock of domestic debt, due to the underestimation of the complexities surrounding the debt conversion and the euro's exchange rate drop since its inception.

EU financial houses and companies are also concerned about the possibility that, unless their governments speed up conversion preparations, they may be prevented from filing accounts and paying taxes in the euro. Many of the large MNCs had indicated that they wanted to switch to euro-based accounting at the start of 1999. Governments that were not ready to accept corporate payments in the euro in 1999 slowed down the adoption of the euro by the corporate sector and thereby distorted competition.

Conclusions

The introduction of EMU and of the euro on January 1 1999 changed the structure and functioning of the international financial markets. The euro changeover costs, in turn, significantly affected the total operating costs of the financial market participants, in particular those of the international banks doing business in the EU.

Due to the economic and technical uncertainties surrounding EMU and the euro, the specific changeover costs are difficult to estimate. However, they are likely to be substantial, particularly during the total transition and final dual currency period between January 1 1999 and July 1 2002, as national currencies co-exist with the euro. The functions that will have to be adjusted range from technical through financial to competitive matters, including the creation of new products. Each of these challenges raises numerous issues that all financial market participants, but particularly the international banks, will have to address in the context of competitive strategy.

Thus, it is surprising that most international banks have been shown to develop a comprehensive euro-strategy focusing on total changeover costs together with an appropriate budget for the final stage of introduction of the cash-based euro. The delay may further complicate an already difficult process, thereby increasing total changeover costs well beyond the currently published estimates.

References

BANK FOR INTERNATIONAL SETTLEMENTS (BIS) (1996) *Central Bank Survey of Foreign Exchange and Derivatives Market Activity 1995*, Bank for International Settlements, Basle, May.

BANK FOR INTERNATIONAL SETTLEMENTS (BIS) (1999) *69th Annual Report*, Bank for International Settlements, Basle, June.

BANKING FEDERATION OF THE EUROPEAN UNION (1995) *Survey*, March.

BLANDEN, M. (1996) Visions of Europe, *Banker*, December.

BMS BOSSARD (1996) *Euro Survey*, BMS Bossard, Paris.

British Bankers Association and the Association of Payment Clearing Services (1995) *Joint 1995 Survey on Euro Changeover Costs*, British Bankers Association, London, and the Association of Payment Clearing Services, London.

DENTON, N. (1997) European monetary union: Impact on IT systems, *Financial Times*, February 5.

EUROPEAN CENTRAL BANK (ECB) (1999) *Annual Report*.

EUROPEAN CENTRAL BANK (ECB) (2000) *Monthly Bulletin*, January, March and April.

EUROPEAN COMMISSION (1997) *Report from the Euro Working Group for the Consumer Committee*, September 15.

FINANCIAL TECHNOLOGY INTERNATIONAL BULLETIN (1995) Europe's bank faces Ecu8–10 billion bill in run-up to EMU, *Financial Technology International Bulletin*, April 1995 and April 1996.

FINANCIAL TIMES (1996) Anxiety over EMU starts to creep in, *Financial Times*, December 3.

MCCAULEY, R. N. and WHITE, W. R. (1997) *The Euro and European Financial Markets* Working Paper No. 41, Monetary and Economics Depart, BIS, Basle, May.

MONTGOMERY, M. J. *The Costs of the Switchover to the European Single Currency for City Banks with Emphasis on the Payment System.*

REHMAN, S. S. (1997) *The path to European Economic and Monetary Union*, Kluwer Academic Publishers, Boston.

SALOMON BROTHERS (1996) What EMU might mean for European banks, *European Equity Research*, October 29.
WHITE, D. (1997) Costs to banks for Euro switch 'overestimated' *Financial Times*, June 10.

Notes

1. In 1995, Austria, Finland and Sweden were admitted and thus EU membership increased to 15.
2. In addition to EMU, the Treaty established the European Union (EU) and officially changed the name of the European Economic Community (EEC) to European Community (EC), recognized the latter as the economic 'pillar' and added the security–foreign policy as well as home affairs–justice 'pillars' to the newly created Union. Under the aegis of the EC, the Treaty calls for the creation of EMU.
3. All existing ecu financial instruments, payments and invoicing arrangements were converted into the euro on January 1 1999.
4. According to the Maastricht Treaty, nations can become EMU members only if they meet the following specific convergence criteria: (1) a country's inflation rate in the year before its performance is examined must not exceed the average of the three best-performing economies by more than 1.5 percentage points (inflation is measured by the consumer price index); (2) the annual general government budget deficit (including social insurance) must not exceed three per cent of GDP while the government debt ratio has to remain below 60 per cent of GDP. Nor can the annual general government budget deficits exceed public investment expenditures; (3) a nation's currency must be a member of the EMS exchange rate mechanism (ERM) within the 'normal' fluctuation margins (+/– 15 per cent) for at least two years prior to examination. Currencies cannot be unilaterally devalued during this period; and (4) in the year before performance is assessed, long-term market interest rates (taking government bonds as a benchmark) must not be more than two percentage points higher than the average comparable interest rates in the three countries with the lowest inflation.
5. Although, not discussed here, there are also substantial changeover costs incurred by national governments, their central banks and non-financial businesses. These costs, in turn, will have an impact on international banks and their changeover costs.
6. It is conceivable that a couple of the remaining four EU non-EMU nations could decide to join EMU over the next three years.
7. Survey conducted by Cap Gemini Sogeti, a Paris-based computer services and consulting group as reported in *Financial Times* (1996).
8. BMS Bossard is part of the Paris-based Cap Gemini Group, a major information technology and management consulting services company.
9. An average of the FX revenues as a percentage of total earnings for four major European banks.
10. As only 11 of the 15 EU nations have joined EMU, there will still be FX activity in EU currencies. This also takes into account possible gains generated by the euro, i.e. new euro FX contracts.

4

A Comparison of the Financial Characteristics of French, German and UK Manufacturing Firms

ILHAN MERIC, BENJAMIN H. EICHHORN, CAROL N. WELSH and GULSER MERIC

Introduction

The subject of integration has received considerable attention in finance literature. Stulz (1981) observes that barriers between countries have a significant effect on international investors' investment decisions and on global financial integration. Gultekin et al. (1989) demonstrate that the removal of barriers in the Japanese financial markets has acted to increase financial integration between the United States and Japan. Bekaert and Harvey (1995) find that barriers affect global financial integration adversely.

The European Union (EU) countries have embarked on a process of removing barriers and integrating their economies since 1958. Several studies have focused on the financial integration of European countries. Schollhammer and Sand (1985) find that the EU has created a high level of interdependence between the member economies. Beckers et al. (1992) study the common factors in European equity markets and conclude that the harmonization of fiscal and monetary policies among the member states of the EU has resulted in an increased integration of their capital markets. Armstrong et al. (1996) examine the relationship between savings and investments within the EU and conclude that the capital markets of the EU member states are integrated. Friedman and Shachmurove (1997) find a greater degree of financial integration between larger European countries than between smaller states.

If the capital markets of the EU countries are integrated, the cost of capital to all firms in the EU would tend to be similar and firms in the same industry with similar business risks would tend to have similar capital structures. Moreover, the free movement of the factors of production and the availability of identical technology throughout the EU would enable firms in all EU member countries to acquire resources at comparable, competitive prices and adopt the best available techniques of production. Therefore, the asset structures of firms in the same industry in different EU countries would also tend to be similar. In this study, we test this hypothesis using a sample of manufacturing firms from three EU member countries: France, Germany, and the UK. While previous studies have investigated various aspects of integration, the effect of integration on the financial characteristics of business firms has not been previously studied.

The paper is organized as follows: in the next section, we explain the data and methodology of the study. Following this, we use the MANOVA (multivariate analysis of variance) technique to compare the financial characteristics of French, German, and UK manufacturing firms. Finally, we summarize our findings and present our conclusions.

Data and Methodology

The data used in this study are drawn from the COMPUSTAT/Global database, using the 1996 year-end financial statements of the studied firms. The research sample includes 50 manufacturing firms from each country; a total of 150 firms from the three countries. The study covers five major industries:

1. Food and kindred products (SIC: 20);
2. Textile products (SICs: 22 and 23);
3. Chemicals and allied products (SIC: 28);
4. Industrial machinery and equipment (SIC: 35); and
5. Electronic and electrical equipment (SIC: 36).

The number of firms included in the study from each industry are presented in Table 4.1.

Comparing the financial characteristics of different groups of firms with financial ratios is a methodology widely used within finance literature (see, for example, Altman, 1968; Edmister, 1972; Belkaoui, 1978; Rege, 1984; Meric and Meric, 1994; and Meric et al., 1997). We use the multivariate analysis of variance (MANOVA)

TABLE 4.1: *Sample used in the study*

Industry Name	France	Germany	UK	Industry Total
	\multicolumn{4}{Number of Firms}			

Industry Name	France	Germany	UK	Industry Total
Food & kindred products tax	10	10	10	30
Textile products	8	8	8	24
Chemicals & allied products	16	16	16	48
Industrial machinery & equipment	6	6	6	18
Electronic & electrical equipment	10	10	10	30
COUNTRY TOTAL	50	50	50	150

method to compare the financial characteristics of French, German, and UK manufacturing firms in terms of various financial attributes represented by ten well-known financial ratios. The financial ratios used in the study are presented in Table 4.2.

The accounting practices in France, Germany and the UK are similar and should not distort our comparisons with financial ratios. Since its foundation, the EU has been making efforts to reduce the differences in accounting practices in member states. The main mechanism used to achieve this is the issuance of Directives, which are binding instructions from the European Council of Ministers to individual member states' governments to enact laws in accordance with their provisions. The Fourth Directive, which was issued in 1978, sets down rules for the preparation of financial statements. The Seventh Directive, which was issued in 1983, seeks to harmonize practice throughout the EU regarding the preparation, audit, and publication of consolidated financial statements (see Coopers and Lybrand, 1993).

TABLE 4.2: *Financial ratios used in the study*

Symbol	Financial Ratios
Liquidity Ratios:	
CR	Current Ratio = Current Assets/Current Liabilities
QR	Quick Ratio = (Current Assets − Inventories)/Current Liabilities
Turnover Ratios:	
ARTURN	Accounts Receivable Turnover = Sales/Accounts Receivable
INVTURN	Inventory Turnover = Sales/Inventories
TATURN	Total Assets Turnover = Sales/Total Assets
Leverage Ratios:	
DEBT/TA	Debt Ratio = Total Debt/Total Assets
LTD/DEBT	Long-Term Debt Ratio = Long-Term Debt/Total Debt
Profitability Ratios:	
PROFMARG	Operating Profit Margin = Operating Profit/Sales
ROA	Return on Assets = Net Income/Total Assets
ROE	Return on Equity = Net Income/Common Equity

MANOVA Tests

France vs. Germany

The ten financial ratios of 100 French and German manufacturing firms were used as input for the SPSSX–MANOVA computer program to determine whether the financial characteristics of manufacturing firms in the two countries are similar or significantly different. The MANOVA test statistics are presented in Table 4.3.

The Wilks Lambda multivariate test statistic indicates that the overall financial characteristics of French and German manufacturing firms (as represented by the ten financial ratios) are significantly different at the one per cent level.

The univariate F Value test statistics indicate that the current ratios of German manufacturing firms are significantly higher than the current ratios of French manufacturing firms at the one per cent level. However, the quick ratios of manufacturing firms in the

TABLE 4.3: *MANOVA test statistics: France vs. Germany*

	Mean Values*		F Value	Significance
	France	Germany		
Liquidity Ratios				
CR	1.81	2.50	8.07	0.01
	(0.78)	(1.52)		
QR	1.23	1.44	1.32	0.25
	(0.59)	(1.15)		
Turnover Ratios				
ARTURN	4.15	6.24	12.59	0.00
	(1.52)	(3.88)		
INVTURN	7.22	8.87	1.69	0.20
	(4.37)	(7.86)		
TATURN	1.21	1.27	0.36	0.55
	(0.54)	(0.56)		
Leverage Ratios				
DEBT/TA	20.32%	24.15%	1.48	0.23
	(13.43%)	(17.73%)		
LTD/DEBT	16.40%	16.36%	0.00	0.99
	(12.43%)	(14.02%)		
Profitability Ratios				
PROFMARG	3.57%	3.03%	0.18	0.68
	(3.45%)	(8.32%)		
ROA	4.11%	2.08%	3.45	0.07
	(4.41%)	(6.32%)		
ROE	9.95%	3.58%	2.07	0.15
	(14.02%)	(27.98%)		

MANOVA statistics: Wilks Lambda = 0.41425 Significance = 0.000
*   The figures in parentheses are the standard deviations.

two countries are not significantly different. This implies that German manufacturing firms carry more inventories as a percentage of current assets than French manufacturing firms.

The univariate tests with the turnover ratios indicate that the inventory turnover and total asset turnover ratios of manufacturing firms in the two countries are not significantly different. However, German manufacturing firms appear to have significantly higher accounts receivable turnover ratios than French manufacturing firms at the one per cent level.

The univariate test results indicate that the leverage and profitability ratios of French and German manufacturing firms are not significantly different at the five per cent level.

France vs. UK

The MANOVA test results for French and UK manufacturing firms are presented in Table 4.4. The Wilks Lambda multivariate test

TABLE 4.4: *MANOVA test statistics: France vs. UK*

	Mean Values*		F Value	Significance
	France	Germany		
Liquidity Ratios				
CR	1.81	1.66	8.77	0.00
	(0.78)	(0.72)		
QR	1.23	0.97	4.58	0.01
	(0.59)	(0.43)		
Turnover Ratios				
ARTURN	4.15	6.57	8.35	0.00
	(1.52)	(3.69)		
INVTURN	7.22	8.43	0.98	0.38
	(4.37)	(5.60)		
TATURN	1.21	1.38	1.34	0.27
	(0.54)	(0.48)		
Leverage Ratios				
DEBT/TA	20.32%	20.14%	1.07	0.35
	(13.43%)	(14.97%)		
LTD/DEBT	16.40%	20.13%	0.98	0.38
	(12.43%)	(19.23%)		
Profitability Ratios				
PROFMARG	3.57%	4.58%	0.76	0.47
	(3.45%)	(6.40%)		
ROA	4.11%	5.22%	3.32	0.04
	(4.41%)	(7.42%)		
ROE	9.95%	11.54%	1.77	0.17
	(14.02%)	(22.93%)		

MANOVA statistics: Wilks Lambda = 0.46952 Significance = 0.000
* The figures in parentheses are the standard deviations.

statistic indicates that the overall financial characteristics of French and UK manufacturing firms (as represented by the ten financial ratios) are significantly different at the one per cent level.

The univariate test statistics indicate that French manufacturing firms have more liquidity than UK manufacturing firms. Both the current ratios and the quick ratios of French manufacturing firms are significantly higher than UK manufacturing firms at the one per cent level.

UK manufacturing firms have significantly higher accounts receivable turnover ratios than French manufacturing firms. However, the inventory turnover and total assets turnover ratios of manufacturing firms in the two countries are not significantly different.

The return on assets ratios of UK manufacturing firms are significantly higher than French manufacturing firms at the five per cent level. However, the profit margin and return on assets ratios of manufacturing firms in the two countries are not significantly different.

Germany vs. UK

The MANOVA test results for German and UK manufacturing firms are presented in Table 4.5. The Wilks Lambda multivariate test statistic indicates that the overall financial characteristics of German and UK manufacturing firms (as represented by the ten financial ratios) are significantly different at the one per cent level.

The univariate test statistics indicate that German manufacturing firms have more liquidity than UK manufacturing firms. Both the current ratios and the quick ratios of German manufacturing firms are significantly higher than UK manufacturing firms at the one per cent level.

The univariate F Value test statistics indicate that the inventory turnover and leverage ratios of German and UK manufacturing firms are not significantly different.

The return on assets ratios in UK manufacturing firms are significantly higher than in German manufacturing firms at the five per cent level. However, the profit margin and return on assets ratios of manufacturing firms in the two countries are not significantly different.

Summary and Conclusions

Previous studies have investigated various aspects of economic and financial integration. However, the effect of integration on the

TABLE 4.5: *MANOVA test statistics: Germany vs. UK*

	Mean Values*		F Value	Significance
	France	Germany		
Liquidity Ratios				
CR	2.50	1.66	12.52	0.00
	(1.52)	(0.72)		
QR	1.44	0.97	7.48	0.01
	(1.15)	(0.43)		
Turnover Ratios				
ARTURN	6.24	6.57	0.19	0.66
	(3.88)	(3.69)		
INVTURN	8.87	8.43	0.11	0.74
	(7.86)	(5.60)		
TATURN	1.27	1.38	1.01	0.32
	(0.56)	(0.48)		
Leverage Ratios				
DEBT/TA	24.15%	20.14%	1.50	0.22
	(17.73%)	(14.97%)		
LTD/DEBT	16.36%	20.13%	1.26	0.27
	(14.02%)	(19.23%)		
Profitability Ratios				
PROFMARG	3.03%	4.58%	1.09	0.30
	(8.32%)	(6.40%)		
ROA	2.08%	5.22%	5.19	0.04
	(6.32%)	(7.42%)		
ROE	3.58%	11.54%	2.42	0.12
	(27.98%)	(22.93%)		

MANOVA statistics: Wilks Lambda = 0.56904 Significance = 0.000
* The figures in parentheses are the standard deviations.

financial characteristics of business firms has not been studied. In this paper, we have compared the financial characteristics of French, German, and UK manufacturing firms using the multi-variate analysis of variance (MANOVA) technique. The MANOVA test statistics indicate that, although France, Germany and the UK are members of the European Union and they have integrated economies and financial markets, the overall financial characteristics of manufacturing firms in these three countries (as represented by ten widely-used financial ratios) are significantly different. The multivariate test statistics indicate that the most significant differences are between the financial characteristics of German and UK manufacturing firms and the least significant differences are between the financial characteristics of French and German manufacturing firms.

The most significant difference between the financial characteristics of manufacturing firms in the three countries is in terms of liquidity. German manufacturing firms have the highest and UK manufacturing firms the lowest liquidity ratios.

The manufacturing firms of the three countries have similar inventory turnover and total assets turnover ratios. However, German and UK manufacturing firms have significantly higher accounts receivable turnover ratios than French manufacturing firms.

The total debt to total assets and long-term debt to total debt ratios of manufacturing firms in the three countries are not significantly different. Manufacturing firms in all three countries appear to use similar degrees of financial leverage in their business operations. This may be the result of integrated financial markets in the European Union enabling manufacturing firms in all three countries to obtain financing at comparable costs.

UK manufacturing firms have significantly higher total assets turnover ratios than French and German manufacturing firms. This indicates that UK manufacturing firms are able to generate more sales on a given amount of investment in assets compared with French and German manufacturing firms.

The profit margin ratios of manufacturing firms in the three countries are not significantly different. This may be the result of integration keeping product prices at comparable levels throughout the European Union and the availability of the same techniques of production to all manufacturing firms throughout the European Union keeping product costs at comparable levels in all three countries.

The return on equity ratios of French, German and UK manufacturing firms are not significantly different. This may be the result of integration and free market economy within the European Union forcing manufacturing firms in all three countries to have comparable levels of return on equity.

References

ALTMAN, E. I. (1968) Financial ratios, discriminant analysis, and the prediction of corporate bankruptcy, *Journal of Finance*, Vol. 23, No. 4, pp. 589–609.

ARMSTRONG, H. W., BALASUBRAMANYAM, V. N. and SALISU, M. A (1996) Domestic savings, intra-national and intra-European capital flows, *European Economic Review*, Vol. 40. pp. 1229–1235.

BECKERS, S., GRINOLD, R., RUDD, A. and STEFEK, D. (1992) The relative importance of common factors across the European equity markets, *Journal of Banking and Finance*, Vol. 16, No. 1, pp. 75–95.

BEKAERT, G. and HARVEY, C. R. (1995) Time varying world market integration, *Journal of Finance*, Vol. 50, No. 2, pp. 403–444.

BELKAOUI, A. (1978) Financial ratios as predictors of Canadian takeovers, *Journal of Business Finance and Accounting*, Vol. 5, No. 1, pp. 93–108.

COOPERS and LYBRAND (International) (1993) *International Accounting Summaries: A Guide for Interpretation and Comparison*, 2nd ed., John Wiley and Sons Inc., New York.

EDMINSTER, R. O. (1972) An empirical test of financial ratio analysis for small business failure prediction, *Journal of Financial and Quantitative Analysis*, Vol. 7, No. 2, pp. 1477–1493.

FRIEDMAN, J. and SHACHMUROVE, Y. (1997) Co-movements of major European Community stock markets: A vector autoregression analysis, *Global Finance Journal*, Vol. 8, No. 2, pp. 257–277.

GULTEKIN, M. N., GULTEKIN, N. B. and PENATI, A. (1989) Capital controls and international capital market segmentation: The evidence from the Japanese and American stock markets, *Journal of Finance*, Vol. 44, No. 4, pp. 849–870.

MERIC, I. and MERIC, G. (1994) A comparison of the financial characteristics of US and Japanese manufacturing firms, *Global Finance Journal*, Vol. 5, No. 1, pp. 205–218.

MERIC, I., ROSS, L. W., WEIDMAN, S. M. and MERIC, G. (1997) A comparison of the financial characteristics of US and Japanese chemical firms, *Multinational Business Review*, Fall, pp. 23–27.

REGE, U. P. (1984) Accounting ratios to locate takeover tagets, *Journal of Business Finance and Accounting*, Vol.11, No.3, pp. 301–311.

SCHOLLHAMMER, H. and SAND, O. (1985) The interdependence among the stock markets of major European countries and the United States: An empirical investigation of interrelationships among national stock market movements, *Management International Review*, Vol. 25, No. 1, pp. 17–26.

STULZ, R. (1981) On the effects of barriers to international investment, *Journal of Finance*, Vol. 36, No. 4, pp. 923–934.

5

Common Information in a Common Market?
Variance Changes in European Capital Markets

ALAN ALFORD, GULSER MERIC and ILHAN MERIC

Introduction

Fischer and Palasvirta (1990) suggest that a common information set is created by capital market integration and that these markets reflect an increased number of common, random shocks across the economies. Ammer and Mei (1996) proffer that integrated markets would have similar reactions to common shocks. Thus, capital market integration should imply a high level of interdependence across capital markets. A shock to one market should quickly be transmitted to other markets.

European countries have integrated their economies over the last 40 years primarily via the goods markets, but this also would affect their capital markets. Wheatley (1988) demonstrates the link between the goods and capital markets using the Consumption Capital Assets Pricing Model (CCAPM). Investors try to hedge against price changes in the basket of goods that they consume. Thus, as investors open up to a greater consumption of non-domestic goods, they will necessarily want to open their portfolios to a greater allocation of international assets. Trade integration leads to capital market integration; thus, European capital markets should exhibit the characteristics set forth by Fischer and Palasvirta (1990) and by Ammer and Mei (1996). Koch and Koch (1991) do find a significant cross-influence of market information for markets that are geographically close, indicating a greater interdependence[1]. However, several empirical examinations of Europe's capital markets tend to contradict the conclusion of greater interdependence across markets.

Schollhammer and Sand (1985) analyse the autocovariances of six selected European capital markets and the United States. The European markets have significant autocovariances, but these intra-European influences are weaker than influences from the United States. Fischer and Palasvirta (1990), using the spectral statistics of world markets, find low coherence, or covariance relation, among the European markets, especially relative to some other market pairs. Eun and Shim (1989) include four European markets in their Vector Autoregression analysis and find little correlation among the errors for the European markets or spillover of information from one market onto another. Beckers et al. (1992), analysing European stock returns using pre-specified factors, conclude that country-specific factors were gaining in significance, not declining. Thus, pan-European information has a diminishing importance in pricing risky European assets. This implies a growing independence for European markets, not a growing interdependence.

This is counter-intuitive to the results expected for integrated markets. Integrated markets should have a common pricing of risk as the influences on the price of risk should be the same. The studies cited above suggest that shocks are totally self-contained within each country with only a minimal spillover; they suggest that there is no commonality of shocks in these capital markets, as events in one country do not necessarily transfer to other countries. In the next section, we propose an alternative test of the spillover effect that explicitly searches for changes in the information set for 12 European countries.

Data and Methodology

This paper tests for explicit shifts in the information set of individual European capital markets and their relation to shifts in the other European markets. The methodology employed aims to detect any shocks that occur in these markets. Points of change are identified and contrasted across European countries. Through this approach, we explicitly examine and test the commonality of shocks for a set of integrated countries. Regardless of an event's origin, an ex-post examination of the returns generated should indicate the event's influence on the risk–return relationship.

In a traditional event study methodology, the researcher examines risk-adjusted returns that occur surrounding a given event. Researchers extract the error terms from the regression to compute Cumulative Abnormal Returns (CAR) for each country over an event window around the event. Statistically significant CARs indicate the importance of the event on the pricing of assets. If the returns are significantly different from zero at a pre-determined level, the event is deemed to have been relevant to the evolution of returns.

In this study, we reverse this process. Inclán and Tiao (1994) describe an alternate methodology for uncovering the event-induced significant change points based upon the Cumulative Sum of Squares (CSS) – the CAR over the entire period in event study terminology – from a regression analysis. This approach provides estimates of points where there are significant shifts in the underlying structure of the regression or significant changes in the risk–return relationship. Aggarwal, Inclán, and Leal (1999) employ this methodology to a set of emerging capital markets – Germany, Japan, the United Kingdom, and the United States – and are able to correlate the indicated change points and events in the underlying capital markets.

Inclán and Tiao (1994) define a D statistic in their equation (2) that is based on the CSS through observation k of the sample period (C_k) and on the CSS of the entire regression (C_T). This equation is reproduced as our equation (1)[2]. The maximum D, in absolute terms, is then multiplied by the square root of the number of observations to develop the test statistic. This statistic is distributed F with T–k and k degrees of freedom. If this value is greater than a predetermined significance level, the point is determined to be significant. Following the suggestion of Inclán and Tiao, we use a five per cent (5%) significance level.

$$D_k = \frac{C_k}{C_T} - \frac{k}{T} \qquad (1)$$

The Inclán–Tiao methodology is recursive. Should this first point be significant, the CSS is then calculated from observations 1 to k and from k+1 to T to check for other significant points. This process identifies j possible points where the variance changes. The D statistic is then recalculated between each identified point and tested for significance[3]. If the D statistic is still significant, the point is retained.

For this study, we employ the log returns with net dividends reinvested from the Morgan Stanley Capital International (MSCI) indices for 12 European countries. Table 5.1 lists the countries that are used in the study and their status in the European Union (EU).

The returns are calculated monthly in the local currency[4]. We estimate a CAPM model, as shown in equations 2a and 2b, using the world market index from MSCI (World) and an arithmetic average for the five original members of the EU (EU5)[5].

$$R_i - R_{f,i} = a_i + \beta_i(R_{World} - R_{f,World}) + \varepsilon_I \qquad (2a)$$

$$R_i - R_{f,i} = a_i + \beta_i(R_{EU5} - R_{f,EU5}) + \varepsilon_I \qquad (2b)$$

where:

R_i = Index returns of country i
$R_{f,i}$ = Risk-free rate of country i
R_{World} = World index returns
$R_{f,World}$ = Average risk-free rate for the world index
$R_{f,EU5}$ = Average risk-free rate for the EU5 countries
a_i = A constant
β_i = Regression coefficient (beta of country i's stock market)
ε_I = Error term of country i's market model

We proxy the risk-free rate with interest rates from *International Financial Statistics (IFS)*. IFS does not report a full series of Swiss interest rates; we take the proxy for the Swiss franc interest rate from the OECD's *Main Economic Indicators*. These interest rates are converted into monthly rates using continuous discounting. We calculate the excess returns for each market as the difference of a country's monthly return and its proxy for the risk-free rate. To calculate the excess returns of the indices, we define the risk-free rate as the arithmetic average of the constituent components of each index.

Break and shifts in the pricing of risky assets occur due to shifts in the information sets. If common sets of information influence all European markets, the Inclán–Tiao methodology will indicate

TABLE 5.1: *European countries included in the study and their EU status*

Original Member	Joined in 1973	Joined in 1986	Joined in 1995	Not a member
Belgium	Denmark	Spain	Austria	Norway
France	United Kingdom	Sweden	Switzerland	
Germany				
Italy				
Netherlands				

common reaction and shifts due to changes in the information set. Therefore, besides allowing an indication of relevant information, we may infer the level of spillover among the various European markets in the study.

Findings

Table 5.2 reports the estimates of the dates where changes take place based on the regressions involving equations (2a) and (2b). No date is significant for all countries, not even for all members of the EU at a given time; rather, a date tends to be associated with only one country. This indicates that shocks are related largely to domestic, not pan-European, events and the effect of any shock is largely confined to

TABLE 5.2: *Dates of significant changes in variance estimated by Inclán–Tiao methodology*

Country	Change Dates	
	World	EU5
Austria	1985:01	1985:01
		1990:09
	1992:09	
Belgium		1980:01
	1981:11	
	1988:02	1988:02
		1993:11
Denmark	1975:07	
	1980:08	
France	1988:05	1988:05
Germany	1975:08	
	1985:04	1985:04
	1990:09	
		1991:05
Italy	1986:07	
Netherlands		1981:02
	1987:12	
		1988:02
Norway	1981:07	
	1992:08	1992:08
Spain	1987:11	
		1988:03
Sweden		1980:10
Switzerland	1975:11	
	1985:05	
	1989:06	
United Kingdom		1977:01
	1977:09	
		1988:02

that country. We find no significant spillover of information across European capital markets. This reinforces the findings of Schollhammer and Sand (1985), Eun and Shim (1989), and Fischer and Palasvirta (1990). Information is not shared across European markets. Certain information catalyses a shift in the asset pricing of one market, but does not shift the way assets are priced in others.

Thus, even in integrated markets, the influence of domestic information is paramount. This is reminiscent of Stehle's (1977) model stressing the importance of both domestic and international factors in the pricing of risky assets. This result also confirms the finding of Beckers et al. (1992) regarding the importance of country-specific factors in pricing European risky assets. A pricing model that neglects domestic factors and events will be misspecified. The true sources of risk will not be included in the analysis and conclusions drawn from those models will be erroneous.

Summary and Conclusions

European countries have taken strong, definitive steps to integrate their capital markets. Capital market integration implies a high level of interdependence across capital markets. Fischer and Palasvirta (1990) and Ammer and Mei (1996) suggest that integrated markets would have similar reactions to random shocks. However, several earlier studies, including Schollhammer and Sand (1985) and Eun and Shim (1989) suggest that, although European capital markets are likely to be integrated, they don't have similar reactions to random shocks. Beckers et al. (1992) conclude that country-specific factors are gaining in significance in European capital markets, not declining, even with regional integration of the goods markets.

We investigated the interdependence of integrated markets using a methodology that explicitly searched for changes in the information set. Further, we also used more recent data to take fuller advantage of the attempts of these countries to integrate. We, like the previous studies, found no significant spillover of information across European capital markets: events are totally self-contained and shifts appear to be related only to domestic factors. This reinforces the importance of domestic factors in asset pricing models, even if the markets are integrated.

References

AGGARWAL, R., INCLÀN, C. and LEAL, R. (1999) Volatility in emerging stock markets, *Journal of Financial and Quantitative Analysis*, Vol. 34, No. 1, pp. 33–35.

AMMER, J. and MEI, J. (1996) Measuring international economic linkages with stock market data, *Journal of Finance*, Vol. 51, No. 5, pp. 1743–1763.

BECKERS, S., GRINOLD, R., RUDD, A. and STEFEK, D. (1992) The relative importance of common factors across the European equity markets, *Journal of Banking and Finance*, Vol. 16, No. 1, pp. 75–95.

EUN, C. S. and SHIM, S. (1989) International transmission of stock market movements, *Journal of Financial and Quantitative Analysis*, Vol. 24, No. 2, pp. 241–256.

FISCHER, K. and PALASVIRTA, A. P. (1990) High road to a global marketplace: The international transmission of stock market fluctuations, *Financial Review*, Vol. 25, No. 3, pp. 371–394.

INCLÀN, C. and TIAO, G. C. (1994) Use of cumulative sum of squares for retrospective detection of changes in variance, *Journal of American Statistical Association*, Vol. 89, pp. 913–923.

KOCH, P. D. and KOCH, T. W. (1991) Evolution in dynamic linkages across daily national stock indices, *Journal of International Money and Finance*, Vol. 10, No. 2, pp. 231–251.

SCHOLLHAMMER, H. and SAND, O. (1985) The interdependence among the stock markets of major European countries and the United States: An empirical investigation of interrelationships among national stock market movements, *Management International Review*, Vol. 25, No. 1, pp. 17–26.

STEHLE, R. (1977) An empirical test of the alternative hypothesis of national and international pricing of risky assets, *Journal of Finance*, Vol. 32, No. 2, pp. 493–502.

WHEATLEY, S. (1988) Some tests of international equity integration, *Journal of Financial Economics*, Vol. 21, No. 2, pp. 177–212.

Notes

1. Among European markets, they consider only Germany, Switzerland, and the United Kingdom in their sample.

2. C_k refers to the Cumulative Sum of Squares from the regression for observations 1 through k. There are a total of T observations included in the regression.

3. For the first observed point, the D statistic is calculated from the first observation (January 1970) through the second observed point. For the final observed point, the D statistic is calculated from the penultimate observed point through the final observation (December 1996 in this study).

4. MSCI also defines a world market index in 'local' currency terms that has no adjustment for exchange rates. This index is used in the estimates involving the local currency.

5. Luxembourg is the sixth original member of the European Union, but its market returns are not included in this study.

volatility than positive innovations. This phenomenon has been linked in the literature to the so-called 'leverage effect.' According to this conjecture, negative stock returns yield a higher debt-to-equity ratio and hence higher volatility. Our study builds on previous research and seeks to shed some additional light on this issue, by investigating the asymmetric transmission of volatility among these five major Asian stock markets. Our empirical findings confirm the claim made by earlier studies that the conventional simple correlations do not reflect the true interrelationships between capital markets. Thus, the use of common correlations between markets in optimal portfolio construction might lead to the implementation of suboptimal portfolios.

The remainder of this paper is organized as follows. First we present the multivariate VAR–EGARCH model. Following this, we describe the data and some preliminary statistics. We then discuss the findings of this investigation, before offering some concluding remarks.

The Multivariate VAR–EGARCH Model

Let $R_{i,t}$ be the logarithmic return at time t for market i where, i = 1, 2, 3, 4, 5 (1=Hong Kong, 2=Japan, 3=Singapore, 4=Korea, and 5=Taiwan), Ω_{t-1} is the information set at time t–1, $\mu_{i,t}$ and $\sigma^2_{i,t}$ the conditional mean and conditional variance respectively, $\varepsilon_{i,t}$ the innovation at time t (i.e., $\varepsilon_{i,t} = R_{i,t} - \mu_{i,t}$), and $Z_{i,t}$ the standardized innovation (i.e., $Z_{i,t} = \varepsilon_{i,t}/\sigma_{I,t}$). The multivariate VAR–EGARCH model is specified as:

$$\mu_{i,t} = \beta_{i,0} + \sum_{j=1}^{5} \beta_{i,j} R_{i,t-1} + \varepsilon_{i,t} \text{ for i, j} = 1, 2, 3, 4, 5 \qquad (1)$$

$$\sigma^2_{i,t} = \exp\{\alpha_{i,0} + \sum_{j=1}^{5} \alpha_{i,j} X_{j,t-1} + \gamma_i \ln(\sigma^2_{i,t-1}) \} \text{ for i, j} = 1, 2, 3, 4, 5 \qquad (2)$$

$$X_{j,t-1} = (| Z_{j,t-1} | - E(| Z_{j,t-1} |) + \delta_j Z_{j,t-1}) \text{ for j} = 1, 2, 3, 4, 5 \qquad (3)$$

$$\sigma_{ij,t} = \rho_{ij} \sigma_{i,t} \sigma_{j,t} \text{ for i, j} = 1, 2, 3, 4, 5 \text{ and i} \neq j. \qquad (4)$$

In equation (1) we specify the conditional mean of country i as a function of the past returns of the other countries as well as its own. The coefficients $\beta_{i,j}$ measure the degree of mean spillover effect across countries. A significant $\beta_{i,j}$ coefficient would imply that market j leads market i or, equivalently, current returns in market j can be used to predict future returns in market i.

Equation (2) describes the conditional variance process as an extended EGARCH process which allows us to test and measure the asymmetric impact of both its own and other countries' past standardized innovations on the conditional variance of a country. The coefficient $\alpha_{i,j}$ in equation (2) captures the effect of innovations from country j on country i.

The variable $X_{j,t-1}$, is specified in equation (3) and is intended to capture the asymmetric effect of past standardized innovations, $Z_{j,t-1}$ ($Z_{j,t-1} = \varepsilon_{j,t-1} / \sigma_{j,t-1}$), on current volatility. The term $|Z_{j,t-1}| - E(|Z_{j,t-1}|)$ measures the size effect, while the term $\delta_j Z_{j,t-1}$ measures the sign effect. If market advances and market declines impact volatility symmetrically, the coefficient δ_j would not be expected to be significant. The degree of asymmetry, or leverage effect, can be measured by the ratio $|(\delta-1)/(1+\delta)|$.[2] However, if stock market declines in country j ($Z_{j,t-1} < 0$) are followed by higher (lower) volatility than stock market advances ($Z_{j,t-1} > 0$), we would expect δ_j to be negative (positive) and significant. Assuming $\alpha_{i,j}$ is positive, the larger the deviation of past standardized innovation from its expected value, the larger the impact (positive or negative) on the current variance. To recapitulate, a significant positive $\alpha_{i,j}$ coupled with a negative δ_j implies that negative innovations in market j have a higher impact on the volatility of market i than positive innovations, i.e., the volatility transmission mechanism is asymmetric. The coefficient γ_i in equation (2) measures the persistence in volatility. If $\gamma_i = 1$, then the unconditional variance does not exist and the conditional variance follows an integrated process of order one. As noted by Hsieh (1989), the exponential specification is less likely to produce integrated variances.

Equation (4) depicts the contemporaneous relationship between the five markets denoted by the covariance and it assumes constant correlation. This is a plausible assumption and it reduces the number of parameters to be estimated.

Assuming that the distribution of returns is normal, the log-likelihood function for the multivariate VAR–EGARCH can be expressed as:

$$L(\Theta) = (1/2)(NT)\ln(2\pi) - (1/2)\sum_{t=1}^{T}(\ln|St| + \varepsilon_t' S_t^{-1} \varepsilon_t) \qquad (5)$$

where Θ is the parameter vector to be estimated. $\varepsilon_t' = [\varepsilon_{1t}, \varepsilon_{2t}, \varepsilon_{3t}, \varepsilon_{4t}, \varepsilon_{5t}]$ is the 1×5 vector of innovations at time t, S_t is the 5×5 time varying conditional variance–covariance matrix with diagonal elements given by equation (2) for i = 1, 2, 3, 4, 5, and cross-diagonal elements given by equation (4) for i, j=1,2,3,4,5 and i≠j. The log-likelihood function in (5) is maximized using the Berndt et al. (1974) algorithm.

Data and Preliminary Findings

The data used in this study are the daily closing stock price indices of the Hong Kong, Japan, Singapore, South Korea, and Taiwan stock markets[3]. This data set covers the period from January 1 1990 to April 28 1995 and contains 1379 observations. Daily percentage returns are calculated as $100*\log(P_t/P_{t-1})$ where P_t is the value of the index at t in terms of local currency.

Table 6.1, panel A, reports results from diagnostic statistics on the distributional properties of the data. Kolmogorov–Smirnov statistics indicate non-normality of unconditional return series for all five markets. All the return series, except for Korea, show negative skewness and all the series have fat tails. The Ljung–Box statistics calculated for both the return and the squared return time series indicate stronger second moment (non-linear) time dependencies. These are typical characteristics of financial series that fit ARCH-type modeling techniques.

TABLE 6.1: *Preliminary statistics on the return time series*

PANEL A: Statistics					
	Hong Kong	Japan	Singapore	Korea	Taiwan
μ	0.0724	–0.0137	0.0468	–0.0010	–0.0361
σ	1.4497	1.5652	1.0173	1.4714	2.3943
S	–0.4381*	–0.3271*	–0.4480*	0.2685*	–0.0275
K	4.0102*	4.3180*	6.3382*	2.9869*	2.6481*
D	0.0571*	0.0762*	0.1465*	0.0379*	0.0543*
LB(10); for R_t	12.5515	25.1389*	63.0358*	9.6790	20.4389
LB(10); for R_t^2	142.2610*	164.2520*	270.8712*	345.7825*	1041.6011*

PANEL B: Correlation matrix					
	Hong Kong	Japan	Singapore	Korea	Taiwan
Hong Kong	1.0000	0.2472	0.4934	0.0785	0.1523
Japan		1.0000	0.3856	0.0783	0.1436
Singapore			1.0000	0.1795	0.2185
Korea				1.0000	0.1052
Taiwan					1.0000

Notes:
The sample spans the period January 1 1990 to April 28 1995. It contains 1379 observations. Daily continuous returns are constructed using the formula $R_t=100*(P_t/P_{t-1})$, where P_t is the value of the price index at time t. μ=sample mean; σ=sample standard deviation; S=skewness; K=excess kurtosis; D=Kolmogorov–Smirnov test for normality (5% critical value is $1.32/\sqrt{T}$, where T is the number of observations); LB(n) is the Ljung–Box statistic for up to n lags (distributed as χ^2 with n degrees of freedom).
Asterisk, *, denotes statistical significance at the 5% level.

Table 6.1, panel B, reports ordinary historical correlations between the markets of the five Asian countries. Singapore and South Korea play a key role in the interdependence of the five markets examined. Singapore has the highest correlation while South Korea has the lowest correlation with all other countries. The low correlation of the Korean market with the remaining markets may be attributed to the corporate restrictions on foreign ownership, which were partially lifted in 1992. The conventional correlations show the average level of correlation during the sample period and are asymptotically efficient only in the case when the mean and variance of the return series are stationary. Since there is statistical evidence that the return series among these countries are heteroskedastic, one would expect the dynamics of these time-dependent correlations to be significantly different from their historical counterparts.

Table 6.2 reports results for the sign bias test, the negative size bias test, the positive size bias test, and the joint F test for the logarithmic returns of the five countries under consideration[4].

According to the t-statistics of this table, the innovations (positive and negative) in Hong Kong, Japan and Singapore have an additional effect on the volatility in these markets, beyond what is predicted by a model with symmetric responses. Based on the size bias tests, it is not possible to identify the source of these effects

TABLE 6.2: *Volatility specification tests based on the news impact curve*

	Hong Kong	Japan	Singapore	Korea	Taiwan
Sign Bias (t-tests)	−3.02*	−2.72*	−6.25*	−0.02	−0.80
Negative Size Bias (t-tests)	2.03*	1.12	6.20*	−1.97*	1.77
Positive Size Bias (t-tests)	2.42*	4.06*	6.19*	−0.42	1.16
F-test; F(3, 1379)	3.30*	6.17*	20.65*	2.17*	1.31

Notes:

The table presents the results of tests for the asymmetric effect of new information on the volatility of stock market returns as developed by Engle and Ng (1993). Let $j = 1, 2, 3, 4, 5$ (1=Hong Kong, 2=Japan, 3=Singapore, 4=South Korea, and 5=Taiwan), $\varepsilon_{j,t}$ is the error from the conditional mean equation of the jth market as of t, and $\sigma_{j,t}$ is the squared root of its conditional variance. These tests are specified as follows:

Sign Bias:	$z^2_{j,t} \equiv (\varepsilon_{j,t}/\sigma_j)^2 = a + b\, S_{-j,t} + e_{j,t}$	(i)
Negative Size Bias:	$z^2_{j,t} \equiv (\varepsilon_{j,t}/\sigma_j)^2 = a + b\, S_{-j,t}\, \varepsilon_{j,t-1} + e_{j,t}$	(ii)
Positive Size Bias:	$z^2_{j,t} \equiv (\varepsilon_{j,t}/\sigma_j)^2 = a + b\, (1 - S_{-j,t})\, \varepsilon_{j,t\,t-1} + e_{j,t}$	(iii)
Joint Test:	$z^2_{j,t} \equiv (\varepsilon_{j,t}/\sigma_j)^2 = a + b_1\, S_{-j,t} + b_2\, S_{-j,t}\, \varepsilon_{j,t-1} + b_3\, (1 - S_{-j,t})\, \varepsilon_{j,t-1} + e_{j,t}$	(iv)

where S_{-t} is a dummy variable that takes the value of one if ε_{t-1} is negative and the value of zero otherwise.

All t-statistics refer to the coefficient b in the regressions (i), (ii), and (iii), while the $F(3,1379)$ is the joint F test.

Asterisk, *, denotes statistical significance at the 5% level.

CHEUNG, Y. W. and NG, L. K. (1992) Stock price dynamics and firm size: An empirical investigation, *Journal of Finance*, Vol. 47, pp. 1985–1997.

CHRISTIE, A. A. (1982) The stochastic behaviour of common stock variances: Value, leverage and interest rate effects, *Journal of Financial Economics*, Vol. 10, pp. 407–432.

CHRISTOFI, A. and PERICLI, A. (1999) Correlation in price changes and volatility of major Latin American stock markets, *Journal of Multinational Financial Management*, Vol. 9, pp. 79–93.

DIVECHA, A. B., DRACH, J. and STEFEK, D. (1992) Emerging markets: A quantitative perspective, *Journal of Portfolio Management*, Vol. 18, No. 1, pp. 41–50.

ENGLE, R. F. and NG, V. K. (1993) Measuring and testing the impact of news on volatility, *Journal of Finance*, Vol. 48, pp. 1749–1778.

ERB, C. B., HARVEY, C. R. and VISKANTA, T. E. (1994) Forecasting international equity correlations, *Financial Analysts Journal*, November/December, pp. 32–45.

EUN, C. S. and RESNICK, B. F. (1989) Estimating the correlation structure of international share prices, *Journal of Finance*, Vol. 41, pp. 313–330.

EUN, C. S. and SHIM, S. (1989) International transmission of stock market movements, *Journal of Financial and Quantitative Analysis*, Vol. 24, No. 2, pp. 241–256.

GRUBEL, H. G. (1968) International diversified portfolios: Welfare gains and capital flows, *American Economic Review*, Vol. 58, pp. 1299–1314.

HAMAO, Y. R., MASULIS, R. W. and NG, V. K. (1990) Correlation in price changes and volatility across international stock markets, *The Review of Financial Studies*, Vol. 3, pp. 281–307.

HARVEY, C. R. (1993) Portfolio enhancement using emerging markets and conditioning information, in S. CLAESSENS and S. GOOPTU, *Portfolio Investment in Developing Countries*, World Bank Discussion Paper 228, September, pp. 110–144.

HARVEY, C. R. (1995) Predictable risk and returns in emerging markets, *Review of Financial Studies*, Vol. 8, No. 3 (Fall), pp. 773–816.

HSIEH, D. (1989) Modeling heteroskedasticity in daily foreign exchange rates, *Journal of Business and Economic Statistics*, Vol. 7, pp. 307–317.

JEON, B. N. and VON FURSTENBERG, G. M (1990) Growing international co-movement in stock price indexes, *Quarterly Review of Economics and Business*, Vol. 30, No. 3, pp. 15–30.

KING, M. A., SENTANA, E. and WADHWANI, S. (1994) Volatility and the links between national stock markets, *Econometrica*, Vol. 62, pp. 901–934.

KING, M. A. and WADHWANI, S. (1990) Transmission of volatility between stock markets, *The Review of Financial Studies*, Vol. 3, pp. 281–307.

KOCH, P. D. and KOCH, T. W. (1991) Evolution in dynamic linkages across daily national stock indices, *Journal of International Money and Finance*, Vol. 10, pp. 231–251.

KOUTMOS, G. (1992) Asymmetric volatility and risk return tradeoff in foreign stock markets, *Journal of Multinational Financial Management*, Vol. 2, pp. 27–43.

KOUTMOS, G. (1996) Modeling the dynamic interdependence of major European stock markets, *Journal of Banking, Finance and Accounting*, Vol. 23, pp. 975–988.

KOUTMOS, G. and BOOTH, G. G. (1995) Asymmetric volatility transmission in international stock markets, *Journal of International Money and Finance*, Vol. 14, No. 5, pp. 747–762.

LESSARD, D. (1974) World, national and industry factors in equity return, *Journal of Finance*, Vol. 26, pp. 379–391.

LEVY, H. and SARNAT, M. (1970) International diversification of investment portfolios, *American Economic Review*, Vol. 60, No. 4 (September), pp. 668–675.

LONGIN, F. M. and SOLNIK, B. (1995) Is the correlation in international equity returns constant: 1960–1990? *Journal of International Money and Finance*, Vol. 14, pp. 3–26.

MATHUR, I. and SUBRAHMANYAM, V. (1990) Interdependencies among the Nordic and US stock markets, *Scandinavian Journal of Economics*, Vol. 92, pp. 587–597.

NELSON, D. B. (1991) Conditional heteroskedasticity in asset returns: A new approach, *Econometrica*, Vol. 59, pp. 347–370.

POON, S-H. and TAYLOR, S. J. (1992) Stock returns and volatility: An empirical study of the UK stock market, *Journal of Banking and Finance*, Vol. 16, pp. 37–59.

SOLNIK, B. H. (1974) Why not diversify internationally rather than domestically? *Financial Analysts Journal*, Vol. 30, pp. 48–54.

SPEIDELL, L. S. and SAPPENFIELD, R. (1992) Global diversification in a shrinking world, *Journal of Portfolio Management*, Vol. 19, No. 1 (Fall), pp. 57–67.

THEODOSSIOU, P. (1994) The stochastic properties of major Canadian exchange rates, *Financial Review*, Vol. 29, pp. 193–221.

THEODOSSIOU, P. and LEE, U. (1993) Mean and volatility slipovers across major national stock markets: Further empirical evidence, *Journal of Financial Research*, Vol. 16, pp. 337–350.

THEODOSSIOU, P. and LEE, U. (1995) Relationships between volatility and expected returns across international stock markets, *Journal of Business Finance and Accounting*, Vol. 22, pp. 289–300.

THEODOSSIOU, P., KAHYA, E., KOUTMOS, G. and CHRISTOFI, A. (1997) Volatility reversion and correlation structure of returns in major international stock markets, *Financial Review*, Vol. 32, pp. 205–224.

Notes

The authors would like to thank Pennoyer Capital Management, Inc. for providing the data.

1.   For a comprehensive review of the literature in this area, the interested reader is referred to Bollerslev et al. (1992 and 1994).

2.   This measure is based on the fact that the slope of $X_{j,t-1}$ is equal to $-1+\delta$ for negative values of $Z_{j,t-1}$ and $1+\delta$ for positive values of $Z_{j,t-1}$ (see Nelson, 1991 and Koutmos and Booth, 1995).

3.   Using data from the same geographical region presents an advantage, as it avoids the problem of asynchronous data which tends to cloud the true transmission of mean and volatility spillover effects.

4.   The sign bias test explores the impact of positive and negative innovations on volatility not predicted by the model. The squared standardized residuals are

regressed against a constant and a dummy S_t^- that takes the value of unity if ε_{t-1} is negative and zero otherwise. The test is carried out based on the t statistic of the coefficient for S_t^-. The negative size bias test examines how well the model captures the impact of large and small negative innovations. It is based on the regression of the squared standardized residuals against a constant and $S_t^- \varepsilon_{t-1}$. Again, the calculated t statistic for the coefficient of $S_t^- \varepsilon_{t-1}$ is used in this test. The positive size bias test examines possible biases associated with positive innovations, both large and small. Here, the squared standardized residuals are regressed against a constant and $(1-S_t^-)\varepsilon_{t-1}$. As before, the t statistic is used for possible biases. A joint F test can also be used even though the individual tests are more powerful (see Engle and Ng, 1993).

5.   This conclusion is consistent with earlier studies by Black (1976), Christie (1982), Nelson (1991), Poon and Taylor (1992), Cheung and Ng (1992), Koutmos (1992, 1996), and Koutmos and Booth (1995). A related study by Erb, Harvey, and Viskanta (1994) found higher correlations in down markets and during recessions.

7

Debt Financing by Industrial Firms in the Pacific Basin: An Empirical Study

LAKSHMAN ALLES, ROSITA P. CHANG and RAMAKRISHNAN S. KOUNDINYA

Introduction

This chapter is an empirical study of the importance of the country factor on the use of debt financing by industrial firms located in the Pacific Basin region. Firms from six industries in Japan, Korea and Taiwan were selected for this study. These three countries are in different stages of capital market development and have varying financial and other institutional infrastructures. More importantly, there is a range of managerial and culture differences across the respective sample countries. Also, regulatory environments, information disclosure requirements and expectations, interrelationships between different stakeholders, and the role of financial intermediaries vary considerably between these countries. Such differences should have noticeable impact on the financing decisions of firms located in these countries and consequently on their capital structures.

Recent and traditional capital structure theories based on market imperfections and product market characteristics have shown capital structure variations, and in turn, propose a variety of hypotheses regarding factors that determine the use of debt financing. While empirical studies on specific variables simplified by theories and assessment of their roles in determining capital structure are ongoing and inconclusive, recent research lends strong support to the relevance of industry and country factors with regard to the use of financial leverage. The rationale for the importance of an industry factor is fairly straightforward. Firms within an industry are, by and large, grouped by commonality from the impact of product market factors and other characteristics. Thus, there is an expectation of a common approach to the determinants of capital structure. This would also mean that differences in the pattern of debt usage among firms across industries could be explained by the industry factor.

Firms located in different countries clearly face different environmental and other country-specific effects indicating the relevance of the country factor as a contributor to the capital structure decision. In a recent cross-sectional study on the use of financial leverage by industrial firms located in Japan, Germany, and USA, Chugh et al. (1996) show that the use of leverage does depend on the country of location. However, the results are mixed for different industries, suggesting the potential impact of international competitiveness on the industries, which may override the country factor.

This study extends the empirical research on the impact of industry and country factors among firms located in the Pacific Basin region. Following is a brief review of related literature. The next section discusses the data source, data selection, and the methodology for the empirical analysis. A discussion of empirical findings follows. The paper concludes with a summary of key findings and scope for other research.

Brief Review of Relevant Literature

For well over the past three decades a continuing research effort has been dedicated to the resolution of what has become known as the 'capital structure puzzle'. From the time of the proposition of the notion of capital structure irrelevance (Modigliani and Miller, 1958, 1963), researchers sought reasons to account for observable regularities in the use of debt financing. Schwarz and Aronson (1967) and Scott (1972) offered some early empirical evidence on the stability of financing patterns and the dependence of debt financing in the context of market imperfections (Jensen and Meckling, 1976; Myers and Majluf, 1984; and Mayer, 1989), and product market strategies (Brander and Lewis, 1986). Empirical research has kept pace with a stream of alternate theoretical views, however the empirical findings are inconclusive in regard to the dominance of any one theory[1].

While empirical findings on the proposed specific determinants are inconclusive there is strong support of the finding of regularity in financing patterns across firms, industries and country of location. While the focus of theories is at a firm level, there are reasons for the prevalence of regularity across industries and country of location. Industry average financing measures have always served as indicators of optimal capital structure. Furthermore, insofar as firms within an industry are in some sense homogeneous, they may all be impacted by similar factors. Thus the industry factor is likely to capture and account for some variations in the financing patterns. A corresponding argument validates the expectation of the impact of country of location factor. The country factor should partially account for the distinct roles played by the capital market and the financial infrastructure in the economies of different countries. Furthermore, market imperfections due to agency costs, information asymmetry and the desire for control would have different implications and responses from the various stake-holders in the respective countries. Remmers et al. (1974), Aggarwal (1981), Errunza (1979), and Collins and Sekley (1983) offered early empirical evidence supporting the importance of country factor in accounting for some regularity in financing differences across locations. Kester (1986) observed that book value based measures of leverage showed significant variations among firms located in the US and Japan. Rutherford (1988), Macclure et al. (1994) provided evidence on observable differences in financing patterns among firms in the US, UK, and Japan using OECD data, and among G7 nations using Disclosure World Scope/Global data, respectively. Rajan and Zingales (1995) reviewed various leverage measures extracted from the Global Vantage database and noted that the UK and Germany have lower leverage ratios while the rest of the G7 countries have similar leverage ratios. No statistical tests were offered on the significance of their observation.

In a recent study, Chugh et al. (1996) examined the financing pattern of firms located in the US, Germany, and Japan for the years 1987–1992. Their sample included nine industries comparable across countries with screened data on leverage measures. They used the financial statements information provided by the Global Vantage database for the selected firms in the respective countries. Their finding strongly supported the significance of a country location factor on debt financing across countries. They observed that equality of mean debt to asset ratio among the population of firms located in US, Germany, and Japan can be rejected at one per cent significance level. However, results for individual industry analyses are mixed. They observed that possible differences in the international competitive posture of different industries could explain such mixed results. This paper extends the investigation on the importance of country of location factor on the use of debt financing by firms located in Pacific Basin countries.

Data Source, Data Selection and Methodology

The Sandra Ann Morsilli Pacific Basin Capital Markets (PACAP) Research Center at the University of Rhode Island has developed a comprehensive, computerized database which traces capital market data for ten Pacific Basin countries: China, Hong Kong, Indonesia, Japan, Korea, Malaysia, the Philippines, Singapore, Taiwan, and Thailand[2]. For each country, the database provides extensive information on security prices and market-related data, economic statistics for the country, and financial statements for all listed companies in the respective countries. For this study, listed companies' financial statements data is used to extract the sample data for analysis. Japan, Korea and Taiwan are selected as representative countries due to the availability of extensive financial statements information in these countries as well as the existence of a wide cross-section of comparable industries. Furthermore, these three countries have an adequate sample of firms so that extreme values can be screened out within each industry[3]. The six industries selected are: food and beverage, textile and clothing, electrical and electronic products, chemicals and plastics, wood and paper, and primary metals. Leverage ratio is proxied by total interest-bearing debt divided by total assets. Firms with debt to total assets ratio of zero or less and firms with debt to total assets and other leverage-related variables were extracted for firms meeting the screening criteria for the years 1985 and 1994.

The one-way analysis of variance (ANOVA) is used to test the significance of the country factor in the aggregate and for selected industry firms respectively. The SAS–GLM procedure is used to execute the ANOVA tests. The procedure test for the equality of means of the study variable is the debt to total assets ratio for selected populations. The importance of the country factor in the aggregate is tested by pooling data for all firms into each respective country's population. The aggregate country population is then disaggregated by industry to test the importance of country factor within each industry group. The importance of the industry factor, holding the country factor constant, is assessed by disaggregating data by country and running the GLM procedure. Reported F tests and probabilities are used to assess the significance of the country and industry factors.

Empirical Results

Mean Debt Ratios Across Three Countries

Table 7.1 summarizes the sample data used in the analysis for six selected industries as well as whole sample for Japan, Korea, and Taiwan. The leverage ratio is proxied by total interest-bearing debt to total assets ratio. As reported in Panel A, for Japan, the total number of observations used is relatively stable for the ten-year period. The mean debt ratios show a generally declining trend for the aggregate data. This declining trend is exhibited by all industries except the electrical and electronics industry. The decline is most pronounced for pulp and paper and primary metal industries. Debt ratios vary, from a high of 60.51 per cent for the pulp and paper industry in 1985, to a low of 26.82 per cent for the food and beverages industry in 1994. These two industries define the upper and lower limits of debt usage in Japan for all years for the sample under study. The pulp and paper industry uses almost twice as much debt as the food and beverage industry per dollar of assets. The primary metal industry has the second highest debt ratios, but exhibits the largest decline.

Panel B of Table 7.1 reports the data for Korea. The usage of debt financing in Korea does not conform to the pattern for Japan in a number of ways. The food and beverages industry has the highest use of debt financing, while the primary metals industry has the lowest debt usage. For the chemical and plastics and electrical and electronics industries, debt usage declined over the years, but this trend was not as pronounced as in Japan. For other industries such as textile and clothing and pulp and paper, the debt ratios actually increased over the years.

Panel C of Table 7.1 reports the mean debt ratios for Taiwan. The trend in the debt ratios confirm the general pattern of declining usage of debt over the study period. Similar to Japan and Korea, the pulp and paper industry has the highest debt ratio. Overall, the use of leverage is higher in Japan and Korea than in Taiwan. This is not surprising, considering the high degree of ownership concentration and affiliation observed in both Japan and Korea[4]. In the aggregate, debt ratios in Japan are higher during 1985–88 and decline to levels closer to those for Korea and Taiwan during 1989–94. For the whole period, the mean debt to asset ratios are 38.70 per cent and 39.36 per cent in Korea and Japan, respectively, while the mean debt ratio for Taiwan is 25.41 per cent. These differences in the aggregate proved to be statistically significant as shown in Table 7.2 that follows[5].

TABLE 7.1: Sample size and mean debt-to-asset ratio: by country and industry

	1985	1986	1987	1988	1989	1990	1991	1992	1993	1994	Tot/Avg
PANEL A: Japan											
Food & beverages											
No. of observation	76	78	77	81	81	80	82	83	84	86	808
Mean debt/asset ratio (%)	30.58	28.74	27.93	28.74	28.00	27.70	26.74	27.00	27.22	26.82	27.91
Textile & clothing											
No. of observation	68	61	62	71	69	72	71	72	65	64	675
Mean debt/asset ratio (%)	48.77	45.30	43.56	42.96	41.23	39.51	39.37	39.58	40.00	39.56	41.92
Pulp & paper											
No. of observation	26	24	27	27	27	26	27	27	25	24	260
Mean debt/asset ratio (%)	60.51	57.92	55.29	52.10	51.70	50.32	51.90	51.78	53.09	53.70	53.78
Chemical & plastics											
No. of observation	151	150	159	160	161	163	163	168	168	167	1610
Mean debt/asset ratio (%)	42.6	42.18	39.39	37.07	35.18	34.91	35.06	34.37	34.04	32.96	36.66
Primary metals											
No. of observation	84	81	85	85	85	83	82	83	76	77	821
Mean debt/asset ratio (%)	57.34	57.58	54.88	50.51	45.97	45.66	45.17	45.71	45.49	44.33	49.34
Electrical & electronics											
No. of observation	31	31	32	32	32	32	32	34	31	29	316
Mean debt/asset ratio (%)	36.64	38.19	38.35	37.73	37.88	39.20	40.15	40.77	41.88	40.73	39.15
Total no. of observations	436	425	442	456	455	456	457	467	449	447	4,490
Mean debt/asset ratio (%)	44.95	43.69	41.85	39.95	38.01	37.51	37.40	37.35	37.17	36.30	39.36
	1985	1986	1987	1988	1989	1990	1991	1992	1993	1994	Tot/Avg
PANEL B: Korea											
Food & beverages											
No. of observation	32	33	30	34	43	43	42	42	41	35	375
Mean debt/asset ratio (%)	48.11	46.03	41.92	42.50	45.17	44.55	44.86	47.82	47.57	44.20	45.36
Textile & clothing											
No. of observation	31	32	32	41	56	58	60	58	56	53	477
Mean debt/asset ratio (%)	37.61	36.12	31.38	36.70	35.66	36.77	39.07	38.32	37.40	36.96	36.85
Pulp & paper											
No. of observation	13	12	12	20	28	31	31	32	31	25	235
Mean debt/asset ratio (%)	46.28	41.93	37.39	40.37	40.91	41.67	40.80	43.47	45.33	41.51	42.11

TABLE 7.1: *Sample size and mean debt-to-asset ratio: by country and industry*

	1985	1986	1987	1988	1989	1990	1991	1992	1993	1994	Tot/Avg
Chemical & plastics											
No. of observation	32	31	36	44	55	57	56	57	58	56	482
Mean debt/asset ratio (%)	39.00	36.17	37.59	34.99	33.21	36.05	37.55	34.71	32.71	32.66	35.17
Primary metals											
No. of observation	15	16	18	25	28	34	36	37	36	29	274
Mean debt/asset ratio (%)	38.01	35.66	36.35	32.83	33.61	35.65	37.45	37.89	36.38	35.21	35.95
Electrical & electronics											
No. of observation	24	26	34	54	69	81	76	74	73	73	584
Mean debt/asset ratio (%)	47.63	45.91	44.06	42.27	36.41	38.15	37.15	36.56	36.77	37.14	38.78
Total no. of observations	147	150	162	218	279	304	301	300	295	271	2,427
Mean debt/asset ratio (%)	42.64	40.42	38.37	38.53	37.15	38.48	39.09	39.03	38.44	37.29	38.70
	1985	1986	1987	1988	1989	1990	1991	1992	1993	1994	Tot/Avg
PANEL C: Taiwan											
Food & beverages											
No. of observation	11	11	13	13	15	16	18	20	23	23	163
Mean debt/asset ratio (%)	40.94	33.40	32.93	32.42	26.09	24.37	26.02	28.50	27.28	26.03	28.91
Textile & clothing											
No. of observation	22	22	23	25	29	30	33	39	42	42	307
Mean debt/asset ratio (%)	36.87	32.91	33.44	31.22	26.78	24.36	25.07	22.99	22.18	24.08	26.90
Pulp & paper											
No. of observation	7	7	7	7	7	7	8	8	8	8	74
Mean debt/asset ratio (%)	38.93	28.10	31.08	36.37	32.09	32.18	31.98	35.20	35.56	35.00	33.69
Chemical & plastics											
No. of observation	11	15	17	20	21	23	24	29	29	31	220
Mean debt/asset ratio (%)	23.46	19.60	19.35	15.47	18.66	15.18	15.16	16.52	16.78	16.19	17.10
Primary metals											
No. of observation	1	1	4	8	9	11	12	16	18	17	97
Mean debt/asset ratio (%)	18.49	20.10	27.97	27.02	31.40	31.23	37.61	34.82	31.20	33.79	32.34
Electrical & electronics											
No. of observation	3	3	4	10	12	15	21	24	27	32	151
Mean debt/asset ratio (%)	26.08	23.50	22.55	25.24	22.16	20.29	25.59	21.84	20.77	20.83	22.19
Total no. of observations	55	59	68	83	93	102	116	136	147	153	1,012
Mean debt/asset ratio (%)	34.34	28.35	28.62	26.92	25.09	22.97	25.03	24.33	23.49	23.75	25.41

ANOVA Tests on Country Factor

Table 7.2 presents the empirical findings of ANOVA tests on the debt to total asset ratio across populations. Values in the last row are the results of tests on the equality of mean debt to total asset ratio across countries in the aggregate. The F statistics and the probability clearly show that the differences are highly significant. The country of location does determine the use of debt financing by firms in the three selected Asian countries: Japan, Korea and Taiwan.

Table 7.2 also presents the results on tests for the equality of means of debt to total asset ratios across the countries by industry groups. As can be noted, the industry results are mixed. The use of debt financing differs significantly among three countries for two out of the six industries (food and beverage and chemical and plastics) for all of the sample years. For the primary metals industry, the hypothesis of equality of mean debt to total asset ratio across three countries can not be rejected at the one per cent significance level only for 1991[5]. For the electrical and electronics industry the differences are not significant at the one per cent level only for years 1985 and 1987. The pulp and paper industry fails to show significant differences for years 1988 and 1989, while the textiles and clothing industry fails to show significant differences across countries for years 1986, 1987 and 1988. It is important to note, however, that the equality of mean debt ratios

TABLE 7.2: *Capital structure by country F ratio and F probability*

	1985	1986	1987	1988	1989	1990	1991	1992	1993	1994
Food & beverage										
F-Ratio	14.94	14.50	9.81	12.87	24.28	24.07	23.5	31.14	30.00	21.14
F-Prob	.0001	.0001	.0001	.0001	.0001	.0001	.0001	.0001	.0001	.0001
Textile & clothing										
F-Ratio	5.77	4.32	4.34	4.44	7.21	9.05	8.31	11.43	13.51	8.94
F-Prob	.0041	.0156	.0152	.0135	.0010	.0002	.0004	.0001	.0001	.0002
Pulp & paper										
F-Ratio	6.00	9.31	8.32	4.19	5.15	4.35	6.92	4.39	4.52	6.28
F-Prob	.0050	.0005	.0009	.0207	.0087	.0147	.0019	.0164	.0148	.0035
Chemical & plastics										
F-Ratio	5.53	12.67	9.96	16.54	12.45	17.79	19.01	16.69	15.69	16.35
F-Prob	.0046	.0001	.0001	.0001	.0001	.0001	.0001	.0001	.0001	.0001
Primary metals										
F-Ratio	11.73	11.52	10.57	16.99	10.48	8.61	3.81	4.79	6.90	4.73
F-Prob	.0001	.0001	.0001	.0001	.0001	.0003	.0247	.0098	.0014	.0105
Electrical & electronics										
F-Ratio	4.42	3.41	4.02	5.55	6.01	11.12	7.47	12.24	14.08	15.46
F-Prob	.0166	.0400	.0199	.0053	.0033	.0001	.0009	.0001	.0001	.0001
All six industries combined										
Total F-Ratios	7.47	17.63	14.44	20.49	26.01	39.84	31.93	38.87	43.62	37.19
F-Prob	.0006	.0001	.0001	.0001	.0001	.0001	.0001	.0001	.0001	.0001

across countries can be rejected at the five per cent level of significance for every industry for every year of study. This result reinforces
the importance of the country factor in the Pacific Basin region.

ANOVA Tests on Industry Factor

Using ANOVA tests, this paper also examines the importance of the
industry factor in each of the country location. Table 7.3 presents the
results of ANOVA tests for Japan, Korea, and Taiwan. For each
country, results for the equality of mean debt to total asset ratio test
across six industries are reported. In the case of Japan, the hypothesis
of equality of mean debt ratio can be rejected at the one per cent
level for all years 1985–94. For Korea and Taiwan, the F ratios are
smaller and the significance levels are lower in all years. Nevertheless,
for all three countries, the differences are statistically significant at
the five per cent level except in the case of Korea in 1991. This
confirms the importance of the industry factor within each country.

Temporal Stability of Leverage Ratio

To assess the temporal stability of debt usage by each industry in the
three countries, ANOVA tests were performed using respective
samples. The results are reported in Table 7.4. A low F ratio will
show that the equality of mean debt ratio across the sample period
cannot be rejected. Except for the chemical and plastics and
primary metals industries in Japan, electrical and electronic
industry in Korea, and textiles and clothing industry in Taiwan, all
other industry debt ratios show temporal stability.

Conclusion

This paper empirically investigated the importance of country of
location on debt financing decisions by companies in the Pacific

TABLE 7.3: *Capital structure by industry F ratio and F probability*

COUNTRY	1985	1986	1987	1988	1989	1990	1991	1992	1993	1994
Japan										
F-Ratio	27.47	24.15	22.45	18.46	16.88	15.07	16.82	16.10	15.06	14.39
F-Prob	.0001	.0001	.0001	.0001	.0001	.0001	.0001	.0001	.0001	.0001
Korea										
F-Ratio	2.65	2.63	2.48	3.08	4.40	2.43	1.78	5.12	6.31	3.29
F-Prob	.0256	.0260	.0340	.0105	.0007	.0214	.1173	.0002	.0001	.0067
Taiwan										
F-Ratio	2.50	2.83	2.49	4.54	2.43	3.10	5.01	4.50	4.43	5.85
F-Prob	.0433	.0241	.0405	.0011	.0409	.0122	.0004	.0000	.0000	.0000

TABLE 7.4: *Temporal stability of capital structure F ratios and F probabilities*

COUNTRY	Japan	Korea	Taiwan
Food & beverages			
F-Ratio	0.46	0.96	2.28
F-Prob	.8990	.4722	.0199
Textile & clothing			
F-Ratio	1.85	0.66	2.75
F-Prob	.0572	.7489	.0042
Pulp & paper			
F-Ratio	1.00	.42	.52
F-Prob	.4431	.9265	.8573
Chemical & plastics			
F-Ratio	6.02	1.08	.82
F-Prob	.0001	.3769	.6008
Primary metals			
F-Ratio	8.28	.34	.62
F-Prob	.0001	.9607	.7777
Electrical & electronics			
F-Ratio	.96	3.44	.39
F-Prob	.4706	.0004	9405

Basin region. Representative countries chosen for the study were Japan, Korea, and Taiwan. Financial leverage was proxied by the debt to total asset ratios and these ratios were used as dependent variables for the analysis of variance (ANOVA) tests. This was to verify the equality of means of the leverage variable across country population of firms first in the aggregate, then by industrial groupings. The country factor proved to be highly significant in the aggregate while the industry results were mixed. However, at a five per cent level of significance, the hypothesis of equality of means of debt to total asset ratio across countries can be rejected both in the aggregate as well as for five out of six industry groups for every year under study. The results confirmed the importance of the country factor in the Pacific Basin region. The study further tested the differences in the financing patterns between industries in the respective countries. The industry factor proved to be a highly significant determinant of debt financing. The results from the analysis of temporal stability of debt usage by each industry in the three countries showed that for most industries, the use of debt is stable over time. Ongoing empirical investigations plan to include a larger cross-section of countries in the region as well as additional industrial groups. Further analysis on the determinants of leverage ratios for each country may also shed light on the importance of the country factor.

References

AGGARWAL, R. (1981) International differences in capital structure norms: An empirical study of large European companies, *Management International Review*, Vol. 1, pp. 75–88.

BRANDER, J. A. and LEWIS, T. R. (1986) Oligopoly and financial structure: The limited liability effect, *American Economic Review*, Vol. 76, pp. 956–970.

CHUGH, L. C., KOUNDINYA, R. and PURI, Y. R. (1996) Financial leverage: A cross-country analysis, *The International Journal of Finance*, Vol. 8, No. 4, pp. 411–424.

COLLINS, J. M. and SEKELY, W. S. (1983) The relationship of headquarters, country and industry classification to financial structure, *Financial Management*, Autumn, pp. 45–51.

ERRUNZA, V. R. (1979), Determinants of financial structure in the Central American common market, *Financial Management*, Autumn, pp. 72–77.

HARRIS, M. and RAVIV, A. (1991) The theory of capital structure, *Journal of Finance*, March, pp. 297–355.

JENSEN, M. and MECKLING, W.H. (1976) Theory of the firm: Managerial behaviour, agency costs and ownership structure, *Journal of Financial Economics*, October, pp. 305–360.

KESTER, C. W. (1986) Capital and ownership structure: Comparison of United States and Japanese manufacturing corporations, *Financial Management*, Spring, pp. 5–16.

MAYER, C. (1989) Financial systems, corporate finance and economic development, in G. R. G. Hubbard (ed.) *Asymmetric Information, Corporate Finance and Investment*, University of Chicago, Chicago, Illinois.

MCCLURE, K., GARY, K. and ATKINSON, S. M. (1994) International capital structures: Are there differences among G7 nations, *Journal of Business and Economic Perspectives*, Vol. 21, p. 2.

MODIGLIANI, F. and MILLER, M. H. (1958) The cost of capital, corporation finance, and the theory of investment, *American Economic Review*, Vol. 48, pp. 261–297.

MODIGLIANI, F. and MILLER, M. H. (1963) Corporate income taxes and the cost of capital: A correction, *American Economic Review*, Vol. 53, pp. 433–443.

MYERS, S. C. and MAJLUF, N. (1984) Corporate financing and investment decisions when firms have information that investors do not have, *Journal of Financial Economics*, Vol. 13, pp. 187–221.

RAJAN, P. and ZINGALES, L. (1995) What do we know about capital structure? Some evidence from international data, *Journal of Finance*, December, pp. 1421–1460.

REMMERS, L., STONEHILL, A., WRIGHT, R. and BEEKHUISEN, T. (1974) Industry and size as debt ratio determinants in manufacturing internationally, *Financial Management*, Summer, pp. 23–32.

RUTHERFORD, J. (1988) An international perspective on the capital structure puzzle, *Midland Corporate Finance Journal*, Fall, pp. 60–72.

SCHWARZ, E. and ARONSON, J. R. (1967) Some surrogate evidence in support of the concept of optimal capital structure, *Journal of Finance*, March, pp. 10–18.

SCOTT, D. (1972) Evidence on the importance of financial structure, *Financial Management*, Summer, pp. 45–50.

Notes

1. Harris and Raviv (1991) offer an extensive review of literature on the capital structure determinants.
2. The data for PACAP Databases – Japan are provided by Daiwa Institute of Research and Toyo Keizai Inc. Other countries' data are obtained directly from each country's stock exchange and central bank.
3. Hong Kong, Malaysia and Thailand were considered initially but had to be dropped from the sample due to insufficient number of firms within each industry.
4. For example, the *keiretsu* affiliation in Japan and the *chaebol* system in Korea.
5. Given that there is only one company in the primary metals industry in Taiwan for 1985 and 1986, we excluded this industry in the ANOVA analysis for the two years.

8

The Causes and Implications of the 1997 Collapse of the Financial Markets in East Asia

M. RAQUIBUZ ZAMAN

Introduction

The rapid economic growth of countries in east and south-east Asia (henceforth referred to as East Asia, EA) in the recent past has been the envy of the developing world. It is to emphasize this achievement that the term Newly Industrialized Countries, NICs, was coined by development economists. The World Bank in its 1993 study went so far as to call it 'The East Asian Miracle'. Indeed, the EA countries of China, Hong Kong, Indonesia, Malaysia, the Philippines, South Korea, Taiwan and Thailand have made significant strides in transforming their economies over the last two decades. The factors that contributed to the economic transformation have been widely discussed by Ranis (1995), Birdsall et al. (1995) and Krueger (1997) and can be summarized as follows.

The EA nations, particularly Taiwan and Korea, launched their economic development with modernization programs in agriculture, followed by promotion of labour-based technologies to increase exports. Simultaneously, they pursued policies to improve literacy and education that emphasized vocational and technical skills, and gradually shifted toward science and technology. Development economists and multilateral agencies, such as The World Bank and the International Monetary Fund (IMF), are of the opinion that public policies in the EA states have accommodated the changing needs of the economies to shelter them from external shocks. Their governments seemed to have provided fiscal, monetary, industrial, and trade policies that helped to accelerate investments and economic growth at the appropriate times. All of these states followed in some sequence policies of import substitution, trade liberalization and export promotion to propel them toward modernization. It is now apparent that some of these policies were pursued more to benefit certain institutions, organizations, and families connected with the governments than for the long-term well-being of the nations concerned.

This chapter purports to examine not only the usual indicators of success of the EA countries, but also the factors that were either overlooked or ignored by the development experts, but have now prominently surfaced and have been identified to be the causes of the recent collapse of the financial markets in the region. It aims to show that the collapse of the financial markets of EA nations in 1997 should have been foreseen by all concerned in the region. Further, it suggests that economic growth and modernization should not be assessed solely in terms of macro-economic aggregates, but also by the nature of the dissemination of wealth among citizens and the extent to which institutions have been developed and nurtured to ensure transparency and accountability of public as well as private enterprises. This chapter concludes with an analysis of the ramifications of the collapse of the financial markets in 1997 on the long-term economic health of not only the EA nations but also their major trading partners in Asia, Europe and North America.

Analysis of Macroeconomic Indicators of EA Countries

The basic indicator for measuring success in economic development is the size and the rate of growth in the Gross Domestic Product (GDP). Table 8.1 presents data on the average annual growth rates in GDP, GDP per head in 1998, and the annual growth rates in volumes of exports and imports for the last two decades or more.

For the 1970–96 period, China experienced the highest average annual rate of growth in GDP, followed by South Korea, Taiwan, Singapore, Hong Kong, Thailand, Malaysia and Indonesia. Only the Philippines lagged behind, averaging a growth rate only slightly higher than that achieved by the developed economies. That the economic growth of the EA region was fueled by export-led development policies can be seen clearly by the size of the increases in their exports relative to their GDPs. Except for Indonesia and the Philippines during 1980–90, the EA states experienced double-digit

TABLE 8.1: *Growth in exports relative to growth in GDP in East Asian economies*

	Annual avg. growth rate in %					GNP/head ($)
	Export of goods & services		GDP			
Country	1980–90	1990–98	1980–90	1990–98	1970–96	1998[a]
China	11.5	14.9	10.2	11.1	9.1	3220
Hong Kong	15.4	15.3[b]	6.9	5.6[b]	7.5	25,400[c]
Indonesia	2.9	8.6	6.1	5.8	6.8	2790
Malaysia	10.9	13.2	5.3	7.7	7.4	6990
Philippines	3.5	11.0	1.0	3.3	3.6	3540
Singapore	10.8	13.3	6.6	8.0	8.2	28,620
South Korea	12.0	15.7	9.4	6.2	8.4	12,270
Taiwan	–	–	–	–	8.3	17,720
Thailand	14.1	11.1	7.6	7.4	7.5	5840
High income economies	5.1	6.1	3.1	2.1	2.7	23,440

Sources: The World Bank, *World Development Report 1999/2000*, Annex Tables 11 and 1.
The Economist (March 7, 1998), Table 3, page 5.
[a] GNP figures are in purchasing power parity.
[b] For 1990–95.
[c] For 1996.
–   Data not available from the World Bank sources.

increases in their exports at rates which were often some multiples of the rates of growth in their GDPs. How these rates of growth in exports were materialized can explain to a large extent the anomaly that surfaced in 1997 and 1998 in their financial sector. More on this shortly.

A second macro indicator for economic modernization could be the size of foreign direct investment (FDI) flows. Table 8.2 presents

TABLE 8.2: *FDI inflows in East Asian economies (billions of dollars)*

Country	1986–91[a]	1992	1993	1994	1995	1996	1997	1998
China	3.1	11.2	27.5	33.8	37.5	42.3	44.2	45.5
Hong Kong	1.7	2.1	1.7	2.0	2.1	2.5	6.0	1.6
Indonesia	0.7	1.8	2.0	2.1	4.5	8.0	4.7	–0.4
Malaysia	1.6	5.2	5.0	4.3	5.8	5.3	5.1	3.7
Philippines	0.5	0.2	1.0	1.5	1.5	1.4	1.2	1.7
Singapore	3.6	2.4	5.0	5.6	5.3	9.4	9.7	7.2
South Korea	0.9	0.7	0.6	0.8	1.5	2.3	2.8	5.1
Taiwan	1.0	0.9	0.9	1.4	1.5	1.4	2.2	0.2
Thailand	1.3	2.1	1.7	0.6	2.3	2.4	3.7	7.0
Total for East Asia	14.4	26.6	45.4	52.1	62.0	75.0	77.4	71.6
EA as % of all developing countries	49.5	48.5	61.9	61.7	62.2	58.3	44.9	43.1

Source: United Nations, 1998 and 1999, *World Investment Report*.
[a] annual average

data on FDI inflows into the EA states between 1983 and 1998. As the data show, these nine countries attracted the bulk of the FDI inflows that the developing countries as a whole received in the last 16 years or so. The FDIs partly financed the growth of the export industries in the region. The developed countries clearly favoured them and their economic policies, and heavily invested in their economies. China, in particular, has been the darling of the industrialized world since at least 1992.

A corollary to the FDI flows in terms of export financing is the increase in external debt. Tables 8.3 and 8.4 present data on external debt profiles of EA and foreign bank debts, respectively. Table 8.4 also presents data on non-performing loans as a percentage of total loans.

Table 8.3 shows that Indonesia is the most indebted country, followed closely by the Philippines. Malaysia, Thailand and China are less indebted in terms of the sizes of their GNPs. This picture changed somewhat by the end of 1997. The total external debts of the countries jumped to US$146.7 billion for China; US$136.2 billion for Indonesia; US$47.2 billion for Malaysia; US$45.4 billion for the Philippines; and US$93.4 billion for Thailand (World Bank, 1999, pp. 270–271). Total external debt as percentage of GNP in 1997 was 13.9 per cent for China, 61.4 per cent for Indonesia, 48.1 per cent for Malaysia, 50.8 per cent for the Philippines, and 55.1 per cent for Thailand (estimated from World Bank, 1998b, 1999). China and the Philippines improved their ratios in 1997. Size of the short-term debt, either as percentage of total debt or the percentage of GDP (see Table 8.4 for the latter), can be a significant measure of the vulnerability of the borrowing country in a volatile economic

TABLE 8.3: *External debt profile of East Asian countries, 1995*

Type of Debt	China	Indonesia	Malaysia	Philippines	Thailand
External debt (in US dollars)	118.1	107.8	34.4	39.4	56.8
External debt (in % GNP)	17.2	56.9	42.6	51.5	34.9
External public debt (in % GNP)	13.8	34.5	19.7	39.1	10.6
External public debt/reserves (%)	1.2	4.4	0.6	3.9	0.5
Short-term debt (% of total debt)	18.9	20.7	21.2	13.4	32.2
Share of long-term debt at variable rates	29.6	48.1	57.3	39.2	62.8
Currency composition of long-term debt (%)					
US dollars	57.9	21.5	45.1	31.5	26.6
Deutschmark	1.7	4.9	1.1	1.5	2.3
Japanese yen	20.7	35.4	31.7	36.9	48.1
Other	19.7	38.2	22.1	30.1	23.0

Source: World Bank, 1997, Table 65, p. 216.

TABLE 8.4: *Foreign bank debt and share of non-performing loans*

Country	Foreign bank debt as % of GDP as of June 1997[a]			Non-performing loans as % of total loans	
	Short-term	Long-term	Total	1995	End March 1999[b]
Thailand	30	15	45	8	52
Indonesia	22	14	36	10	55
Malaysia	17	13	30	6	24
South Korea	16	7	23	1	16
Philippines	9	8	17	–	–
Taiwan	7	2	9	3	–
China	3	3	6	–	–

Sources: The Economist, 1998d; IMF, 1999, p. 58. *The Economist*, 1998.
[a] Percentages are approximate. Calculated from *The Economist*.
[b] IMF
– Data not available.

situation. Thailand, Indonesia, Malaysia, and South Korea borrowed significantly in the short term, and the events of 1997 and 1998 proved how vulnerable their economies could be. Non-performing loans as percentage of total loans jumped from eight per cent in 1995 to 52 per cent in March 1999 for Thailand. These figures for Indonesia were ten per cent in 1995 and 55 per cent in March 1999; for Malaysia six per cent and 24 per cent; for Korea one per cent and 16 per cent, respectively. (The corresponding figures for the Philippines, Taiwan, and China were not available.) The collapse of the financial markets in 1997 was particularly devastating for the banking sector.

Data on domestic borrowing are more difficult to assess since the lenders and the borrowers are, at times, the same party. The debt-to-equity ratio of 400 per cent for the largest 30 *chaebols* in Korea (The Economist, 1998d, p. 6) clearly indicates bank lending has been rather reckless in the EA region. Just ten big *chaebols* accounted for 19 per cent of all bank lending in 1997 (The Economist, 1998a, p. 82). In Thailand, roughly 25 per cent of all bank loans are in arrears (The Economist, 1998c, p. 81). The situation in Indonesia was equally grim. Malaysia faced a similar situation. Table 8.5 summarizes the predicaments of the banking and finance companies in some of the EA countries.

Thailand, which experienced financial trouble earlier than its neighbouring countries, already closed or suspended operation of 56 financial institutions. Indonesia, South Korea, Malaysia and Singapore also faced closures and consolidations. These are some of the symptoms of troubled economies. Let us examine the nature of the ailment from which the EA nations need to recover to propel their economies forward.

TABLE 8.5: *Status of bank and finance companies in East Asia*

Country	# of banks & finance companies July 1997	Closed/ suspended operation	Nationalized/ administered by restructuring agency	Planning to merge	Foreign-bought majority stake
Thailand	108	56	4	0	4
Malaysia	60	0	0	41	0
Singapore	13	0	0	4	0
Indonesia	228	16	56	11	0
South Korea	56	16	2	0	0

Source: The Economist, 1998c.

The Causes and Implications of Financial Turmoil

The economic crisis in the EA region has been in the making for some time. Rampant corruption that resulted in misallocation of investment funds into government-favoured industries, institutions or families has been reported from time to time by the business periodicals (i.e., Worthy, 1989; The Economist, 1995; Brull and Lee, 1997) even before the financial crisis became apparent. Corruption in Indonesia has enriched the family members of the long-term President Suharto (Thoenes, 1998; The Economist, 1997b and 1997a, pp. 12–16 of the survey), while in all the states of the region it has led to excessive borrowing and over-building in industries and sectors favoured by corrupt officials. Some blame the Asian Crisis on 'the legacy of so-called Japanese development model, and its perverse consequences'. (Wolf, 1998). The model professed the virtue of targeting industries with export potential for preferred access to capital and protection from competition in the domestic market.

Export-led economic growth may eventually cause economic imbalances domestically by promoting islands of economic prosperity at the expense of neglecting sectors which cater to domestic demand. Often such policies fail to promote adequate domestic demand for consumption that can sustain economic growth in the face of external shocks. This is happening to Japan (Montagnon, 1998) and the other East Asian nations that have been following the Japanese model (or variations thereof). The push for exports is also responsible for excessive borrowing and investing in industries such as automobile, shipbuilding, steel, consumer electronics, and even aircraft (in Indonesia and Korea, for example). Indiscriminate investments have created overcapacity in such industries, while shortages loom elsewhere in the economy (Wolf, 1998). Lack of transparency in the EA economies have accentuated the problems

(Stiglitz, 1998; Johnston, 1997) that led to the financial market crash.

Decades of economic growth have prompted the EA countries to embark on grandiose schemes to dominate the world market and/ or to show off to the world their economic successes. The tallest towers, largest airports, seaports, or highways to nowhere were pursued by EA countries. What they have to show for this is nearly US$1 trillion in bank debts that are now threatening to bankrupt the financial system in the region (The Economist, 1998a and 1998c).

It should have come as no surprise to Malaysia, Indonesia, Hong Kong and South Korea to see the collapse of their currencies in the third and fourth quarters of 1997 after what Thailand faced in July. After all, these countries pursued similar economic policies with similar consequences. There has been a failure on the part of the world's multilateral agencies, such as the World Bank and the IMF, as well as the various financial institutions and professional financial analysts, to warn investors all around the world about the impending collapse of the financial markets in EA. Instead, until very recently, they have been praising these economies for their vigorous economic growth and transformation. The fault for the collapse is now being pinned on 'bad private-sector decisions' by Stiglitz, the Senior Vice President and Chief Economist of the World Bank (Stiglitz, 1998). It seems that the implications of the Japanese model of economic growth have not yet been fully comprehended by the development economists or by the development institutions and agencies. A decade-long economic recession and stagnation have not brought home to the Japanese the need for fundamental reforms in their economic institutions and policies. The nations of East Asia should have guarded themselves from policies that did not work for Japan, the second largest economy in the world.

The World Bank, in its East Asia: The Road to Recovery (World Bank, 1998a), summarized the causes of the East Asian financial crises of 1997 as follows:

- First, rapid economic growth in the absence of sophisticated financial markets and institutions along with the heavy presence of government in the economic sector encouraged the private sector corporations and financial institutions to meet the needs of long-term financing through short-term borrowing, mainly from abroad.
- Second, rapid economic growth put severe strain on the basic system of protection of the elderly, the sick, and the unemployed

by the family unit. Instead of personal savings to meet such needs, increasing reliance was put on economic growth to finance this. Large-scale migration of labour to cities and urban areas further weakened the support system. The tradition among the richer countries in the region of providing lifetime employment guarantees worked contrary to the need for flexible labour forces in rapidly growing economies.

- Third, the rapid economic growth in the region was achieved more due to the over-exploitation of natural resources such as forestry, fisheries and agricultural lands than any significant growth in productivity. The World Bank, which coined the term 'The East Asian Miracle' in 1993, now admits that there was no miracle (World Bank, 1998a). Growth in productivity of the region was in line with those of the other developing countries.

- Fourth, large-scale availability of short-term foreign funds seeking higher returns at a time when the governments of the region pursued macro-economic policies that encouraged such inflows created a credit boom. According to The World Bank, "The credit boom, in turn, led to an increase in asset's prices, creating the appearance of high returns. Property values in Bangkok, Seoul, and Jakarta rose at double-digit rates through 1996. Rising asset prices provided greater collateral to banks, and led to greater lending. At the same time, middle- and upper-class owners of these assets, feeling more well-heeled, consumed more freely. Rising aggregate demand encouraged yet more foreign borrowing." (World Bank, 1998a) This exposed the countries to sudden reversals in capital inflows.

Financial liberalization without adequate regulations to ensure proper management of currency risks increased the possibility of a financial crash through its effect on international liquidity (Chang and Velasco, 1998, p. 29; see also Guitian, 1998). The contraction of exports in 1996, after growing 20 per cent in 1995, started the chain reaction of events that ultimately led to the large-scale outflow of funds from Thailand. Under a severe pressure on its currency Thailand had to abandon its peg to dollar in July 1997. This ushered in the financial crisis in East Asia.

The contagion spread rapidly across all trading nations. News of trouble in the banking and financial sectors brought immediate devaluations in their currencies, which in turn caused securities markets to plummet, not only in the EA region, but also in Europe, North America and South America. Even though the financial markets have bounced back since the October 1997 crash, the markets seemed to have become much more volatile since then. The Brazilian currency crisis of early 1999 and the crash of the Russian rouble in summer 1999 are examples of the lingering fallout of the East Asian crisis of 1997.

The EA crisis brought to the forefront the basic weakness of the policies pursued by the IMF and The World Bank in monitoring the economic activities of its member countries. The insistence of the IMF that the governments of the affected countries follow tight monetary policies to suppress inflationary tendencies led to the soaring domestic interest rates. This, in turn, facilitated the heavy inflow of foreign capital that took flight when Thailand failed to support its currency in July 1997. The prescription that the IMF imposed on these countries after the collapse also caused consider-able suffering among the people. Malaysia, which went against the wishes of the IMF and imposed restrictions on capital movements, came out of the crisis earlier than Thailand and Indonesia, the countries that followed the IMF's solutions. However, a report by the IMF suggests that capital controls do not always work at all times for all countries (Lachica, 2000), possibly to fend off widespread criti-cisms of its lack of foresight in stemming the crisis (see also Eichen-green and Portes, 2000).

One of the major factors in the financial markets crisis was the prevalence of widespread corruption and lack of general account-ability in the region. The crisis of 1997 does not seem to have made significant changes in the way business is practised there. A survey of 600 regional businesses in 1999 records the sorry state of affairs in EA. Table 8.6 shows that corruption is still endemic in the region, except to a lesser extent in Singapore. Indonesia is still the most corrupt and the least transparent country.

Restructuring and recapitalization of the banking sector were thought to be a major priority for the EA countries to avert future

TABLE 8.6: *Corruption and transparency in East Asia: 1999*[1]

Country	Scale: 0=best; 10=worst		
	Corruption	Transparency	Potential for social unrest
Indonesia	9.91	8.00	9.64
Malaysia	7.50	6.50	4.88
Philippines	6.71	6.29	4.43
Singapore	1.55	4.55	1.18
Thailand	7.57	7.29	3.86
Japan	4.25	7.13	0.88

Source: The Economist, 2000.
[1]   Ranking by 600 regional businessmen.

TABLE 9.2: *The Wilcoxon test for the comparison of the ROE ratios of US and the PRC*

PAIR	$\sum_{i=1}^{n} ROEUS_{ki}$	$\sum_{i=1}^{n} ROEPRC_{ki}$	DK	RD	NRS
1	16.70	12.36	4.34	3.00	22
2	22.60	7.93	14.67	8.00	
3	30.50	20.90	9.60	4.00	
4	9.30	19.30	−10.00	6.00	6.00
5	10.20	13.04	−2.84	2.00	2.00
6	14.50	13.21	1.29	1.00	
7	28.99	16.99	12.00	7.00	
8	19.19	9.52	9.67	5.00	
					T=8

Source. Calculated from the data provided by *Global Company Handbook 1993* and CD Rom *Disclosure/World Scope 1998*.

$ROEUS_{ki}$ = ROE of the kth US. industry in the ith year;
$ROEPRC_{ki}$ = ROE of the kth PRC's industry in the ith year;
i = 1…8; k = 1…7

$$DK = \sum_{i=1}^{n} ROEUS_{ki} - \sum_{i=1}^{n} ROEPRC_{ki}$$

RD = Rank of DK
NRS = Negative rank sum

TABLE 9.3: *The Wilcoxon test for the comparison of the ROA ratios of US and the PRC industries*

PAIR	$\sum_{i=1}^{n} ROAUS_{ki}$	$\sum_{i=1}^{n} ROAPRC_{ki}$	DK	RD	NRS
1	4.20	2.01	2.19	5.00	
2	10.50	5.07	5.43	7.00	
3	10.70	10.48	0.22	1.00	
4	6.40	5.88	0.52	3.00	
5	5.70	5.24	0.46	2.00	
6	6.40	10.28	−3.88	6.00	6.00
7	17.68	7.09	10.59	8.00	
8	5.79	4.00	1.79	4.00	
					T=6

Source. Calculated from the data provided by *Global Company Handbook 1996* and CD Rom *Disclosure/World Scope 1998*.

$ROAUS_{ki}$ = ROA of the kth US industry in the ith year;
$ROAPRC_{ki}$ = ROA of the kth PRC industry in the ith year;
i = 1…8; k = 1…7

$$DK = \sum_{i=1}^{n} ROAUS_{ki} - \sum_{i=1}^{n} ROAPRC_{ki}$$

RD = Rank of DK
NRS = Negative rank sum

TABLE 9.4: *The Wilcoxon test for the comparison of the ROS ratios of US and PRC industries*

PAIR	$\sum_{i=1}^{n} \text{ROSUS}_{ki}$	$\sum_{i=1}^{n} \text{ROSPRC}_{ki}$	DK	RD	NRS
1	9.00	14.80	−5.80	6.00	6.00
2	11.50	7.15	4.35	5.00	
3	16.00	3.60	12.40	8.00	
4	4.08	11.52	−7.45	7.00	7.00
5	5.20	3.72	1.48	3.00	
6	8.60	7.05	1.55	4.00	
7	4.44	3.47	0.97	2.00	
8	4.47	4.88	−0.41	1.00	1.00
					T=14

Source: Calculated from the data provided by *Global Company Handbook 1996* and CD Rom *Disclosure/World Scope 1998*.
ROSUS_{ki} = ROS of the kth US industry in the ith year;
ROSPRC_{ki} = ROS of the kth PRC industry in the ith year;
i = 1…8; k = 1…7

$$DK = \sum_{i=1}^{n} \text{ROSUS}_{ki} - \sum_{i=1}^{n} \text{ROSPRC}_{ki}$$

RD = Rank of DK
NRS = Negative rank sum

TABLE 9.5: *The Wilcoxon test for the comparison of the ATO ratios of US and PRC industries*

PAIR	$\sum_{i=1}^{n} \text{ATOUS}_{ki}$	$\sum_{i=1}^{n} \text{ATOPRC}_{ki}$	DK	RD	NRS
1	0.04	0.14	−0.09	1.00	1.00
2	0.46	0.71	−0.25	3.00	3.00
3	0.40	2.91	−2.51	8.00	8.00
4	0.28	0.51	−0.23	2.00	2.00
5	0.69	1.41	−0.71	4.00	4.00
6	0.37	1.46	−1.09	5.00	5.00
7	0.64	2.04	−1.40	7.00	7.00
8	2.15	0.82	1.33	6.00	
					T=30

Source: Calculated from the data provided by *Global Company Handbook 1996* and CD Rom *Disclosure/World Scope 1998*.
ATOUS_{ki} = ATO of the kth US industry in the ith year;
ATOPRC_{ki} = ATO of the kth PRC industry in the ith year;
i = 1…8; k = 1…7

$$DK = \sum_{i=1}^{n} \text{ATOUS}_{ki} - \sum_{i=1}^{n} \text{ATOPRC}_{ki}$$

RD = Rank of DK
NRS = Negative rank sum

TABLE 9.6: *The Wilcoxon test for the comparison of the EM ratios of US and PRC industries*

PAIR	$\sum\limits_{i=1}^{n} EMUS_{ki}$	$\sum\limits_{i=1}^{n} EMPRC_{ki}$	DK	RD	NRS
1	24.33	6.15	18.18	8.00	
2	2.12	1.56	0.56	3.00	
3	0.94	2.00	−1.05	5.00	5.00
4	12.56	3.28	9.27	7.00	
5	3.00	2.49	0.51	2.00	
6	3.23	1.29	1.94	6.00	
7	1.59	2.40	−0.81	4.00	4.00
8	2.86	2.38	0.48	1.00	
					T=9

Source: Calculated from the data provided by *Global Company Handbook 1996* and CD Rom *Disclosure/World Scope 1998*.
$EMUS_{ki}$ = EM of the kth US industry in the ith year;
$EMPRC_{ki}$ = EM of the kth PRC industry in the ith year;
$i = 1\ldots8; k = 1\ldots7$

$$DK = \sum_{i=1}^{n} EMUS_{ki} - \sum_{i=1}^{n} EMPRC_{ki}$$

RD = Rank of DK
NRS = Negative rank sum

Then these differences are ranked on the basis of their absolute values. Next, the sum of the ranks of the negative differences is used as the test statistic T.

The results of the test are shown in Tables 9.2 through 9.6. The values of the test statistic (T) in these tables indicate that only the null hypothesis regarding ROA can be rejected at the five per cent level of significance.

Concluding Remarks

To the extent that the data are not biased in the context of the limitations set in this study, the foregoing analysis suggests the following conclusions:

1. The absence of statistically significant differences between the ROE of the US and the ROE of PRC industries suggests that they are similar to each other with respect to their profitability, as measured by the rate of return on equity.
2. The ROA in US industries are higher than the ROA of their similar industries in PRC. This implies that US industries are more

efficient in terms of asset utilization as compared to their PRC counterparts.

3. The absence of statistically significant differences between the ROS of US industries as compared to their similar PRC industries implies that US industries and PRC industries are similar with respect to the efficiency by which they produce their products.

4. The absence of statistically significant differences between the ATO of US industries as compared to their similar PRC industries implies that US industries and PRC industries are similar with respect to the efficiency by which they utilize their plant.

5. The absence of statistically significant differences between the EM of US industries as compared to their similar PRC industries implies that these industries are similar with respect to their financial leveraging.

Given the aforementioned results, it is no wonder that the Pacific Rim Countries (PRC) had been forging ahead with a staggering double-digit growth rate far exceeding those of Japan, the US and Europe. It would be helpful to compare the financial ratios of PRC industries with those of the Japan and Europe to see if PRC firms are as efficient as their counterparts in the US and Europe. This could be a subject of further research in this area.

References

ASHEGHIAN, P. and FOOTE, W. (1985) The productivities of US multinationals in the industrial sector of the Canadian economy, *Eastern Economic Journal*, April/June, pp. 123–133.

BUCKLEY, P., DUNNING, J. H. and PEARCE, R. D. (1978) The influence of firm size, nationality and degree of multinationality on the growth and profitability of the world's largest firms, *Welwirtschaftliches Archiv* 114, No. 2, pp. 243–257.

LARRY, H. B. (1968) *Imports of Manufacturers from Less Developed Countries*, National Bureau of Economic Research, Columbia Press, New York.

MENDENHALL, W., MCCLARIE, J. T. and RAMMEY, M. (1977) *Statistics for Psychology*, 2nd ed., Dubury Press, Massachusetts, pp. 143–154.

SHAPIRO, A. C. (1983) *Multinational Financial Management*, Allyn and Bacon, London.

SIEGEL, S. (1956) *Nonparametric Statistics for the Behavioral Sciences*, McGraw Hill, New York.

VAZIRI, M. T. and SHALCHI, H. (1992) Are the US firms inferior to Japanese firms in profitability and management, in K. FATEMI, ed., *International Trade and Finance in a Rapidly Changing Environment*, International Trade and Finance Association, Loredo, Texas.

10

Return and Variance Parities of ASEAN-5 Country Funds and International Equity Index Investments

CHEE K. NG

Introduction

A country fund is a closed-end fund that invests in the shares of only one country. Country funds are closed-end funds because, unlike open-end mutual funds, being so makes share redemption unnecessary, thus relinquishing respective sponsors of any potentially binding restrictions on the cross-border withdrawal of capital[1]. The withdrawal restrictions will cause problems for mutual funds that may have to sell shares in order to either pay shareholders who wish to redeem shares or to meet the SEC (Securities & Exchange Commission) and IRS (Internal Revenue Service) diversification requirements[2].

Two benefits of closed-end funds are: (i) they can provide access to local capital markets and help investors achieve international diversification, and; (ii) they can circumvent short-term foreign investment restrictions. Fraser (1993) maintains that "closed-end funds can be the best way to invest in emerging markets; sometimes they are the only way". Moreover, investing in country funds helps to circumvent any short-term portfolio investment restriction imposed against foreigners by the local government that attempts to decelerate rapid short-term portfolio flows, especially in response to a widespread financial crisis. A recent example was the currency control measures imposed by the Malaysian government on September 2, 1998.

Another form of international equity investment available in the US that does not require explicit currency exposure is World Equity Benchmark Shares (WEBS). WEBS are indeed open-end funds, and to date there are 17 WEBS for 17 different economies[3]. The 17 WEBS funds started their debut exclusive trading in the American Stock Exchange on March 18, 1996. WEBS are distributed by Morgan Stanley Dean Witter, and managed by Barclays Global Investors of the UK. Being open-end funds, each WEBS fund can issue more shares or redeem some shares as investors buy or sell, respectively. Recently, each WEBS fund has been renamed iShares MSCI followed by the name of the economy it represents[4].

In this study, we compare the return and variance of investing with three investment strategies: (i) invest in the NYSE-listed closed-end country funds of Indonesia, Malaysia, the Philippines, Singapore and Thailand (ASEAN-5 countries), (ii) invest in the iShares MSCI Malaysia and iShares MSCI Singapore funds, and; (iii) invest in each of the five ASEAN-5 countries by making currency conversions, investing in the respective countries' major equity index, and converting the wealth back to US dollars. The five country funds are chosen for their historic economic accomplishments realized in the last two decades, for their founding membership in the Association of Southeast Asian Nations (thus the abbreviation ASEAN-5), for their geographical proximity to each other, and for their homogeneity in other economic parameters.

Table 10.1 presents some salient descriptive statistics for the international funds used in the study. The statistics are obtained from Compustat's *Research Insight* for the five closed-end country funds, one for each of the ASEAN-5 nations, plus the iShares MSCI Malaysia Fund, and the iShares MCSI Singapore Fund[5]. Surprisingly, the two iShares funds are also coded with the same SIC code of 6726 which stands for unit investment trust closed-end management, despite the fact that the iShares MSCI funds are open-end funds.

Hypothesis Development

In international investment, the following return parity condition is well-known. Sharpe et al. (1998), for example, show that

$$(1 + r_{Total}) = (1 + r_{LE})(1 + r_C)$$

where r_{Total} = total rate of return by investing offshore

TABLE 10.1: *Salient descriptive statistics for the five closed-end country funds for the ASEAN-5 nations, and for the iShares MSCI Malaysia and iShares MSCI Singapore funds*

Fund	Ticker symbol	Stock exchange	Managed by	Fund type	Created on	Beta in Feb 2000	NAV on Feb 29 00 (US$)	Price on Feb 29 00 (US$)
Indonesia fund	if	NYSE	Credit Suisse	Closed	Mar 5 90	1.547	3.280	4.44
Malaysia fund	mf	NYSE	Morgan Stanley	Closed	Nov 5 87	1.787	7.100	6.88
First Philippine	fpf	NYSE	Clemente Capital	Closed	Nov 8 89	1.673	6.550	4.875
Singapore fund	sgf	NYSE	Daiwa Securities	Closed	Jul 25 90	1.565	9.960	7.875
Thailand fund	ttf	NYSE	Morgan Stanley	Closed	Feb 17 88	1.616	4.960	6.31
iShare MSCI Malaysia	ewm	Amex	Barclays Global Investors	Open	Mar 16 98	2.116	5.590*	7.31
iShare MSCI Singapore	ews	Amex	Barclays Global Investors	Open	Mar 16 98	1.785	7.930*	7.19

*   The net asset value (NAV) data for EWM and EWS are for August 1999 since these are the latest data available from Compustat.

$$r_{LE} \quad = \text{local equity's rate of return}$$
$$r_C \quad = \text{rate of currency appreciation or depreciation.}$$

The total rate of return in offshore investment, r_{Total}, is the return realized after accounting for currency change and local equity return realized by an offshore investor. The local equity's rate of return, r_{LE}, is the return earned either by domestic investors or by foreign investors who have to first convert their wealth into the local currency and then invest in a particular country. For example, if the British local equity index yields five per cent, then r_{LE} will equal five per cent to either a British investor or an American investor who buys the British equity index. The American investor also faces another type of risk, the currency return (r_C) risk, since the spot exchange rate between the dollar and the pound fluctuates constantly[6]. The American investor's total rate of return, as denominated in US dollars, is given by the above equation while the British investor's total rate of return, as expressed in British pounds, is simply r_{LE}.

We utilize the following numerical example that has a binomial discrete stock price-currency rate combination to further illustrate the above return parity condition. Assume that the initial exchange rate between the US dollar and the Thai baht is 42 baht/$, and that an American investor starts with an initial wealth of $1000. After converting his wealth into baht, the American investor buys a Thai stock that sells for 100 baht per share and obtains 420 shares. Ignoring transaction costs and tax withholding, let's assume a binomial outcome of either (110 baht/share, 44.1 baht/$) or (88 baht/share, 40 baht/$) for the next period. We summarize the mutually exclusive binomial outcomes in Table 10.2.

From the above two-outcome numerical example, the American investor's total return factor in an offshore investment is equal to the product of the local equity return factor and the currency return factor. Consistent with the return parity condition, we test the return parity condition of investing in each closed-end country fund and the two iShares MSCI funds against the (convert–invest offshore–convert) alternative for each of the five ASEAN-5 nations. More specifically, we test the following parity condition:

$$(1 + r_{CF}) = (1 + r_{LEI})(1 + r_C)$$

Or after simplifying, we have the following first testable model:

$$r_{CF} = r_{LEI} + r_C + r_{LEI}\, r_C$$

where r_{CF} = rate of return on a country-fund or an iShares MSCI fund

r_{LEI} = rate of return on local equity index

TABLE 10.2: *A numerical example with a mutually exclusive binomial stock price-currency rate combination. Initially, the American investor starts with $1,000 which he sells at the spot exchange rate of 42 baht/$, and buys 420 shares of a Thai stock at price of 100 baht/share*

Binomial outcome → Returns and wealth estimates at t=1↓	(110 baht/share, 44.1 baht/$)	(88 baht/share, 40 baht/$)
Thai equity return[a], r_{LE}	10%	–12%
Currency return[b], r_{curr}	–4.762%	5%
Wealth in Thai baht	46,200 baht	36,960 baht
Wealth in US$	$1047.62	$924
Hence, total return[c], r_{Total}	4.762%	–7.6
$(1 + r_{LE})*(1 + r_{curr})$	1.1 * (1 – .04762) = 1.04762	(1 – .12)*1.05 = .9024 = 1 – .076

[a]   The return for equity is estimated as $(P_1 - P_0)/P_0$.

[b]   The currency return is estimated as $(1/e_1 - 1/e_0)/(1/e_0)$ where e_t is the spot exchange rate for time t (expressed in European-style quotation). If the exchange rate is expressed in American-style quotation, then the currency return will be estimated as $(e_1 - e_0)/e_0$.

[c]   The total return is estimated simply as (final $ wealth – initial $ wealth)/(initial $ wealth).

r_C = rate of return on spot currency exchange rate

$r_{LEI}r_C$ = interactive return term.

Consistent with Markowitz's theory on mean-variance dominance, we continue to test the parity of the return variance on the country-fund investment and the return variance of the convert–invest offshore–convert investment alternative. We take the variance on both sides of the above equation and obtain the following second testable model:

$$\sigma^2_{CF} = \sigma^2_{LEI} + \sigma^2_C + \sigma^2_{IA} + 2\sigma_{LEI,C} + 2\sigma_{LEI,IA} + 2\sigma_{C,IA}$$

The σ^2 terms are the variances of returns on the country funds or the iShares MSCI funds (α^2_{CF}), the return on the local equity index (α^2_{LEI}), the return on the currency (α^2_C), and the return on the interactive term (α^2_{IA}), respectively. The double-subscripted $\sigma_{i,j}$ terms are the covariances between the returns on the local equity index, the returns on the currency, and the returns on the interactive term in the equation.

In addition to comparing the return and variance parities between the closed-end country and iShares MSCI funds and the convert–invest offshore–convert strategy, we also compare the return and variance parities between the closed-end country funds and the two iShares MSCI funds. The latter comparisons are important for two reasons: (i) Karmin (1999) documents that the iShares MSCI funds are the more cost-efficient substitutes for the country funds, and (ii) when Malaysia imposed currency controls on September 2, 1998, the iShares MSCI Malaysia Fund essentially became a closed-end country fund. The results of any comparisons between the Malaysia Fund and the iShares MSCI Malaysia Fund, dichotomized as pre-September 2, 1998 and post-September 2, 1998, have implications for both foreign investors and policy-makers. Thus, the third testable model is:

$$r_{CF} = r_{iSh} \ and \ \sigma^2_{CF} = \sigma^2_{iSh}$$

and the fourth testable model is, for both pre- and post-September 2, 1998:

$$r_{MF} = r_{EWM}$$

$$\sigma^2_{MF} = \sigma^2_{EWM}$$

Data

Our data window begins on either January 1, 1990 or the inception date of the fund (for the funds that were created after January 1, 1990), and ends on July 14, 2000. The daily unadjusted price data are obtained from DataStream International. From the unadjusted prices, and following Klibanoff et al. (1998), we estimate the daily returns by finding the log difference between consecutive daily prices as $[\ln(P_t/P_{t-1})]$. The daily local equity indices and the currency exchange rates are also obtained from DataStream International. Other less frequently-reported fund-specific financial data are obtained from Compustat's *Research Insight.*

Empirical Results

The results in Table 10.3 suggest that there is no statistically significant difference between the daily returns of the closed-end country funds and the daily returns from the convert–invest–convert strategy. The tests with the monthly and annual returns yield similar results for all five funds (the test results are available from the author). However, the returns from the closed-end funds are consistently lower, although the difference is not statistically insignificant, than the returns from the returns of the convert–invest–covert strategy for all five closed-end country funds.

The results in the last two rows in Table 10.3 show that both the iShares Malaysia Fund and the iShares Singapore Fund yield statistically significant lower returns than the convert–invest–convert strategies. The results of lower period frequencies, both monthly and annually, are similar to the daily results reported here (the test results with lower period frequencies are available from the author).

The results in Table 10.4 show that the variances of the Indonesia, Malaysia, Philippines, and Thailand country funds are significantly higher than the variances of the convert–invest–convert strategies. Even though the Singapore Fund does not show significantly higher variance of returns than the convert-invest-convert strategy, the relative magnitude of the two variances is still consistent with those of the other four country funds.

These high volatilities are consistent with those documented by Brown (1999), and Malhotra and McLeod (2000). Brown attributes the high volatility to 'noise' traders' irrational sentiment, whereas Malhotra and McLeod posit that the volatility originates from expense ratio variability.

TABLE 10.3: *Testing the parity of average daily returns* $r_{cf} = r_{lei} + r_c + r_{lei}r_c$ *between the closed-end country funds of ASEAN-5, the iShares MSCI Malaysia and iShares MSCI Singapore funds, and the round-trip foreign equity index investment*

Fund	(I) r_{cf}	r_{lei}	(II) r_c	$r_{lei}r_c$ [a]	(III) Σ(II)	(IV) (I) – (III) [b]	t(IV)
if	–.000263711	–.00017543	.00013252	.00002782	–.00001509	–.000248621	–1.53
mf	–.000351228	–.00018326	.00010250	.00003619	–.00004457	–.000306658	–1.46
fpf	–.000102538	–.00020231	.00009897	.00002982	–.00007352	–.000029018	–.88
sgf	–.000032490	.00009654	.00010054	.00006724	.00026432	–.000296810	–1.39
ttf	–.001267491	–.00087392	.00025862	.00006982	–.00054548	–.000721992	–1.65
ewm	–.000639238	–.00018326	.00010250	.00003619	–.00004457	–.000594668	–2.34**
ews	–.000452459	.00009654	.00010054	.00006724	.00026432	–.000716779	–1.75*

[a]   The value in this column need not be the product of the previous two columns. To obtain the values in this column, each product of the corresponding values in the previous two columns is first obtained, and the average of the product terms is then estimated. That is, product of the averages need not equal the average of the products.

[b]   The t-value for the difference between both sides of the return parity equation, $r_{cf} = r_{lei} + r_c + r_{lei}r_c$, is estimated using the following formula.

$$t = \frac{\bar{x}_1 - \bar{x}_2}{\sqrt{s_p^2\left(\frac{1}{n_1} + \frac{1}{n_2}\right)}} \ where \ s_p^2 = \frac{s_1^2(n_1-1) + s_2^2(n_2-1)}{n_1+n_2-2}$$

with d.f. = $(n_1 - 1) + (n_2 - 1) = n_1 + n_2 - 2$.

*(**) Statistically significant at the five(one) per cent level of significance.

The results in the last two rows of Table 10.4 show that the volatilities of the iShares Malaysia and iShares Singapore funds are both significantly higher than the respective variances of the convert–invest–convert strategies. The results of lower periodic frequencies, though not reported here, are similarly significant (the test results with lower periodic frequencies are available from the author).

TABLE 10.4: *Testing the parity of average daily variances* $[\sigma_{cf}^2 = \Sigma(3 \ variances) + 2\Sigma(3 \ covariances)]$ *between the closed-end country funds of ASEAN-5, the iShares MSCI Malaysia and iShares MSCI Singapore funds, and the round-trip foreign equity index investment*

Fund	(I) σ_{cf}^2	(II) Σ 3 var.	(III) 2Σ (3 cov.)	(IV) (II) + (III)	(V) (I) – (IV)	t(V)
if	.000851362	.00038574	–.00025872	.00012702	.000724342	2.59**
mf	.000663943	.00028668	–.00012487	.00016181	.000502133	1.99*
fpf	.000568622	.00030385	–.00018972	.00011413	.000454492	2.21*
sgf	.000485010	.00010987	–.00009589	.00001398	.000471030	1.87
ttf	.000754985	.00038853	–.00010134	.00028719	.000467795	2.56**
ewm	.001073058	.00028668	–.00012487	.00016181	.000858728	2.87**
ews	.000600153	.00010987	–.00009589	.00001398	.000471030	2.11*

*(**) Statistically significant at the five(one) per cent level of significance.

The results suggest that investing in the closed-end country funds of ASEAN-5 is mean-variance inefficient in the Markowitz sense. An American investor can earn the same return and bear lower variance by converting US dollars into the local currency, investing in the local equity index, and subsequently converting the wealth back into US dollars[7].

The results further suggest that investing in the iShares funds for the two ASEAN countries for which iShares funds have been created is also mean-variance inefficient in the Markowitz sense compared with the convert–invest–convert strategy. An American investor can earn higher returns and bear lower risk by pursuing the convert–invest–convert investment strategy rather than investing either in the iShares Malaysia Fund or in the iShares Singapore Fund. These results are consistent with those reported by Willoughby (1998) who conjectures that the need for WEBS to comply with the SEC and IRS concentration restrictions entails constant portfolio balancing, hence making them cost-inefficient, and oftentimes requires involuntary liquidation in order to meet the concentration restriction requirements.

Table 10.5 presents the mean-variance comparisons between the two closed-end country funds that have iShares-fund counterparts. The means and variances for the country funds in Table 10.5 have also been synchronized with the beginning date of the iShares funds on March 18, 1996. In Table 10.5, we observe that the mean returns of both the Malaysia Fund and the Singapore Fund are significantly higher than those of their iShares-fund counterparts. Further, the return variance of the iShares Malaysia Fund is significantly higher than that of the Malaysia Fund. This makes the Malaysia Fund mean-variance dominant over the iShares Malaysia Fund. Although the return variance of the iShares Singapore Fund is not significantly higher than that of the Singapore Fund, the significantly higher yield of the Singapore Fund over the yield of the iShares Singapore Fund is a sufficient condition that makes the Singapore Fund dominant over iShares Singapore in the Markowitz sense.

TABLE 10.5: *Comparing the means and variances of the closed-end country funds and the open-end iShares MSCI Malaysia and iShares MSCI Singapore funds for the period March 18 1996–July 14 2000*

Country funds	Mean and variance		IShares MSCIs	Mean and variance		t(C.F. – iShares)
mf	μ	–.000401286	ewm	μ	–.000639238	2.04*
	σ^2	.000987543		σ^2	.0010730581	–2.49**
sgf	μ	–.00037842	ews	μ	–.000452459	2.87**
	σ^2	.000543741		σ^2	.000640153	1.56

*(**) Statistically significant at the five(one) per cent level of significance.

TABLE 10.6: *Comparing the means and variances of the Malaysia Fund and the iShares Malaysia Fund before and after the imposition of currency controls on September 2 1998*

Period before currency controls: March 18 1996 through September 1 1998

Country funds		Mean and variance	iShares MSCIs		Mean and variance	t(C.F. – iShares)
mf	μ	–.000261247	ewm	μ	–.0004158	1.99*
	σ^2	.000865432		σ^2	.00099204	1.24

Period after currency controls: September 2 1998 through July 14 2000
| mf | μ | –.00077846 | ewm | μ | –.0008062 | 1.19 |
| | σ^2 | .0011983 | | σ^2 | .0012687 | 1.03 |

*(**) Statistically significant at the five(one) per cent level of significance.

In Table 10.6, we present the mean-variance comparisons between the Malaysia Fund and the iShares Malaysia Fund, dichotomized into pre- and post-currency control periods. In the pre-currency control period, the return on the Malaysia Fund is significantly higher than that of the iShares Malaysia Fund. The Malaysia Fund's variance is, however, not significantly different from the variance of the iShares Malaysia Fund in the same period. Taken collectively, we observe that the closed-end Malaysia Fund is mean-variance dominant over the open-end iShares Malaysia Fund in the pre-currency control period. During the post-currency control period, the returns of the Malaysia Fund are not significantly different from those of the iShares Malaysia Fund. The difference between the return variances is also statistically insignificant. These results seem to support the conjecture that the open-end iShares Malaysia Fund and the closed-end Malaysia Fund have indeed become structurally more similar to each other after the imposition of the currency controls. We have also estimated the difference between the variances between the pre- and post currency-control periods for both the Malaysia Fund and the iShares Malaysia Fund. We have found that there is statistically significant inter-temporal increase in the variance only for the iShares Malaysia Fund, but the inter-temporal increase in variance is statistically insignificant for the closed-end Malaysia Fund.

Summary and Conclusions

In this study, I have found empirical evidence that the convert–invest–convert strategy is mean-variance dominant (same mean, significantly lower variance) over the closed-end country funds for the five ASEAN-5 nations in the period 1990–2000. Evidence also suggests that the convert–invest–convert strategy is mean-variance dominant (significantly higher mean, significantly lower variance) over the more recent innovation of iShares Malaysia and iShares Singapore funds. The Malaysia and Singapore country funds in turn dominate their respective iShares MSCI counterparts since the latter's inception in March 1996 through July 2000. The currency controls imposed by Malaysia's Central Bank since September 2, 1998 seem to have made the return–risk structure of the open-end iShares MSCI Malaysia Fund closer to that of the closed-end Malaysia Fund.

References

BONSER-NEAL, C., BRAUER, G., NEAL, R. and WHEATLEY, S. (1990) International investment restrictions and closed-end country funds, *Journal of Finance*, Vol. 45, No. 2, pp. 523–547.

BROWN. G. W. (1999) Volatility, sentiment and noise traders, *Financial Analysts Journal*, Vol. 55, No. 2, pp. 82–90.

FRASER, K. (1993) The odd ways of closed-end funds, *Euromoney*, July, pp. 88–89.

JOHNSON, G., SCHNEEWEIS, T. and DINNING, W. (1993) Closed-end country funds: exchange rate and investment risk, *Financial Analysts Journal*, Vol. 49, No. 6, pp. 74–82.

KARMIN, C. (1999) More efficient WEBS provide alternative closed-end funds, *Wall Street Journal*, July 6.

KARP, R. (2000) Doomed dinosaurs, *Barron's*, Vol. 80, No. 9 (February), pp. 27–28.

KLIBANOFF, P., LAMANT, O. and WIZMAN, T. (1998) Investor reaction to salient news in closed-end country funds, *Journal of Finance*, Vol. 53, No. 2, pp. 673–699.

MALHOTRA, D. K. and MCLEOD, R. W. (2000) Closed-end fund expenses and investment selection, *Financial Review*, Vol. 35, No. 1, pp. 85–104.

SHARPE, W. F., ALEXANDER, G. J. and BAILEY, J. V. (1998) *Investments*, 6th ed., Prentice Hall, Upper Saddle River, New Jersey.

WILLOUGHBY, J. (1998) Caught in the WEBS, *Institutional Investor*, Vol. 32, No. 12, p. 164.

Notes

1. Post IPO, a closed-end fund cannot issue more shares. It can only raise additional capital by selling preferred stock, commercial paper or right offerings, or by getting bank loans. Thus, a closed-end fund can become a leveraged investment vehicle. See Karp (2000).

2. The SEC requires that the top five assets in an investment company cannot exceed 50 per cent of the fund's portfolio value. The IRS requires that if the top asset in a fund exceeds 25 per cent of the fund's value, the fund will be taxed as a corporation. To meet these concentration restrictions, fund managers regularly have to liquidate the appreciating shares involuntarily.

3. The 17 economies with WEBS are Australia, Austria, Belgium, Canada, France, Germany, Hong Kong, Italy, Japan, Malaysia, Mexico, the Netherlands, Spain, Singapore, Sweden, Switzerland, and the UK.

4. We use the term *economy* instead of *country* because Hong Kong is a part of the country of China, despite the fact that it is being ruled as a separate economic unit.

5. The other three ASEAN-5 nations (Indonesia, the Philippines, and Thailand) do not have any iShares MSCI funds created based on their respective local equity markets.

6. Following Bonser-Neal et al. (1990), we assume that there is either lack of hedging using the forward contracts or forward hedges are cost-prohibitive such that currency translations occur at the contemporaneously observed spot exchange rate.

7. The assumption of a perfect market with frictionless transactions is made for the statement to hold.

Part IV
US and Latin American Markets

11

When the US Sneezes, Does the World Catch a Cold?

ALAN ALFORD and VANITHA RAGUNATHAN

Introduction

The state of any economy influences the perception of both risk and return for securities in that economy. Several factors such as inflation, industrial production, term and default spread and interest rates have been shown to impact on stock returns. The empirical evidence suggests that economic expansion tends to lead to stronger stock returns and contraction tends to lead to lower returns. Moreover, several studies link changes in the evolution of returns and of risks for US securities to shifts in the direction of monetary policy. Patelis (1997) holds that monetary policy shocks affect expected excess returns from holding stocks. King et al. (1994) find that an increase in the variance of interest rate innovations decreases the required rate of return on risky assets. Thorbecke (1997), though, estimates that a one standard deviation increase in the Federal Funds rate decreases the return of US stocks by 0.8 per cent monthly on average. Further, this result is found to vary across size and industry portfolios. Jensen et al. (1996) find evidence that the parameters of risk shift between times of contraction and expansion in US monetary policy.

This imposes a level of interest rate risk on risky assets – not just bonds, but stocks as well. Campbell and Ammer (1993) conclude that the covariance between excess stock returns and excess bond returns has increased over time due, in part, to increases in the influence of real interest rates relative to inflation effects. Solnik et al. (1996) find, however, that there is only a very weak relation between innovations in bond market volatility and stock market volatility without commenting on the influence of short-term rates on either market.

Leibowitz et al. (1994) suggest the full influence of volatility in the risk-free rate on portfolio development. If managers have a set required return, their portfolio allocations necessarily vary as interest rate levels vary. Portfolio managers must increase their risk exposure to other market factors in order to achieve required returns. Litterman and Winkelmann (1996) indicate that this parallels the management of any other risk from an allocation standpoint. They criticize, though, the duration analysis of a portfolio followed by Leibowitz et al. Duration analysis implicitly assumes that all shifts are parallel across all assets. As demonstrated in Thorbecke's analysis, this is not the case with shifts in the risk-free rate. Litterman and Winkelmann advise an examination of volatilities and correlations to refine the portfolio allocation to hedge against these types of risk.

Rational investors would hope to smooth the effects of a domestic contraction through international diversification. This necessitates that there exists a stable covariance structure for international security returns that is independent of the direction of the domestic economy. Without the ability to predict the covariance relationships accurately, the ability to diversify risk or to hedge optimally is restricted.

In general, many studies find instability in the covariance relationship among capital markets, especially at the shorter horizons. Shaked (1985) suggests that this move towards stability over time may be caused by frictions in the transmission of longer-term information. Few studies have attempted to explain the types of information frictions that may lead to the instability of the covariance matrix. Erb et al. (1994) find differences in correlations for the G7 countries between up markets and down markets. Ragunathan et al. (1999) support this conclusion for the Australian and US markets, but find the US influence greater than Australia's when the two markets are out of phase. All these studies find fewer diversification opportunities when returns fall; exactly when most investors want to be able to remove risk from their portfolios. Erb et al. as well as King et al., indicate that covariances among risky assets may be influenced by certain economic variables. Ammer (1996) also demonstrates that correlation between two assets will rise when a common factor becomes riskier. This suggests that a spillover of increased risk from US monetary policy changes may impact correlation across international markets.

The purpose of this paper is twofold. First, we extend the research on the influence of US monetary policy to international markets to test for spillover effects on the world economy and, thus, on world stock returns. If the state of the US economy proxies, or influences, the state of the world economy, there would be an increased correlation and fewer diversification opportunities from international investment during contraction. We examine how risks and returns differ according to contractions and expansions in the US economy using a simple CAPM approach. Second, we investigate how the correlation structure of international stock market returns varies given shifts in US monetary policy. We employ a bivariate GARCH model to extract correlations between individual markets and the world market. We test these correlations for differences across monetary policies. In both areas, we adapt our methodology to examine the influence of interest rate surprises, a proxy for subsequent reinforcement of the Federal Reserve's policy, on our results.

Interest Rates, Stock Returns, and Higher Moments

We can examine the influence of US monetary policy on international stock returns by looking at the variation in the excess returns of international stock markets across policy shifts. To investigate these relationships, we utilize monthly Morgan Stanley Capital International (MSCI) indices with net dividend reinvested for eighteen countries. The market portfolio is proxied by the MSCI World index. These indices are denominated in US dollars and the period of analysis is January 1971 to December 1997. All returns are calculated in excess of the one-month Eurodollar interbank rates taken from the Federal Reserve Board's statistical release. The dates for changes in US monetary policy are obtained from Jensen et al. (1996). The changes in monetary policy in April 1994 and in February 1996 are confirmed by changes in the Fed Funds rate.

In Table 11.1 we demonstrate that excess returns do vary across US monetary policy. As would be expected, most markets show statistically significantly higher returns during US monetary expansion than during contraction. For five countries – Australia, Austria, Japan, Norway, and Spain – the excess returns cannot be differentiated from zero, in either expansion or contraction, at conventional significance levels. Only the UK, the US, and the World indices exhibit returns that are statistically different from zero during

TABLE 11.1: *The impact of US monetary policy on returns of 19 MSCI country and world indices*

Country	Expansion	Contraction	R^2	Wald Statistic
Australia	0.0085	–0.0102	0.0145	4.7230
	(0.13)	(0.12)		(0.03)
Austria	0.0047	–0.0011	0.0023	0.7397
	(0.29)	(0.82)		(0.39)
Belgium	0.0131	–0.0056	0.0290	9.6217
	(0.00)	(0.21)		(0.00)
Canada	0.0066	–0.0060	0.0135	4.4006
	(0.10)	(0.18)		(0.04)
Denmark	0.0106	–0.0022	0.0137	4.4866
	(0.01)	(0.63)		(0.03)
France	0.0097	–0.0055	0.0122	3.9773
	(0.05)	(0.33)		(0.05)
Germany	0.0112	–0.0055	0.0197	6.4704
	(0.01)	(0.27)		(0.01)
Hong Kong	0.0210	–0.0097	0.0177	5.7932
	(0.01)	(0.31)		(0.02)
Italy	0.0152	–0.0089	0.0328	10.3921
	(0.00)	(0.11)		(0.00)
Japan	0.0051	–0.0079	0.0071	2.3052
	(0.37)	(0.22)		(0.13)
Netherlands	0.0159	–0.0063	0.0465	15.6533
	(0.00)	(0.13)		(0.00)
Norway	0.0049	0.0002	0.0009	0.2861
	(0.39)	(0.97)		(0.59)
Singapore	0.0142	–0.0084	0.0168	5.5025
	(0.03)	(0.25)		(0.02)
Spain	0.0048	–0.0032	0.0037	1.1959
	(0.32)	(0.56)		(0.27)
Sweden	0.0127	–0.0011	0.0119	3.8654
	(0.01)	(0.83)		(0.05)
Switzerland	0.0143	–0.0065	0.0349	11.6414
	(0.00)	(0.16)		(0.00)
UK	0.148	–0.0096	0.0307	10.2138
	(0.00)	(0.10)		(0.00)
US	0.0102	–0.0067	0.0369	12.3642
	(0.00)	(0.06)		(0.00)
World	0.0110	–0.0078	0.0519	17.6240
	(0.00)	(0.02)		(0.00)

*   p-values in parentheses.

periods of contractionary monetary policy. The results are generally consistent with evidence provided by Jensen and Johnson (1995) that stock returns are higher in periods characterized by interest rate decreases (expansionary periods). In all but four cases, the Wald statistics indicate that returns in expansionary periods are statistically different from those in contractionary periods.

It is also easy to determine US monetary policy's influence on the risk–return relationship by estimating a CAPM type model allowing for different risk premia and betas during contractionary periods. Equations (1a) and (1b) modify the CAPM and the GARCH (1,1) model to capture the differing regimes. The former equation, the mean equation, allows for differential intercepts and betas when US monetary policy is contractionary. The latter equation, the variance equation, allows for the unconditional variance to differ during periods of contraction.

$$R_{i,t} - R_{f,t} = \beta_0 + \beta_{1,\text{Contract}} + \beta_2 (R_{m,t} - R_{f,t})$$
$$+ \beta_{2,\text{Contract}} (R_{m,t} - R_{f,t}) + \varepsilon_t \quad (1a)$$

where, $\varepsilon_{it} \sim N(0, h_t)$

$$h_t = \gamma_0 + \gamma_{0,\text{Contract}} + \gamma_1 \varepsilon_{i,t-1}^2 + \gamma_2 h_{t-1} \quad (1b)$$

Table 11.2 contrasts the intercepts as well as the betas estimated using the above model. All country indices seem to be fairly priced. No intercept, with the exception of Hong Kong and the Netherlands, is significantly different from zero at conventional levels; equally, no country demonstrates significant intercepts during periods of contractionary policy. This result infers that there are no gains from segmentation available over the time period of the study.

We find that systematic risk for most countries does not differ across different monetary policies. In four cases, beta estimates are larger in times of contraction than in expansion. Hong Kong is the most extreme example of this feature: its beta in contraction shows the largest increase in terms of magnitude and in terms of percentage change of the eighteen countries. Only Italy has a significantly higher beta during expansion than during contraction.

Table 11.2 also reports the differences between the variance estimates between monetary policies. The US index does have higher unconditional variance in contraction as do most countries, consistent with Jensen et al. (1996). Only four countries – Netherlands, Norway, Spain, and Switzerland – report no change in their unconditional variance. Thus, a shift in monetary policy may influence the level of total risk and returns, but not necessarily the diversifiable risk of a specific market. Changes in risk must be due to changes in covariances between assets, not due to their relative volatilities.

From a portfolio point of view, international asset allocations may be influenced by the state of the US economy. The correlation

TABLE 11.2: *The impact of monetary policy on returns and risk*

Country	β_0	$\beta_{1,Contract}$	β_2	$\beta_{2,Contract}$	α_0	α_1	β_1	β_2	$\Sigma\alpha_1+\beta_1$	R^2
Australia	-0.0039 (0.33)	0.0018 (0.78)	0.9903 (0.00)	0.2984 (0.05)	$7.10*10^{-5}$ (0.28)	0.0905 (0.00)	0.8984 (0.00)	$-1.68*10^{-5}$ (0.82)	0.9889	0.3407
Austria	-0.0026 (0.48)	0.0012 (0.82)	0.3966 (0.00)	0.0562 (0.69)	0.0001 (0.00)	0.1411 (0.00)	0.8143 (0.00)	$3.54*10^{-5}$ (0.55)	0.9554	0.1103
Belgium	0.0035 (0.22)	0.0014 (0.75)	0.6857 (0.00)	0.2302 (0.02)	$-5.12*10^{-7}$ (0.97)	0.0645 (0.00)	0.9307 (0.00)	$2.64*10^{-5}$ (0.32)	0.9952	0.4173
Canada	-0.0003 (0.29)	0.0041 (0.39)	0.8489 (0.00)	0.1231 (0.19)	0.0008 (0.10)	0.1518 (0.05)	0.2304 (0.58)	0.0001 (0.47)	0.3822	0.4979
Denmark	0.0024 (0.54)	-0.0003 (0.96)	0.6922 (0.00)	-0.0789 (0.56)	0.0001 (0.07)	0.0606 (0.09)	0.8853 (0.00)	$-6.06*10^{-5}$ (0.14)	0.9459	0.2569
France	-0.0013 (0.69)	0.0052 (0.43)	0.9427 (0.00)	0.2385 (0.11)	0.0005 (0.04)	0.2025 (0.00)	0.5617 (0.00)	0.0005 (0.01)	0.7642	0.4091
Germany	0.0021 (0.57)	-0.0020 (0.72)	0.6817 (0.00)	0.1949 (0.10)	0.0002 (0.12)	0.0989 (0.04)	0.8067 (0.00)	$4.73*10^{-5}$ (0.55)	0.9056	0.3298
Hong Kong	0.0119 (0.06)	-0.0068 (0.47)	0.8950 (0.00)	0.6956 (0.00)	0.0009 (0.00)	0.3562 (0.00)	0.5964 (0.00)	0.0002 (0.67)	0.9526	0.2382
Italy	0.0022 (0.58)	-0.0036 (0.52)	1.3028 (0.00)	-0.3775 (0.00)	0.0010 (0.11)	0.1295 (0.04)	0.4564 (0.10)	$-3.98*10^{-5}$ (0.85)	0.5859	0.4856
Japan	-0.0073 (0.20)	0.0042 (0.60)	0.9142 (0.53)	-0.1321 (0.10)	0.0005 (0.08)	0.0595 (0.05)	0.8471 (0.00)	-0.0002 (0.11)	0.9066	0.1997
Netherlands	0.0065 (0.01)	-0.0047 (0.20)	0.8957 (0.00)	0.0582 (0.47)	$3.58*10^{-5}$ (0.42)	0.0426 (0.12)	0.9229 (0.00)	$6.65*10^{-6}$ (0.71)	0.9655	0.5733
Norway	-0.0061 (0.17)	0.0117 (0.16)	0.9909 (0.00)	0.0888 (0.58)	0.0028 (0.16)	0.0606 (0.36)	0.1030 (0.86)	0.0019 (0.16)	0.1636	0.2809
Singapore	$5.35*10^{-5}$ (0.99)	0.0003 (0.96)	1.0237 (0.00)	0.1683 (0.24)	0.0003 (0.01)	0.2159 (0.00)	0.7485 (0.00)	$2.53*10^{-6}$ (0.68)	0.9644	0.3102
Spain	-0.0045 (0.43)	0.0064 (0.36)	0.9254 (0.00)	-0.2184 (0.13)	0.0011 (0.16)	0.0682 (0.17)	0.6612 (0.00)	-0.0006 (0.16)	0.7294	0.2596
Sweden	0.0040 (0.36)	0.0031 (0.61)	0.7622 (0.00)	0.1413 (0.35)	0.0005 (0.21)	0.0917 (0.10)	0.7520 (0.00)	-0.0002 (0.29)	0.8437	0.3285
Switzerland	0.0044 (0.13)	-0.0033 (0.48)	0.8753 (0.00)	0.0679 (0.55)	0.0002 (0.29)	0.0743 (0.20)	0.7394 (0.00)	0.0001 (0.19)	0.8137	0.4744
UK	0.0045 (0.13)	-0.0030 (0.48)	0.9497 (0.00)	0.1907 (0.11)	$8.54*10^{-5}$ (0.11)	0.1655 (0.00)	0.8166 (0.00)	$-3.64*10^{-5}$ (0.43)	0.9821	0.4781
US	$-1.86*10^{-5}$ (0.99)	0.0008 (0.76)	0.9049 (0.00)	0.0398 (0.53)	$2.41*10^{-5}$ (0.08)	0.0857 (0.01)	0.8644 (0.00)	$1.85*10^{-5}$ (0.23)	0.9501	0.6759

* p-values in parentheses.
This table represents the preliminary results of the impact US monetary policy has on the various stock markets. The impact on returns is modelled by the modified CAPM model and the variance is captured by the GARCH model.

among assets determines how best to construct the portfolio. A shift in correlations may affect the development of these portfolios. From the following mean model, shown in equation (2), we extract point estimates for the correlation between the two sets of returns over time and regress these against the dummy variables that capture periods of expansion and of contraction. If correlations, or equivalently the diversifiable risk of a market, are independent of the direction of US monetary policy, there will be no statistical difference between the coefficients.

$$R_{i,t} - R_{f,t} = \mu_i + \varepsilon_t \tag{2}$$

$$R_{m,t} - R_{f,t} = \mu_m + \varepsilon_t$$

where μ is a vector of constants and $\varepsilon_t = [\varepsilon_{it}, ..., \varepsilon_{nt}]'$ is an n*1 vector such that $\varepsilon_t \sim N(0,H_{it})$, where H_{it} is the time-varying variance–covariance matrix conditioned on information available at time t–1. H_{it} is defined in equation (3). To test the influence of US monetary policy on correlations, we construct a bivariate GARCH model.

$$H_{it} = \begin{bmatrix} h_{11,t} & h_{12t} \\ h_{21,t} & h_{22t} \end{bmatrix} \tag{3}$$

In the interest of parsimony we use a GARCH (1,1) model. The problem normally encountered using a bivariate GARCH approach is the number of parameters that need to be estimated[1]. In the case of a full bivariate GARCH (1,1) model there are 21 parameters. There is a range of ways of reducing the number of parameters. One such way is Engle and Kroner's (1988) BEKK model, as shown in equation (4) which reduces the number of parameters to eleven.

$$H_{t+1} = C'C + B'H_tB + A'E_t'A \tag{4}$$

From the BEKK model, we extract point estimates for the correlation between the two sets of returns over time and regress these against the dummy variables that capture periods of expansion and of contraction. If correlations, or equivalently the diversifiable risk of a market, are independent of the direction of US monetary policy, there will be no statistical difference between the coefficients.

Table 11.3 examines the difference in correlations across different monetary policies. There are differences in each market's correlations with the world market portfolio across the two different

TABLE 11.3: *Correlations and monetary policy*

	Contraction	Expansion	R^2	Wald Statistic
Australia	0.6046	0.5799	0.0132	4.3082
	(0.00)	(0.00)		(0.04)
Austria	0.3068	0.3269	0.0035	1.1256
	(0.00)	(0.00)		(0.29)
Belgium	0.6587	0.6305	0.0273	9.0242
	(0.00)	(0.00)		(0.00)
Canada	0.6763	0.6768	0.0000	0.0015
	(0.00)	(0.00)		(0.97)
Denmark	0.5099	0.4935	0.0039	1.2880
	(0.00)	(0.00)		(0.26)
France	0.6475	0.6309	0.0055	1.7593
	(0.00)	(0.00)		(0.18)
Germany	0.5542	0.5239	0.0142	4.6098
	(0.00)	(0.00)		(0.03)
Hong Kong	0.5246	0.4825	0.0113	3.6771
	(0.00)	(0.00)		(0.06)
Italy	0.6933	0.7044	0.0111	3.5892
	(0.00)	(0.00)		(0.06)
Japan	0.4557	0.4151	0.0433	14.5248
	(0.00)	(0.00)		(0.00)
Netherlands	0.7309	0.7490	0.0171	5.5927
	(0.00)	(0.00)		(0.02)
Norway	0.4580	0.5236	0.0335	11.1252
	(0.00)	(0.00)		(0.00)
Singapore	0.5168	0.5176	0.0000	0.0026
	(0.00)	(0.00)		(0.96)
Spain	0.4969	0.5063	0.0027	0.8555
	(0.00)	(0.00)		(0.35)
Sweden	0.5778	0.5472	0.0195	6.3841
	(0.00)	(0.00)		(0.01)
Switzerland	0.6835	0.6807	0.0014	0.4435
	(0.00)	(0.00)		(0.51)
UK	0.6910	0.7097	0.0138	4.5013
	(0.00)	(0.00)		(0.03)
US	0.8271	0.8328	0.0015	0.4718
	(0.00)	(0.00)		(0.49)

* p-values in parentheses.

policies, but these differences are statistically negligible for all but ten countries. In six cases we find that the correlations increase during periods of contraction, reflecting the results found by Erb et al. (1994). The greatest difference occurs for Norway, which has a larger correlation with the world market during times of expansion.

Returns, risks, and correlations do vary internationally depending on the monetary policy being followed by the Federal Reserve. However, the influence on diversifiable risk appears to be negligible. The impact on portfolio design may be minimal. The direction of US monetary policy does appear to spillover onto the rest of the world. Our focus now shifts to the influence of subsequent reinforcements of US monetary policy.

Stock Returns, Risk, and Interest Rate Shocks

Thorbecke indicates that the effect of policy changes differs directly with the strength of the change. Within a given contractionary (expansionary) policy, the Federal Reserve will raise (lower) interest rates on several occasions to strengthen the effects of the policy on the economy[2]. As the Fed moves to reinforce its policy by raising (lowering) interest rates, stock markets may further react. We can model simply these shifts, and other interest rate shocks, as 'surprises' in the risk-free rate (u_t) to be captured by the error term from equation (5). We segment this variable into positive and negative errors $(u_t^+$ and u_t^-, respectively) to test for differential effects of bad and good surprises on returns, as in equation (6a). Further, these surprises are incorporated into the volatility equation of excess returns, as in equation (6b). This incorporates the shifts in volatilities and correlations as suggested by Litterman and Winkelmann. Finally, we allow the intercept in all three equations to vary across monetary regimes.

$$\Delta R_{f,t} = \alpha_0 + \alpha_{0,Contract} + \alpha_1 R_{f,t-1} + \alpha_{1,Contract} R_{f,t-1} + u_t \tag{5}$$

$$R_{i,t} - R_{f,t} = \beta_0 + \beta_{0,Contract} + \beta_1 (R_{m,t-1} - R_{f,t}) + \beta_{1,Contact}(R_{m,t-1} - R_{f,t}) + \beta_2 u_t^+ + \beta_3 u_{t-} + \varepsilon_{it} \tag{6a}$$

$$h_t = \gamma_0 + \gamma_{0,Contract} + \gamma_1 \varepsilon_{i\,t-1}^2 + \gamma_2 h_{t-1} + \gamma_3 u_t^+ + \gamma_4 u_t^- \tag{6b}$$

Table 11.4 indicates that there is a difference in the evolution of interest rates across different policy regimes. The regression indicates the previous month's interest rate should be higher than the current month's when the Federal Reserve is pursuing an accommodative monetary policy. During times of contractionary monetary policy, the markets should expect a steady increase in interest rates over the period. Efficient markets would incorporate this

TABLE 11.4: *Evolution of interest rates over time*

	α_0	$\alpha_{0,Contract}$	α_1	$\alpha_{1,Contract}$
Coefficients	0.0008	−0.0010	0.8397	0.2032
	(0.00)	(0.00)	(0.00)	(0.00)

information and adjust the price of risky assets to incorporate this evolution over time. If interest rates evolve according to this pattern, markets should not react to shifts in interest rates. Deviations from this relationship constitute shocks that become relevant to the pricing of those assets and to the determination of risks.

Table 11.5 demonstrates a lack of influence of unanticipated changes of interest rates on asset returns. Italy responds positively to higher-than-expected US interest rates, but Switzerland falls with the same news. Singapore, on the other hand, rises when the US interest rates are lower than expected. Interestingly, Hong Kong does not respond to surprises in US interest rates. The true effect of interest rate shocks is seen in the volatility equation. Four countries respond to positive and negative surprises, three to positive surprises, and two to negative surprises.

Overall, the results indicate that the shift from expansion to contraction, or vice versa, affects returns. Subsequent shocks have limited, if any, impact on asset returns. These shocks, though, do influence the unconditional volatility of the realized returns, adding a dimension of interest rate risk to international investing and portfolio allocations.

Conclusion

Patelis indicates that if equities are claims on future output and if monetary policy affects real economic output, then stock prices, and ultimately stock returns, should be influenced by the direction of monetary policy. Thorbecke, as well as Jensen et al., demonstrates the full influence of policy shifts by the Federal Reserve on the US stock market. The evolution of stock returns is sensitive to the direction of interest rates. This implies a level of interest rate exposure for US securities. Interest rates themselves then become a risk factor for pricing US risky assets.

This study extends this analysis into international markets. We document an international influence of US monetary policy on world stock returns. Using the Morgan Stanley Capital International Indices, we find that the world market portfolio yields, on average, over 110 basis points in excess of the one-month Eurodollar rate when the US is in expansion, but over 78 basis points less when the US is in contraction. Further, it appears that most countries have significantly larger unconditional variances and higher correlations with the world market during US monetary contraction than during expansion. However, betas are largely the same across the two regimes.

TABLE 11.5: *The influence of interest rate surprises on returns and variances*

Country	β_0	$\beta_{0,Contract}$	β_1	$\beta_{1,Contract}$	β_2	β_3	γ_0	$\gamma_{0,Contract}$	γ_1	γ_2	γ_3	γ_4
Australia	-0.0042	0.0044	0.0263	0.2772	3.2094	-11.4590	$2.97*10^{-5}$	$-7.60*10^{-5}$	-0.0087	0.9899	0.5478	0.1136
	(0.38)	(0.52)	(0.00)	(0.05)	(0.78)	(0.19)	(0.35)	(0.06)	(0.27)	(0.00)	(0.00)	(0.35)
Austria	-0.0022	0.0026	0.3374	0.0494	-4.6907	2.1951	0.0003	-0.0001	0.1679	0.7619	0.3623	0.5122
	(0.63)	(0.64)	(0.00)	(0.71)	(0.61)	(0.68)	(0.00)	(0.13)	(0.00)	(0.00)	(0.09)	(0.00)
Belgium	0.0037	0.0004	0.6589	0.2299	-3.2025	-3.2536	$4.94*10^{-5}$	0.0001	0.0738	0.7139	1.1839	-0.4294
	(0.25)	(0.93)	(0.00)	(0.02)	(0.74)	(0.79)	(0.41)	(0.04)	(0.07)	(0.00)	(0.01)	(0.13)
Canada	-0.0021	0.0036	0.8146	0.1446	-9.2548	-4.3145	0.0009	0.0002	0.1362	-0.0006	0.6168	-0.5795
	(0.57)	(0.44)	(0.00)	(0.14)	(0.25)	(0.62)	(0.04)	(0.39)	(0.07)	(0.99)	(0.22)	(0.33)
Denmark	0.0074	-0.0076	0.7027	-0.0665	2.6542	-3.4656	$1.36*10^{-5}$	$-3.12*10^{-5}$	-0.0131	1.0048	0.1469	0.0598
	(0.02)	(0.08)	(0.00)	(0.59)	(0.76)	(0.59)	(0.56)	(0.29)	(0.03)	(0.00)	(0.00)	(0.32)
France	-0.0009	0.0065	0.9714	0.1980	-1.8031	2.7863	0.0006	0.0005	0.2406	0.2739	2.6156	-0.2619
	(0.83)	(0.31)	(0.00)	(0.20)	(0.87)	(0.81)	(0.02)	(0.07)	(0.01)	(0.11)	(0.01)	(0.68)
Germany	0.0040	-0.0011	0.6812	0.1632	-11.2977	-0.1644	$4.11*10^{-5}$	$-5.52*10^{-5}$	-0.0163	1.0057	0.2035	0.1784
	(0.33)	(0.82)	(0.00)	(0.14)	(0.12)	(0.98)	(0.07)	(0.08)	(0.42)	(0.00)	(0.00)	(0.00)
Hong Kong	0.0111	-0.0079	0.9406	0.6075	14.9571	10.0057	0.0009	$-9.30*10^{-5}$	0.3040	0.4783	5.1311	-3.5243
	(0.20)	(0.45)	(0.00)	(0.01)	(0.49)	(0.65)	(0.02)	(0.85)	(0.00)	(0.00)	(0.08)	(0.10)
Italy	-0.0016	-0.0028	1.3606	-0.3954	17.6574	2.3239	0.0009	$-1.55*10^{-5}$	0.1068	0.4099	0.0269	-0.5245
	(0.73)	(0.63)	(0.00)	(0.00)	(0.03)	(0.83)	(0.18)	(0.94)	(0.12)	(0.25)	(0.94)	(0.36)
Japan	-0.0059	0.0069	1.0193	-0.2107	-10.1179	7.8625	0.0002	-0.0002	-0.0704	1.0076	0.1145	-1.0278
	(0.34)	(0.30)	(0.00)	(0.25)	(0.38)	(0.56)	(0.00)	(0.01)	(0.00)	(0.00)	(0.05)	(0.00)
Netherlands	0.0088	-0.0038	0.8859	0.0055	-9.3211	9.1927	$1.90*10^{-5}$	$-1.47*10^{-6}$	-0.0058	0.9506	0.1592	-0.0721
	(0.00)	(0.32)	(0.00)	(0.95)	(0.14)	(0.16)	(0.56)	(0.92)	(0.76)	(0.00)	(0.14)	(0.17)
Norway	-0.0024	0.0102	0.9949	0.0513	-10.5648	9.8700	0.0007	0.0004	0.0694	0.6853	1.3569	0.3415
	(0.66)	(0.18)	(0.00)	(0.74)	(0.46)	(0.37)	(0.19)	(0.31)	(0.11)	(0.00)	(0.21)	(0.59)
Singapore	-0.0091	0.0033	0.9644	0.2472	16.3493	-32.8794	0.0002	$-9.07*10^{-5}$	0.2059	0.7536	0.8053	-0.1204
	(0.12)	(0.64)	(0.00)	(0.10)	(0.29)	(0.00)	(0.10)	(0.50)	(0.00)	(0.50)	(0.13)	(0.71)
Spain	-0.0046	0.0068	0.9003	-0.2095	-1.6658	-0.5669	0.0014	-0.0007	0.0798	0.5968	-0.1797	0.1685
	(0.48)	(0.35)	(0.00)	(0.15)	(0.87)	(0.95)	(0.16)	(0.16)	(0.17)	(0.02)	(0.62)	(0.68)
Sweden	0.0019	0.0021	0.7339	0.1692	6.6368	-6.8148	0.0006	-0.0002	0.1070	0.7087	-0.2883	-0.4099
	(0.70)	(0.73)	(0.00)	(0.27)	(0.48)	(0.35)	(0.24)	(0.26)	(0.11)	(0.00)	(0.32)	(0.27)
Switzerland	0.0076	-0.0025	0.8397	0.0882	-17.3275	3.7029	0.0002	0.0001	0.0879	0.7454	0.1705	-0.1052
	(0.02)	(0.57)	(0.00)	(0.44)	(0.03)	(0.66)	(0.31)	(0.14)	(0.14)	(0.00)	(0.51)	(0.64)
UK	0.0064	-0.0054	0.9254	0.2039	-5.5647	1.7726	$6.52*10^{-5}$	$-4.69*10^{-5}$	0.1340	0.7989	-0.1070	-0.7654
	(0.09)	(0.21)	(0.00)	(0.12)	(0.50)	(0.85)	(0.33)	(0.39)	(0.01)	(0.00)	(0.46)	(0.01)
US	0.0004	0.0005	0.8732	0.0789	-3.5809	-0.4633	$2.13*10^{-5}$	$1.77*10^{-5}$	0.0528	0.9125	0.0127	0.0488
	(0.85)	(0.85)	(0.00)	(0.24)	(0.32)	(0.92)	(0.07)	(0.13)	(0.03)	(0.00)	(0.58)	(0.08)

* p-values in parentheses.

We further analyse how subsequent reinforcements of Fed policy, through subsequent interest rate shifts, influence the results. We develop a crude measure of interest rate surprises for the one-month Eurodollar interest rate. We re-examine our previous analysis to explore how subsequent interest rate changes may influence the evolution of returns and variances over time. These shocks tend not to have a significant impact on the asset returns, but do impact the unconditional variances.

Monetary policy and interest rate surprises do influence expectations for returns, variances, and risk. Monetary policy has a largely uniform influence–returns and correlations, ceteris paribus, tend to be higher in expansion than in contraction. Our results largely confirm similar studies that examine only the US stock market. Interest rate surprises, however, have differential effects; country indices react in different directions and with different magnitudes to different types of shocks. Thus, this type of risk may be best mitigated through the diversification of portfolios.

References

AMMER, J. (1996) Macroeconomic state variables as determinants of asset price co-movements, *International Finance Discussion Paper 553,* Board of Governors of the Federal Reserve.

CAMPBELL, J. Y. and AMMER, J. (1993) What moves the stock and bond markets? A variance decomposition for long-term asset returns, *Journal of Finance,* Vol. 48, pp. 3–37.

ENGLE, R. F. and KRONER, K. (1995) Multivariate simultaneous GARCH, *Econometric Theory,* Vol. 11, 122–150.

ERB, C. B., HARVEY, C. R. and VISKANTA, T. E. (1994) Forecasting international equity correlations, *Financial Analysts Journal,* November/December, pp. 32–45.

JENSEN, G. R. and JOHNSON, R. R. (1995) Discount rate changes and security returns in the US, 1962–1991, *Journal of Banking and Finance,* Vol. 19, No. 1, pp. 79–95.

JENSEN, G. R., MERCER, J. M. and JOHNSON, R. R. (1996) Business conditions, monetary policy, and expected security returns, *Journal of Financial Economics,* Vol. 40, pp. 213–237.

KING, M. A., SENTANA, E. and WADHWANI, S. (1994) Volatility and the links between national stock markets, *Econometrica,* Vol. 62, pp. 901–934.

LEIBOWITZ, M. L., KOGELMAN, S., BADER, L. N. and DRAVID, A. R. (1994) Interest rate sensitive asset allocation, *Journal of Portfolio Management,* Spring, pp. 8–15.

LITTERMAN, R. and WINKELMANN, K. (1996) Managing market exposure, *Risk Management Series,* Goldman Sachs.

PATELIS, A. D. (1997) Stock return predictability and the role of monetary policy, *Journal of Finance,* Vol. 52, pp. 1951–1972.

RAGUNATHAN, V., FAFF, R. W. and BROOKS, R. D. (1999) Correlations, business cycles and integration, *Journal of International Financial Markets, Institutions and Money*, Vol. 9, pp. 75–95.

SHAKED, I. (1985) International equity markets and the investment horizon, *Journal of Portfolio Management*, Winter, pp. 80–84.

SOLNIK, B. H., BOUCRELLE, C. and LE FUR, Y. (1996) International market correlation and volatility, *Financial Analysts Journal*, Vol. 52, No. 5 (September/October), pp. 17–34.

THORBECKE, W. (1997) On stock market returns and monetary policy, *Journal of Finance*, Vol. 52, pp. 635–654.

Notes

This paper was written while the authors were at the School of Economics and Finance, RMIT. The authors would like to thank Robert Brooks, Sinclair Davidson and seminar participants at RMIT for their comments. We are especially grateful to Steve Gray for his helpful suggestions and comments and assistance with GAUSS.

1. The number of parameters to be estimated is given by $\{[n\ (n+1)]\ [1+n\ (n+1)\ (p+q)/2]\}/2$.

2. Over the period of this study, there is a median of five interest rate decreases for each expansionary period and a median of three increases during contractionary periods.

12

Asset-Liability Management Strategy, Performance and Efficiency of Multinational Banks in the United States

IFTEKHAR HASAN, TANWEER HASAN and ROSWELL MATHIS III

Introduction

Foreign banking activity in the US, including the ownership of US banks by foreign multinational banks, has escalated in recent decades. This activity has attracted substantial attention in banking literature[1]. One widely debated issue is whether foreign-owned US banks enjoy a comparative cost advantage over their US-owned peers in the production of banking services. A relative cost advantage could result from different operating strategies, different organization structures, differences in regulatory requirements and/or support from home governments. If such an advantage exists, US banks will have to undertake additional efforts to increase operating efficiency in order to remain competitive.

However, there are several factors that could mitigate the ability of US-based, foreign-owned banks to exploit any comparative cost advantages. Included among these factors are a lack of exposure and training in the US market and the lack of stringent monitoring of the bank's operations by the senior management in the home country. Empirical findings suggest that foreign-owned US banks do not enjoy any comparative advantages vis-à-vis domestically-owned banks that result solely from their foreign ownership. Houpt (1983) found no major difference between the financial performance of foreign-acquired banks and their US-owned counterparts. Similarly,

Goldberg (1982) found that, on a total cost of funds basis, US subsidiaries of foreign banks appeared to have no comparative advantage over their domestic peers.

It should be noted that the results cited above only address the scale and scope aspects of productive efficiency. Recent research examining managerial efficiency (inefficiency) in banking has shown that the potential gains resulting from scale and scope economies are dominated by those which arise through the elimination of managerial inefficiencies. For example, Berger et al. (1993) suggest that differences in managerial ability to control costs or maximize revenues account for as much as 20 per cent of the costs in banking, while scale and scope inefficiencies account for only about five per cent of costs. Thus, it is important to examine whether there are significant differences in managerial efficiency between foreign-owned multinational banks (FOMNBs) and US-owned multinational banks (USMNBs). Comparing managerial inefficiency between FOMNBs and USMNBs, Chang et al. (1998) and DeYoung and Nolle (1996) reported significant differences between the groups with superior performance by the USMNBs.

The above papers on multinational banks either address the scale and scope aspects of productive efficiency or simply focus on return on assets, return on equity, or managerial efficiency without investigating the interconnected relationship of operational strategies and performance. Moreover, in determining the key factors associated with performance, these papers primarily focused on the estimation of Ordinary Least Square (OLS) regressions. Since an OLS approach ignores the simultaneous nature of depository institution input, output, pricing, and performance it may not be adequate or appropriate for the examination of the relative importance of different factors in determining performance (Graddy and Kyle, 1979).

This study extends the literature by providing empirical evidence on the asset management, financing strategy, noninterest or managerial efficiency and performance of multinational banks operating in the US during the period 1984–89, through the use of a simultaneous regression approach. Interestingly, the paper also uses a stochastic frontier technology to calculate profit (performance) and non-financial management efficiency variables. Over all, the results portray weaker performance by the subsidiaries of foreign multinational banks in US compared to their US counterparts, which is largely due to their lack of diversification in lending and higher noninterest operating (managerial) inefficiency. However, once adjusted for experience in the US market, the differences narrow substantially. The differences also narrow once the Japanese-owned sub-sample is excluded. The results of this study should enhance efforts to establish efficient criteria for evaluating multinational bank management strategy in competitive and integrated banking activities.

The paper is structured as follows. The next section examines the recent literature on multinational cross-country banking; following this we describe the empirical methodology and describes the data used in the estimation. The final sections present the results and conclude the paper.

Recent Literature on Multinational Cross-Country Banking

Banks expand in other countries to exploit economies of scale, reduce risks, increase profitability and counter the moves of competitors. Many banking analysts believe that multinational banks possess firm-specific advantages which they can exploit in foreign markets (see Casson, 1990 and Gray and Gray, 1981). When these advantages can be transferred at little total cost or utilized at lower marginal cost, multinational banks may enjoy competitive advantages relative to local banks or local multinational banks (Lewis and Davis, 1987). On the other hand, when there are significant costs associated with transferring these advantages or dealing with the idiosyncratic features of the local customer and service delivery systems, FOMNBs may operate at a competitive disadvantage.

It is well-known that differences in expertise and strategic objectives between FOMNBs and USMNBs can lead to differences in product lines. For example, Cooper et al. (1989) found significant differences in the portfolio behaviour of Pacific and European FOMNBs operating in the US, which resulted from significant relative differences in the economic, financial, and policy conditions between their home nations and the US. In addition, USMNBs tend to serve retail customer bases whereas FOMNBs are oriented more toward wholesale business (Goldberg, 1981). This is demonstrated by the heavy concentration of commercial and industrial loans in their portfolios (Damanpour, 1990). Other studies have found that FOMNBs pay higher prices on average than USMNBs to acquire local banks. In addition, their capital infusion after acquisition was found to be substantially higher (Walter, 1981 and Damanpour, 1990).

Less is known about the costs incurred by FOMNBs in transferring firm-specific and home country procedures and techniques to new markets, the costs incurred in adapting customer and service delivery systems to these new markets; and the resulting impact on the efficiency of FOMNBs. Using a data envelopment analysis and a cross-sectional sample for the year 1988, Elyasiani and Mehdian (1992) did not find any significant statistical evidence of cost efficiency differences between the USMNBs and FOMNBs. They, however, argued and provided evidence that the two groups may have different technologies. On the contrary, studies have reported a higher cost efficiency (Chang et al., 1998) and profit efficiency (DeYoung and Nolle, 1996) for the USMNBs. DeYoung and Nolle portrayed that foreign banks traded lower profits in exchange for market shares. Such claims are consistent with Calomiris and Carey (1994) which reported that institutions may produce higher quality products and services in order to capture market share.

The X-efficiency literature on cross-country comparisons of banking institutions has two perspectives. One deals with the comparison of foreign-owned banks with domestic-owned banks in the context of a single country. The other concentrates on cross-country comparisons among banking institutions. In the first category, local business environmental factors are ignored as banks compete in the same market within the country (Hasan and Hunter, 1996; Mahajan et al., 1996; DeYoung and Nolle, 1996; Chang et al., 1998; and Peek et al., 1999). The overall evidence here portrays foreign-owned banks as relatively less efficient than their domestic counterparts. These papers conclude that, in general, the foreign banks' capacity to transfer their unique ability and management skills in a different country is outweighed by the advantages associated with performing business in the home country. However, these findings do not extend uniformly for similar comparisons in non-US settings.

Comparing acquiring institutions in Europe, Vander Vennet (1996) did not find significant differences in cost efficiency between foreign-owned and domestic-owned institutions. The author further reported that, over the period studied, foreign-owned banks tended to become more efficient institutions. Once adjusted for production technology differences (Mester, 1993) by estimating separate frontiers for foreign-owned and domestic-owned banking institutions in Spain, Hasan and Lozano-Vivas (1998) found no significant differences between the two groups.

Berger et al. (2000) extended the literature by comparing foreign-owned and domestic-owned banks in several countries. Their paper stresses the importance of disaggregated and separate frontier estimations based upon the nation of origin. Evidence indicates no clear-cut dominance ('home field advantage') for local banks relative to the foreign banks' ability ('global advantage') to transfer their unique management efficiency abroad. An in-depth analysis of banks by foreign nation of origin portrays mixed results, where foreign-owned and domestic-owned banks both outperform each other under certain categories or groupings.

In the second category of the literature, most papers focus on the efficiency of banks in multi-country comparisons. These papers trace variability in bank performance across nations by setting a common frontier for all institutions. This assumes that any differences in efficiency between countries can be explained by country-specific banking technology (Fecher and Pestieau, 1993; Berg et al., 1995; Allen and Rai, 1996; Ruthenberg and Elias, 1996; Pastor et al., 1997; and Bikker, 1999). Most of these studies are based on European institutions, however, the results did not reveal any definite status of or trends in banking efficiency. Recently, Hasan et al. (2000), in an analysis of banking sectors in Europe, defined a common frontier that incorporates the country-specific environmental conditions.

However, the vast literature discussed above fails to examine the effect on the relative performance of FOMNBs and USMNBs of inter-connected asset–liability management strategies and managerial efficiency. This paper attempts to address this gap by introducing a simultaneous system of equations that capture the interrelated nature of depository institutions' asset management, financing strategy, pricing, and performance perspectives.

Empirical Methodology and Data

In carrying out the empirical analysis, several approaches used separately in the literature were combined. A Two Stage Least Squares (2SLS) regression analysis was used to determine the relationship between performance, asset management, financing strategy, and managerial efficiency for the sample MNBs[2]. As mentioned earlier, Ordinary Least Squares (OLS) regression is not adequate or appropriate for analysing the performance of depository institutions since it ignores the simultaneous nature of depository institution input, output, pricing, and performance (Graddy and Kyle, 1979). This point has been echoed by Clark (1986a, 1986b) and Lindley et al. (1992).

The simultaneous equation regression system incorporates four dependent variables: profit inefficiency (PINEFF) or return on assets (ROA) as performance measures; risky assets (RASST) as a proxy for asset management; purchased funds (PFUND) as a proxy for financing strategy; and noninterest inefficiency (NIINEFF) or noninterest cost to asset ratio (NICOSTR) to represent management efficiency and ability in controlling noninterest cost. The objective is to determine simultaneously the key factors associated with the dependent variables.

The four basic regression equations can be summarized as follows:

PINEFF OR ROA	= Intercept + b_1 Risky Assets Ratio + b_2 Purchased Fund Ratio + b_3 Noninterest Inefficiency (Cost) + b_4 FOREIGN MNB + b_5 Percentage of Foreign Owned + b_6 Foreign Asset Share + b_7 Mega-Foreign Multinational Banks + b_8 Bank Holding Companies + b_9 Log of Age + b_{10} Log of Total Assets	(1)
RASST	= Intercept + y_1 Purchased Fund Ratio + y_2 Noninterest Inefficiency (Cost) + y_3 FOREIGN MNB + y_4 Percentage of Foreign-Owned + y_5 Foreign Asset Share + y_6 Mega-Foreign Multinational Banks + y_7 Bank Holding Companies + y_8 Log of Age + y_9 Log of Total Assets	(2)
PFUND	= Intercept + z_1 Profit Inefficiency (ROA) + z_2 Noninterest Inefficiency (Cost) + z_3 FOREIGN MNB + z_4 Percentage of Foreign-Owned + z_5 Foreign Asset Share + z_6 Mega-Foreign Multinational Banks + z_7 Bank Holding Companies + z_8 Log of Total Age + z_9 Log of Total Assets	(3)
NIINEFF OR NICOSTR	= Intercept + q_1 Risky Assets Ratio + q_2 Purchased Fund Ratio + q_3 FOREIGN MNB + q_4 Percentage of Foreign-Owned + q_5 Foreign Asset Share + q_6 Mega-Foreign Multinational Banks + q_7 Bank Holding Companies + q_8 Log of Total Age + q_9 Log of Total Assets	(4)

In determining PINEFF and NIINEFF, the methodology developed by Aigner et al. (1977) and Meeusen and Broeck (1977) was used, i.e., an economic frontier approach to calculate a measure of inefficiency scores in each category for each multinational bank in our sample. These scores are used to gain further insight into the determination of performance[3].

The use of profit inefficiency (PINEFF) and return on assets (ROA) as alternative performance measures are consistent with other studies of depository institution performance (DeYoung and Hasan, 1998; Clark, 1986a; and Lindley et al. 1992). Risky assets (RASST) is defined to include all assets other than cash, government securities, one to four family permanent mortgage loans, and mortgage-backed securities. RASST serves as a measure of the aggressiveness of the bank's asset management policies. Purchased funds (PFUND), a proxy for financing strategy, include all deposits except retail and demand deposits. The effect of this variable on performance can be ambiguous. On one hand, purchased funds (mostly certificates of deposit) can be used for profitable lending. Alternatively, they may be indicative of management which was either ineffective in raising core deposits or simply poor at managing risks. Noninterest inefficiency (NIINEF) or noninterest cost to asset ratio (NICOSTR) attempts to capture the extent to which management was successful in optimizing the cost associated with employee and office expenses. The use of these dependent variables representing asset management, financing strategy and management efficiency is consistent with banking research on other topics (Lindley et al., 1992 and Hasan et al., 1995).

Foreign multinational bank (FOMNB) is a binary variable which has a value of one to indicate foreign multinational banks and zero to indicate US multinational banks. The percentage of foreign ownership binary variable (PFOWN) takes a value of one if a majority (50 per cent or more) of the institution is controlled by foreign ownership, otherwise PFOWN takes a value of zero. Foreign Asset Share (FSHARE) represents the amount of assets the sample multinational banks held outside the US. A binary variable, Mega-foreign multinational bank (M-FOMNB), is used to distinguish the largest foreign banks from relatively smaller foreign institutions. The bank holding company (BHC) binary variable has a value of one if the financial institution is some form of bank holding company; otherwise, BHC takes a value of zero – indicating banking institutions that are controlled by either individuals, the government, or a non-banking agency. The age variable captures the number years the bank has conducted business in the US – reflecting their market experience. The logarithm of the total assets variable controls for asset size. All data were obtained from

TABLE 12.1: *Frequency distribution of multinational banks operating in the US*

	Number of Banks					
	1984	1985	1986	1987	1988	1989
Foreign-owned multinationals						
Total banks	77	80	76	77	75	74
Percentage of foreign ownership:						
Below 50%	12	10	11	11	9	8
50% and over	65	70	65	66	66	66
Types of foreign ownership:						
Owned by individuals and others	31	34	30	28	27	25
Owned by bank holding companies	46	46	46	49	48	49
US-owned multinationals						
Total banks	174	180	170	164	166	159
Combined multinational banks	251	260	246	241	241	233

commercial bank Reports of Condition (Call Reports) and Income filed with the Federal Reserve. All FOMNBs and USMNBs that were in business during the period 1984–89 were included in the sample.

Results

Table 12.1 summarizes the ownership characteristics of the foreign banks in the sample. The number of foreign multinational banks ranged from 74 to 80 during the sample years. The majority of these banks (over 85 per cent) had over 50 per cent foreign ownership. Almost half of the sample FOMNBs had a holding company organizational structure. There were over twice as many US-owned multinational banks as FOMNBs in the sample – ranging from 159 to 180 during the sample period.

Table 12.2 presents summary data for the variables used in the estimation of the efficiency variables. With average total assets of US$2.76 billion, the FOMNBs were significantly smaller than their USMNB counterparts, who posted average assets of US$4.95 billion. The input prices paid by FOMNBs were observed to be significantly higher, on average, than those paid by USMNBs. In terms of asset portfolio composition, USMNBs held smaller percentages of their assets in money market forms and larger percentages in other types of loans. Although USMNBs held significantly more commercial and industrial loans than FOMNBs, these loans as a percentage of assets did not statistically differ for the two groups of banks. USMNBs also held fewer foreign assets, both in absolute terms and as a percentage of assets, than did FOMNBs. Total measured costs were significantly higher at the USMNBs in absolute terms, but not

TABLE 12.2: *Descriptive statistics for multinational banks*

Variables	FOMNBs	% Assets	USMNBs	% Assets
Profit and cost function inputs:				
Price of labour	33.65		29.36*	
	(11.32)		(8.74)	
Price of capital	6.13		.417*	
	(.468)		(.244)	
Price of funds	.061		.056[+]	
	(.056)		(.013)	
Profit and cost function outputs (millions)				
All money market assets	789.0	35.51	1173.0*	25.64*
	(1655)	(17.96)	(1327)	(12.28)
Commercial/industrial loans	677.0	22.54	1180.0*	21.56
	(1452)	(11.57)	(1676)	(8.38)
Other loans	958.0	32.26	1934.0*	39.66
	(2111)	(14.51)	(1916)	(11.51)
Other bank outputs	23.0	9.70	4954*	1.16*
	(54)	(0.86)	(5235)	(1.99)
Total assets (millions)	2755		4954*	
	(5428)		(5235)	
Foreign assets (millions)	399	14.50	267*	5.40*
	(1050)		(748)	
Total profit	46.2	1.51	93.8*	1.90*
	(11.7)	(0.97)	(20.3)	(0.76)
Noninterest costs (millions)	64.6	2.01	84.8*	1.69*
	(32.8)	(1.59)	(27.3)	(1.02)
Total costs (millions)	229	8.00	399*	7.70
	(485)	(3.55)	(467)	(2.15)

*   Difference in means significant at the one per cent level.
[+]   Difference in means significant at the five per cent level.
Standard deviations are in parentheses.

as a percentage of assets. The smaller size and higher input prices at FOMNBs relative to USMNBs is suggestive of managerial inefficiencies. This is especially the case given the more liquid asset portfolios and larger percentages of foreign assets held by FOMNBs. However, the total costs for FOMNBs was significantly lower than that for USMNBs.

Utilizing a normalized version of the translog function and the inefficiency estimation procedure discussed earlier, profit and noninterest inefficiency scores for the sample banks were calculated. These results, which are displayed in Table 12.3, demonstrate that both USMNBs and FOMNBs yielded a profit efficiency level that was 28 per cent lower on average than the best performing multinational bank in the sample. In addition, both types of MNBs displayed noninterest cost efficiency levels that were on average 20

TABLE 12.3A: *Descriptive statistics for profit inefficiency scores (combined pooled sample)*

Sample	Mean	Std. Dev.	Min	Max
Foreign-owned multinationals	35.08*	18.51	14.80	59.30
Percentage of foreign ownership:				
Below 50%	30.61	18.53	14.80	50.64
50% and over	40.55*	11.76	15.32	59.30
Types of foreign ownership:				
Owned by individuals and others	39.61*	14.52	15.63	59.30
Owned by bank holding companies	33.50*	18.51	14.80	50.64
US-owned multinationals	26.02	13.54	11.65	40.74
Combined multinational banks	28.33	14.03	11.65	59.30

TABLE 12.3B: *Descriptive statistics for noninterest cost inefficiency scores (combined pooled sample)*

Sample	Mean	Std. Dev.	Min	Max
Foreign-owned multinationals	24.30*	19.65	7.54	86.35
Percentage of foreign ownership:				
Below 50%	22.18	10.03	7.54	75.09
50% and over	30.14*	12.82	9.38	86.35
Types of foreign ownership:				
Owned by individuals and others	27.45*	9.51	9.38	86.35
Owned by bank holding companies	23.06	11.33	7.54	75.09
US-owned multinationals	19.14	11.58	4.36	70.36
Combined multinational banks	20.03	15.92	4.36	86.35

*   Denotes that the average inefficiency score of FOMNBs is different from the average inefficiency of USMNBs at one per cent significant level.

per cent higher than the best possible efficiency attained by a bank in the sample.

The average profit inefficiency score of the USMNBs (26.02 per cent) was significantly lower than the average noninterest inefficiency score posted by the FOMNBs (35.08 per cent). Only the subsample of the FOMNBs with less than 50 per cent foreign ownership had an average profit inefficiency score somewhat close to the scores of USMNBs. The most profit-inefficient banks were FOMNBs with foreign ownership exceeding 50 per cent[4]. Higher levels of profit inefficiency were also observed in cases where the FOMNB was not owned by a bank holding company. This could result from agency or monitoring problems on the part of the foreign controlling interests (individuals, government or governmental agencies) or simply the lack of an organizational structure amenable to transferring home country advantages at low cost.

The average noninterest inefficiency score of the USMNBs (19.14 per cent) was significantly lower than the average noninterest inefficiency score posted by the FOMNBs (24.3 per cent). The FOMNBs with foreign ownership exceeding 50 per cent reported a high inefficiency score of 30.64 per cent. Thus, it appears that the larger the foreign presence in terms of ownership, the more inefficient the bank was in controlling noninterest cost. This could be the result of difficulties encountered by FOMNBs in adapting customer and service delivery systems to the US market. Also, banks without holding company affiliation reported higher noninterest inefficiency.

The 2SLS regressions were estimated to examine the correlation between firm performance and asset–liability management, firm performance and cost management, and their interrelationship. Specific attention is given to the organizational structure of the multinational banking institutions. Money Market Assets, Capital Assets Ratio, Number of Branches, and Yearly Per Capita Income in the United States were treated as instrumental variables in the estimation of the simultaneous equations. The results from the regressions are displayed in Tables 12.4 and 12.5. Table 12.4 includes efficiency scores with performance (PINEFF) and management efficiency (NIINEFF) as dependent variables representing performance and management efficiency, whereas Table 12.5 replaces these two variables with ROA and NICOSTR respectively.

Regressions were also estimated separately for each year using a similar format to that used in the combined estimates except that the yearly per capita income variable was excluded. The results of the yearly estimates were less pronounced; however, they were not significantly different to impact the overall conclusions obtained from the combined estimates for all six years. For brevity, only the combined estimates are reported.

As indicated in the tables, the results were quite similar in almost all cases (parameters) irrespective of whether efficiency scores or simple ratios were used to capture performance and noninterest cost (Tables 12.4 and 12.5 respectively). The explanations given below address the overall results.

The foreign ownership dummy variable (FOMNB) variable had a significant impact on the performance variables. In both cases, the FOMNB was found to be negatively associated with performance, i.e., a positive association with profit inefficiency and a negative association with ROA. Similarly, the coefficient of the percentage of foreign ownership variable (PFOWN) and the extent of sales in foreign market variable (FSHARE) reflect that higher foreign

TABLE 12.4: *Two-stage least squares combined regression results*

INDEPENDENT VARIABLES	PROFIT INEFFCIENCY (PINEFF)	RISKY ASSETS (RASST)	PURCHASED FUNDS (PFUND)	NON INTEREST COST INEFFICIENCY (NIINEFF)
Intercept	0.165	0.103	0.125	0.147
	(3.23)*	(5.90)*	(5.61)*	(2.36)⁺
Profit Inefficiency	–	–	0.112	–
(PINEFF)			(1.09)	
Risky Assets to Total Assets	−0.018	–	–	−0.129
(RASST)	(2.52)⁺			(2.18)⁺
Purchased Funds to Total	0.157	0.066	–	−0.103
Liabilities (PFUND)	(1.42)	(4.30)*		(1.49)
Noninterest Cost	0.081	−0.159	−0.124	–
Inefficiency (NIINEFF)	(1.84)#	(2.24)⁺	(1.69)#	
Foreign Multinational	0.046	−0.012	0.253	0.065
Banks (FOMNB)	(3.73)*	(1.42)	(4.69)	(5.37)*
Percentage of Foreign	0.018	−0.136	0.013	0.120
Owned (PFOWN)	(4.51)*	(1.07)	(1.80)#	(3.21)*
Foreign Assets Share	0.102	−0.102	0.027	0.117
(FSHARE)	(3.78)*	(1.48)	(1.58)	(2.54)⁺
Mega Foreign	−0.134	0.093	0.066	0.040
Multinational Bank	(1.02)	(1.37)	(2.32)⁺	(0.75)
(M-FOMNB)				
Bank Holding Companies	−0.089	0.248	−0.138	−0.141
(BHC)	(1.97)⁺	(1.59)	(0.56)	(1.89)#
Log of Age (AGE)	−0.021	0.014	−0.027	−0.051
	(2.56)⁺	(1.16)	(0.90)	(1.60)
Log of Total Assets	−0.001	−0.010	0.071	−0.006
(ASSETS)	(2.42)⁺	(1.09)	(1.60)	(2.73)⁺
	MODEL STATISTICS			
Adjusted R-Square	11.46	8.08	11.70	9.36
F-Statistic	25.58*	20.29*	18.14*	11.20*
Number of Observations	1472	1472	1472	1472

Note: * = one per cent significance level, ⁺ = five per cent significance level, # = ten per cent significance level. The t-statistics are in the brackets. Money Market Assets, Capital Asset Ratio, Number of Branch, and Yearly Per Capita Income in the United States are considered as Instrumental Variables.

ownership and higher involvement of business activities outside the US impacted performance negatively.

These results are consistent with the observations derived from the earlier tables (the descriptive statistics) that the FOMNBs were less efficient than their USMNB counterparts. Additionally, such differences were more apparent when the foreign samples included sub-samples with higher foreign involvement both with respect to

TABLE 12.5: *Two-stage least squares combined regression results*

INDEPENDENT VARIABLES	RETURN ON ASSETS (ROA)	RISKY ASSETS (RASST)	PURCHASED FUNDS (PFUND)	NON INTEREST COST TO ASSET (NICOSTR)
Intercept	0.074	0.112	0.098	0.095
	(2.60)$^+$	(4.87)*	(4.74)*	(1.97)$^\#$
Return on Assets (ROA)	–	–	0.176	–
			(0.83)	
Risky Assets to Total Assets	0.035	–	–	–0.056
(RASST)	(3.96)*			(1.99)$^+$
Purchased Funds to Total	–0.103	0.043	–	–0.083
Liabilities (PFUND)	(1.26)	(3.60)*		(1.56)
Noninterest Cost to Assets	–0.081	–0.092	0.101	–
Ratio (NICOSTR)	(2.07)$^+$	(3.05)*	(1.08)	
Foreign Multinational	–0.193	–0.026	0.186	0.073
Banks (FOMNB)	(5.06)*	(1.01)	(4.02)*	(4.54)*
Percentage of Foreign	–0.124	–0.092	0.012	0.091
Owned (PFOWN)	(3.98)*	(1.03)	(1.78)$^\#$	(3.78)*
Foreign Assets Share	–0.095	–0.063	0.022	0.124
(FSHARE)	(3.02)*	(1.30)	(1.66)$^\#$	(2.07)$^+$
Mega Foreign	0.048	0.088	0.060	0.058
Multinational Bank	(0.73)	(1.56)	(1.99)$^+$	(1.02)
(M-FOMNB)				
Bank Holding Companies	0.053	0.153	–0.102	–0.103
(BHC)	(1.84)$^\#$	(1.71)$^\#$	(0.42)	(1.97)$^+$
Log of Age (AGE)	0.016	0.013	–0.018	–0.066
	(2.85)$^+$	(1.04)	(1.01)	(1.51)
Log of Total Assets	0.001	–0.010	0.036	–0.005
(ASSETS)	(3.50)*	(1.23)	(1.51)	(2.48)$^+$
MODEL STATISTICS				
Adjusted R-Square	18.30	10.08	16.44	10.02
F-Statistic	30.15*	19.38*	23.16*	11.85*
Number of Observations	1472	1472	1472	1472

Note: * = one per cent significance level, $^+$ = 5 per cent significance level, $^\#$ = ten per cent significance level. The t-statistics are in the brackets. Money Market Assets, Capital Asset Ratio, Number of Branch, and Yearly Per Capita Income in the United States are considered as Instrumental Variables.

percentage of ownership and the extent of business involvement abroad. The bank holding company (BHC) parameter indicated that multinationals adopting such organizational form performed relatively better although the statistical significance of such relationship is marginal in the second estimate.

The risky assets variable indicates that risk (asset management strategy) and return (performance) variables were positively associated. The role of purchase funds as a liability strategy was not significant in explaining performance. Bigger institutions were associated with less noninterest inefficiency (cost). Higher noninterest inefficiency (expenses) negatively impacted performance as indicated by the NIINEFF and NICOSTR parameters. Overall, the bigger institutions (by assets size, ASSET) were better performers during the sample period. The AGE coefficient showed a significant negative association with the profit inefficiency variable and a positive association with the ROA. This indicates that as the multinationals gained more experience in the market, their performance tended to improve. Additional estimations (not reported) showed that an interactive variable incorporating FOMNB and AGE provided even stronger t-statistics supporting the fact that experience in the new market helps performance.

In examining the relative importance of RASST, institutions with higher involvement in purchased funds were found to be more prone to invest in risky assets. Institutions with higher noninterest inefficiency or cost were less likely to have a higher asset concentration in risky assets. In determining the extent of involvement in purchase funds, it is evident that foreign MNBs were significantly associated with this liability strategy. Finally, with respect to noninterest cost inefficiency (or noninterest cost) regressions, FOMNBs were associated with higher noninterest costs and thus noninterest inefficiency. It is also apparent that banks with BHC organizational structure were more successful in lowering noninterest cost (or noninterest inefficiency). This ability to control cost led to better performance in the ROA or PINEFF regressions as evidenced from the ASSET and BHC parameters.

Overall, the results from both univariate and multivariate analyses portray that FOMNBs are more conservative, concentrating in liquid assets with less involvement in high return risky assets. Moreover, these institutions with less experience and understanding in the US market incurred higher noninterest expenses. These factors contributed to lower relative performance for FOMNBs compared to USMNBs. Further investigations (not reported) of the data were conducted by excluding the Japaneses FOMNBs from the sample. Lower performance by FOMNBs was still detected; however, the statistical significance of the FOMNB parameters was weaker than the reported results. This is consistent with the earlier findings by Hasan and Hunter (1996). For other parameters, the results of these additional sub-samples were similar to the pooled combined reported results.

Conclusion

Overall, the results of the regression analyses indicate that foreign-owned multinational banks operating in the US are less efficient than their US-owned multinational counterparts. While the specific sources of this difference in performance are difficult to specify, the results of the empirical analysis suggest that, to some extent, the asset–liability management strategy, management efficiency, extent of business in foreign countries and organization structure play active roles. Large banks and banks in a holding company network with fewer foreign assets tend to be significantly more efficient. This finding suggests that the ability of the bank holding company form of organization to transfer comparative advantages to new markets while managing foreign assets in other more suitable units of their networks allows these banks to outperform banks which are not affiliated with a holding company network. In addition, the ability of the bank holding company structure to minimize agency problems (for example, through decentralization) may also contribute to efficient production. Also, once adjusted for experience in the US market, the differences in performance between USMNBs and FOMNBs narrow substantially. This is also true when the Japanese sub-sample is excluded from the FOMNB group. The results of this study should enhance efforts in establishing efficient criteria for evaluating multinational bank management strategy in competitive and integrated banking activities in the US and other parts of the world.

References

AIGNER, D. J., LOVELL, C. A. and SCHMIDT, P. (1977) Formulation and estimation of stochastic frontier production function models, *Journal of Econometrics*, December, pp. 21–37.

ALLEN, L. and RAI, A. (1996) Operational efficiency in banking: An international comparison, *Journal of Banking and Finance*, Vol. 20, pp. 655–672.

BERG, S. A., BUKH, P. N. D. and FORSUND, F. R. (1995) *Banking Efficiency in the Nordic Countries: A Four-Country Malmquist Index Analysis*, Working Paper, University of Aarhus, Denmark.

BERGER, A. N. and DEYOUNG, R. (1997) Problem loans and cost-efficiency in commercial banks, *Journal of Banking and Finance*, Vol. 21, pp. 849–870.

BERGER, A. N., DEYOUNG, R., GENAY, H. and UDELL, G. (2000) The globalization of financial institutions: Evidence from cross-border banking performance, *Brookings–Rochester Economic Series*, forthcoming.

BERGER, A. N. HUNTER, W. C. and TIMME, S. G. (1993) The efficiency of financial institutions: A review and preview of research past, present and future, *Journal of Banking and Finance*, Nos. 2–3, pp. 221–249.

BIKKER, J. A. (1999) *Efficiency in the European Banking Industry: An Explanatory Analysis to Rank Countries,* De Nederlandsche Bank, Amsterdam, The Netherlands.

CASSON, M. (1990) Evolution of multinational banks: A theoretical perspective, in G. Jones (ed.) *Banks As Multinationals,* Routledge, London, pp. 14–29.

CHANG, C. E., HASAN, I. and HUNTER, W. C. (1998) Efficiency of multinational banks: An empirical investigation, *Applied Financial Economics,* December, pp. 689–696.

CLARK, J. A. (1986a) Market structure, risk and profitability: The quiet life hypothesis revisited, *Quarterly Review of Economics and Business,* Spring, pp. 45–56.

CLARK, J. A. (1986b) Single-equation, multiple-regression methodology: Is it an appropriate methodology for the estimation of the structure–performance relationship in banking? *Journal of Monetary Economics,* November, pp. 295–312.

COOPER, S., FRASER, D., ROSE, P. and WOLKEN, L. (1989) US activities of Pacific-Rim and European banks: Evidence for a global integrated market for bank credit? *The Review of Research in Banking and Finance,* Fall, pp. 1–25.

DAMANPOUR, F. (1990) *The Evolution of Foreign Banking Institutions in the United States,* Quorum Books, New York.

DEYOUNG, R. and HASAN, I. (1998) The performance of De Novo commercial banks: A profit efficiency approach, *Journal of Banking and Finance,* May, pp. 565–587.

DEYOUNG, R. and NOLLE, D. E. (1996) Foreign-owned banks in the United States: Earning market share or buying it, *Journal of Money, Credit and Banking,* May, pp. 622–636.

ELYASIANI, E. and MEHDIAN, S. M. (1990) A nonparametric approach to measurement of efficiency and technological change: The case of large US commercial banks, *Journal of Financial Services Research,* August, pp. 157–168.

ELYASIANI, E. and MEHDIAN, S. M. (1992) *A Nonparametric Frontier Model of Internationally-Owned and Domestically-Owned Bank Cost Structures,* Paper presented at the Financial Management Association Meetings.

FECHER, F. and PESTIEAU, P. (1993) Efficiency and competition in OECD financial services, in H. O. FRIED, C. A. K. LOVELL and S. S. SCHMIDT (eds.), *The Measurement of Productive Efficiency Techniques and Applications,* Oxford University Press, Oxford, pp. 374–385.

GOLDBERG, E. (1981) Analysis of current operations of foreign-owned US banks in US, in US Comptroller of the Currency, *Foreign Acquisition of US Banks,* Robert. R. Dame, Richmond, Virginia, pp. 343–368.

GOLDBERG, E. (1982) Comparative cost analysis of foreign-owned US banks, *Journal of Bank Research,* Vol. 13, pp. 144–159.

GOLDBERG, L. and SAUNDERS, A. (1981a) The determinants of foreign banking activities in the United States, *Journal of Banking and Finance,* March, pp. 17–32.

GOLDBERG, L. and SAUNDERS, A. (1981b) The growth of organizational forms of foreign banks in the US, *Journal of Money, Credit and Banking,* Vol. 13, pp. 365–374.

GRADDY, D. B. and KYLE, R. III (1979) The simultaneity of bank decision-making, market structure, and bank performance, *Journal of Finance,* Vol. 34, pp. 1–18.

GRAY, P. and GRAY, J. (1981) The multinational bank: A financial MNC? *Journal of Banking and Finance,* March, p. 33–63.

GROSSE, R. and GOLDBERG, L. (1991) Foreign banking activity in the United States: An analysis of country of origin, *Journal of Banking and Finance*, December, pp. 1093–1112.

HASAN, I., HASAN, T. and PICKERAL, R. (1995) Are mortgage specialized thrifts viable? An empirical analysis, *International Review of Economics and Finance*, Vol. 4, No. 2, pp. 189–204.

HASAN, I. and HUNTER, T. W. (1996) Efficiency of Japanese multinational banks in the United States, *Research in Finance*, Vol. 14, pp. 157–173.

HASAN, I. and LOZANO-VIVAS, A. (1998) *Foreign Banks, Production Technology, and Efficiency: Spanish Experience*, Working Paper presented at the Georgia Productivity Workshop III, Athens, Georgia.

HASAN, I., LOZANO-VIVAS, A. and PASTOR, J. (2000) *Cross-border Performance in European Banking*, Paper presented at the Wharton School and Frankfurt Finance Centre Conference.

HOUPT, J. (1983) Foreign ownership of US banks: Trends and effects, *Journal of Bank Research*, Vol. 14, pp. 144–156.

HULTMANN, C. and McGEE, L. (1989) Factors affecting the foreign banking presence in the US, *Journal of Banking and Finance*, October, pp. 383–396.

LEWIS, M. and DAVIS, K. (1987) *Domestic and International Banking*, MIT Press, Cambridge, Massachusetts.

LINDLEY, J. T., GUP, B. E., McNULTY, J. E. and VERBRUGGE, J. A. (1992) Investment policy, financing policy and performance characteristics of De Novo Savings and Loan Association, *Journal of Banking and Finance*, April, pp. 313–330.

MAHAJAN, A., RANGAN, N. and ZARDKOOHI, A. (1996) Cost structures in multinational and domestic banking, *Journal of Banking and Finance*, Vol. 20, pp. 238–306.

MESTER, L. (1993) Efficiency in the savings and loan industry, *Journal of Banking and Finance*, April, pp. 267–286.

MEEUSEN, W. and BROECK, J. (1977) Efficiency estimation from Cobb–Douglas production function with composed error, *International Economic Review*, June, pp. 435–444.

PASTOR, J. M., PÉREZ, F. and QUESADA, J. (1997) Efficiency analysis in banking firms: An international comparison, *European Journal of Operational Research*, pp. 119–223.

PEEK, J., ROSENGREN, E. S. and KASIRYE, F. (1999) The poor performance of foreign bank subsidiaries: Were the problems acquired or created? *Journal of Banking and Finance*, Vol. 22, No. 6, pp. 799–819.

RUTHENBERG, D. and ELIAS, R. (1996) Cost economies and interest rate margins in a unified European banking market, *Journal of Economics and Business*, Vol. 48, pp. 231–249.

VANDER VENNET, R. (1996) The effects of mergers and acquisitions on the efficiency and profitability of EC credit institutions, *Journal of Banking and Finance*, Vol. 20, No. 9, pp. 1531–1558.

WALTER, A. (1981) Supervisory performance of foreign-controlled US banking organization, in US Comptroller of the Currency, *Foreign Acquisition of US Banks*, Robert R. Dame, Richmond, Virginia, pp. 329–342.

Notes

The authors thank Ilhan Meric and Gulser Meric (editors), Asokan Ananadarajan and Jane-Ruang Lin for suggestions and comments. Usual caveats apply.

1. See Goldberg and Saunders (1981a, 1981b), Hultman and McGee (1989), Damanpour (1990), and Grosse and Goldberg (1991) for extensive discussions of these developments.

2. Three-Stage Least Squares (3SLS) regressions were also estimated. The results were similar to the ones reported in the text. These results are available upon request.

3. The econometric frontier approach (EFA) was used to estimate profit and noninterest cost inefficiency. In EFA models, a frontier is estimated using a statistical procedure that decomposes the error term into two parts. One part of the error term captures random disturbances and is assumed to follow a symmetric normal distribution around the frontier that captures a phenomenon beyond the control of management (e.g., local or regional economic conditions, luck, labour strikes or machine performance). The other part of the error term is assumed to capture inefficiency that is assumed to follow a positive half-normal distribution below (above) the profit (cost) frontier and represent individual firm profit (cost) deviations or errors due to factors under management control (technical and allocative inefficiency). This represents poor managerial performance (e.g., incompetent asset–liability management, expense preference behaviour, agency problems, etc.). A Fourier-flexible, alternative, or nonstandard profit function was used to estimate separate annual frontiers for banks during each sample year. This functional form combines a standard translog functional form with the nonparametric Fourier functional form. The translog form is a local approximation that performs well for banks close to the sample means, but can perform poorly for particularly small or large banks. In the Fourier-flexible form, trigonometric transformations of the translog variables are added so that the function globally approximates the underlying profit or cost function over the entire range of data. Berger and DeYoung (1997) found that the Fourier-flexible form dominates the translog. This type of functional form is appropriate for analysing the multinational banks with a wide range of asset sizes.

4. The following Fourier-flexible profit (noninterest cost) function was estimated:

$$
\begin{aligned}
\ln P \,(\ln C) = {} & \alpha_0 + \sum_{j=1}^{3} \beta_j \ln Y_j + \frac{1}{2} \sum_{j=1}^{3} \sum_{k=1}^{3} \beta_{jk} \ln Y_j \ln Y_k + \sum_m^{2} \gamma_m \ln W_m \\
& + \frac{1}{2} \sum_{m=1}^{2} \sum_{n=1}^{2} \gamma_{mm} \ln W_m \ln W_n + \sum_{j=1}^{3} \sum_{m=1}^{2} \rho_{jm} \ln Y_j \ln W_m \\
& + \sum_{j=1}^{5} \left[\delta_j \cos Z_j + \theta_j \sin Z_j \right] + \sum_{j=1}^{5} \sum_{k=1}^{5} \left[\delta_{jk} \cos\!\left(Z_j + Z_k \right) + \theta_{jk} \sin\!\left(Z_j + Z_k \right) \right] \\
& + \sum_{j=1}^{5} \sum_{k=j}^{5} \sum_{l=k}^{5} \left[\delta_{jkl} \cos\!\left(Z_j + Z_k + Z_l \right) + \theta_{jkl} \sin\!\left(Z_j + Z_k + Z_l \right) \right] + \eta
\end{aligned}
$$

where the subscript that identifies individual banks has been dropped for simplicity. P is the after-tax profit (C is noninterest cost); Y is a vector of outputs, and W is a vector of inputs. The Z's are functions that rescale the $\ln Y_j$ and the $\ln W_m$ terms so that they fall on specific intervals. The error term η is a composite expression: $\eta = \ln U + \ln V$, where $\ln U$ captures profit (cost) inefficiency and is distributed as a truncated normal variable, and $\ln V$ captures random error and is distributed as a normal variable. Three outputs included are measured as the dollar value of (1) all money market assets, (2) commercial and industrial loans, and (3) other assets. Labour, physical capital, and funds (including deposits) are treated as inputs that are intermediated to produce bank assets. The price of labour, P_1, is calculated by dividing total salaries and fringe benefits by the number of full-time equivalent employees (including bank officers). The price of physical capital, P_2, is equal to the ratio of total expenses of premises and fixed assets to total assets. The price of funds, P_3, is calculated by dividing the total interest expense paid on deposits, Federal funds purchased, and securities sold under agreements to repurchase, demand notes issued to the US treasury, mortgage indebtedness, subordinated debts and debentures, and other borrowed money, by the sum of funds from these sources. In calculating noninterest inefficiency, the cost function only includes total noninterest cost in the left-hand side of the equation whereas the only input variable considered in the right-hand side is the cost of funds.

Further investigation of the efficiency score by age group shows that FOMNBs that are in the business in US market more than ten years record a better inefficiency score (30.03 per cent), still significantly lower than the USMNB average of 26.02 per cent. Also, once the Japanese FOMNBs are excluded, we find some improvement in the inefficiency score with an average of 31.07 per cent. These additional statistics are available upon request.

13

Selecting a Portfolio with Skewness: Recent Evidence from Latin American Equity Markets

ARUN J. PRAKASH, THERESE E. PACTWA, CHUN-HAO CHANG and MICHAEL A. SULLIVAN

Introduction

Researchers have long argued that the higher moments of return distributions cannot be neglected unless there is reason to believe that the asset returns are normally distributed and the utility function is quadratic, or that the higher (than two) moments are irrelevant to the investor's decision (e.g., Arditti, 1967; Samuelson, 1970; Rubinstein, 1973). Many have provided evidence that returns are not symmetrical. Others have shown that the assumption of a quadratic utility function is appropriate only for relatively low returns, which precludes its use for many types of investments. The important role of skewness in portfolio decision making has been demonstrated[1].

As is shown in Arditti (1967), an investor's preference for skewness in the return is consistent with the notion of decreasing absolute risk aversion. This is because positive skewness refers to a right-handed, elongated tail for the density function. Positive skewness is desirable, since increasing skewness decreases the probability of large negative returns, and increases the probability of large positive returns. Based on the previous research, e.g. Stephens and Proffitt (1991), we also assume that the higher moments of return distributions are relevant to the investor's decision and cannot be neglected.

Similar to Lai (1991) and Chunhachinda et al. (1997), we incorporate an investor's preference for skewness while applying goal programming to portfolio selection. Goal programming is a multi-objective technique which analyses the properties, such as mean, variance, skewness and kurtosis, of the return distribution. Results of the goal programming model provide a set of weights to compose an optimal investment portfolio. This optimal portfolio addresses the trade-offs between objectives, such as maximizing expected returns and skewness, and minimizing risk. This research updates the previous work of Chunhachinda et al. (1997) and extends the analysis to include more international markets.

Consistent with the results of the seminal work by Meric and Meric (1989), Chunhachinda et al. (1997) found that there exists inter-temporal stability among 14 international stock markets during the time period of January 1988 to December 1993. Meric and Meric utilized data from 1973 to 1987. We examine data from 1993 to 1998. The stability of international stock markets is important in helping investors realize the potential gains from international diversification. If the observed structural relationships are stable over time, the investors can use the ex post patterns of co-movement to proxy the ex ante co-movements. Both studies by Meric and Meric and Chunhachinda et al. find that the longer the time period, the more the ex post patterns of co-movement will be better proxies for the ex ante co-movements. The important implication to this finding to the portfolio decision is that the portfolio efficient frontier may be considered relatively stable over time.

The remaining sections of this paper are arranged as follows. A literature review of the related concepts and economic justifications is provided next, followed by a description of the data. Then we present our goal programming approach to combine forecasts based on distributions of previous returns and the mathematical programming formulation. The last section concludes the study with suggestions for future research.

Previous Literature on Higher-Moment Portfolio Selection and Polynomial Goal Programming

Although numerous researchers have documented the existence of a risk premium with skewness, only a few studies to date have contributed to the construction of a portfolio with skewness. In the presence of skewness, selecting a portfolio is a trade-off between competing and conflicting objectives. On one hand, investors try to maximize expected return and skewness, and on the other hand, they try to minimize the variance of the portfolio returns. To solve this problem, therefore, portfolio selection must depend on an investor's subjective judgments and relative preferences on objectives.

Arditti and Levy (1975) suggest a nonlinear mathematical program to solve the mean-variance–skewness efficient set in a multi-period framework. However, Lai (1991) points out that Arditti and Levy's assumption that the third moment in a multi-period model is insignificant can result in an inefficient portfolio. Kumar et al. (1978) proposes that linear goal programming can be used to solve the goal conflicts inherent in the portfolio selection of dual-purpose mutual funds, such as growth and income funds.

Lai (1991) demonstrates that investor preferences can be incorporated into polynomial goal programming, introduced by Tayi and Leonard (1988), from which portfolio selection with skewness is determined. The optimal portfolio is chosen from a sample of five domestic stocks. The important features of polynomial goal programming are the existence of an optimal solution, the flexibility of incorporating investor preferences, and the relative computational simplicity.

Chunhachinda et al. (1997) apply polynomial goal programming to construct portfolios chosen from among 14 international stock market indexes based on the data from January 1988 to December 1993. Using the Wilk–Shapiro test, they find that the returns of these 14 stock markets are not normally distributed. They show that the incorporation of skewness into an investor's portfolio decision causes a major change in the construction of the optimal portfolio. The evidence also indicates that investors trade expected return for skewness.

The Data

The sample data consists of monthly rates of return for seven international stock market indices for various emerging markets in Latin America. The indices include those of Argentina, Brazil, Chile, Colombia, Mexico, Peru and Venezuela. The data source for these indices was the Morgan Stanley Capital Markets International Returns Index (MSCI), available from DataStream, for the period April 1993 through March 1998[2]. MSCI reports the international assets' returns as converted into US dollars at the appropriate period's spot foreign exchange rate. Thus, no analysis is needed of currency hedging issues. The indices are also adjusted for dividends. The monthly risk-free rates of return are obtained from the three-month US Treasury bill rates as reported by DataStream during the same time period as the returns.

Empirical Analysis

The methodology employed in this study can be summarized in several parts. First, the return distribution of each international index is tested for normality. Next, the variances and covariances of the monthly returns are examined. Then, with different combinations of an investor's preferences for objectives, optimal portfolio selections with skewness are determined.

Testing for Normality of Return Distributions

The empirical analysis initially examines the normality of the return distributions of the seven Latin American stock market indices. This test provides the groundwork for our constructing an optimal portfolio with skewness. If the test results support the non-normality of return distributions and the evidence also supports the skewed returns, we will construct an optimal portfolio with skewness. The Jarque–Bera test is selected as the methodology to test the normality of the returns[3].

Table 13.1 provides details of the summary statistics. During the time period of this study, none of the mean returns were negative. In addition, the Latin American markets showed wide variations in both the means and the standard deviations. For example, the highest mean return occurred in Brazil (2.82 per cent) and the lowest in Mexico (0.76 per cent). The highest standard deviation was in Venezuela (14.02 per cent) and the lowest in Chile (6.72 per cent).

This table also provides the values of skewness and kurtosis for each of the indices' rates of return. Skewness and kurtosis represent

TABLE 13.1: *Summary statistics and results for normality tests, April 1993–March 1998*

	Argentina	Brazil	Chile	Colombia	Mexico	Peru	Venezuela
Mean	0.0155	0.0282	0.0120	0.0116	0.0076	0.0216	0.0281
Median	0.0296	0.0263	0.0004	0.0031	0.0290	0.0139	0.0101
Maximum	0.1894	0.3581	0.1727	0.1589	0.2078	0.3611	0.3176
Minimum	−0.1945	−0.2411	−0.1483	−0.1408	−0.3540	−0.1961	−0.4713
Std. Dev.	0.0876	0.1062	0.0672	0.0703	0.1067	0.0993	0.1402
Coeff. of Var.	5.6443	3.7688	5.5943	6.0582	13.9891	4.5947	4.9823
Skewness	−0.4256	0.3919	0.1564	0.1246	−0.9939	0.7727	−0.5753
Kurtosis	2.7319	4.9484	2.7425	2.1878	4.3010	4.7483	4.7571
Jarque–Bera	1.9914	11.0263	0.4103	1.8045	14.1100	13.6123	11.0288
Probability	0.3695	0.0040	0.8145	0.4056	0.0009	0.0011	0.0040
Observations	60	60	60	60	60	60	60

Note: Under the null hypothesis of a normal distribution, the Jarque–Bera statistic follows a Chi-Squared distribution with two degrees of freedom. The indicated probability shows the probability of observing a larger statistic under the null.

the third and fourth *standardized* moments of the rates of return, respectively[4]. The kurtosis of a data set can sometimes be examined to provide an informal check of normality; the kurtosis of a normal distribution is zero. It has been argued by Krauss and Lizenberger (1976) that any moments higher than the third cannot be behaviourally justified and should be ignored. The evidence indicates that four out of seven of the Latin American markets (Brazil, Chile, Columbia and Peru) exhibit positive skewness. The information provided indicates that the kurtosis of all seven of the international stock markets are far from zero.

The results of the test for normality of return distributions using the Jarque–Bera test are also provided in Table 13.1. Under the null hypothesis of a normal distribution, the Jarque–Bera statistic follows a Chi-squared distribution with two degrees of freedom. The indicated probabilities in the table show the probability of observing a larger statistic under the null. Thus, if the Jarque–Bera statistic is greater than 5.99, the null hypothesis of normality cannot be supported at the five per cent level of significance. The probability associated with the Jarque–Bera statistic indicates that the null hypothesis of a normal distribution cannot be supported for four of the seven Latin American markets (Brazil, Mexico, Peru and Venezuela) at the five per cent level of significance. These four markets also exhibited significant skewness.

The greater variation of the results of the means of the returns and the standard deviations, taken together with the higher incidence of skewness and kurtosis, emphasizes the problem of using a mean-variance model, especially when dealing with emerging markets. These findings further support the investigation of alternative risk measures that, unlike variance, do not rely an assumption of normality. In the presence of skewness, selecting a portfolio is a trade-off between competing and conflicting objectives, i.e., the investor tries to maximize expected return and skewness, while simultaneously minimizing variance. To solve this multi-objective portfolio problem, we utilize polynomial goal programming, which incorporates investor preferences for skewness.

Examining the Variances, Covariances and Correlations of Monthly Returns across Countries

Table 13.2 provides the mean values of the variances and covariances for the monthly rates of return for the Latin American stock markets. The values appearing in bold represent the variances, and

TABLE 13.2: *Summary of covariances of monthly returns: Latin American markets, April 1993–March 1998*

	x_1	x_2	x_3	x_4	x_5	x_6	x_7
Argentina (x_1)	0.00755						
Brazil (x_2)	0.00384	0.01109					
Chile (x_3)	0.00283	0.00315	0.00444				
Colombia (x_4)	0.00042	0.00069	0.00104	0.00486			
Mexico (x_5)	0.00651	0.00602	0.00281	0.00008	0.01119		
Peru (x_6)	0.00419	0.00478	0.00397	0.00112	0.00502	0.00970	
Venezuela (x_7)	0.00087	0.00278	0.00198	0.00203	0.00014	0.00170	0.01934

The covariance is determined by multiplying x_i by x_j (for $i, j = 1, \ldots, 10$).

all other values represent the covariances. As can be seen, all covariances are relatively low compared to the variances. The evidence implies that after forming a portfolio, a substantial amount of unsystematic risk is diversified.

Table 13.3 provides correlations, a measure of dependence between two variables, for the Latin American markets. The Latin American markets in general exhibit low correlation. The lowest correlation appears between Venezuela and Mexico (0.0098); whereas the highest correlation is between Mexico and Argentina (0.7084). There are other interesting patterns between markets. For example, Mexico appears to be the most diverse, as it ranked high in both the highest and the lowest correlations.

Solving the Multi-Objective Portfolio Problem

As was argued in the previous section, skewness cannot be ignored. In this section, we briefly describe a multi-objective portfolio selection model based on Lai (1991), which incorporates the skewness of the return distribution. Using the information from Table 13.1, and the following notation, portfolio selection allowing no short sales is determined. We define the following variables for the stock indices:

TABLE 13.3: *Summary of correlations of monthly returns, April 1993–March 1998*

	x_1	x_2	x_3	x_4	x_5	x_6	x_7
Argentina (x_1)	1						
Brazil (x_2)	0.4201	1					
Chile (x_3)	0.4893	0.4485	1				
Colombia (x_4)	0.0697	0.0933	0.2243	1			
Mexico (x_5)	0.7084	0.5407	0.3993	0.0105	1		
Peru (x_6)	0.4892	0.4604	0.6050	0.1627	0.4816	1	
Venezuela (x_7)	0.0722	0.1902	0.2140	0.2090	0.0098	0.1241	1

n = number of stock indices

t = number of periods in sample

k_t = return over period t on each index, $n{\times}1$ vector

k = mean return, $(1/t)\Sigma_t k_t$, $n{\times}1$ vector

V = variance-covariance matrix, estimated by $(1/t)\Sigma_t (k_t{-}k)(k_t{-}k)'$, $n{\times}n$ matrix

S = third central moment matrix, estimated by $(1/t)\Sigma_t (k_t{-}k)(k_t{-}k)'$ $\otimes (k_t{-}k)'$, $n{\times}n^2$ matrix

Skewness for a given random variable = (third central moment)/ (standard deviation)^3

And for the portfolio:

r = riskless rate

w = portfolio weights, $n{\times}1$ vector

$k_p(w)$ = expected excess return on portfolio, $w'(k{-}r)$; expected return on portfolio is $k_p(w){+}r$

$v_p(w)$ = variance of portfolio, $w'Vw$

$s_p(w)$ = third central moment of distribution of portfolio returns, $w'S(w{\otimes}w)$

w_{MV} = mean-variance efficient portfolio, unit variance, no short sales

w_{SV} = skewness-variance efficient portfolio, unit variance, no short sales

$w_{MVS}(s)$ = mean-variance-skewness efficient portfolio, unit variance, no short sales, where $\bar{s}$ is a fixed skewness

$w_{PGP}(a,b)$ = solution to polynomial goal programming problem, unit variance, no short sales, where a and b are parameters in the objective function

The solution of the mean-variance efficient portfolio is given by:

w_{MV} which solves $\quad \overset{Max}{_w} k_p(w) \qquad$ s.t. $w{\geq}0$ and $v_p(w) = 1$

The skewness-variance efficient portfolio is provided by:

w_{SV} which solves $\quad \overset{Max}{_w} s_p(w) \qquad$ s.t. $w{\geq}0$ and $v_p(w) = 1$

The polynomial goal programming problem is:

w_{PGD} which solves $\quad \overset{Min}{_w} \{k_p(w_{MV}) - k_p(w)\}^a + \{s_p(w_{SV}) - s_p(w)\}^b$

$$\text{s.t. } w{\geq}0 \text{ and } v_p(w) = 1$$

While the mean-skewness efficient frontier is determined by:

w_{Max} which solves $\quad \overset{Min}{_w} k_p(w) \qquad$ s.t. $w{\geq}0$, $v_p(w) = 1$ and $s_p(w)$

$$= \bar{s} \text{ where } s_p(w_{MV}) \leq \bar{s} \leq s_p(w_{SV})$$

TABLE 13.4: *Polynomial goal programming: minimize weighted deviations from maximums*

Parameters						
a	1	0	1	2	1	2
b	0	1	1	1	2	2

Optimal Portfolio Composition						
Argentina	0.4702	0	0	0	0	0
Brazil	5.5547	0.6238	1.5750	0.8045	4.3748	2.6399
Chile	0	0.9212	0.6865	0.8684	0.4422	0.4109
Colombia	2.4653	0	0	0	0	0
Mexico	0	0	0	0	0	0
Peru	2.6522	9.432	8.9657	9.3531	6.9019	8.3551
Venezuela	3.1567	0	0	0	0	0

Optimal Portfolio Statistics (all are unit variance)						
Mean	0.2756	0.1853	0.1980	0.1878	0.2270	0.2106
Skewness	–01865	0.7804	0.7743	0.7802	0.6917	0.7534

Note: The weight in the goal programming model on deviation from maximum return is a, the weight on deviation from maximum skewness is b.

Table 13.4 presents the optimal portfolio solution when short sales are not allowed, i.e. the portfolio weight x_i can take on only positive values. The results show that different combinations of the parameters *a* and *b* (weights on the deviation from maximum return and on the deviation from maximum skew, respectively) result in different portfolio compositions. The combination of a = 1, b = 0 represents the mean-variance efficient portfolio (the shaded column in Table 13.4). The other combinations represent the mean-variance-skewness efficient portfolio. Skewness represents the third central co-moments of the optimal portfolio return. Clearly, the evidence demonstrates that the incorporation of skewness into an investor's portfolio decision causes a major change in the construction of the optimal portfolio.

For the optimal portfolios for the Latin American markets, Mexico is not included in any combination of *a* and *b*. In addition, Argentina, Colombia and Venezuela only show up in the mean-variance efficient portfolio (these are the three markets that exhibited negative skewness). Chile does not appear in the mean-variance efficient portfolio, yet it appears in all of the mean-variance-skewness efficient portfolios. Other than in the mean-variance efficient portfolio, Peru consistently has the largest component in the optimal portfolio. These are all markets with distinguished performance within the period studied. For example, Mexico had the lowest mean return, and one of the highest standard deviations. Peru exhibited a high mean and the highest skew. Venezuela had the highest standard deviation, while Chile, Columbia, and Argentina revealed the lowest.

Generally, the mean-variance-skewness efficient portfolios seem to be dominated by the investment components of only three markets: Brazil, Chile and Peru. These markets seem to be relatively highly correlated (for Latin American countries), and have either a relatively high mean return, low standard deviation, or high skewness.

As reported in Table 13.4, the mean-variance efficient portfolio has the highest expected return of 0.2756. This evidence is consistent with the notion that the expected return of the mean-variance efficient portfolio must dominate any other portfolio, given the same level of variance. On the other hand, all skewness of the mean-variance-skewness efficient portfolios are much greater than that of the mean efficient portfolio (which shows negative skewness). This implies that the investor will trade the expected return of the portfolio for the skewness. However, the optimal portfolios obtained from polynomial goal programming may not retain their optimal status for long due to the changing nature of correlation structure. Thus, the optimal portfolio must be periodically revised by rerunning the model.

Conclusions

In this study, we test the return distributions of seven international stock market indices for normality using the Jarque–Bera test. The evidence indicates that, in general, the international markets, especially those in Latin America, exhibit significant skewness. This confirms our argument that higher moments cannot be neglected in portfolio selection. As a result, we present a multi-objective approach to constructing an optimal portfolio of international stock market indices. This approach creates portfolios based on mean, variance and skewness of investment returns. As shown by our analysis, the benefits of this approach become more apparent when the markets exhibit higher volatility and instability. Thus, the approach is especially useful for investors in the emerging markets. A suggestion for future research would be to extend the model to the recent data for developed markets.

References

ARDITTI, F. D. (1967) Risk and the required return on equity, *Journal of Finance*, Vol. 22, pp. 19–36.

ARDITTI, F. D. and LEVY, H. (1975) Portfolio efficiency analysis in three moments: The multi-period case, *Journal of Finance*, Vol. 30, pp. 797–809.

CHUNHACHINDA, P., DANDAPANI, K., HAMID, S. and PRAKASH, A. J. (1997) Portfolio selection and skewness: Evidence from international stock markets, *Journal of Banking and Finance*, Vol. 21, pp. 143–167.

KRAUSS, A. L. and LIZENBERGER, R. H. (1976) Skewness preference and the valuation of risk assets, *Journal of Finance*, Vol. 31, No. 4, pp. 1085–1100.

KUMAR, P. C., PHILIPPATOS, G. C. and EZZELL, J. R. (1978) Goal programming and the selection of portfolios by dual-purpose funds, *Journal of Finance*, Vol. 33, pp. 303–310.

LAI, T. Y. (1991) Portfolio selection with skewness: A multiple-objective approach, *Review of Quantitative Finance and Accounting*, Vol. 1, pp. 293–305.

MERIC, I. and MERIC, G. (1989) Potential gains from international portfolio diversification and inter-temporal stability of international stock market relationships, *Journal of Banking and Finance*, Vol. 13, pp. 627–640.

RUBINSTEIN, M. (1973) The fundamental theorem of parameter preference security valuation, *Journal of Financial and Quantitative Analysis*, Vol. 8, pp. 61–69.

SAMUELSON, P. (1970) The fundamental approximation of theorem of portfolio analysis in terms of means, variances and higher moments, *Review of Economic Studies*, Vol. 37, pp. 537–542.

STEPHENS, A. and PROFFITT, D. (1991) Performance measurement when return distributions are nonsymmetric, *Quarterly Journal of Business and Economics*, Vol. 30, pp. 23–41.

TAYI, G and LEONARD, P. (1988) Bank balance-sheet management: An alternative multi-objective model, *Journal of the Operational Research Society*, Vol. 39, pp. 401–410.

Notes

The views expressed here are those of the authors solely, and not of the Office of the Comptroller of the Currency.

1. See Chunhachinda et al. (1997) for a detailed discussion of these studies.
2. DataStream International, 120 Wall Street, 15th Floor, New York, NY 10005.
3. For more on this statistic, see the Shazam Econometrics Computer Program, User's Reference Manual, Version 7.0, McGraw Hill Book Company, Vancouver, Canada, 1993, p. 5.
4. Skewness = (third central moment)^2/(variance)^3 and kurtosis = [(fourth central moment)/(variance)^2] – 3.

14

Financial Liberalization and the Mexican Stock Market Beyond the 1994 Crisis

ALEJANDRA CABELLO

Introduction

Financial liberalization has invariably led to increased risk and crisis within emerging markets during the last two decades. One important aspect of increased risk has been unstable international financial flows, particularly large withdrawals from foreign portfolio investors at critical times. Coupled with inadequate macroeconomic policies, fragility of domestic financial systems, weak corporate governance, and ill-prepared financial and capital account liberalization, massive capital withdrawals have been the cause for a large incidence of financial crises among developing countries since the 1980s (see: World Bank, 1998). In Mexico, the 1994 macro peso devaluation and resulting sharp economic crisis were partly due to massive withdrawals from foreign investments made at the local money and capital markets (Ortiz, 2000a). Previously, symptoms of the crisis were clear, but were ignored because portfolio investments strengthened the capital account, disregarding their volatility and weak links with the real sectors of the economy[1]. Currently, 'hot money' and in general portfolio investments not associated with real investments continue as the most significant area of investment made in this market. This potentially explosive situation has been induced by further financial liberalization policies, ignoring the lessons from the 1994–1995 crisis.

This chapter examines this situation. The work is organized in the following manner. Following this brief introduction, the next section examines financial liberalization policies, stressing those related to the financial markets; it also identifies the main characteristics of the Mexican stock market, largely induced by financial deregulation and financial liberalization policies. After this, an analysis is presented of the performance of the Mexican capital and money markets, following the 1994–1995 crisis. This is followed by a short conclusion.

Financial Liberalization and the Mexican Stock Market

One of the most important impacts of the Mexican debt crisis of the 1980s comprised deregulation and liberalization of the real and financial markets. Previously, the Mexican economy was characterized by a strong intervention of the State in the economy, protectionism, and repressed financial markets. Reforms in the financial sector started as early as the mid-1970s; then multiple banking (e.g., universal banking) was approved to promote economies of scale and better banking services. The stock markets of Guadalajara, Monterrey and Mexico City were also merged, and Certificados de Tesoreria, (CTs), Mexican Treasury Bills, began to be traded by the end of the decade. Reforms in the real sector continued during the following decade, spurred on by the need to meet the challenges of the debt crisis and economic globalization. Many commercial barriers were eliminated and soon Mexico joined GATT. However, financial reforms remained at a standstill because the banking sector was nationalized in 1982. Nonetheless, the Mexican government continued the process of banking mergers that had started before nationalization. From 60 nationalized institutions, the banking system was restructured into 18 larger banks, with national, regional or local coverage (Cabello, 1997).

By the end of the 1980s, Mexican authorities accelerated economic and financial liberalization processes. Indeed, 1989 can be identified as the end of financial repression in Mexico. In December 1989, President Salinas de Gortari submitted a set of financial reforms to the Mexican Congress which were approved by the Congress without a thorough discussion. Three additional reform packages were later submitted to the Mexican Congress from 1991 to 1994. The financial system was transformed profoundly; there were many changes aimed at eliminating state participation in the control of interest rates, and in directing credit rigidly to 'priority sectors'; as well as reforms aimed at promoting a strong participation of private investors in the banking sector, and in promoting the internationalization of the Mexican securities markets. Foreign investments in the local securities market were approved, as well as the participation of local companies at the international capital markets via American Depository Receipts and Global Depository Receipts. Thus, the Mexican Stock Market (MSM) became a very important target for financial liberalization and a key sector for supporting economic liberalism in Mexico.

From 1989 to 1993, foreign investors actively participated in the capital and money markets: the market value of holdings from foreign residents at the Mexican stock market increased from US$808 million in 1989 to US$54.5 billion by 1993. Investments at the money markets increased from US$5.5 billion in 1991 to US$22.0 billion by the end of 1993. Similarly, leading macroeconomic indicators, particularly those related to output, inflation control and public deficit control, seemed to indicate that the Mexican economy was evolving favourably, and that the Mexican securities markets were strong and liquid. However, these welcome trends ended abruptly by the end of 1994; the good performance of the Mexican economy could not be sustained. Reasons given for this today stress the fact that the good performance of the Mexican economy and its failure during the early 1990s were the result of policies based on a short-term vision (Kessler, 1999: 116). Liquidity was high in the secondary markets but investments in the local capital market did not have a significant impact on important productive projects; similarly, the economy was never really strong, especially its external sector. Persistent trade and current account deficits were never corrected, and the peso was overvalued. Besides, most upward trends of the Mexican stock market were limited to few securities; investments concentrated in shares of a few, large private companies, such as Telmex's and Televisa's via ADRs. Thus, profound adjustments were overdue and needed by the end of 1994. Since policy-makers held on any decision for nearly two years and only undertook a mild devaluation at the beginning of President Zedillo's term, foreign portfolio holders lost confidence in the Mexican economy and its financial markets and overreacted, making massive withdrawals from funds invested in Mexico. Local enterprises and investors also attempted to cover their monetary positions and speculated, making massive dollar demands. As a result, Mexico's international reserves were nearly depleted and the peso was devalued nearly 100 per cent (Cabello, 1999). In relative terms, this depreciation was actually 146 per cent by the end of 1995. The stock and money markets became the leading mechanisms to continue the crisis and transmit it to other sectors of the economy, because massive outflows originated in these markets put national reserves under pressure. Moreover, the fall of the Mexican stock market reaffirmed the loss of confidence that both local and foreign investors had in the Mexican economy.

Spurred by financial deregulation and financial liberalization, the Mexican stock and money markets showed impressive results from January 1989 to November 1994. Good performance was partly due to large foreign portfolio investments enhanced by economic and financial liberalization policies enforced during that period. Among the policies that must be mentioned are the privatization of public enterprises, the re-privatization of the banking system, the creation of a retirement fund managed by banks (Sistema para el Ahorro del Retiro, SAR), which invested in the securities markets, and the free convertibility of the peso. Several new financial laws were also approved, liberalizing the banking system, non-banking financial intermediaries, the Mexican securities markets, and granting autonomy to Banco de Mexico, Mexico's central bank. Regulating agencies were also restructured and their supervisory role was redefined, stressing precautionary regulation. The role of the supervisory commissions was redefined to conform to the emerging new architecture of the Mexican financial sector: a commission to supervise banking activities (Comisión Nacional Bancaria), a commission to supervise the securities markets (Comisión Nacional de Valores), and a commission to supervise insurance companies and other non-banking intermediaries (Comisión Nacional de Seguros).

However, financial liberalization during the 1989–1994 period was disorderly and did not follow a well-thought sequence. Indeed, Mexico's 1994–1995 crisis can be partly attributed to this fact. Many analysts attribute Mexico's banking crisis to poor re-privatization and poor financial liberalization and deregulation processes; ownership concentrated among a few owner–administrators, who had little experience in banking activities. Supervision was also limited and on offer were 100 per cent (implied) guarantees to bank savings and deposits. This led to severe problems of adverse selection and moral hazard which ended in large and badly-performing credits. To insure savings, a special agency was created in 1991, Fondo Bancario para la Protección del Ahorro (FOBAPROA). Because its resources were limited and protection to savings was unlimited, the government was forced to implement a huge banking rescue package in 1995. Because this package was implemented without approval from the Congress, after an intense debate in the Congress, a new agency was created in 1999: Instituto para la Protección al Ahorro Bancario (IPAB). To date, banking debts assumed by this institute amount to US$96 billion, which will be finally billed to the Mexican taxpayer[2].

In relation to the securities market, following the 1994–1995 crisis, the role of the supervisory commissions was restructured again. Reforms approved in 1993 allowed the formation of financial groups (e.g., universal banking). The holding group can be comprised of banks, stock brokerage houses, insurance companies and other non-banking intermediaries; it can be headed, according to the law, either by a banking institution or by an investment banking institution (*casa de bolsa*). For this reason, to strengthen supervisory activities, seeking consistency with the emerging institutional setup, the banking and securities commissions were merged in January 1995. The supervisory agencies now are Comisión Nacional Bancaria y de Valores and Comisión Nacional de Seguros y Finanzas. Financial opening has been also increased since 1995. Above all, the regulations regarding the entry of foreign capital have been loosened. Before the 1990s, financial institutions were totally owned by the state or local investors. As a result of financial liberalization policies and the signing of trade agreements with other nations, particularly the North American Free Trade Agreement (NAFTA), the entry of foreign capital was allowed but in a gradual and limited way. Originally, foreign ownership on local financial intermediaries had a cap changing from five per cent in 1994 to a maximum of 25 per cent of total capital by 2005, for the banking sector; for securities firms the initial cap was ten per cent increasing to 20 per cent in 1994. In fact, from 2000 on, the limits would be relaxed, but Mexico retained the right to impose limits if aggregates of Canadian and US ownership move beyond 25 per cent of domestic capital. The reasoning behind these rules was a desire to have a financial system owned and managed mainly by Mexican nationals (Armendariz and Mijangos, 1995). As a result of the 1994 crisis, these rules have been relaxed and now even 100 per cent foreign ownership is allowed both in commercial and investment banking.

Attempting to prevent future financial crisis, the retirement system was reformed, creating special institutions for the management of pension funds (Afores). Two other regulatory commissions were also created: one to regulate operations of pension funds (Comisión Nacional del Sistema de Ahorro para el Retiro, CONSAR) and the other to protect customers from

TABLE 14.1: *Main characteristics of the Mexican stock market*

	1989	1990	1991	1992	1993	1994	1995	1996	1997	1998
Number of Companies	170	199	207	199	190	206	185	193	198	195
Principal Market	170	199	207	199	162	154	138[b]	158	155	152
Enterprises	127	119	126	122	97	93		111	116	116
Financial Institutions	43	80	81	77	65	61	47[b]	47	39	36
Intermediate[a]					28	52		35	39	39
International System of Quotations									4	4
In Million Dollars										
Capitalization	26,563	40,940	101,719	138,749	200,613	129,850	90,939	106,780	156,182	91,746
Trade Value	6161	12,103	31,500	44,566	62,411	84,101	34,646	43,134	48,726	33,841
Stock Market Index										
Pesos	419	629	1432	1759	2603	2376	2779	3361	5229	3960
Pesos 78=100	290	334	639	704	963	821	632	599	805	511
Dollars	156.31	213.87	466.27	565.73	836.85	475.13	260.84	428.15	648.8	401.38
Real Returns in Pesos	65.35	15.64	91.31	10.04	37.17	-15.01	-22.55	-5.27	34.72	-36.51
Returns in Dollars	68.85	36.8	118.74	20.98	48.55	-42.54	-24.81	18.35	51.18	-37.96

Source: Developed from Bolsa Mexicana de Valores, *Anuario Bursátil*, various issues.
a Intermediate = Market for Medium-Sized Companies
b Include intermediate Mexican Enterprises and Financial Institutions.

financial institutions (Comisión para la Protección de los Usuarios de los Servicios Financieros).

Further financial liberalization implemented during the last few years has deepened the growth and structural changes of the Mexican stock market[3]. As shown in Table 14.1, market capitalization increased explosively from US$26.6 billion in 1989 to US$200.6 billion in 1993. Traded value also increased from US$6.15 billion to US$62.4 billion by 1993. Finally, returns also increased significantly. The Mexican stock exchange index rose from 419 points in 1989 to 2602.6 points in 1993. The accumulated return in dollars for the period was an impressive yield of 293.9 per cent; in 1991 alone returns reached a peak of 118.7 per cent for the year. Finally, it is worth noting that the number of companies slightly increased from 170 companies listed in 1989 to 190 companies listed in 1993[4].

Table 14.1 also shows that the 1994 macro peso devaluation impacted the Mexican stock market negatively. Market capitalization measured in nominal pesos increased slightly during 1994. However, measured in dollars, market capitalization plummeted from US$200.6 billion in 1993 to US$129.8 billion in 1994 and US$90.9 billion in 1995. The following years, a clear growing tendency characterized market capitalization in this market. A similar trend of sharp decay and some recuperation was followed by the traded value. It is worth noting that by 1995 traded value had declined to a low point of US$ 34.6 billion, nearly 2.5 times lower than the traded value of the previous year. Returns also declined significantly as a result of the 1994 crisis. From the peak returns of the previous period, for three consecutive periods, the Mexican stock market showed negative returns. During the period 1994–1996 the accumulated negative real return amounted to 42.8 per cent. The stock market index declined from 2602.6 points in 1993 to 2375.7 in 1994. Finally, the number of firms listed increased during the critical year of 1994, but the following year, 21 companies dropped from the stock market. During the following years, some new companies entered the market; hence, by 1997 there were 198 companies listed in Bolsa Mexicana de Valores.

A clarification needs to be made regarding the number of companies listed in the market. During the period 1995–1998, some companies changed their listing from the principal market to the intermediate market created in 1993 for medium-sized corporations. Some new companies also entered this market. Thus, by 1998, the number of companies listed in the main market is only

152, comprising 116 non-financial corporations and 36 financial institutions; in the intermediate market 39 companies were listed in 1998. From 1997 on, the listing also comprised four companies in the international system of quotations.

In short, the Mexican stock market has grown significantly since financial liberalization and deregulation policies were enforced in Mexico in 1989. However this growth has been unstable and the market is still small and thin. It can be affirmed that financial reforms have not yielded the desired results. Particularly, added capital from foreign partnerships and ownership have not solved the fragility and inefficiencies of the Mexican banking system. Similarly, the Mexican capital and money markets are still very volatile and inefficient. Foreign portfolio holdings have increased since the drop to US$18.9 billion in early 1995; but their growth has been very irregular. Following the 1994 peso devaluation, further reforms and liberalization of the financial markets have been enforced; associated with these changes, the Mexican securities markets show a volatile behaviour similar to that preceding the 1994 peso crisis, which is analysed next.

Mexico's Securities Market Performance after the 1994 Crisis

Trends of the Mexican Stock and Money Markets after the Crisis

By 1993, the Mexican money and capital markets showed impressive results. A very important factor contributing to this performance were foreign portfolio investments. The failure of the Mexican economy in 1994 disappointed policy-makers, entrepreneurs, investors and citizens alike. Further, foreign portfolio investors made massive withdrawals from the financial markets, focusing their attention on short-term rapid returns, taking advantage of currency convertibility and all facilities granted to them by financial liberalization laws to de-invest and repatriate their profits. A long-term vision on the strengths of the Mexican economy and the potential for high returns in its financial markets was lacking. However, it is worth noting that investors, local and foreign, did not make their decisions simply as a reaction to the December 1994 peso devaluation. Indeed, during the entire of 1994, investors became aware of and nervous about Mexico's economic disequilibria, which was compounded by several unfavourable local political events. As shown in Table 14.2, during that year, foreign investors decreased their holdings at the Mexican Stock Market from US$54.5 billion in December 1993 to US$50.3 billion by November 1994. Similarly,

TABLE 14.2: *Market value/participation of foreign portfolio holdings in the Mexican stock market*

	TOTAL[a]	ADRs	FUND MEXICO	FREE SUBSCRIPTION[a]	FUND NEUTRO	OTHERS[c]
Market Value (million dollars)						
1989	808.00	402.00	264.00	107.00	35.00	
1990	4079.46	2086.83	243.85	1072.74	676.03	
1991	18,542.51	13,733.46	499.33	2960.96	1348.76	
1992	28,668.00	21,153.95	619.00[b]	5096.98	1798.08	
1993	54,484.29	33,959.55	1238.06	12,906.07	6380.61	
Nov 94	50,311.45	29,056.66	1183.25	12,968.64	7102.89	
Dec 94	34,395.00	21,163.00	766.00	8100.00	4348.00	19.00
Jan 95	22,973.00	14,681.00	562.00	4791.00	2913.00	26.00
Feb 95	18,946.00	12,612.00	450.00	3549.00	2292.00	43.00
1995	24,515.59	15,223.50	750.27	5884.28	2620.28	36.25
1996	30,978.67	15,108.14	920.17	11,418.62	3506.59	0.00
1997	48,967.99	23,135.13	1311.26	19,498.34	4891.65	0.00
1998	32,613.00	18,625.09	790.56	11,044.05	2884.88	0.00
Mar 99	41,731.92	14,372.14	3731.26	23,618.29	992.89	0.23
Participation (%)						
1989	100.00	49.75	32.67	13.24	4.33	
1990	100.00	51.15	5.98	26.30	16.57	
1991	100.00	74.06	2.69	15.97	7.27	
1992	100.00	73.79	2.16	17.78	6.27	
1993	100.00	62.33	2.27	23.69	11.71	
Nov 94	100.00	57.75	2.35	25.78	14.12	
Dec 94	100.00	61.53	2.23	23.55	12.64	0.06
Jan 95	100.00	63.91	2.45	20.85	12.68	0.11
Feb 95	100.00	66.57	2.38	18.73	12.10	0.23
1995	100.00	62.10	3.06	24.00	10.69	0.15
1996	100.00	48.77	2.97	36.86	11.32	0.00
1997	100.00	47.25	2.68	39.82	9.99	0.00
1998	100.00	57.11	2.42	33.86	8.85	0.00
Mar 99	100.00	34.44	8.94	56.62	2.38	0.00

Source: Developed from: Bolsa Mexicana de Valores, *Anuario Bursátil*, various issues.

[a]   Figures at end of December.
[b]   Valuation at October 1992.
[c]   Warrants & Nmex.

foreign investors changed their preferences from Certificados de Tesoreria or CTs (Mexican Treasury bills), to Tesobonos, indexed to the dollar. Public debt Tesobonos increased from US$1.2 billion in 1993 to US$15.6 billion by November 1994, while holdings in CTs decreased from a peak of US$15.5 billion in 1993 to US$6.0 billion by November 1994 (as shown later in Table 14.5).

By the end of November 1994 the market value of foreign portfolio holdings amounted to US$54,484.3 billion; favourable trends were sustained during 1994 until November; however, by December of 1994, these trends were reversed. As shown in Table 14.2, the market value of foreign investments at the MSM decreased dramatically to US$34.5 billion by the end of the year. By February 1995 the market value of these investments fell down to US$18,946 billion. This was the result of a drop in the prices of shares, as well as of massive withdrawals by institutional and individual investors. The crisis lasted almost two years. By 1997, the MSM started to recover. By September of that year, the market value of foreign portfolio investments reached almost the 1993 levels, amounting US$53,386 billion; however, by the end of 1997, a declining tendency became clear; foreign portfolio holdings decreased to US$48.9 billion, further decreasing to US$32.6 billion by the end of 1998, a level even lower than that reached in December 1994. However, during the following months, foreign investments at the Mexican Stock Market tended to increase, ending at US$41.7 billion by March 1999.

Examining by types of security, it is clear that the preference of foreign investors is for ADRs; however, it is tending to become less favoured because free subscription shares have started to get more attention.

These trends fully reflect the performance of and the expectations built on the Mexican economy following the 1994 peso devaluation and the crash of the financial markets. As seen in Table 14.3, during 1995, GDP decreased by 6.2 per cent; however, the following three years, the economy recovered significantly; particularly, in 1997, the economy reached an impressive growth of 7 per cent induced by greater control on inflation (down from 35 per cent in 1995 to 20.6 per cent in 1997), improved performance in the external sector and a sharp increase in international reserves.

Market Value vs. Real Portfolio Investments

It is important to note that market value does not represent the value of original levels of portfolio and stock market investments made. Table 14.4 shows the stock and flows of foreign portfolio investments made in recent years. Apparently since the 1994 crisis a favourable trend has ensued: direct investments have tended to become more important than portfolio investments, reverting the situation existing from 1992 to 1994; it is worth noting that in 1993 foreign portfolio investments for the year amounted to US$28.9 billion, while direct investments amounted to only US$4.4 billion,

TABLE 14.3: *Mexican economic trends*

	1994	1995	1996	1997	1998
MILLION PESOS OF 1993:					
GDP	1,312.200.4	1,230,608.0	1,294.151.7	1,384,824.5	1,447,946.0
% (VAR)	4.5	(6.2)	5.2	7.0	4.6
INFLATION (VAR %)	7	35	34.4	20.6	15.4
MILLION DOLLARS:					
COMMERCIAL BALANCE:	(18,400.0)	7000.0	6531.0	623.6	(7742.2)
EXPORTS	60,900.0	79,500.0	96,000.0	110,431.4	117,500.3
IMPORTS	79,300.0	72,500.0	89,469.0	109,807.8	125,242.5
CURRENT ACCOUNT	(29,400.0)	(700.0)	(2330.3)	(7448.4)	(15,786.4)
INTERNATIONAL RESERVES	6400.0	15,700.0	17,509.0	28,003.0	30,139.0
CHANGE INTNAL. RESERVES	(18,400.0)	9592.8	1809.0	10,494.0	2136.9
EXCHANGE RATE $-usd	5.325	7.6425	7.8509	8.0833	9.865
VAR (%)[a]	71.45	43.52	2.726	2.96	22.04

Source: Banco de Mexico, *The Mexican Economy,* 1996; Nafinsa, *El Mercado de Valores,* March 1998, p. 57;
Banco de Mexico, *Indicadores Economicos,* March 1999.

[a]   In 1993 = 3.1059.

showing a decreasing trend from previous years. During the crisis, large capital reversals in foreign portfolio holdings led to a net de-investment equal to US$9.7 billion. During the 1995 critical year, foreign direct investment increased significantly to US$9.5 billion, an amount nevertheless insufficient to cover withdrawals from the securities markets. Total foreign investments decreased in 1995 by US$188.4 million. Considering the Mexican stock market, it is worth noting that, except for 1997, most foreign investments between 1995 and 1998 were made in Mexican paper abroad. In 1995 and 1996, foreign investments in Mexican securities contracted abroad amounted to US$3.6 and US$9.7 billion, respectively, while foreign investments at the local markets reached levels of only US$519.2 million and US$3.0 billion for the same years, respectively.

Comparing the stock and flows of foreign portfolio holdings with their market value uncovers a striking situation. Due to its explosive growth, market value is considerably higher than the original investments made at the stock market by foreign nationals. Table 14.4 shows the cumulative balance for these items. Assuming that foreign investors had decided to realize their gains, it is worth noting that

TABLE 14.4: *Direct and portfolio foreign investments in Mexico (million dollars)*

Values

	ANNUAL			PORTFOLIO FOREIGN INVESTMENT					CUMULATIVE BALANCE				
					MONEY MARKET								
	TOTAL	DIRECT SUBTOT	PORTFOLIO SUBTOT	TOTAL	PUBLIC DEBT	BONDS & COM PAPER	MEXICAN PAPER IN ABROAD	STOCK MARKET	TOTAL A+b	DIRECT A	STOCK MARKET B	STK MKT VALUE C	CAPITAL GAINS C/B
1988	2,594.6	2,594.6	–	–	–	–	–	–	24,087	24,087	–	–	–
1989	2,913.7	2,499.7	414.0	–	–	–	–	414.0	27,001	26,587	414	808	2.0
1990	4,978.4	3,722.4	1,256.0	–	–	–	–	1,256.0	31,980	30,310	1,670	4,080	2.4
1991	9,897.0	7,015.2	2,881.8	–	–	–	–	2,881.8	41,877	37,325	4,552	18,543	4.1
1992	22,433.9	4,392.8	18,041.1	8,146.9	8,146.9	0.0	5,111.1	4,783.1	51,052	41,718	9,335	28,668	3.1
1993	33,308.1	4,388.8	28,919.7	7,405.7	7,012.7	393.0	10,797.0	10,717.0	66,158	46,106	20,052	54,484	2.7
1994	16,165.8	7,979.6	8,186.2	(2,225.3)	(1,942.3)	(283.0)	6,323.8	4,087.7	78,226	54,086	24,140	34,395	1.4
1995	(188.4)	9,526.3	(9,714.7)	(13,859.6)	(13,790.6)	(69.0)	3,625.7	519.2	88,271	63,612	24,659	24,516	1.0
1996	21,781.7	8,168.9	13,612.8	907.5	948.5	(41.0)	9,710.4	2,994.9	99,435	71,781	27,654	30,979	1.1
1997	17,082.7	12,100.6	4,982.1	584.8	490.1	94.7	1,182.0	3,215.3	84,687	53,818	30,869	48,968	1.6
1998	11,530.4	10,237.5	1,292.8	214.1	290.2	(76.1)	1,744.3	(665.6)	86,547	56,344	30,203	32,613	1.1

Percentages

	ANNUAL			PORTFOLIO FOREIGN INVESTMENT					CUMULATIVE BALANCE				
					MONEY MARKET								
	TOTAL	DIRECT SUBTOT	PORTFOLIO SUBTOT	TOTAL	PUBLIC DEBT	BONDS & COM PAPER	MEXICAN PAPER IN ABROAD	STOCK MARKET	TOTAL A+b	DIRECT A	STOCK MARKET B	STK MKT VALUE C	CAPITAL GAINS C/B
1988	100	100	0	–	–	–	–	–	100	100	0	–	–
1989	100	86	14	–	–	–	–	100	100	98	2	–	–
1990	100	75	25	–	–	–	–	100	100	95	5	405	25
1991	100	71	29	–	–	–	–	100	100	89	11	355	67
1992	100	20	80	45	45	0	28	27	100	82	18	55	(25)
1993	100	13	87	26	24	1	37	37	100	70	30	90	(12)
1994	100	49	51	(27)	(24)	(3)	77	50	100	69	31	(37)	(48)
1995	100	(5,056)	5,156	143	142	1	(37)	(5)	100	72	28	(29)	(30)
1996	100	38	62	7	7	(0)	71	22	100	72	28	26	13
1997	100	71	29	12	10	2	24	65	100	64	36	58	42
1998	100	89	11	17	22	(6)	135	(51)	100	65	35	(33)	(32)

Sources: Secofi; Banco de México, *Indicadores Económicos*, June 1998; *Anuario Bursátil*, various issues;
Banco de México, *Informe Anual*, 1998; IMF, *International Financial Statistics*, February 1998.

a Figures in June 1997.

they would have taken out about US$4.1 for each US$1.0 invested in from 1989 to 1991 and US$3.1 for each US$1.0 invested from 1989 to 1992. The outlook of the MSM became less positive during the following years to the point that, during the crisis years, no capital gains would have been realized by foreign investors. This situation becomes even more dramatic if withdrawals from the money markets are considered. Besides reflecting the instability of Mexican stock market returns, this situation reflects the potential danger of capital reversals to the Mexican economy. Over a medium- and long-term basis, the Mexican Stock Market will tend to recover. However, growth of this market and foreign investments made there cannot be necessarily associated with economic stability and growth, considering the experience of 1994–1995. Hence, growth of the Mexican money and capital markets need to be monitored. Rather than further liberalization of these markets, regulation to promote the stability of foreign portfolios should be considered.

Performance of the Money Market

Table 14.5 summarizes the main trends of foreign portfolio investments in the Mexican money market. Foreign investments in this market tended to decrease after 1994. In 1993, these investments amounted to US$22,083.2 billion, and reached a peak of US$23,293 billion by November 1994. Then, impacted by the peso devaluation, foreign holdings in Mexican debt securities decreased by near US$4 billion by December 1994, falling further to US$17.4 billion by February 1995. Of the total, 77.8 per cent was represented by Tesobonos. Debt contracted via this instrument was paid back by the Mexican government during the following months, until February of 1996. It became a heavy burden on the nation's international reserves; about US$16,000 billion were necessary to amortize it. Since then, investment holdings by foreigners in the money market have decreased sharply. By the end of 1998, those investments only amounted to US$2.5 billion and US$2.3 billion by the end of March 1999. Since no further Tesobonos have been issued, CTs are again the preferred short-term government debt security for foreign residents. Foreign investments in CTs by March of 1999 amounted to US$1,871 million, 80.65 per cent of total foreign investment in the money market; this amount was smaller than the levels attained in 1991. The success of this market in attracting foreign investors, especially from 1991 to February of 1995, resulted in a heavy dollar pressure on the Mexican economy. The Tesobonos experience also

TABLE 14.5: *Foreign investment/participation in the Mexican money market*

	TOTAL	CETES	PAGAFES	BONDES	TESOBONOS	AJUBONOS	UDIBONOS
Investment (million dollars)							
1991	5,466.28	2,952.34	21.08	725.84	257.03	1,509.99	
1992	14,206.87	9,150.98	0.00	1,236.64	197.37	3,641.12	
1993	22,083.15	15,478.45	0.00	836.53	1,241.78	4,526.40	
Nov 94	23,292.80	6,071.20	0.00	187.70	15,654.70	1,379.10	
Dec 94	19,576.80	2,531.70	0.00	28.60	16,491.00	524.70	
Jan 95	19,411.90	2,870.00	0.00	16.10	16,052.60	473.30	
Feb 95	17,424.30	3,393.60	0.00	41.50	13,552.90	436.30	
1995	3,338.51	2,738.88	0.00	109.25	186.19	304.19	
1996	3,394.38	3,028.47	0.00	326.19	0.00	37.65	2.07
1997	3,320.74	2,997.96	0.00	256.10	0.00	7.73	58.95
1998	2,476.15	2,198.41	0.00	244.39	0.00	1.93	31.43
Mar 99	2,319.81	1,870.92	0.00	378.97	0.00	5.04	64.88
Participation (%)							
1991	100.00	54.01	0.39	13.28	4.70	27.62	
1992	100.00	64.41	0.00	8.70	1.39	25.63	
1993	100.00	70.09	0.00	3.79	5.62	20.50	
Nov 94	100.00	26.06	0.00	0.81	67.21	5.92	
1994	100.00	12.93	0.00	0.15	84.24	2.68	
Jan 95	100.00	14.78	0.00	0.08	82.69	2.44	
Feb 95	100.00	19.48	0.00	0.24	77.78	2.50	
1995	100.00	82.04	0.00	3.27	5.58	9.11	0.00
1996	100.00	89.22	0.00	9.61	0.00	1.11	0.06
1997	100.00	90.28	0.00	7.71	0.00	0.23	1.78
1998	100.00	88.78	0.00	9.87	0.00	0.08	1.27
Mar 99	100.00	80.65	0.00	16.34	0.00	0.22	2.80

Source: Developed from Bolsa Mexicana de Valores, *Anuario Bursátil*, various issues.

illustrates how dangerous it can be to denominate domestic debt in foreign currencies (Mishkin, 1998: 117).

Conclusions

Financial reforms and financial liberalization of the Mexican financial markets have continued to be implemented after the 1994 crisis. These policies are now aimed at solving problems caused by earlier liberalization and deregulation schemes implemented from 1989 to 1994. Hence, investments at the local money and capital markets have continued to operate basically under the same rules that led the banking system to severe adverse selection and moral hazard problems, and in the money and capital markets to massive withdrawals by foreign investors. Further, because the Mexican economy has not yet fully recovered, the Mexican money and capital markets show a poor and irregular performance. Moreover, although direct investments have again become more important than foreign portfolio investments, foreign institutions and individuals continue investing in Mexico with a short-term vision, disregarding the high potential Mexico and its financial markets have for high and stable growth and returns.

References

ALLEN, F. and GALE, D. (2000) *Comparing Financial Systems*, MIT Press, Boston, Massachusetts.

ARMENDARIZ, P. and MIJANGOS, M. (1995) Retos de la liberalización en el tratado de libre comercio: El caso de los servicios bancarios, in A. GIRÓN, E. ORTIZ and E. CORREA (eds.), *Integración Financiera y TLC. Retos y Perspectivas*, Siglo XXI, Mexico, DF.

BLANCO, G. H. and VERMA, S. (1996) *The Mexican Financial System*, Captus Press, North York, Ontario.

CABELLO, A. (1997) Liberalization and deregulation of the Mexican stock market, in D. K. GHOSH and E. ORTIZ (eds.), *The Global Structure of Financial Markets*, Routledge, London.

CABELLO, A. (1999) *Globalización y Liberalización Financieras y Bolsa Mexican de Valores. Del Auge a la Crisis*, Plaza y Valdés, Mexico, DF.

DE ALBA MONROY, J. DE J.A. (2000) *El Mercado de Dinero y Capitales y El Sistema Financiero Mexicano*, Editorial Pac, Mexico, DF.

HUERTA, A. (1997) *Carteras Vencidas, Inestabilidad Financiera. Propuestas de Solucion*, Diana, Mexico, DF.

KESSLER, T. P. (1999) *Global Capital and National Politics. Reforming Mexico's Financial System*, Praeger, London.

LOPEZ OBRADOR, A. M. (1999) *Fobaproa: Expediente Abierto*, Grijalbo, Mexico, DF.

MENCHACA TREJO, M. (1998) *El Mercado de Dinero en Mexico*, Trillas, Mexico, DF.

MISHKIN, F. S. (1998) The Mexican financial crisis of 1994–95: An asymmetric information analysis, in S. S. REHMAN (ed.), *Financial Crisis Management in Regional Blocs*, Kluwer Academic Publishers, Boston.

ORTIZ, E. (2000a) La inversión extranjera de portafolios en los mercados de dinero y capital de Mexico y su impacto en la crisis Mexicana, in I. MANRIQUE-CAMPOS (ed.), *Arquitectura de la Crisis Financiera*, Miguel Angel Porrua, Mexico, DF.

ORTIZ, E. (2000b) *Crisis and the Future of the Mexican Banking System*, Working Paper, Universidad Nacional Autónoma de México.

STANDARD and POOR'S (2000) *Emerging Stock Markets Factbook 2000.*

SZEKELY, G. (1999) *Fobaproa e IPAB: El Acuerdo que no Debio Ser*, Oceano, Mexico, DF.

WORLD BANK, THE (1998) *Global Economic Prospects and the Developing Countries. Beyond Financial Crisis*, The World Bank, Washington DC.

Notes

The author acknowledges the support from Programa de Apoyo a Proyectos de Investigación e Innovación Tecnológica (PAPIIT), Project IN 312798, from Direccion

General de Asuntos del Personal Academico from Universidad Nacional Autonoma de Mexico.

1. A triple financial crisis took place in Mexico in 1994–1995: currency crisis, banking crisis, and stock market crisis. Poor policy-making and fragility of the banking system, and a declining and volatile stock market preceded the currency crisis. The currency crisis triggered the full manifestation of the banking and stock market crisis which in turn fed back the currency crisis and became the leading mechanism fuelling a fully-fledged economic crisis (Ortiz, 2000b). For a historical review on the nature of financial crisis see chapter 2 in Allen and Gale (2000).

2. The FOBAPROA and IPAB problems have been widely analysed in Mexico. See: Szekely (1999), Huerta (1997), and Lopez Obrador (1999).

3. For a detailed account of the Mexican money and capital markets see: Blanco and Verma (1996); Menchaca Trejo (1998), and De Alba Monroy (2000).

4. The Emerging Markets Fact Book, however, reports 204 firms for 1989.

15

Co-movements of US and Latin American Stock Markets during the 1997–1998 Emerging Markets Financial Crisis

GULSER MERIC, RICARDO P.C. LEAL, MITCHELL RATNER and ILHAN MERIC

Introduction

The world economy has experienced more than 200 episodes of financial crisis between 1975 and 1998 (see: Christoffersen and Errunza, 2000). Some of these crises are local in nature and some have worldwide implications. One of the most important global events was the 1987 global stock market crash, which affected the stock markets of almost all countries (see: Roll, 1988; Malliaris and Urrutia, 1992; Arshanapalli and Doukas, 1993; McInish and Lau, 1993; Lee and Kim, 1993; Meric and Meric, 1997, 1998; and Aggarwal et al., 1999). Another recent global event is the 1997–1998 emerging markets crisis. This crisis started in the Southeast Asian countries in 1997, led to the Russian default of August 17 1998, culminating with the flotation of the Brazilian real on January 15 1999, after a series of speculative attacks in 1998.

In this chapter, we study the co-movements of the US, Argentinian, Brazilian, Chilean, and Mexican stock markets during the 1997–1998 emerging markets crisis. The latter are the four largest stock markets in Latin America. Their combined market capitalization constitutes more than 90 per cent of the market capitalization of all Caribbean and Latin American equity markets during the sample period (see: Standard and Poor's, 2000).

Latin American stock markets receive considerable attention in recent finance literature (see, for example, Urrutia, 1995; Ratner and Leal, 1996; Domovitz et al., 1997; Meric et al., 1998; Aggarwal et al., 1999; and Ojah and Karemera, 1999). However, co-movements between Latin American stock markets and the US stock market during a crisis period have not been sufficiently studied. The objective of this chapter is to undertake such a study.

The chapter is organized as follows. The next section describes our data and methodology. There then follow studies of the correlation between the US, Argentinian, Brazilian, Chilean and Mexican stock markets during the 1997–1998 crisis. Next, vector autoregression (VAR) analysis is used to study the linkages between the five stock markets during the crisis period. Finally, we summarize our findings and present our conclusions.

Data and Methodology

The impact of the Southeast Asian crisis is first observed in the US stock market and in the stock markets of Argentina, Brazil, Chile and Mexico during the summer of 1997. The effect of the crisis on these stock markets continues during the remainder of 1997, including the Russian default and the strong speculative attacks on the Brazilian real throughout 1998. Therefore, our sample period covers the period from May 5 1997 to December 30 1998.

The daily index returns in US dollars are used in the study. The closing daily index levels for the US stock market are obtained for the S&P 500 index. The closing daily index levels for the four Latin American stock markets are obtained for the General Index (Argentina), the IBOVESPA Index (Brazil), the IGPA Index (Chile), and the IPC Index (Mexico). The daily index returns are computed as the natural log difference in the indices, ln $(I_{i,t}/I_{i,t-1})$. Daily index levels and foreign exchange rates are provided by the *Economatica* database.

We first study the co-movements of the five stock markets and the correlation between their index returns during the crisis period. We use period and rolling correlations to study the co-movement patterns and fluctuations of the markets. We present the index returns and rolling correlations on graphs, and analyse the co-movement patterns with the help of graphs.

We apply vector autoregression analysis (VAR) to the data and study the linkages between the five markets during the crisis period. We use Sims' (1980) likelihood ratio test to determine the optimum

TABLE 15.1: *Average daily US$ index returns and volatility of the markets during the 1997–1998 crisis*

Stock market	Mean return	Standard deviation
Argentina	−0.00021	0.009671
Brazil	−0.00053	0.015154
Chile	−0.00054	0.004447
Mexico	−0.00021	0.011743
United States	0.00049	0.005016

lag length in the model. Granger's (1969) causality test is used to perform innovation accounting. The impulse analysis is used to study the responses of the five markets to one another.

Correlation Analysis

The daily mean index returns and standard deviations, of the five stock markets during the period May 5 1997–December 30 1998 are presented in Table 15.1. Except the US stock market, all the other stock markets have a negative mean daily index return during the crisis period. The Chilean and Brazilian stock markets have the highest negative daily index returns and the Mexican and Argentinian stock markets have the lowest negative daily index returns. The standard deviation figures in the table indicate that the Brazilian stock market is the most volatile market and the Chilean stock market is the least volatile market during the crisis period.

The daily index returns of the five stock markets during the study period are presented in Figure 15.1. The horizontal axis represents the trading days in all markets during the period studied. The same daily index return range is used on the vertical axis in all five graphs to facilitate comparison. The graphs clearly indicate that Brazil is the most volatile market during the crisis period. The Mexican and Argentinian stock markets are also quite volatile. However, in the US and Chilean stock markets, extreme volatility is limited to certain periods.

The first strong impact of the Southeast Asian crisis is felt in the United States in July 1997. There is a sharp fall in the index returns followed by a sharp recovery (the period between observations 121 and 136 on the graph). As can be easily seen on the graphs, all four Latin markets also experienced sharp falls followed by sharp recoveries during the same period. The impact is the greatest on the Mexican stock market. The Brazilian and Argentinian stock markets are also strongly affected. However, the effect on the Chilean stock market is less pronounced.

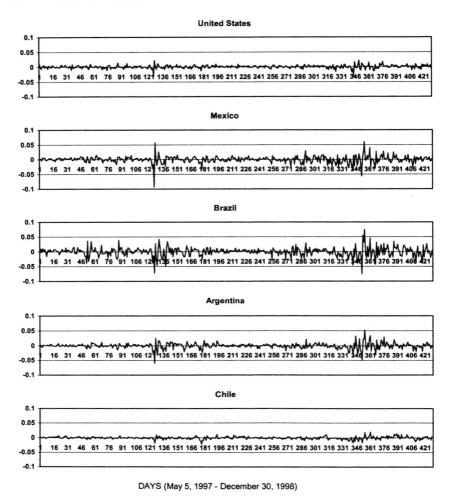

DAYS (May 5, 1997 - December 30, 1998)

FIGURE 15.1: *Country stock market returns during the crisis period*

After about a year of relative stability in the US stock market, the second sharp impact, now due to the Russian default, is experienced in July and August of 1998. As can be seen on the graphs between observations 346 and 376, all five markets respond. This time, the greatest effect is on the Brazilian stock market (Brazil was perceived to be the next large emerging market to have to devalue its currency and was losing about US$1 billion a day in investment outflows after the Russian default). Baig and Goldfajn (2000) study the contagion of the Russian crisis on Brazil and conclude that the contagion was due to international investors' panic from the Russian crisis and joining locals in speculating against the Brazilian real.

The Mexican and Argentinian stock markets are also strongly affected. Argentina is a partner of Brazil in the Mercosur customs union and Brazil is its main trade partner. A depreciation of the Brazilian real would strongly affect Argentina's exports to Brazil and its trade balance. Due to the convertibility law of Argentina, it cannot issue pesos unless they are fully backed by US dollars. A negative trade balance would lead Argentina into a monetary crunch and into a recession, which eventually happened in 1999–2000. Although the Chilean stock market is again less affected than the other Latin stock markets, the effect of the July/August 1998 turbulence is greater on the Chilean stock market than the effect of the July 1997 turbulence. This is not surprising because Chile is an associate member of Mercosur and both Argentina and Brazil are among its main trade partners.

The correlation matrix of the five stock markets during the study period is presented in Table 15.2. The figures indicate that there is a high level of correlation between the markets. The average correlation coefficient for all stock markets is about 0.638. Meric et al. (1998), using monthly index return figures, find that the average correlation coefficient between these five countries during the 50-month period after the October 1987 global stock market crash is 0.273. These figures imply that the co-movements of the five stock markets are extremely close during the 1997–1998 emerging markets crisis. There is mounting evidence that correlations rise during periods of crisis, as occurs during the emerging markets crisis of 1997–1998.

Correlation coefficients between pairs of countries during the study period are presented in Table 15.3. Among the ten pairs of stock markets, the Brazilian and Argentinian stock markets have the highest correlation and the US and Chilean stock markets have the lowest correlation. The Brazilian, Argentinian, and Mexican stock markets appear to have higher correlations between each other

TABLE 15.2: *Correlation matrix of the five stock markets during the 1997–1998 crisis*

	Argentina	Brazil	Chile	Mexico
Brazil	0.803			
Chile	0.604	0.528		
Mexico	0.790	0.718	0.553	
United States	0.654	0.598	0.469	0.650

TABLE 15.3: *Most correlated and least correlated markets during the 1997–1998 crisis*

Stock market pairs	Correlation coefficient
	(most correlated)
Brazil–Argentina	0.803
Mexico–Argentina	0.790
Mexico–Brazil	0.718
United States–Argentina	0.654
United States–Mexico	0.650
Argentina–Chile	0.604
United States–Brazil	0.598
Mexico–Chile	0.553
Brazil–Chile	0.528
United States–Chile	0.469
	(least correlated)

than with the US stock market. Argentina and Brazil are closely associated through Mercosur. Mexico, as the second largest Latin economy, could also suffer from a general Latin markets crisis and fall in disfavour among international investors.

We have computed an average correlation coefficient for each of the five stock markets by finding the arithmetic average of each market's correlation coefficients with the other four stock markets. A high average correlation coefficient for a stock market indicates that the stock market has the closest co-movements with the other stock markets during the period May 5 1997–December 30 1998. The results are presented in Table 15.4. The figures in the table indicate that the Argentinian stock market has the closest co-movements and the Chilean stock market has the least close co-movements with the other stock markets. The low correlation of the Chilean stock market with the other markets is the result of its relatively subdued response to the crisis compared with the other markets as observed in Figure 15.1. Chile has always been perceived as the least risky economy among the largest Latin American economies, with the best credit rating in the region. Its macroeconomic

TABLE 15.4: *Average Correlation Coefficients*

Stock market	Average correlation coefficient
	(most correlated)
Argentina	0.713
Mexico	0.678
Brazil	0.662
United States	0.593
Chile	0.539
	(least correlated)

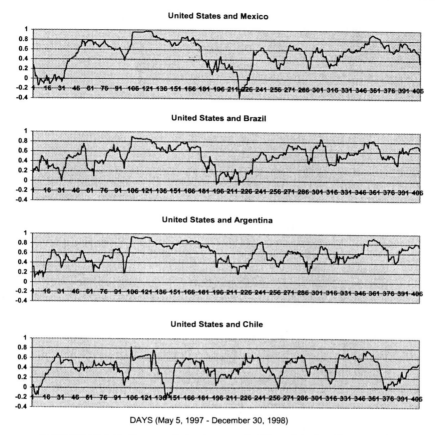

FIGURE 15.2 *Rolling correlation between the US and the four Latin markets*

stability, low risk, and capital flow restrictions probably made Chile the country that was affected the least by the emerging markets crisis. One reason that Chile may have weathered the crisis with less volatility is that foreign investors were not permitted to repatriate investments within one year. Aggarwal et al. (1999) found a similar result for the period 1985–1995.

Rolling correlation is a useful tool used in the finance literature to study the correlation patterns of international stock markets over time (see, for example, Solnik et al., 1996). We use rolling correlation analysis to study the changes in the correlation patterns of the five stock markets during the crisis period.

Starting with the first month, monthly correlation coefficients are computed by rolling the sample period ahead one trading day at a time. Specifically, the latest daily observation is added while the earliest observation is deleted. A total of 409 correlation coefficients are computed for all ten pairs of equity markets. The rolling correlation results for the US stock market with the Mexican, Brazilian, Argentinian and Chilean stock markets are presented in Figure 15.2. The rolling correlations between the four Latin stock markets are presented in Figure 15.3.

The rolling correlation patterns in Figure 15.2 are similar across the four Latin markets. The correlations are not stable as evidenced

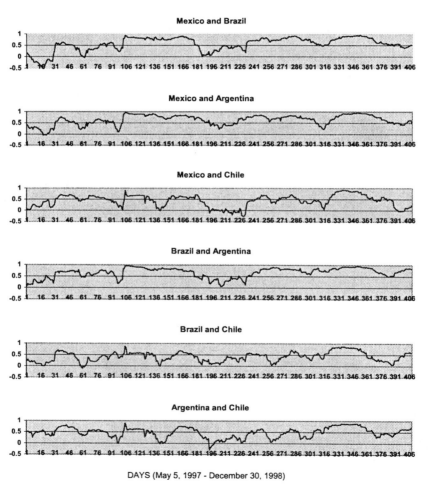

DAYS (May 5, 1997 - December 30, 1998)

FIGURE 15.3 *Rolling correlation between the four Latin markets*

by the considerable fluctuation throughout the crisis period. The correlation with the Argentinian stock market remains positive throughout the period. However, the correlations with the other three Latin markets even become negative during some short periods. The correlation between the US stock market and the Latin stock markets reach their highest positive levels during the periods when the crisis impacted the US stock market the most (between observations 106–121 and 346–361).

The graphs in Figure 15.3 indicate that the four Latin American stock markets also had a very high level of correlation between them during the second half of 1997 and in 1998. However, the rolling correlation patterns in the six graphs imply a great degree of instability in the correlations between the four Latin stock markets during the crisis period. The correlation coefficients between the four markets often reach the maximum level of +1. However, it is even negative between some markets during some short periods.

The mean values, standard deviations, and coefficients of variation of the rolling correlations between the five stock markets are presented in Table 15.5. The mean correlation figures show that the highest correlation is between the Brazilian and Argentinian stock markets and the lowest correlation is between the US and Chilean stock markets during the crisis period. The coefficient of variation figures indicate that the most volatile correlation is between the Mexican and Chilean stock markets, and the most stable correlation is between the US and Argentinian stock markets.

TABLE 15.5: *Mean and standard deviations of rolling correlations*

Stock market pair	Mean correlation	Standard deviation	Coefficient of variation
			(most volatile)
Mexico–Chile	0.434	0.264	0.633
Mexico–Brazil	0.561	0.308	0.549
United States–Mexico	0.527	0.286	0.543
Brazil–Chile	0.417	0.216	0.518
United States–Chile	0.406	0.201	0.495
Argentina–Chile	0.477	0.230	0.482
United States–Brazil	0.515	0.219	0.425
Mexico–Argentina	0.633	0.223	0.352
Brazil–Argentina	0.664	0.221	0.333
United States–Argentina	0.589	0.195	0.331
			(most stable)

Vector Autoregression (VAR) Analysis

The VAR Model

Vector autoregression (VAR) analysis is a technique widely used in the economics and finance literatures to analyse dynamic interactions between time series variables (see, for example, Eun and Shim, 1989; Lee, 1992; and Park and Ratti, 2000). We use VAR analysis to study the dynamic linkages between the five stock markets during the 1997–1998 crisis. Impulse responses and forecast error variance decompositions are used to obtain inferences about the linkages. The VAR model can be stated as folllows:

$$X_t = A_0 + \Sigma_{k=1 \text{ to } p} A_k X_{t-k} + \varepsilon_t \qquad (1)$$

where X_{t-k} is a nx1 column vector of n variables (five country index returns in our study) at time t–k, A_0 is an nx1 column vector of intercept terms (constants), A_k is an nxn matrix of coefficients, p is number of lags, and ε_t is a nx1 column vector of white-noise disturbances that may be correlated (innovation terms).

Underidentification Problem and the Ordering of Variables

The estimated VAR is underidentified. Therefore, additional restrictions must be imposed on the VAR system to identify the impulse responses (see Enders, 1995). Choleski decomposition is one possible identification restriction generally used in empirical studies (see, for example, Eun and Shim, 1989 and Park and Ratti, 2000). The system is constrained by ordering the variables and assuming that the contemporaneous value of variable X_i does not have any effect on the contemporaneous value of variable X_{i-1}. However, there is an indirect effect of the lagged values of X_i on the contemporaneous value of X_{i-1}.

The vector autoregression model with the following ordering of the variables is used in this study: VAR(US,MEX,BRA,ARG,CHI). Based on the findings of previous studies (see, for example, Ratner and Leal, 1996), the US stock market is likely to be the most dominant market in the group with strong contemporaneous influence on the other stock markets. Therefore, the US is ordered as the first country in the VAR model. Because of its high contemporaneous correlation with and its geographical proximity to the US, Mexico is ordered as the second country. Since the Brazilian stock market is the largest stock market in South America, it is likely to be influenced contemporaneously by the North American markets and it is also likely to influence the other South American markets contemporaneously. Therefore, Brazil is ordered as the third country. Due to its larger size relative to Chile and geographical proximity to Brazil, Argentina is ordered as the fourth country. Chile is ordered last, because it is the smallest of the four Latin markets with the lowest contemporaneous correlation during the crisis period.

Lag Length Selection

In VAR analysis, appropriate lag length selection can be of critical importance. If the lag length selected is too short, the model is misspecified. If the lag length is too long, degrees of freedom are wasted. We use Sims' (1980) likelihood ratio test to determine the optimum lag length. The following statistic has the asymptotic Chi-square distribution with degrees of freedom equal to the number of restrictions in the VAR system:

$$(T-c)(\log |\Sigma_r| - \log |\Sigma_u|) \qquad (2)$$

where T is number of observations, c is number of parameters estimated in each equation of the unrestricted system, Σ_u and Σ_r are the variance/covariance matrices of the residuals in the unrestricted and restricted systems, respectively, and $|\Sigma_u|$ and $|\Sigma_r|$ are the determinants of Σ_u and Σ_r, respectively. The VAR is initially estimated with u lags and it is re-estimated over the same period with r lags. The test statistic is compared to a Chi-square distribution with degrees of freedom equal to number of restrictions. We have applied the Sims (1980) test to the data and determined that five-period (five trading days) lags are optimum for the study.

Granger Causality

The covariance/correlation matrix of the residuals from the variables are presented in Table 15.6. The figures indicate a high

TABLE 15.6: *Covariance/correlation matrix of residuals*

	United States	Mexico	Brazil	Argentina	Chile
United States	0.00002812	0.65918340	0.60949922	0.65349988	0.50470509
Mexico	0.00003977	0.00012945	0.71304606	0.79025621	0.58497678
Brazil	0.00004645	0.00011661	0.00020659	0.81298817	0.57393261
Argentina	0.00003241	0.00008410	0.00010930	0.00008750	0.63345219
Chile	0.00001087	0.00002702	0.00003349	0.00002406	0.00001649

TABLE 15.7: *Granger causality test results*

Independent variables	F-statistic	Significance
Dependent Variable: United States		
United States	0.5264	0.756
Mexico	0.7691	0.572
Brazil	0.6354	0.673
Argentina	1.6479	0.146
Chile	0.5576	0.733
Dependent Variable: Mexico		
United States	1.5446	0.175
Mexico	1.6690	0.141
Brazil	0.6460	0.665
Argentina	1.4744	0.197
Chile	0.1984	0.963
Dependent Variable: Brazil		
United States	2.6382	0.023
Mexico	2.3006	0.044
Brazil	1.2261	0.296
Argentina	2.4095	0.036
Chile	1.0146	0.409
Dependent Variable: Argentina		
United States	2.1266	0.061
Mexico	1.1964	0.310
Brazil	0.2222	0.953
Argentina	1.9797	0.081
Chile	0.5391	0.747
Dependent Variable: Chile		
United States	0.4750	0.795
Mexico	0.8347	0.526
Brazil	0.5624	0.729
Argentina	1.3079	0.260
Chile	5.8275	0.000

level of correlation between the innovations in the five stock markets.

Since there are 25 lags in each of the five VAR equations (a total of 125 coefficients), to conserve space, t-statistics for the individual lags are not given. The results of the tests for the joint hypothesis of zero coefficients on all five lags for each variable are presented in Table 15.7.

The significance levels of the F statistics in the table indicate that neither their own lagged index returns nor the lagged index returns of the other stock markets can help forecast the index returns of the US, Mexican and Argentinian stock markets. However, the lagged index returns of the US, Argentinian and Mexican stock markets can help forecast the index returns of the Brazilian stock market (i.e., the US, Argentinian and Mexican stock market index returns Granger cause the Brazilian stock market index returns) at the five per cent significance level.

Although the index returns of the Chilean stock market are not significantly affected by the lagged index returns of the other four stock markets, they are significantly affected by the Chilean stock market's own lagged index returns at the one per cent level. Since none of the other stock markets' own lagged index returns significantly affect their forecasted index returns, this implies that the Chilean stock market may be less efficient compared with the other four stock markets.

Impulse Simulation

By using the decomposition implied by the elements of the VCV (variance/covariance) matrix, we have obtained 1-step-ahead through 12-step-ahead forecast errors and impulse responses for the five index returns. The impulse responses of the five stock markets to one another are plotted in Figures 15.4 and 15.5. The horizontal axis measures number of lags in trading days. The vertical axis measures the responses of the markets in standard deviations.

The responses of the other markets to the innovation in the US and Mexican markets are plotted in Figure 15.4. A comparison of the five graphs in Figures 15.4 and 15.5 clearly indicates that the US stock market has the greatest influence on the other stock markets. One standard deviation shock in the US stock market index returns produces about 1.7, 1.4, 1.2, and 0.4 standard deviation contemporaneous changes in the Brazilian, Mexican, Argentinian and Chilean stock market index returns, respectively. However, the effect of the shock on all countries dies down quickly except in Brazil. The impact almost completely disappears on all markets after the fifth lag.

The effect of the Mexican stock market on the other Latin stock markets is also strong, although not as strong as the effect of the US stock market. The Mexican stock market has no contemporaneous effect on the US stock market (assumed by the Choleski ordering of the variables). One standard deviation shock in the Mexican stock market index returns produces about 0.7, 0.5, and 0.15 standard deviation contemporaneous changes in the Brazilian, Argentinian and Chilean stock market index returns, respectively. The impact

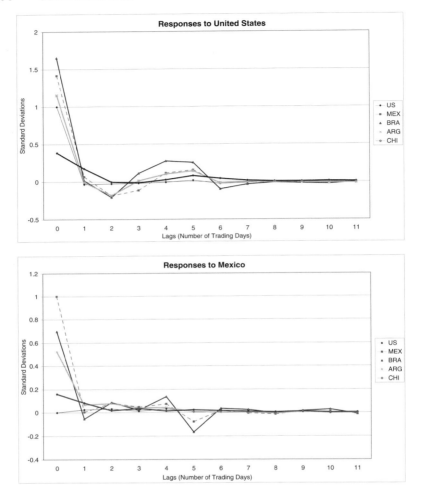

FIGURE 15.4 *Impulse simulation: responses to United States and Mexico*

continues to be strong on the Brazilian stock market for several periods. However, the impact on all markets virtually dies down completely after the fifth period.

The first graph of Figure 15.5 shows the responses of the other stock market index returns to the Brazilian stock market index returns. No contemporaneous response is assumed in the US and Mexican stock markets to shocks in the Brazilian stock market (the Choleski ordering). One standard deviation shock in the Brazilian stock market index returns produces about 0.3 and 0.1 standard

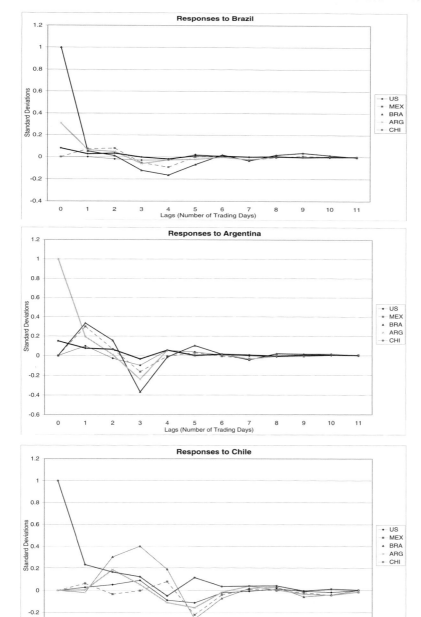

FIGURE 15.5 *Impulse simulation: responses to Brazil, Argentina and Chile*

deviation contemporaneous changes in the Argentinian and Chilean stock market index returns, respectively. The lagged responses of the other stock markets to the Brazilian stock market are insignificant and all impact virtually dies down after the fifth lag.

The Choleski ordering of the variables assumes that there are no contemporaneous responses in the US, Mexican, and Brazilian markets to changes in the Argentinian stock market. However, one standard deviation change in the Argentinian stock market index returns produces about 0.15 standard deviation contemporaneous change in the Chilean stock market index returns. The graph indicates that the Argentinian stock market has somewhat strong lagged influences on the Brazilian stock market. However, all influences virtually die down after the fifth lag.

The last graph in Figure 15.5 shows that there is no contemporaneous influence of the Chilean stock market on the other stock markets (using the Choleski ordering of the variables). However, the Chilean stock market appears to have somewhat strong lagged influence on the Brazilian stock market for several days. For the Chilean stock market, as is the case for all the other four stock markets, all influences also virtually die down after the fifth lag. As we explained above, the Sims (1980) likelihood ratio test also indicates that more than five lags would have no significant effects on the model.

Summary and Conclusions

The 1997–1998 emerging markets financial crisis affected virtually all emerging and developed stock markets in the world. In this chapter, we have studied the effects of the crisis on the US, Mexican, Brazilian, Argentinian and Chilean stock markets and on the co-movements of these markets during the crisis period. We have found that all five markets are strongly affected by the crisis and they have extremely close co-movements during the crisis period.

All five stock markets experience extreme volatility during the months of July 1997 (Asian crisis), and July–August 1998 (Russian default), when the crisis has its most severe impact on the US stock market. Although the Mexican, Brazilian and Argentinian stock markets have substantial volatility throughout the crisis period (May 1997–December 1998), the Chilean stock market remains relatively stable.

Although the emerging markets crisis causes substantial volatility in the US stock market, it does not affect stock market returns adversely. The S&P500 index increases about 51 per cent from May 1997 through December 1998. However, the Chilean, Brazilian, Argentinian and Mexican stock market indices decrease sharply by about 40.7 per cent, 40.4 per cent, 18.5 per cent, and 16.1 per cent, respectively, in constant dollars, during the same period.

The VAR analysis indicates that the five stock markets have some influence on each other with a time lag of up to five trading days. All influences virtually die down after five trading days and the remaining influences are statistically insignificant. The Granger causality test indicates that the lagged influences of the US, Argentinian and Mexican stock markets on the Brazilian stock market are statistically significant (i.e., the US, Argentinian and Mexican lagged stock market index returns Granger cause the Brazilian stock market index returns).

Among the five stock markets, only the lagged index returns of the Chilean stock market can explain its contemporaneous index returns significantly. This implies lower efficiency in the Chilean stock market compared with the other stock markets, which may lead to the development of trading strategies to earn abnormal contemporaneous profits based on information from the lagged index values. However, these strategies may not be profitable, as indicated by Ratner and Leal (1999).

The impulse simulation results indicate that the five markets mainly have contemporaneous effects on each other and that the lagged influences are minimal during the 1997–1998 emerging markets crisis. Our results also suggest that countries which are perceived as less risky, such as Chile, are less subject to contagion than countries perceived as more vulnerable, such as Brazil, Mexico or Argentina.

References

AGGARWAL, R., INCLÀN, C. and LEAL, R. (1999) Volatility in emerging stock markets, *Journal of Financial and Quantitative Analysis*, Vol. 34, No. 1, pp. 33–35.

ARSHANAPALLI, B. and DOUKAS, J. (1993) International stock market linkages: Evidence from the pre- and post-October 1987 period, *Journal of Banking and Finance*, Vol. 17, No. 1, pp. 193–208.

BAIG, T. and GOLDFAJN, I. (2000) *The Russian Default and the Contagion to Brazil*, PUC-Rio, Department of Economics Working Paper #420, Brazil (obtained from www.puc-rio.br/economia).

CHRISTOFFERSEN, P. and ERRUNZA, V. (2000) Towards a global financial architecture: Capital mobility and risk management issues, *Emerging Markets Review*, Vol. 1, No. 1, pp. 3–20.

DOMOWITZ, I., GLEN, J. and MADHAVAN, A. (1997) Market segmentation and stock prices: Evidence from an emerging market, *Journal of Finance,* Vol. 52, pp. 1059–1085.

ENDERS, W. (1995) *Applied Econometric Time Series,* John Wiley and Sons, Inc., New York.

EUN, C. S. and SHIM, S. (1989) International transmission of stock market movements, *Journal of Financial and Quantitative Analysis,* Vol. 24, No. 2, pp. 241–256.

GRANGER, C. W. (1969) Investigating causal relations by econometric models and cross-spectral models, *Econometrica,* Vol. 37, pp. 424–438.

LEE, B. S. (1992) Causal relations among stock returns, interest rates, real activity and inflation, *Journal of Finance,* Vol. 47, No. 4, pp. 1591–1603.

LEE, S. B. and KIM, K. J. (1993) Does the October 1987 crash strengthen the co-movements among national stock markets? *Review of Financial Economics,* Vol. 3, No. 1, pp. 89–104.

MALLIARIS, A. G. and URRUTIA, J. L. (1992) The international crash of October 1987: Causality tests, *Journal of Financial and Quantitative Analysis,* Vol. 27, No. 3, pp. 353–364.

MCINISH, T. H. and LAU, S. T. (1993) Co-movements of international equity returns: A comparison of the pre- and post-October 19, 1987 periods, *Global Finance Journal,* Vol. 4, No. 1, pp. 1–19.

MERIC, I. and MERIC, G. (1997) Co-movements of European equity markets before and after the 1987 crash, *Multinational Finance Journal,* Vol.1, No.2, pp.137–152.

MERIC, I. and MERIC, G. (1998) Correlation between the world's stock markets before and after the 1987 crash, *Journal of Investing,* Vol. 7, No. 3, pp. 67–70.

MERIC, I., RATNER, M., LEAL, R. and MERIC, G. (1998) Co-movements of Latin American equity markets, *International Journal of Finance,* Vol. 10, No. 3, pp. 1163–1178.

OJAH, K. and KAREMERA, D. (1999) Random walks and market efficiency tests of Latin American equity markets: A revisit, *Financial Review,* Vol. 34, No. 2, pp. 57–72.

PARK, K. and RATTI, R. A. (2000) Real activity, inflation, stock returns and monetary policy, *Financial Review,* Vol. 35, No. 2, pp. 59–78.

RATNER, M. and LEAL, R. (1996) Causality tests for the emerging markets of Latin America, *Journal of Emerging Markets,* Vol. 1, No. 1, pp. 29–40.

RATNER, M. and LEAL, R. (1999) Tests of technical trading strategies in the emerging markets of Latin America and Asia, *Journal of Banking and Finance,* Vol. 23, No. 12, pp. 1887–1905.

ROLL, R. (1988) The international crash of October 1987, *Financial Analysts Journal,* Vol. 44, No. 5, pp. 19–35.

SIMS, C. (1980) Macroeconomics and reality, *Econometrica,* Vol. 48, No. 1, pp. 1–49.

SOLNIK, B. H., BOUCRELLE, C. and LE FUR, Y. (1996) International market correlation and volatility, *Financial Analysts Journal,* Vol. 52, No. 5, September/October, pp. 17–34.

STANDARD AND POOR'S (2000) *Emerging Stock Markets Factbook 2000.*

URRUTIA, J. L. (1995) Test of random walk and market efficiency for Latin American equity markets, *Journal of Financial Research,* Vol. 18, pp. 299–309.

Part V

Emerging Markets

16

An Analysis of Country, Industry and Company Influences on Returns of Equities from Emerging Stock Markets

S.G.M. FIFIELD, C.D. SINCLAIR, A.A. LONIE and D.M. POWER

Introduction

A significant transformation in the operation of global financial markets has taken place since the late 1980s. The increased integration and liberalization of many large developed markets has led to a flurry of cross-border investment activity. In recent years however, the spotlight has tended to focus increasingly on the developing world. A sizeable increase in the capital flows from the industrialized countries has followed on from the relaxation of foreign investment restrictions in many emerging markets. Gross portfolio flows increased more than elevenfold over the period 1989–1995, peaking at US$99.7 billion in 1993 (World Bank, 1996). Equity financing is an essential component of these portfolio flows. Equity flows experienced a more than sixfold increase over the 1989–1995 period, reaching a level of US$22 billion in 1995. In short, developing country equity markets are evolving into an increasingly well-developed and well-researched arena for global financial investment.

The growing interest of foreign investors in emerging markets has been fuelled by high levels of real and nominal growth which have been achieved by equities in many of these developing countries (Hale, 1994; Kuczynski, 1994; El-Erian and Kumar, 1995; Smith and Walter, 1996). Furthermore, not only have investors come to expect extraordinarily high returns, but the international portfolio diversification (IPD) benefits have also been exceptional, due primarily to the existence of relatively low correlations between emerging stock market (ESM) returns and the returns of major market indices (Errunza, 1994; Speidell and Sappenfield, 1992). International investors have therefore been able to achieve both lower risk and higher returns by devoting a portion of their portfolio to the securities of emerging market firms (Divecha et al., 1992; Speidell and Sappenfield, 1992; Harvey, 1993 and 1994).

However, several researchers have queried whether these benefits from diversification can be sustained over the long run. Since the benefits of diversification depend crucially on the degree of market segmentation that exists, and the degree of correlation between markets, concern has arisen that these benefits may have been eroded as emerging markets have become increasingly integrated with world financial markets; specifically increased integration may result in a rise in return correlations between countries and hence a decline in the diversification value of ESM investment. This concern is addressed in the present study by initially investigating, on an ex-post basis, the potential gains that could have been achieved by diversifying into ESMs in a relatively recent time period, 1991–1996. The paper then examines a simple strategy for portfolio selection; it assesses whether some of the gains documented in ex-post IPD analyses can also be achieved on an ex-ante basis. As a final consideration, the paper examines the role of country and industry effects in explaining the returns of individual shares that are traded on emerging markets.

To provide a backcloth against which to compare the results, a number of aspects of the literature on IPD are briefly rehearsed in the next section. The subsequent section supplies details about the dataset. Further sections critically examine the case for diversifying into ESMs, both on an ex-post and on an ex-ante basis, followed by an exploration of the nature of any gains from ESM investment. The final section offers a number of concluding comments.

A Brief Survey of the Literature

The benefits of incorporating the securities of less developed countries into diversified portfolios was documented in studies by Levy and Sarnat (1970), Lessard (1973) and Errunza (1977) as early as the 1970s. In more recent investigations of emerging markets, academics such as Harvey (1993, 1994 and 1995) have systematically examined the impact of emerging equity markets on global investment strategies. Employing monthly index returns for 20 ESMs and data on 21 developed stock markets (DSMs) over the period January 1976–June 1992, Harvey investigated whether the addition of emerging markets to an institutional portfolio enhanced the reward to risk profile of his sample. His findings confirm the results of previous studies which suggest that a shift in the mean-variance efficient frontier can give rise to theoretical gains for investors who diversify their portfolio holdings into emerging stock markets (for example, Bailey and Stulz, 1990; Bekaert, 1993 and 1995; Diwan et al., 1993, De Santis, 1993). These results suggest that investors who spread their investments across developed markets can improve the performance of their portfolios *significantly* by also investing in the stock markets of emerging economies.

In contrast to the virtual unanimity among different researchers about the existence of benefits from emerging market diversification, the question of how large a portion of an investor's portfolio should be allocated to the securities of developing countries remains the subject of controversy. For example, Hartmann and Khambata (1993) point out that the addition of any emerging market equity component to a portfolio could result in enhanced performance: an investment of any size in the IFC Composite index increased portfolio efficiency for both domestic US and international investors. Adopting the perspective of a UK investor, Avgoustinos, Lonie, Power and Sinclair (1994) arrived at a similar conclusion. However, Divecha et al. (1992) argue that diversification benefits can fall once investment moves beyond a 20 per cent ESM component. Other writers advocate a still more prudent 10 to 15 per cent ESM weighting (for example, Speidell and Sappenfield, 1992; Poshakwale, 1996).

Several investigators have also investigated the optimal composition of the emerging market component of a portfolio. The analysis of Hartmann and Khambata (1993) suggests that when a portfolio's weights do not conform to weights employed by the IFC Composite index, a considerable improvement in the risk/return trade-off can be achieved. Furthermore, Hartmann and Khambata argue that diversification benefits vary according to the geographic composition of the ESM component: the risk, return and efficiency of their test portfolios varied dramatically with changes in the geographical composition of the investment. The subsequent results of Avgoustinos et al. (1994) corroborate this finding. Their mean return per unit of risk optimal portfolio consisted of four non-indexed EXM components from different geographical regions; importantly however, these analyses do not contradict the notion that gains are available from investment in a single geographical area. Indeed there is a great deal of evidence which suggests that the concentration of investment into the emerging economies of a single region can yield substantial diversification benefits (Lessard, 1973; Bailey and Stulz, 1990; Greenwood, 1993; Poshakwale, 1996; Islam and Rodriguez, 1998).

An Overstatement of Gains?

The classical ex-post mean-variance framework has primarily been used to study the diversification benefits of emerging market investment. Such studies assume that the required inputs to the portfolio analysis (returns, variances and covariances) are known with certainty (for example, Levy and Sarnat, 1970; Errunza, 1977; Bailey and Stulz, 1990; Diwan et al., 1993). Empirical studies that rely on these assumptions do not therefore reflect the realities under which actual investment decisions are made. For the practitioner, the volatile nature of equity returns makes the selection of an optimal investment strategy extremely difficult. Such an exercise becomes even more precarious however, if the variance–covariance/correlation matrices between market returns display inter-temporal instability; it is ex-ante stability of the correlation matrix that provides the basis for the portfolio investment decision. Evidence does exist suggesting that the inter-temporal correlations between emerging market returns may be unstable. For example, Sinclair et al. (1994) examined monthly return indices for nine ESMs drawn from four geographical regions, over the period 1977–1992. By employing a battery of tests, the authors concluded that "no signs of stability were identified in any of the time-series patterns of the variance/covariance matrices", (p. 17), except for the period spanning the October 1987 crash. Cheung and Ho (1991) arrived at a similar conclusion when they investigated the issue of stability for seven Asian–Pacific ESMs and four DSMs over the period 1977–1988. Using various analytical techniques, they demonstrated that the whole correlation matrix, incorporating both developed markets and Asian emerging markets was not stable inter-temporally, thus rendering the ex-ante identification of optimal portfolio investment extremely hazardous.

Although the inter-temporal correlations between returns appear to be unstable, early evidence suggests that the employment of a simple method of forecasting covariance matrices can result in effective IPD, and form the basis of a potentially successful portfolio strategy (for example, Elton and Gruber, 1973; Elton et al., 1978; Sinclair et al., 1994). Elton and Gruber (1973) found that most of the ex-post gains available from IPD could be achieved on an ex-ante basis by predicting future variance/covariance matrices from past data, and by assuming that means and standard deviations can be easily forecast with precision. Sinclair et al. (1994) also reported evidence of predictability in covariance matrices which offered hope to practitioners attempting to achieve some of the diversification gains that might be available from investing in emerging stock markets.

An Industry or a Country Effect?

Ever since the benefits of international diversification were first documented, researchers have sought to split risk and return into their constituent sources in order to explain the low co-movement between the returns from different markets. In particular, researchers have investigated the competing roles of country and industry effects in international stock returns. However early papers by Grinold et al. (1989) and Divecha et al. (1992) were unable to disentangle the two components. Zervos (1996) was more successful in her attempt to measure the influence of country and industry components in individual stock returns over the period 1976–1992. She found that, although both country- and industry-specific disturbances are important factors in understanding emerging market returns, industry effects explain very little of the cross-sectional variations in returns and return volatility. In fact, she concluded that the low correlations between various markets are primarily due to country-specific factors. Moreover, her results indicated that country effects have increased in importance over time, while the impact of industry grouping has fallen sharply since 1986; this finding contradicts the conventional wisdom that greater market integration has reduced the importance of country effects in the determination of share returns in ESMs. Furthermore, in comparing emerging and developed markets, Grinold et al. (1989) and Divecha et al. (1992) suggest that, whilst a country factor dominates returns from both sets of markets, it plays a larger role in explaining emerging market returns than in explaining developed market returns; industry effects are more prominent in returns of equities from developed markets. The importance of country selection in emerging markets investment is demonstrated very effectively in the Hartmann and Khambata (1993) study; the widely disparate performance of portfolios consisting of equally-weighted investments in three different ESMs from three different geographical regions illustrated the enormous impact that country selection could have on both portfolio risk and return.

Data

Datastream was used to obtain weekly nominal share price data for a selection of shares traded in 17 ESMs, over the six-year period 1991–1996. In particular, the top 20 shares, by market value, traded in Argentina (ARG), Chile (CHL), Greece (GRE), Hong Kong (HK), India (IND), Indonesia (INO), Korea (KOR), Malaysia (MAL), Mexico (MEX), the Philippines (PHI), Portugal (POR), South Africa (SAF), Singapore (SIN), Sri Lanka (SRL), Taiwan (TAI), Thailand (THA) and Turkey (TUR) were included in the study. These countries represent the population of emerging markets for which data were available for the time period considered. The sample represents a good geographical spread of countries including ten Asian and Far Eastern countries, three Latin American countries, two European countries, one African country and one Middle Eastern country. The results should therefore not be specific to any one sub-group of emerging market countries. In addition, data for the world market were obtained for comparative purposes.

All share prices were obtained in their local currency and converted to returns in pounds sterling (£) according to the formula:

$$R_{it} = \mathrm{Ln}\ [(P_{it}/P_{it-1})(X_{t-1}/X_t)] \tag{1}$$

where R_{it} is the return on share i in week t, P_{it} is the price level of the share in week t, X_t is the exchange rate for the period and Ln is the natural logarithm.

The Morgan Stanley Capital International (MSCI) Emerging Markets Industrial Classification scheme was used to assign each of the sample companies to one of seven broad industry groupings: Capital equipment, Consumer goods, Energy, Finance, Materials, Multi-industry and Services. The industrial composition of companies varied widely across the countries studied. For example, Greece, Hong Kong and Singapore had a heavy concentration of firms in the finance sector, while the materials sector was prominent in India and South Africa. In contrast, countries such as Mexico and

TABLE 16.1: *Statistics for the largest 20 firms in each emerging market country*

	MEAN			STDEV			MRPUR		
	Mean	Min	Max	Mean	Min	Max	Mean	Min	Max
ARG	0.005	−0.001	0.010	0.097	0.071	0.140	0.053	−0.013	0.125
CHL	0.004	0.000	0.007	0.050	0.037	0.072	0.081	−0.008	0.158
GRE	−0.001	−0.009	0.003	0.067	0.035	0.229	−0.010	−0.087	0.081
HK	0.005	0.002	0.007	0.042	0.034	0.048	0.111	0.034	0.196
IND	0.002	−0.004	0.007	0.058	0.045	0.077	0.039	−0.069	0.138
INO	0.000	−0.004	0.008	0.067	0.039	0.135	0.001	−0.053	0.119
KOR	−0.001	−0.003	0.003	0.049	0.042	0.063	−0.024	−0.077	0.054
MAL	0.002	0.000	0.006	0.041	0.031	0.055	0.062	0.008	0.151
MEX	0.005	0.001	0.009	0.053	0.038	0.083	0.107	0.022	0.186
PHI	0.004	−0.002	0.009	0.068	0.040	0.154	0.064	−0.050	0.180
POR	0.000	−0.004	0.007	0.044	0.025	0.070	0.011	−0.063	0.199
SAF	0.002	0.000	0.005	0.043	0.031	0.065	0.061	0.010	0.153
SIN	0.002	0.000	0.006	0.032	0.019	0.046	0.060	−0.003	0.129
SRL	0.001	−0.004	0.007	0.074	0.045	0.122	0.008	−0.031	0.090
TAI	0.002	0.000	0.004	0.049	0.033	0.061	0.038	−0.008	0.097
THA	0.000	−0.006	0.006	0.053	0.040	0.065	0.004	−0.100	0.151
TUR	0.010	0.005	0.015	0.112	0.086	0.139	0.094	0.037	0.141
AVG	0.002	−0.002	0.007	0.055	0.038	0.093	0.042	−0.031	0.138
WLD	0.002	−0.042	0.054	0.014	–	–	0.133	–	–

MEAN is the mean weekly return for the period 1991–1996, STDEV is the standard deviation of the weekly returns, and MRPUR is the ratio of MEAN to STDEV. The column headed Mean contains the average statistic over the 20 firms, while Min and Max contain the smallest and largest statistic respectively.

Turkey had a more even distribution of firms across industries. The sample highlights the fact that the geographical distribution of industries is not uniform across countries.

A number of descriptive statistics were calculated for the weekly return series of all 20 firms in each ESM and for the world market over the whole six-year period. In particular, the mean (MEAN), the standard deviation (STDEV), and the ratio of mean to standard deviation (MRPUR) were estimated and are summarized in Table 16.1.

Several points emerge from an analysis of the descriptive statistics. First, average returns varied widely across the ESMs. Turkish firms performed best over the period, earning a mean weekly return of 1.0 per cent. The worst performances were achieved by firms in Korea and Greece which earned negative returns (−0.1 per cent) on average. Second, the overall average weekly return of companies in all 17 ESMs was 0.2 per cent, matching the return of 0.2 per cent earned by the world market portfolio over the six-year period, although the average risk of ESM companies, as measured by

TABLE 16.2: *Companies that make up the optimal return per unit risk equally-weighted optimal portfolio for each year*

Country	1991	1992	1993	1994	1995	1996
ARG	11,18	–	2,6	16	19	7,11,19
CHL	2,5,18	4,17	1,2,7,10,18	7,19	16	15
GRE	6	–	1,2,5,13	6,12	6,8,9,12	1,9,11,18
HK	1,14,18	2	18	–	–	15,18
IND	2,6,7,10,15,17	2	7,9,12	2,8,14	1,4,10	7
INO	–	14	4,10,12	8	7	3
KOR	7	–	12	3,13,17	9,14	–
MAL	–	16,17,18	1,7,18	–	4,6,13,17	7,12,14,19,20
MEX	11,12,15,19	1,19	5,7,15,19	3,10,11,13	6,15	3,9,10,11,13
PHI	1,9,11,19	6,7,10,14,19	6,10,12,16,17,19	17,19	14	1,6,15
POR	15,19	5,20	1,2,9,12,15,18	6,7,13,18,19	1,3,20	2,3,6,10,12,13,14,15,19
SAF	1,2,5,9,14,19	19	2,13	1,10,15	–	3
SIN	11,13,19	9,18,19	1,3,18	7,13,18	12,13	18
SRL	1,6,7,8,9,10,18,19	1	7,11,12	1	–	2,8,18
TAI	–	11,14	–	8,10,14	–	4,5
THA	3,10,12,14	7,14	10,16	9	10,16	11,15,18
TUR	–	12	2,7,17	–	2,6	18
Number	47	27	51	34	28	45

The companies in each market are identified by the numbers 1 to 20.

standard deviation, was four times that of the world market portfolio over the same period.

Third, the ESM returns were highly volatile. Singaporean firms experienced the lowest total risk among the ESM companies, recording a standard deviation of 3.2 per cent. By contrast, Turkish and Argentinian firms were associated with particularly volatile returns, with standard deviations of 11.2 per cent and 9.7 per cent, respectively. Fourth, although portfolio theory associates higher risk with higher return, average returns for firms in eleven of the emerging markets (Greece, India, Indonesia, Korea, Malaysia, Portugal, Singapore, South Africa, Sri Lanka, Thailand and Taiwan) were either lower than or the same as that for the world market portfolio, despite the fact that the level of total risk was substantially higher.

These observations tend to suggest that, over the period from 1991 to 1996, it would have been possible for a global investor to benefit by investing in particular companies in almost any of the emerging markets in our study.

Diversification and Ex-Post Optimal Portfolios

To investigate the recent IPD benefits of ESM equities, the study examines the risk–return advantages of a portfolio composed entirely of emerging market securities for the period 1991–1996. For the whole six-year period and in each one-year sub-period, equally-weighted ex-post portfolios were constructed and the MRPUR behaviour of these portfolios was examined. In each test period, the MRPUR-optimal (highest MRPUR) portfolios were identified using a forward selection procedure in which the best single company was initially selected and extra companies were added to the portfolio in an iterative process in which the company included in the portfolio at each stage was the one that would result in the best return per unit of risk. The process was continued until all 340 companies were included in the portfolio. The maximum MRPUR portfolio was then identified.

A number of points that are relevant to the construction of an optimal portfolio emerge from an analysis of Table 16.2. First, to reap the benefits from IPD fully, a minimum of 27 companies spread over at least 13 of the emerging markets was required; indeed, in two of the sub-periods (1991 and 1993) the minimum requirement was closer to 50 companies. Second, over the six years of the study, firms in some countries appeared more frequently in the optimal portfolio than the firms in other countries. Indeed, a formal Chi-squared test conclusively rejects homogeneity of frequency of occurrence (p-value 0.0007). Firms in Portugal (27), Mexico (21) and the Philippines (21) appeared relatively frequently, while firms in Hong Kong (7), Indonesia (7), Korea (7), Taiwan (7) and Turkey (7) appeared less often than average. Third, the propensity for some firms to appear in the optimal portfolio in more than one of the six years under study varied from country to country. The hypothesis that the number of times in which a single country appears in the optimal portfolio is equal across countries is rejected by a Chi-squared test (p=0.0021). Countries whose firms are relatively persistent in their appearance in the optimal portfolio (i.e., that have a low proportion of single occurrences) include Portugal (19 per cent), Mexico (21 per cent) and the Philippines (21 per cent). On the other hand, firms in Indonesia and Korea only feature in the optimal portfolio in a single year.

Table 16.3 permits an examination of the performance of the ex-post MRPUR-optimal emerging market portfolios in each of the six years of the study. The table clearly illustrates that the MRPUR ratio for the optimal ESM portfolio was significantly greater than that for the world market portfolio in every test period. The most striking results were obtained for 1994, when the MRPUR-optimal portfolio achieved a reward to risk ratio of 1.749, chiefly as a result of the low standard deviation of ESM returns in this period. This ratio is approximately 33 times greater than the MRPUR for the corresponding world market portfolio (0.052). Overall, the results shown in the table reveal that there was considerable scope for potential (theoretical) benefits from this particular form of IPD, due to a combination of larger mean weekly returns and smaller variability in weekly returns in the optimal ESM portfolio as compared to the world market portfolio.

TABLE 16.3: *Risk–return characteristics of the ex-post MRPUR optimal portfolios*

	Return from the ESM portfolio			Return from the world portfolio		
Year	MEAN	STDEV	MRPUR	MEAN	STDEV	MRPUR
1991	0.0112	0.0058	1.942	0.0029	0.0178	0.162
1992	0.0050	0.0041	1.204	−0.0016	0.0149	−0.105
1993	0.0117	0.0045	2.606	0.0035	0.0118	0.299
1994	0.0068	0.0039	1.769	0.0006	0.0115	−0.052
1995	0.0070	0.0066	1.060	0.0033	0.0118	0.277
1996	0.0053	0.0035	1.521	0.0022	0.0127	0.171

Diversification for Ex-Ante Optimal Portfolios

The outcomes from the above analysis would have proved difficult to achieve by a portfolio manager who was not blessed with perfect foresight. One persistent problem is that ex-post efficient portfolios from one period do not necessarily turn out to be optimal ex-ante, since the stock returns, variances and covariances between each pair of investments all tend to change over time. Consequently, studies which utilize an ex-post framework potentially overstate the true level of gains which can be obtained from diversifying into ESMs in practice and are of limited value to the portfolio manager who is searching for an operational approach to global portfolio construction. This section addresses this problem and investigates whether, by using a simple strategy to construct portfolios, some of the theoretical gains that are available from ex-post analyses of IPD can be achieved in practice.

The procedure adopted is based on the notion that, instead of using the optimum equally-weighted portfolio developed in the formation period, a sub-optimal, more diversified portfolio is chosen to permit the achievement of *momentum* in the equity selection. In particular, the subsequent one-year performances of portfolios that attained 95, 90, 85, 80 and 75 per cent of the optimum portfolio return in the formation year are analysed in Table 16.4; the performance of each of these ESM portfolios and the MRPUR of the world

TABLE 16.4: *Summary of the characteristics of the ex-ante emerging market portfolios by year*

Formation year	Test year		Emerging market ex-ante portfolio						World portfolio
			100%	95%	90%	85%	80%	75%	
1991	1992	mean	**0.0006**	0.0002	0.0004	0.0004	0.0001	0.0001	−0.0016
		stdev	0.0144	0.0223	0.0123	0.0127	0.0112	**0.0111**	0.0150
		mrpur	**0.038**	0.014	0.029	0.034	0.010	0.005	−0.1054
1992	1993	mean	0.0088	0.0031	**0.0102**	0.0101	0.0095	0.0098	0.0035
		stdev	0.0149	0.0146	0.0116	0.0117	**0.0115**	0.0117	0.0118
		mrpur	0.587	0.215	**0.877**	0.864	0.827	0.842	0.2996
1993	1994	mean	**0.0021**	−0.002	0.0014	0.0013	0.0010	0.0010	0.0006
		stdev	0.0165	0.0205	**0.0115**	0.0158	0.0154	0.0153	**0.0115**
		mrpur	**0.126**	−0.098	0.123	0.081	0.064	0.067	0.0525
1994	1995	mean	−0.001	−0.0007	−0.0010	−0.0011	−0.0008	−0.0013	**0.0033**
		stdev	0.0118	0.0128	**0.0105**	0.0111	0.0111	0.0112	0.0118
		mrpur	−0.103	−0.063	−0.093	−0.100	−0.070	−0.119	**0.2770**
1995	1996	mean	0.002	0.0004	0.0021	0.0020	0.0020	0.0019	**0.0022**
		stdev	0.0113	0.012	0.0087	0.0087	**0.0086**	0.0093	0.0127
		mrpur	0.177	0.029	**0.243**	0.227	0.231	0.200	0.1706

For each year the largest MEAN and MRPUR and the smallest STDEV are emboldened, while the corresponding figures for emerging market portfolios are underlined.

market portfolio are compared. The results indicate that opportunities existed for profitable IPD by employing a forward-looking strategy based on historic data. At least five of the six ex-ante strategies achieved higher mean returns than did the world market portfolio in four years out of five, while five of the six ex-ante portfolios had smaller standard deviations of returns than did their world counterpart in three of the five periods. Because of these higher returns and lower standard deviations, at least five of the six ex-ante strategies achieved higher return per unit of risk than did the world market portfolio in four years out of five. Finally, a comparison of the six strategies suggests that, in forming an ex-ante portfolio for the succeeding period, it is worth increasing the number of firms in the ex-post optimal portfolio for the current formation period until its MRPUR drops to 90 per cent of the optimal value.

Table 16.5 describes the performance of each of the ESM portfolios in the four quarters following the formation year. It is evident from the data that the emerging market portfolio has a significantly higher MRPUR in the first quarter following the formation period, in four out of the five test years; only the emerging market portfolio formed in 1995 performed much worse than the world market portfolio. However, in each test year the advantage of the emerging market portfolio had disappeared by the second quarter. Again, diversification beyond the ex-post optimal portfolio of 90 per cent of the optimal value offers the best results.

The findings from the analysis therefore suggest that some of the gains from IPD which have been highlighted in the literature may be achievable on an ex-ante basis, but that these gains are likely to be short-term in character.

Country and Industry Factors

The analysis presented in the previous sections suggests that substantial gains may exist from investing in emerging market securities rather than the world market portfolio. In this section, the nature of these gains is explored by investigating the sources of variation in the returns earned by ESM securities. Evidence on the structure of ESM returns is of critical importance to investors; it would indicate how the investment process should be structured and research resources efficiently allocated.

The data were analysed to determine whether the returns earned by equities traded in developing countries vary in a systemic fashion (1) over time; (2) across countries; (3) across different industries; and (4)

TABLE 16.5: *Return per unit of risk for the ex-ante emerging market portfolios by quarter, for the first four quarters following formation*

		Emerging market ex-ante portfolio				World portfolio
		100%	95%	90%	80%	
1992	Q1	0.415	0.450	0.640	0.897	−0.691
1992	Q2	−0.408	−0.181	−0.290	−0.418	0.301
1992	Q3	−0.336	−0.467	−0.500	−0.472	−0.088
1992	Q4	0.136	0.133	0.139	0.147	0.037
1993	Q1	0.915	0.484	0.779	1.643	0.663
1993	Q2	−0.014	0.075	0.437	1.628	0.158
1993	Q3	0.873	1.068	1.097	1.023	0.480
1993	Q4	0.970	1.099	1.542	0.989	0.053
1994	Q1	0.197	0.088	−0.014	−0.069	−0.010
1994	Q2	−0.103	−0.130	−0.051	−0.037	0.197
1994	Q3	0.555	0.648	0.879	0.811	0.161
1994	Q4	−0.244	−0.294	−0.201	−0.268	−0.060
1995	Q1	−0.752	−0.691	−0.750	−0.587	0.263
1995	Q2	−0.091	−0.065	−0.017	−0.024	0.210
1995	Q3	0.685	0.666	0.593	0.578	0.305
1995	Q4	−0.288	−0.242	−0.219	−0.183	0.315
1996	Q1	0.371	0.664	0.686	0.693	0.231
1996	Q2	−0.024	−0.003	−0.015	0.015	0.185
1996	Q3	0.013	0.008	−0.038	−0.060	0.039
1996	Q4	0.336	0.294	0.412	0.374	0.232

according to the size of the company. In order to decompose the variance of emerging market company level share returns into their individual components, an analysis of covariance was carried out, with time, country, and industry and their interactions as explanatory factors and with the log of the market value of each company as a covariate.

Table 16.6 presents summary statistics from the analysis described above. Six main points emerge from an analysis of this table. First, when all the factors in the table are taken together a substantial proportion (42 per cent) of the total variance of returns is explained. Second, the market value covariate is extremely significant (second only to year) and has a positive relationship with returns (coefficient 0.0062, t-value 6.97), implying that companies with larger market values tend to outperform their smaller-sized counterparts; there is some evidence of a reverse-size effect in these 17 emerging markets as a whole. Third, while the year factor is the most significant of the three main effects, the month factor and the interaction between months and years are also extremely important, implying that returns vary significantly, on an inter-temporal basis, both from year to year and from month to month. The monthly

TABLE 16.6: *Analysis of variance of monthly sterling returns for 17 emerging stock markets over the six-year period 1991–1996*

Source of variation	Sum of squares	DF	Mean square	F	Signif. of E
ln(market value)	0.47	1	0.4695	48.81	0.0000
Country	3.69	16	0.2307	24.03	0.0000
sector	0.12	6	0.0206	2.15	0.0451
Country by sector	0.42	74	0.0057	0.59	0.9979
residual firm level	1.43	243	0.0059		
firm total	5.67	339			
year	7.41	5	1.4817	154.34	0.0000
month	2.88	12	0.2401	25.01	0.0000
year by month	22.76	60	0.3794	39.52	0.0000
Time total	33.05	77			
Country by year	15.67	80	0.1959	20.40	0.0000
residual firm level by year	14.77	1615	0.0091		
firm by year total	30.44	1695			
Country by month	21.66	192	0.1128	11.75	0.0000
residual firm level by month	38.73	3876	0.0100		
firm by month total	60.39	4068			
Country by year by month	99.98	960	0.1041	10.85	0.0000
residual firm level by year by month	186.06	19380	0.0096		
firm by year by month	286.04	20340			
error (combined residuals)	240.99	25114	0.0096		
model	174.60	1405			
Total	416.13	26519			

DF denotes degrees of freedom. Signif. of F denotes the p-value for the variance ratio test.

pattern also changes over the six years studied. Fourth, the country main effect is extremely significant, as are the two-factor interactions between country and year and between country and month. The three-factor interaction between country, month and year is also important, implying that returns vary significantly on a geographical basis and that differences between the mean returns from various countries change from one year to the next, and from one month to the next; the monthly pattern in returns also varies from year to year. Fifth, the sector main effect is barely significant at the five per cent level, while the interactions between sector and other factors (country, year, month) all have p-values greater than 0.05.

The results from this analysis of covariance suggest that, when investing in emerging market equities, fund managers and investors should (a) focus on the task of choosing the right *countries* instead of directing their principal efforts towards the selection of industrial sectors; (b) concentrate on companies with larger market value; and (c) review their portfolio rather frequently, perhaps at quarterly intervals.

Conclusion

This study has investigated a number of issues relevant to investment in emerging stock markets. Employing weekly disaggregated data over the period 1991–1996 the paper examined the case for investing in a portfolio composed of ESM securities. Relative to the benefits from investing in a portfolio consisting entirely of developed market equities, the analysis demonstrated that emerging markets offered global fund managers excellent opportunities for increasing portfolio returns, while simultaneously reducing portfolio risk. In addition, an investigation into the structure of emerging market returns advocated a geographic top-down approach to ESM investment: the choice of industries or individual securities is likely to have less influence on the performance of an ESM portfolio than the selection of the right countries in which to invest.

References

AVGOUSTINOS, P., LONIE, A. A., POWER, D. M. and SINCLAIR, C. D. (1994) An examination of the argument for increased investment in emerging equity markets, *Dundee Discussion Papers in Accountancy and Business Finance*, FIN/9402, pp. 1–19.

BAILEY, W. and STULTZ, R. (1990) Benefits of international diversification: The case of Pacific Basin stock markets, *Journal of Portfolio Management*, Vol. 16, No. 4 (Summer), pp. 57–61.

BEKAERT, G. (1993) Market integration and investment barriers in emerging equity markets, in S. Claessens and S. Gooptu, *Portfolio Investment in Developing Countries*, World Bank Discussion Paper 228, September, pp. 221–251.

BEKAERT, G. (1995) Market integration and investment barriers in emerging equity markets, *World Bank Economic Review*, Vol. 9, No. 1 (January), pp. 75–107.

CHEUNG, Y. W. and HO, Y. (1991) The intertemporal stability of the relationships between the Asian emerging equity markets and the developed equity markets, *Journal of Business Finance and Accounting*, Vol. 18, No. 2 (January), pp. 235–254.

DE SANTIS, G. (1993) Asset pricing and portfolio diversification: Evidence from emerging financial markets, in S. CLAESSENS and S. GOOPTU, *Portfolio Investment in Developing Countries*, World Bank Discussion Paper 228, September, pp. 145–168.

DIVECHA, A. B., DRACH, J. and STEFEK, D. (1992) Emerging markets: A quantitative perspective, *Journal of Portfolio Management*, Vol. 18, No. 1 (Fall), pp. 41–50.

DIWAN, I., ERRUNZA, V. R. and SENBET, L. W. (1993) Country funds for emerging economies, in S. CLAESSENS and S. GOOPTU, *Portfolio Investment in Developing Countries*, World Bank Discussion Paper 228, September, pp. 252–286.

EL-ERIAN, M. A. and KUMAR, M. S. (1995) Emerging equity markets in Middle Eastern countries, *IMF Staff Papers*, Vol. 42, No. 2 (June), pp. 313.–343.

ELTON, E. J. and GRUBER, M. J. (1973) Estimating the dependence structure of share prices – implications for portfolio selection, *Journal of Finance*, Vol. 28, No. 5 (December), pp. 1203–1232.

ELTON, E. J., GRUBER, M. J. and URICH, T. (1978) Are betas best? *Journal of Finance*, Vol. 33, No. 5 (December), pp. 1375–1384.

ERRUNZA, V. R. (1977) Gains from portfolio diversification into less developed countries' securities, *Journal of International Business Studies*, (Fall), pp. 83–99.

ERRUNZA, V. R. (1994) Emerging markets: Some new concepts, *Journal of Portfolio Management*, Vol. 20, No. 3 (Spring), pp. 82–87.

GREENWOOD, J. G. (1993) Portfolio investment in Asian and Pacific economies: Trends and Prospects, *Asian Development Review*, Vol. 11, No. 1, pp. 20–150.

GRINOLD, R., RUDD, A. and STEFEK, D. (1989) Global factors: Fact or fiction? *Journal of Portfolio Management*, Vol. 16, No. 1 (Fall), pp. 79–88.

HALE, D. D. (1994) Stock markets in the new world order, *Columbia Journal of World Business, Focus Issue: Emerging Capital Markets*, Vol. 29, No. 2 (Summer), pp. 14–28.

HARTMANN, M. A. and KHAMBATA, D. (1993) Emerging stock markets: Investment strategies of the future, *Columbia Journal of World Business*, Summer, pp. 82–104.

HARVEY, C. R. (1993) Portfolio enhancement using emerging markets and conditioning information, in S. CLAESSENS and S. GOOPTU, *Portfolio Investment in Developing Countries*, World Bank Discussion Paper 228, September, pp. 110–144.

HARVEY, C. R. (1994) Conditional asset allocation in emerging markets, *NBER Working Paper 4623*, January, pp. 1–45.

HARVEY, C. R. (1995) Predictable risk and returns in emerging markets, *Review of Financial Studies*, Vol. 8, No. 3 (Fall), pp. 773–816.

ISLAM, M. M. and RODRIGUEZ, A. J. (1998) Evidence on the benefits of portfolio investment in emerging capital markets in Latin America, in J. C. BAKER (ed.), *Selected International Investment Portfolios*, Elsevier Science B.V., pp. 75–89.

KUCZYNSKI, P. (1994) Why emerging markets? *Columbia Journal of World Business, Focus Issue: Emerging Capital Markets*, Vol. 29, No. 2 (Summer), pp. 8–13.

LESSARD, D. (1973) International portfolio diversification: A multivariate analysis for a group of Latin American countries, *Journal of Finance*, Vol. 28, No. 3 (June), pp. 619–633.

LEVY, H. and SARNAT, M. (1970) International diversification of investment portfolios, *American Economic Review*, Vol. 60, No. 4 (September), pp. 668–675.

POSHAKWALE, S. (1996) Emerging markets as new channels for international diversification, *Manchester Business School*, pp. 6–7.

SINCLAIR, C. D., POWER, D. M., LONIE, A. A. and AVGOUSTINOS, P. (1994) An investigation of the stability of relationships between returns from emerging stock markets, *Dundee Discussion Papers in Accountancy and Business Finance*, FIN/9406, pp. 3–35.

SMITH, R. C. and WALTER, I. (1996) Rethinking emerging markets, *Washington Quarterly*, Vol. 19, No. 1, pp. 45–64.

SPEIDELL, L. S. and SAPPENFIELD, R. (1992) Global Diversification in a Shrinking World, *Journal of Portfolio Management*, Vol. 18, No. 1 (Fall), pp. 57–67.

WORLD BANK, THE (1996) *Global Economic Prospects and the Developing Countries*, The World Bank, Washington DC.

ZERVOS, S. J. (1996) Industry and Country Components in Emerging Market Stock Returns, *Discussion Paper 96-02*, Centre for Empirical Research in Finance, Brunel University.

17

Portfolio Performance and Returns Due to Global Diversification with Emerging Markets

TULIN SENER

Introduction

The enhancement of the compound return as a result of diversification is not widely recognized. In fact, there is very little empirical evidence for the direct measurement of the return enhancement effects of diversification in the literature (Booth and Fama, 1992 and Gastineau, 1995). The degree of association between the asset returns creates the effects of return enhancement as well as risk reduction. The greater the diversification effects, the higher the rewards.

As shown by Markowitz (1991, p. 122) and Booth and Fama (1992), the compound return on an asset is not the correct measure of the return contribution of the asset to the compound return on a portfolio. The return contribution of each asset exceeds its compound return by an incremental amount. This incremental amount stems from the risk reduction effect of diversification and is called the return due to diversification.

As is well known, the success of global portfolios depends on the countries and asset classes chosen, as well as the assigned portfolio weights and time periods. Recently, high returns and low correlations of emerging markets (EMS) have attracted international portfolio flows to EMS (Divecha, 1994; Errunza, 1994; and Michaud et al., 1996). Further, various studies indicate that country risk ratings are correlated with fundamental valuation attributes and they have the explanatory power for the country selection (Erb et al., 1996 and Macedo, 1995).

In this study, I contribute to the work of Booth and Fama (1992) in two ways. First, I use optimal weights for the asset allocation, which will provide the best diversification effects. Second, I extend global portfolios with EMS and EMS regional indexes as well as with a chosen country index based on the country risk ratings. The findings show that these portfolios perform better. For asset evaluation, if return contributions are used rather than annualized simple or compound returns, the US Small Stock, the IFCG composite and regional indexes would have the highest premiums.

This paper is organized as follows. Following the introduction, I provide the theory and data as well as the estimation procedures. Next, the empirical findings are analysed. Finally, the summary and concluding remarks are given.

Optimal Asset Allocation and the Return Due to Diversification

Optimal Asset Allocation Weights

The optimal weights are obtained from the tangency portfolio. That is:

$$\underset{\{w_j\}}{\text{Max SR}} = \frac{Er_p - r_f}{SD_p}$$

$$= \sum_{j=1}^{n} w_j \, (ER_j - r_f) / \sum_{i=1}^{n} \sum_{j=1}^{n} w_j \, w_i \, Cov_{ij})^{50} \qquad (1)$$

$$\text{Subject to} \sum_{j=1}^{n} w_j = 1.0$$

where SR, SD_p and r_f refer respectively to the Sharpe (reward to variability) ratio, the standard deviation of returns on the portfolio and the risk-free interest rate; ER and w depict the expected (average) return and the portfolio weight; and Cov. stands for the covariance term.

Here, as proven by Tobin (1958), the mixture of the tangency portfolio is independent of the investors' preference structure (Eun and Resnick, 1994).

The Return Due to Diversification

Markowitz (1991, p.122) and Booth and Fama (1992) prove that the compound returns (continuously compounded) on any asset $_j$ (C_j) and on a portfolio p (C_p) can be approximated as follows:

$$C_j = \ln(1 + ER_j) - \frac{Var_j}{2(1 + ER_j)^2} \tag{2}$$

$$C_p = \ln(1 + ER_p) - \frac{Var_p}{2(1 + ER_p)^2} \tag{3}$$

Here Var depicts the variance term and ln (1 + ER) is the average return expressed as a continuously compounded return.

Equations (2) and (3) indicate that the higher the variance of returns, the lower the compound returns. Also, it should be noted that variance is an appropriate measure of risk for a portfolio, but not for an asset in a diversified portfolio. The risk of the asset is less than the variance of the asset's returns, because of the risk reduction coming from the diversification effects. The risk reduction due to diversification is the reason why an asset's compound return is smaller than the return contribution of the asset.

The return contribution of an asset j (D_j) is formulated as:

$$D_j = \frac{ER_j}{Er_p} \ln(1 + ER_p) - \frac{\beta_{jp} Var_p}{2(1 + ER_p)^2} \tag{4}$$

Where:

$$\beta_{jp} Var_p = Cov_{jp} \tag{5}$$

and β indicates the beta coefficient.

Finally, the return due to diversification for an asset $_j$ (RDD_j) can be obtained by subtracting the compound return from the return contribution. That is:

$$RDD_j = D_j - C_j \tag{6}$$

It is expected that the higher the diversification effect, or the negative covariance between the returns on asset $_j$ and portfolio $_p$, the greater the return due to diversification to the asset$_j$. Also, it should be noted that:

$$C_p = \sum_{j=1}^{n} w_j D_j \tag{7}$$

Why Should Returns Due to Diversification Be Higher for EMS?

Unlimited expansion of investment opportunities makes global investing more attractive than domestic investing. Global diversification is based on the assumption that countries experience different business cycles and the returns over countries balance each other out (Solnik, 1995; Solnik et al., 1996; and Akdogan, 1996). In addition, diversification into other countries can further reduce the systematic risk associated with single market investment.

Recently, the increased integration of the developed countries (DCS) has started to raise the question of positive correlation risk. As institutional trading and global events decrease the degrees of segmentation in DCS, diversification effects with EMS become more important. EMS have structural differences from DCS and they are less affected by global events. They experience higher returns with higher volatility and have lower correlations with DCS. Thus, global portfolios with EMS are expected to have greater diversification effects and larger returns due to diversification.

Data and Estimation Procedures

Data

The time periods of the study are 1926–1996, 1970–1996 and 1988–1996. However, the time spans of the global portfolios with EMS is limited to the 1988–1996 period. Monthly total returns on the major domestic and international asset classes come from the *Ibbotson Associates' Database.* Monthly total returns on the IFCG composite and regional indexes for the EMS are taken from the *IFC Factbooks.* Country credit ratings are from the *Institutional Investors' Semiannual Reports* (1988–1996).

Estimation Procedures

The asset classes that are used for the construction of the domestic portfolio are: (1) S&P500, (2) US Small Stock, (3) US LT Govt Bond, (4) US LT Corp Bond, (5) US IT Govt Bond and (6) One-Month T-Bill. The asset classes for other DCS include MSCI/EAFE and SB World Govt Bond[1]. As for the EMS, IFCG is used as the composite index. Regional indexes are available for Latin America and Asia in the IFC Factbooks.

However, in the case of the Europe/Middle East/Africa region (EMEA), a surrogate regional index is created. The sample countries are Greece, Hungary, Jordan, Nigeria, Poland, Portugal, South Africa, Turkey and Zimbabwe. In addition, a chosen country index is originated by screening the countries with average credit ratings below 30. The screened countries are Argentina, Chile, Peru, Philippines, Pakistan, Jordan, Nigeria, Poland and Zimbabwe.

Optimal portfolio weights, returns, standard deviations and Sharpe ratios are derived from the *Ibbotson Associates' Optimizer.* Portfolios are set up for an investor who takes moderate risk (e.g., position 50). Finally, the statistics that have been obtained from the Optimizer are applied to the formulas given in equations (1) through (5), to calculate the returns due to diversification.

Empirical Findings

Cross Correlations of Dollar Returns

Tables 17.1 and 17.2 provide cross-correlations of dollar returns for the 12 major asset classes.

The S&P500 has high positive cross-correlations with the US Small Stock (71–80 per cent) and, in the short run, with the domestic bonds (60–73 per cent). However, it has low and moderate correlations with the MSCI/EAFE (41–53 per cent) and, in the long run, with all bond classes (10–50 per cent). The market index has the lowest positive or negative cross-correlations with the US T-Bills (–4–27 per cent), and with the indexes of IFCG (21 per cent), MEEAF (–3 per cent) and Asia (14 per cent).

TABLE 17.1: *Cross-correlations of dollar returns for the domestic portfolio*

	S&P 500	US Small Stock	US LT Corp Bond	US Lt Govt Bond	US IT Govt Bond	US T-Bill
Domestic portfolio (January 1926–December 1996)						
S&P500	1.00	–	–	–	–	–
US Small Stock	0.81	1.00	–	–	–	–
US LT Corp. Bond	0.25	0.11	1.00	–	–	–
US LT Govt Bond	0.18	0.03	0.94	1.00	–	–
US IT Govt Bond	0.10	–0.03	0.90	0.91	1.00	–
US T-Bill	–0.04	–0.09	0.22	0.24	0.50	1.00
Domestic portfolio (January 1970–December 1996)						
S&P500	1.00	–	–	–	–	–
US Small Stock	0.72	1.00	–	–	–	–
US LT Corp. Bond	0.51	0.24	1.00	–	–	–
US LT Govt Bond	0.46	0.21	0.96	1.00	–	–
US IT Govt Bond	0.37	0.13	0.93	0.93	1.00	–
US T-Bill	–0.05	0.01	–0.04	–0.02	0.23	1.00

TABLE 17.2: *Cross-correlations of dollar returns for the global portfolios*

	S&P 500	US Small Stock	US LT Corp. Bond	US LT Govt Bond	US IT Govt Bond	US T-Bill	MSCI EAFE	SB World Govt	IFCG Compo	MEEAF	Asia	Latin America	Chosen Country Index
Global portfolio with DCS (January 1970 – December 1996),													
S&P500	1.00												
US Small Stock	0.72	1.00											
US LT Corp Bond	0.51	0.24	1.00										
US LT Govt Bond	0.46	0.21	0.95	1.00									
US IT Govt Bond	0.37	0.13	0.93	0.93	1.00								
US T-Bill	-0.05	0.01	-0.04	-0.02	0.23	1.00							
MSCI EAFE	0.53	0.37	0.20	0.21	0.04	-0.22	1.00						
SB World	0.39	0.13	0.63	0.62	0.67	0.23	0.62	1.00					
Global portfolio with DCS and EMS regional indexes (January 1988–December 1996)													
S&P500	1.00												
US Small Stock	0.71	1.00											
US LT Corp. Bond	0.73	0.59	1.00										
US LT Govt Bond	0.69	0.54	0.98	1.00									
US IT Govt Bond	0.60	0.41	0.95	0.94	1.00								
US T-Bill	0.27	-0.36	0.24	0.18	0.34	1.00							
MSCI EAFE	0.41	0.55	0.25	0.31	0.08	-0.27	1.00						
SB World Govt	0.42	0.38	0.72	0.75	0.75	-0.03	0.05	1.00					
IFCG Composite	0.21	0.33	0.16	0.20	0.11	-0.13	0.81	-0.26	1.00				
MEEAF	-0.03	-0.25	-0.05	0.09	0.08	-0.08	0.33	0.13	0.21	1.00			
Asia	0.14	0.25	0.09	0.13	0.01	-0.11	0.78	-0.39	0.93	0.08	1.00		
Latin America	0.35	0.60	0.31	0.23	0.30	0.00	0.52	-0.01	0.56	0.20	0.31	1.00	
Chosen Country	0.42	0.37	0.25	0.25	0.27	0.08	0.60	0.06	0.34	0.49	0.15	0.55	1.00

TABLE 17.3: *Risk and return of the domestic portfolio (January 1926–December 1996)*

	S&P 500	US Small Stock	US IT Govt Bond	Portfolio
Portfolio Weights	48.58	28.19	23.23	100.00
Average Annual Returns	12.67	17.66	5.36	12.38
Standard Deviations	20.32	34.13	5.77	18.65
Annualized continuously compounded returns				
Portfolio Return	10.32			
Return of Each Asset and the Average	10.30	12.06	5.07	9.58
Return Due to Diversification	0.31	2.53	−0.37	0.78
Return Contribution	10.61	14.58	4.70	10.32

The US Small Stock (1–60 per cent), the IFCG composite index (–13–33 per cent) and the MSCI/EAFE (–27–55 per cent) have low or moderate correlations, while the US T-Bills have the best negative correlations (–27–8 per cent). As for the bonds, high correlations exist among the domestic bond classes (90–96 per cent), but moderate correlations are observed between the domestic and international ones (62–75 per cent). Finally, all regional indexes are advantageous for the benefits of risk reduction and return enhancement.

Domestic Portfolios

As it can be seen in Tables 17.3 through 17.5, for the three periods, the annualized return contributions for the S&P500 are 10.61 per cent, 11.95 per cent and 15.53 per cent. The corresponding return contributions for the Small Stock are 14.58 per cent, 14.70 per cent and 15.15 per cent. The returns due to diversification are 0.31 per cent, 0.33 per cent and 0.47 per cent for the S&P500, and 2.53 per cent, 1.37 per cent, 0.93 per cent for the Small Stock.

The Small Stock has the greatest returns due to diversification. Evaluations on the basis of return contributions give a much higher premium to the Small Cap, particularly for the long run. For the three periods, the differences between the return contributions of the Small Cap and the S&P500 are 3.97 per cent, 2.75 per cent and –0.38 per cent. The corresponding differences between the compound returns are 1.76 per cent, 1.70 per cent and –0.52 per cent.

There are three major explanations for these findings. First, in equation (2), the Small Stock has high return variance, which lowers its compound return. Second, Tables 17.1 and 17.2 reveal the

TABLE 17.4: *Domestic and global portfolios with DCS (January 1970–December 1996)*

	S&P 500	US Small Stock	US IT Govt Bond	Portfolio
Domestic Portfolio Weights	20.33	40.97	38.70	100.00
Average Annual Returns	13.47	16.58	9.25	13.11
Standard Deviations	16.14	23.36	7.02	12.09
Annualized continuously compounded returns				
Portfolio Return				11.66
Return of Each Asset and the Averag	11.63	13.33	8.64	11.17
Return Due to Diversification	0.33	1.37	–0.20	0.55
Return Contribution	11.95	14.70	8.44	11.72
Global portfolio with DCS	US Small Stock	MSCI EAFE	SB World Govt	Portfolio
Portfolio Weights	44.93	9.75	45.31	100.00
Average Annual Returns	16.58	15.34	13.22	14.94
Standard Deviations	23.36	2.29	8.35	12.94
Annualized continuously compounded returns				
Portfolio Return				13.29
Return of Each Asset and the Averag	13.33	12.30	12.14	12.69
Return Due to Diversification	1.28	1.24	–0.10	0.65
Return Contribution	14.62	13.55	12.04	13.34

fact that, compared to the Large Cap, the Small Stock is not highly correlated with other asset classes. Its risk in a diversified portfolio (the covariance of its returns with portfolio returns) is much less than its return variance. In equation (4), this diversification benefit substantially increases the return contribution of the Small Stock to the compound returns on portfolios. Third, the high average annual asset return itself raises the return due to diversification for that particular asset.

Global Portfolios

For the periods of 1970–1996 and 1988–1996, Tables 17.4 through 17.6 present the results for eleven internationally diversified portfolios. In Table 17.4, the returns due to diversification for the Small Stock and MSCI/EAFE are 1.28 per cent and 1.24 per cent respectively, and none for the SB World Govt Bond. In Table 17.5, the return due to diversification for the IFCG composite index, 3.05 per cent and 3.10 per cent, dominates the S&P500 and the SB World Bond significantly. In Table 17.6, I observe more striking results for the portfolios with regional indexes. Latin America, Asia and

TABLE 17.5: *Domestic and global portfolios with DCS and EMS (January 1988–December 1996)*

	S&P 500	US Small Stock	US IT Govt Bond	SB World Govt	IFCG Compo	Portfolio
Domestic portfolio						
Portfolio Weights	63.33	8.18	28.49	–	–	100.00
Average Annual Returns	17.24	17.29	8.53	–	–	13.89
Standard Deviations	14.30	18.99	6.93	–	–	10.33
Annualized continuously compounded returns						
Portfolio Return	–	–	–	–	–	13.58
Return of Each Asset	15.16	14.64	7.98	–	–	13.07
Return Due to						
Diversification	0.47	0.93	–0.22	–	–	0.31
Return Contribution	15.53	15.15	7.62	–	–	13.38
Global portfolio with DCS						
Portfolio Weights	61.02	3.09	–	35.89	–	100.00
Average Annual Returns	17.24	17.29	–	9.59	–	14.49
Standard Deviations	14.30	18.99	–	6.22	–	10.31
Annualized continuously compounded returns						
Portfolio Return	–	–	–	–	–	13.13
Return of Each Asset	15.16	14.64	–	9.00	–	12.93
Return Due to						
Diversification	0.45	0.88	–	0.19	–	0.24
Return Contribution	15.62	15.52	–	8.81	–	13.17
Global portfolio with DCS and EMS						
Portfolio Weights	61.35	–	–	31.97	6.92	100.00
Average Annual Returns	17.24	–	–	9.59	15.14	14.66
Standard Deviation	14.30	–	–	6.22	32.15	10.31
Annualized continuously compounded returns						
Portfolio Return	–	–	–	–	–	13.28
Return of Each Asset	15.16	–	–	9.00	10.20	12.86
Return Due to						
Diversification	0.50	–	–	0.13	3.05	0.80
Return Contribution	15.66	–	–	8.87	13.25	13.34
Global portfolio with EMS						
Portfolio Weights	58.67	–	–	–	41.33	100.00
Average Annual Returns	17.24	–	–	–	22.98	19.61
Standard Deviation	14.30	–	–	–	37.03	19.35
Annualized continuously compounded returns						
Portfolio Return	–	–	–	–	–	16.60
Return of Each Asset	15.16	–	–	–	16.15	15.57
Return Due to						
Diversification	–0.17	–	–	–	3.10	1.18
Return Contribution	14.99	–	–	–	19.26	16.75

TABLE 17.6: *Global portfolios with DCS and EMS regional indexes (January 1988–December 1996) (in per cent)*

	S&P 500	US Small Stock	SB World Govt	Latin America	Asia	MEEAF	Chosen Country Index	Portfolio
Global portfolio with DCS and Latin America								
Portfolio Weights	56.83	–	–	43.17	–	–	–	100.00
Average Annual Returns	17.24	–	–	34.24	–	–	–	24.59
Standard Deviations	14.3	–	–	47.3	–	–	–	24.47
Annualized continuously compounded returns								
Portfolio Return	–	–	–	–	–	–	–	20.06
Return of Each Asset	15.16	–	–	23.24	–	–	–	18.65
Return Due to Diversification	–0.60	–	–	4.39	–	–	–	1.55
Return Contribution	14.56	–	–	27.63	–	–	–	20.20
Global portfolio with DCS and Asia								
Portfolio Weights	61.44	–	31.37	–	7.19	–	–	100.00
Average Annual Returns	17.24	–	9.59	–	16.41	–	–	14.78
Standard Deviations	14.3	–	6.22	–	39.5	–	–	10.31
Annualized continuously compounded returns								
Portfolio Return	–	–	–	–	–	–	–	13.38
Return of Each Asset	15.16	–	9.00	–	9.44	–	–	12.82
Return Due to Diversification	0.51	–	–0.12	–	4.80	–	–	0.62
Return Contribution	15.68	–	8.88	–	14.24	–	–	13.44
Global portfolio with DCS and MEEAF								
Portfolio Weights	–	46.85	–	–	–	53.15	–	100.00
Average Annual Returns	–	17.29	–	–	–	17.99	–	17.66
Standard Deviations	–	18.94	–	–	–	46.22	–	23.92
Annualized continuously compounded returns								
Portfolio Return	–	–	–	–	–	–	–	14.20
Return of Each Asset	14.64	–	–	–	–	8.87	–	11.57
Return Due to Diversification	0.42	–	–	–	–	5.34	–	3.03
Return Contribution	15.05	–	–	–	–	14.21	–	14.61
Global portfolio with DCS and the chosen index								
Portfolio Weights	63.88	–	–	–	–	–	36.12	100.00
Average Annual Returns	17.24	–	–	–	–	–	29.48	21.66
Standard Deviations	14.3	–	–	–	–	–	35.91	18.77
Annualized continuously compounded returns								
Portfolio Return	–	–	–	–	–	–	–	18.42
Return of Each Asset	15.16	–	–	–	–	–	21.99	17.63
Return Due to Diversification	–0.30	–	–	–	–	–	2.99	0.89
Return Contribution	14.86	–	–	–	–	–	24.98	18.52

MEEAF indexes provide quite high returns due to diversification. The corresponding figures are 4.39 per cent, 4.80 per cent and 5.34 per cent respectively. The explanation for this is the same as in the case of the Small Stock.

The S&P500 benefits the least from diversification among other equity classes and usually has a large weight in the portfolios with the lowest returns due to diversification. In the optimization process, if the return contributions are used rather than the compound returns, the S&P500 index would have taken lower weights. The differences between the return contributions are much higher than those between the compound returns.

Finally, the returns due to diversification for the bond classes are, in general, lower than those for the equities. In fact, many of them have negative values. The bond classes have, on average, low returns and variances, and have moderate or high positive correlations.

Comparative Performance of the Portfolios

The Sharpe ratios given in Table 17.7 indicate that the best performances are obtained for the period 1988–1996. Three portfolio combinations, (Domestic & DCS & Asia), (Domestic & DCS & IFCG) and (Domestic & DCS) yield the best results, with a Sharpe ratio slightly greater than 1.40. Those combinations include the domestic market and DCS in all cases. The addition of the IFCG composite index, or the Asia index, contributes little to the reward to variability ratio. It is noteworthy to see that the Domestic portfolio for the period 1988–1996 ranks fourth, with a Sharp ratio of 1.34, although the long-term Domestic portfolio has the lowest Sharpe ratio (66%) and has been dominated by all other portfolios.

As for the returns due to diversification, other three portfolio combinations, (Domestic & DCS & MEEAF) (3.03 per cent), (Domestic & DCS & Latin America) (1.55 per cent) and (Domestic & IFCG) (1.18 per cent) rank at the top. At the same time, as can be expected, these portfolios are the highest return/risk portfolios.

For the period 1988–1996, the shift from 'Domestic & DCS' to 'Domestic & IFCG' portfolio raises the return to diversification by 94 basis points. The corresponding shifts to portfolios with 'Latin America' and 'MEEAF' increase the returns due to diversification by 131 and 279 basis points. The chosen country index does not produce the expected results.

TABLE 17.7: *Comparative performance of the portfolios for all periods (in per cent)*

Asset Mixture	Time Span	Annualized continuousl compounded returns			Annualized simple returns		
		Comp. Return	Return Due to Div.	Portfolio Return	Expected Return	Standard Deviation	Sharpe Ratio*
Domestic Portfolio	1926–96	9.58	0.78	10.32	12.38	18.65	0.66
Domestic Portfolio	1970–96	11.17	0.55	11.72	13.11	12.09	1.08
Domestic & DCS	1970–96	12.69	0.65	13.34	14.94	12.94	1.15
Domestic Portfolio	1988–96	13.07	0.31	13.38	13.89	10.33	1.34
Domestic & DCS	1988–96	12.93	0.24	13.17	14.49	10.31	1.41
Domestic & DCS & IFCG	1988–96	12.86	0.8	13.34	14.66	10.31	1.42
Domestic & IFCG	1988–96	15.57	1.18	16.75	19.61	19.35	1.01
Domestic & DCS & Lat.Am.	1988–96	18.65	1.55	20.20	24.59	24.47	1.01
Domestic & DCS & Asia	1988–96	12.82	0.62	13.44	14.78	10.31	1.43
Domestic & DCS & MEEAF	1988–96	11.57	3.03	14.61	17.66	23.92	0.74
Domestic & DCS & Chosen	1988–96	17.63	0.89	18.52	21.66	18.77	1.15

* Sharpe ratio is obtained by dividing the expected return into the standard deviation.

Summary and Conclusions

Findings of the study show that the risk reduction and return enhancement benefits of global diversification still continue. Moreover, global portfolios without EMS also still perform well. The findings do not imply serious correlation risk or complete integration of financial markets. The lower cross-correlations between DCS and EMS regional indexes indicate a lower degree of segmentation between the two.

When annualized simple returns are used for the optimization, the contributions of EMS and regional indexes to the global portfolios are positive. However, in regard to the Sharpe ratios, the addition of the IFCG composite index or the regional indexes to the global portfolios make very little difference. The country risk criterion does not contribute at all.

However, the findings regarding the returns due to diversification imply that if Sharpe ratios were calculated from the portfolio return and risk based on the return contributions, not the compound or simple returns, the results for the portfolio performance would be different.

The findings for the returns due to diversification conform with the conclusions of Booth and Fama (1992). Since optimal weights are used, the returns due to diversification are larger in this study than theirs, as was expected.

References

AKDOGAN, H. (1996) A suggested approach to country selection in international portfolio diversification, *Journal of Portfolio Management*, (Fall), pp. 33–39.

BOOTH, D. G. and FAMA, E. F. (1992) Diversification returns and asset contributions, *Financial Analysts Journal*, (May/June), pp. 26–32.

DIVECHA, A. B. (1994) Emerging markets and risk reduction, in J. LEDERMAN and R.A. KLEIN (eds.), *Global Asset Allocation*, John Wiley and Sons, Inc., New York, pp. 340–348.

ERB, C. B., HARVEY, C. R. and VISKANTA, T. E. (1995) Country risk and global equity selection, *Journal of Portfolio Management*, (Winter), pp. 74–83.

ERRUNZA, V. R. (1994) Emerging markets: Some new concepts, *Journal of Portfolio Management*, Vol.20, No. 3 (Spring), pp. 82–87.

EUN, C. S. and RESNICK, B. F. (1994) International diversification of investment portfolios: US and Japanese perspectives, *Management Science*, January, pp. 140–161.

GASTINEAU, G. L. (1995) The currency hedging decision: A search for synthesis in asset allocation, *Financial Analysts Journal*, May/June, pp. 8–16.

MACEDO, R. (1995) Value, relative strength and volatility in global equity country selection, *Financial Analysts Journal*, March/April, pp. 70–78.

MICHAUD, R. O., BERGSTROM, G. M., FRASHURE, R. D. and WOLAHAN, B. K. (1996) Twenty years of international equity investing, *Journal of Portfolio Management*, (Fall), pp. 9–22.

MARKOWITZ, H. (1991) *Portfolio Selection: Efficient Diversification of Investments*, Blackwell, Oxford.

SOLNIK, B. H. (1995) Why not diversify internationally rather than domestically? *Financial Analysts Journal*, January/February, pp. 89–93.

SOLNIK, B. H., BOUCRELLE, C. and LE FUR, Y. (1996) International market correlation and volatility, *Financial Analysts Journal*, Vol. 52, No. 5 (September/October), pp. 17–34.

TOBIN, J. (1958) Liquidity preference as behavior towards risk, *Review of Economic Studies*, No. 1, pp. 65–86.

Notes

1. The MSCI/EAFE composite index includes 21 DCS, excluding USA and Canada. The SB World Govt Bond index is comprised of intermediate term bonds.

18

The Analysts' Recommendations and the Effects of Second-Hand Information on Stock Prices: Emerging Market Evidence

HALIL KIYMAZ

Introduction

The question of whether or not trading based on a particular set of information can lead investors to obtain excess returns has been an interesting topic to study in finance literature. There are several studies investigating the effect of analysts' recommendations on stock prices. Analyst recommendations are regular feature of financial publications and contain the opinions of security analysts, who are likely to release such information to their firms' clients first. The main purpose of this study is to investigate whether stock prices of firms appearing in a 'recommended' column react to the information provided in an emerging market setting. Specifically, the study examines the impact of analysts' recommendations (second-hand information), reported in the 'Stock Recommendations' column of '*Para* (Money)' weekly magazine, on stocks traded at Istanbul Stock Exchange. Furthermore the following questions are addressed in the study:

1. Is the price reaction related to the price pressure created by the column itself?
2. Can an investor benefit from trading based on the information provided by the column?
3. Are there any differences in price reaction with respect to firm size?

Studies on analysts' recommendations are mainly related to the market efficiency hypothesis. The strong form of the efficient market hypothesis assumes that all information, whether public or private, is so rapidly incorporated into security prices that no investor can use it to earn excess returns. The empirical studies in this subject report mixed results, although the majority of studies in published literature seem to refute the market efficiency hypothesis in its strongest form. Diefenback (1972) and Logue and Tuttle (1973) are two initial studies reporting that analysts' recommendations have no value for investors. Later studies, on the other hand, report that information heard on the street or provided by analysts contains valuable information to the investor. Lloyd-Davies and Canes' (1978) study focuses on financial analysts' recommendations as discussed in the HOTS column of WSJ. They report that buy recommendations provide significant positive abnormal returns, while sell recommendations are associated with significant negative abnormal returns on the day of publication. They conclude that analysts and investment advisors provide a valuable service to investors. Liu et al. (1990) extend the Lloyd-Davies and Canes (1978) study with more recent samples and further analyse the effects of the single-company versus multi-company recommendations, and the trading volume around the publication day. Their findings are in line with those of former study. Moreover, the results indicate that investors respond earlier to the information and single-company recommendations have greater impact on the stock prices than those of multi-company recommendations.

There are also studies investigating the factors influencing the magnitude of stock market reaction to the analysts' information or recommendation provided by various publications. Beneish (1991) investigates explanations for the significant stock price reaction to analysts' information reported in the 'HOTS' column of the WSJ. The results indicate that market reaction persists after controlling for confounding releases. Furthermore, stock prices adjust prior to publication when recommendations are reported on a single firm. Huth and Maris (1992) examine the same issue in terms of the usefulness to short-term trade decision-making and firm size. The findings indicate that information obtained from columns can produce statistically significant stock price movements. Firm size is found to be important only for negative comments in the column. Barber and Loeffler's (1993) study analyses the stock price and volume behaviours using recommendations published in the Dartboard column of the WSJ. They report average positive abnormal returns of 4 per cent in two days following publication. Furthermore, the average volume was double the normal volume level in the same period.

More recently, Mathur and Waheed (1995) investigated the stock price behaviour of firms that were favourably mentioned in the 'Inside Wall Street' column of Business Week. The results reveal the existence of positive significant abnormal returns on the day before the publication date, the publication date, and two days after the publication date. The study suggests that information provided by the column is valuable to short-term traders if transaction costs are low. Furthermore, the results indicate that investors who invest long term, based on information, obtain rate of returns below market return.

One of the proposed explanations of finding positive abnormal returns around the publication date is that analysts often recommend securities that have recently performed well (Stickel, 1985). Almost all of the studies reporting positive abnormal returns around the publication date utilize a pre-event estimation period to determine market model parameters. The use of the pre-event estimation period may result in biased market model parameters. Specifically, use of a pre-estimation period may result in upward-biased alphas in the market model regression. To avoid such bias, a post-event estimation period is also employed in the study and the results are compared with those of the pre-estimation period to answer the question of whether the stock price reaction is related to the price pressure created by publicity.

The final issue investigated in the paper is related to the size of the firm. Dimson and Marsh (1986) and Huth and Maris (1992) report that returns to investors from published stock recommendations are inversely related to the firm size. Such effect may be an important explanation of the price movements in an emerging market.

The reminder of the study is organized as follows. First I present a brief overview of Istanbul Stock Exchange, followed by the data and methodology. The next section reports and discusses empirical findings, and the final section summarizes and concludes the paper.

Istanbul Stock Exchange

The Istanbul Stock Exchange (ISE) is the only stock exchange in Turkey, and it began operations in 1986. Turkey has a long stock market history dating back to the nineteenth century. The first

Ottoman stock exchange was established in Istanbul after the Crimean War. It closed as a result of the disintegration of the Ottoman Empire, and the outbreak of World War I. In the 1980s the economic liberalization and the applications of free market principles have reemerged. The ISE in its present form, as recognized by international investors, began operation in 1986 following the setting up of the Capital Market Board in 1982. The development of the ISE since its establishment is outlined in Table 18.1.

The number of companies traded on the exchange climbed from 80 at the end of 1986 to 277 at the end of 1998. There are four different markets at the ISE: National Market, Regional Market, New Companies Market, and Watch-List Companies Market. However, the most of firms (94 per cent) are traded at National Market. The total market capitalization of the firms traded has increased from US$938 million at the end of 1986 to US$33.6 billion at the end of 1998. While the number of firms traded has more than tripled over the last 12 years, the total trading value sharply increased from only US$13 million in 1986 to over US$68 billion in 1998.

Data and Methodology

The study uses analysts' recommendations published in the 'Stock Recommendations (SR)' column of '*Para* (Money)' weekly magazine in the period 1995–1997. The SR page is published every week in *Para* magazine. The recommendation clearly states the suggested action to take on a particular stock. The purpose of the page is to

TABLE 18.1: *Developments at the ISE 1986–1998*

Years	Number of Firms	Traded Value (Million US$)	Market Value of Firms (Million US$)
1986	80	13	938
1987	82	118	3125
1988	79	115	1128
1989	76	773	6756
1990	110	5854	18,737
1991	134	8802	15,564
1992	145	8567	9,922
1993	160	21,771	37,824
1994	176	23,203	21,785
1995	205	52,357	20,782
1996	228	37,737	30,797
1997	258	56,015	61,095
1998	277	68,478	33,645

TABLE 18.2: *Sample selection*

	Number of recommendations
Panel A: Sample selection	
All recommendations	797
Less: Subsequently repeated recommendations	109
Less: Missing data	86
Net sample	602
Panel B: Classification of net sample	
Buy recommendations	535
Sell recommendations	67
Total	602

inform investors of the opinions of experts in the market, and facilitate the information flow to individual investors.

Table 18.2 reports the sample selection and the division of final sample based on the type of recommendation. During this period, a total of 797 recommendations are identified. From this sample, recommendations published concerning the same firm in subsequent weeks are eliminated (109). Furthermore, firms with missing stock price data (86) are eliminated. The net sample consists of 602 recommendations.

I, then, classify the net sample based on the type of recommendations. Accordingly, the sample consists of 535 buy recommendations and 67 sell recommendations. Other researchers also note relatively smaller numbers of sell recommendations[1].

The event study methodology is employed to analyse the effects of analysts' recommendations on stock prices as surveyed by Brown and Warner (1985). The following market model is employed.

$$R_{i,t} = \alpha_i + \beta \, R_{m,t} + \varepsilon_{i,t} \qquad (1)$$

Where:
$R_{i,t}$ = return on the common stock of firm i on the day t
$R_{m,t}$ = return on the ISE Composite Index on day t
α, β = regression coefficients
$\varepsilon_{i,t}$ = stochastic error term for firm i on day t.

For each sample observation, calendar time is converted to event time by defining the date of publication as event day 0 (zero)[2]. I estimate the market model for each of the recommendations in the sample, using daily observations of return for the 180 trading days spanning the period from (–210) through (–30), (pre-estimation period), and spanning from (+31) to (+210), (post-estimation period), where day 0 is the publication date of the analysts' recommendation. The analysis period extends from event day −30 to +30. I test for the abnormal performance in the analysis period. For each event i, abnormal returns ($AR_{i,t}$), are calculated for each day in the analysis period.

$$AR_{i,t} = R_{i,t} - (\alpha_i + \beta_i R_{m,t}) \tag{2}$$

Where:
$AR_{i,t}$ = abnormal return for security i on day t
$R_{i,t}$ = observed return for security i on day t
$(\alpha_i + \beta_i R_{m,t})$ = expected return for security i on day t.

The abnormal returns are calculated for each of the 60 days surrounding the event day. Average abnormal returns (AAR_t) across all firms (N) in the sample are calculated for each day in the analysis period.

$$AAR_t = (1/N). \sum_{i=1}^{N} \varepsilon_{i,t} \tag{3}$$

The null hypotheses to be tested are the average abnormal returns in the event period are equal to zero. The following test statistic is used.

$$t_t = (\frac{1}{\sqrt{N}}). \sum_{i=1}^{n} \frac{\varepsilon_{i,t}}{\sigma_i} \tag{4}$$

Where $\varepsilon_{i,t}$ is the error term and σ_i is the standard deviation in the estimation period. Finally, cumulative abnormal returns are calculated in the analysis period.

$$CAR = (1/N) \sum_{t=d_j}^{d_2} \sum_{i=1}^{n} \varepsilon_{i,t} \tag{5}$$

The corresponding test statistic for CARs is calculated as follows:

$$t = \sqrt{(\frac{1}{N.k})}. \sum_{t=d_1}^{d_2} \sum_{i=1}^{n} \frac{\varepsilon_{i,t}}{\sigma_i} \tag{6}$$

Empirical Results

To determine how stock prices are influenced by analysts' recommendations, I initially pose three period analyses. The first examines the effect of recommendations around the publication date. The second looks for unusual activity prior to publication of the recommendations. Finally, I analyse price movement after the publication date.

The empirical results obtained from using the pre-estimation period are reported on Tables 18.3 and Table 18.4. The daily average abnormal returns (AARs) for all recommendations as well as buy and sell recommendations are calculated over −30 and +30 period relative to the event day 0. Only AARs for −10 and +10 period are reported on Table 18.3. The results indicate that the whole sample experiences statistically significant positive abnormal returns prior to publication of recommendation. The AARs are 0.33 per cent, 0.60 per cent, 0.82 per cent, and 0.25 per cent for the days −4, −2, −1 and +1 respectively. These results are statistically significant, where AARs in days −2, and −1 are highly significant. The AARs after day +1 are mostly negative and statistically significant on day +2. These results show a significant price reversal after the publication. For example, AARs are −0.10 per cent on day +2, −0.42 per cent on day +3, −0.20 per cent on day +4, and −0.05 per cent on day +5. Only AARs on day +3 is statistically significant at the one per cent level.

The findings of buy and sell recommendations are also reported in Table 18.3. The results of buy recommendations are similar to those of the whole sample. The AARs are positive and statistically significant in days prior to publication and the day after publication. The magnitude of AARs appears to be larger. For example, the AARs on days −2 and −1 are 0.72 per cent and 0.91 per cent, and highly significant. Furthermore, there appears to be greater price reversal in the days after day +1. For example, AARs on day +2 and +6 are −0.48 per cent and −0.35, and both are statistically significant: 0.82 per cent, and 0.25 per cent for the days −4, −2, −1 and +1 respectively. These results are statistically significant, where AARs in days −2 and −1 are highly significant. The AARs after day +1 are mostly negative and statistically significant on day +2.

Sell recommendations, on the other hand, experience mostly negative, statistically insignificant stock price reaction in pre- and post-publication periods. For example, the AARs on day −3 and −2 are −0.60 per cent and −0.38 per cent and on day +1 and +2 are −0.06 per cent and 0.04 per cent respectively.

TABLE 18.3: *Daily Average Abnormal Returns (AARs) using pre-estimation period*

Event days	All Recommendations (n=602)		Buy Recommendations (n=535)		Sell Recommendations (n=67)	
	AARs (%)	t-value	AARs (%)	t-value	AARs (%)	t-value
−10	0.10	0.70	0.09	0.83	0.20	0.23
−9	0.02	0.09	0.07	0.39	−0.35	−0.82
−8	−0.10	−0.53	−0.21	−0.99	0.74	1.21
−7	0.33	2.18**	0.30	1.87*	0.65	1.25
−6	0.20	1.33	0.25	1.59	−0.27	−0.52
−5	0.02	0.20	0.06	0.04	−0.26	−0.72
−4	0.33	2.53**	0.30	2.20**	0.58	1.38
−3	0.08	0.97	0.16	1.41	−0.60	−1.06
−2	0.60	4.25***	0.72	4.73***	−0.38	−0.61
−1	0.82	5.84***	0.91	6.11***	0.04	0.28
0	–	–	–	–	–	–
+1	0.25	1.91*	0.29	2.03**	−0.06	−0.01
+2	−0.10	−0.87	−0.12	−0.94	0.04	0.05
+3	−0.42	−2.75***	−0.48	−3.05***	0.07	0.37
+4	−0.20	−1.10	−0.14	−0.64	−0.67	−1.53
+5	−0.05	−0.14	−0.12	−0.49	0.56	0.97
+6	−0.26	−1.80	−0.35	−2.16**	0.42	0.71
+7	−0.15	−0.86	−0.15	−0.76	−0.12	−0.44
+8	−0.17	−1.01	−0.11	−0.56	−0.65	−1.45
+9	0.11	1.02	0.09	0.98	0.27	0.28
+10	−0.15	−0.35	−0.16	−0.27	−0.08	−0.27

***, **, and * are statistically significant at 1%, 5% and 10% respectively.
Event day (0) represents the day of publication of recommendations and corresponds to Sundays.

To get a better view of the stock price reaction to the published recommendations, the average cumulative abnormal returns (CARs) for all sample and sub-samples are reported on Table 18.4, which has three parts. In the first part of the table, CARs in and around the publication date are reported. The results indicate that firms experience statistically significant positive abnormal returns in event windows (−1, +1), (−2, +2), (−5, +5), and (−10, +10). For example, during (−1, +1), (−2, +2), and (−5, +5) periods, CARs are 1.06 per cent, 1.56 per cent, and 1.33 per cent respectively. All of them are statistically significant at the one per cent level. In longer time periods firms experience negative insignificant abnormal returns. For example, during the (−30, +30) period, CARs are −1.62 per cent. Similar results are obtained in buy recommendations with the magnitude of abnormal returns being higher. For example, the CARs are 1.20 per cent and 1.80 per cent in event windows (−1, +1) and (−2, +2) respectively. Sell recommendations, on the other hand,

TABLE 18.4: *Cumulative Abnormal Returns (CARs) using pre-estimation period*

Windows	All Recommendations (n=602)		Buy Recommendations (n=535)		Sell Recommendations (n=67)	
	CARs (%)	t-value	CARs (%)	t-value	CARs (%)	t-value
Combined periods						
(−1,+1)	1.06	5.49***	1.20	5.75***	−0.02	−0.20
(−2,+2)	1.56	5.57***	1.80	5.96***	−0.36	−0.13
(−5,+5)	1.33	3.31***	1.57	3.59***	−0.66	−0.26
(−10,+10)	1.26	2.51**	1.40	2.76***	−0.14	−0.25
(−20,+20)	0.27	1.19	0.70	1.76*	−3.12	−1.42
(−30,+30)	−1.62	−0.41	−1.37	−0.08	−3.58	−1.26
Prior to publication date						
(−5,−1)	1.84	5.99***	2.15	6.47***	−0.61	−0.32
(−10,−1)	2.40	5.43***	2.66	5.75***	0.35	0.04
(−20,−1)	2.01	3.60***	2.37	4.06***	−0.82	−0.65
After publication date						
(+1,+5)	−0.51	−1.32	−0.57	−1.38	−0.05	−0.04
(+1,+10)	−1.14	−1.88*	−1.25	−1.86*	−0.21	−0.40

***, **, and * are statistically significant at 1%, 5% and 10% respectively.
Event day (0) represents the day of publication of recommendations and corresponds to Sundays.

seem to yield negative insignificant stock price reaction during all event periods under consideration. Based on these results, one would conclude that second-hand analyst buy recommendations provide valuable information to investors. Trading based on recommendations would provide statistically significant abnormal returns. But these returns may not be economically significant when the transaction costs are taken into the account.

I further analyse the behaviour of stock prices in the period prior to and following the publication of recommendations. In the middle part of Table 18.4, the CARs in the pre-publication period for several windows are reported. The CARs in the pre-publication periods are positive and statistically significant. For example during the (−20, −1), (−10, −1) and (−5, −1) periods, the CARs are 2.01 per cent, 2.40 per cent and 1.84 per cent respectively. They are all statistically significant at the one per cent level. The significant stock price reaction in pre-publication days may suggest that the information provided by the analysts to their clients has value. Those who possess the information initially can benefit from the recommendations. The second possible interpretation can be attributed to the nature of the Recommendations column itself. Typically, the stocks

TABLE 18.5: *Daily Average Abnormal Returns (AARs) using post-estimation period*

Event days	All Recommendations (n=602)		Buy Recommendations (n=535)		Sell Recommendations (n=67)	
	AARs (%)	t-value	AARs (%)	t-value	AARs (%)	t-value
−10	0.20	1.70*	0.17	1.39	0.40	1.17
−9	0.07	0.31	0.13	0.79	−0.41	−1.31
−8	−0.13	−0.69	−0.22	−1.16	0.61	1.21
−7	0.44	3.07***	0.40	2.52**	0.76	2.06**
−6	0.30	2.12**	0.36	2.34**	−0.17	−0.26
−5	0.05	0.21	0.09	0.50	−0.20	−0.77
−4	0.39	3.01***	0.34	2.42**	0.82	2.19**
−3	0.21	1.79*	0.30	2.32**	−0.48	−1.20
−2	0.72	5.82***	0.85	6.30***	−0.36	−0.37
−1	0.86	6.38***	0.98	6.68***	−0.04	−0.26
0	−	−	−	−	−	−
+1	0.30	2.28**	0.34	2.41**	−0.02	−0.03
+2	−0.04	−0.17	−0.07	−0.45	0.25	0.76
+3	−0.25	1.88*	−0.30	−2.07**	0.15	0.22
+4	−0.08	−0.49	0.00	0.03	−0.68	−1.60
+5	0.03	0.09	−0.05	−0.51	0.64	1.18
+6	−0.14	−1.06	−0.21	−1.49	0.45	1.03
+7	−0.08	−0.55	−0.07	−0.53	−0.17	−0.13
+8	−0.06	−0.57	−0.01	−0.14	−0.55	−1.32
+9	0.28	2.02**	0.26	1.78**	0.40	1.08
+10	−0.03	−0.01	−0.01	−0.01	−0.16	−0.62

***, **, and * are statistically significant at 1%, 5% and 10% respectively.
Event day (0) represents the day of publication of recommendations and corresponds to Sundays.

mentioned in the column are those that recently have been performing well. This issue is elaborated later in this paper.

Finally, in the last part of Table 18.4, CARs in the post-publication period are analysed. The CARs for (+1, +5), and (+1, +10) windows are negative for all recommendations, buy recommendations and sell recommendations. For example, the buy recommendations experience CARs of −0.57 per cent, and −1.24 per cent during the event windows of (+1, +5) and (+1, +10) respectively. Only window (+1, +10) is statistically weakly significant. These results would suggest that an investor buying a stock at the first day closing price would not benefit from recommendations. The negative gains in the post-publication period would support the view that trading based on published recommendations would not benefit investors and that the information has no value.

In general the empirical results, using the pre-estimation period, indicate the existence of positive statistically significant abnormal

TABLE 18.6: *Cumulative Abnormal Returns (CARs) using post-estimation period*

Windows	All Recommendations (n=602)		Buy Recommendations (n=535)		Sell Recommendations (n=67)	
	CARs (%)	t-value	CARs (%)	t-value	CARs (%)	t-value
Combined periods						
(−1,+1)	1.16	6.13***	1.31	6.42***	−0.06	−0.21
(−2,+2)	1.84	7.15***	2.09	7.47***	−0.16	−0.34
(−5,+5)	2.21	5.33***	2.47	5.57***	0.08	0.22
(−10,+10)	3.05	5.19***	3.28	5.21***	1.23	0.81
(−20,+20)	4.28	5.47***	4.68	5.62***	1.08	0.57
(−30,+30)	4.56	5.01***	4.78	4.89***	2.82	1.21
Prior to publication date						
(−5,−1)	2.24	7.70***	2.55	8.15***	−0.25	−0.05
(−10,−1)	3.12	7.50***	3.39	7.62***	0.92	0.94
(−20,−1)	3.72	6.70***	4.04	6.85***	1.17	0.71
After publication date						
(+1,+5)	−0.03	−0.16	−0.08	−0.26	0.33	0.27
(+1,+10)	−0.06	−0.16	−0.11	−0.24	0.30	0.20

***, **, and * are statistically significant at 1%, 5% and 10% respectively.
Event day (0) represents the day of publication of recommendations and corresponds to Sundays.

returns in the pre-publication period of recommendations. Such findings would refute the strong form of market efficiency, which is in line with existing literature. The statistically significant abnormal returns, however, may not be economically profitable when the transaction costs are taken into account. The findings pertaining to the post-publication period of recommendations, on the other hand, reveal that there are statistically insignificant negative abnormal returns. This suggests that investment strategies based on the published analyst recommendations would not generate any wealth gains to investors, implying that information provided by the column has no value at all.

To investigate the issue of whether the analysts recommend the stocks that have been performing well recently, I test the robustness of previous findings pertaining to the reaction of stock prices by employing post-estimation period data. Using post-event period data instead of pre-estimation period data may eliminate the bias introduced in market model parameters in using a pre-estimation period. The results of analysis by employing post-event estimation period data are reported in Tables 18.5 and 18.6. The AARs in prior to the publication day appears to be higher. AARs on the four days prior to publication day and on the actual day of publication range between 0.21 per cent and 0.86 per cent for the whole sample, 0.30 per cent and 0.98 per cent for buy recommendations. They are all statistically significant at least the five per cent level. An important finding is the existence of statistically significant positive abnormal returns for sell recommendations on days −7 and −4. The CARs pertaining to the use of the post-estimation period are reported on Table 18.6. All CARs in combined and pre-publication event windows are positive and statistically highly significant. For example, (−20, +20) and (−20, −1) windows experience CARs of 4.28 per cent and 3.72 per cent, respectively. Both are statistically significant at the one per cent level. During the post-publication periods, all CARs are negative for all recommendations and buy recommendations and positive for sell recommendations. None of these results are statistically significant. Furthermore, the magnitude of positive abnormal returns appears to be higher when post-estimation period data is employed. These findings suggest that there is not a significant price reversal when the post-estimation period data is employed, implying that analyst recommendations provide valuable information in the pre-publication period regardless of the types of estimation periods utilized. Hence, the results show that abnormal returns are not due to recommending stocks which recently perform well, but are rather due to the valuable information provided by analysts to their clients.

Finally, to evaluate the relationship between the firm size and market reaction to published analysts' recommendations; the firms are classified into large firms and small firms using the market value of equity. While firms with market values above five trillion TL are classified as large firms, firms with market values below one trillion TL are classified as small firms[3]. This classification yielded 107 small firms and 161 large firms in buy recommendations, and 15 small and 29 large firms in sell recommendations. Tables 18.7 and 18.8 show results for the small and large firms in buy and sell recommendations. With respect to buy recommendations, small firms experience higher abnormal returns than larger firms do. For example; AARs on day −2 and −1 are 1.26 per cent and 1.56 per cent respectively for small firms, while the AARs on day −2 and −1 are 0.40 per cent and 0.80 per cent for large firms. Panel B of Table 18.7 reports CARs for small and large firms with respect to sell recommendations. The magnitude of abnormal returns for small firms is almost twice as much as those of larger firms. The difference is more pronounced in pre-publication period CARS. For example, during the (−20, −1) window, small firm CARs are 5.98 per cent compared to 2.57 per cent for the large firms sample. These results seem to be in line with the interpretation that the stocks of smaller firms are more responsive to the release of the analysts' recommendations to their firm's clients than are the prices of larger firms. These findings are similar to those reported by Huth and Maris (1992) with respect to size effects and analysts' recommendations. Another interesting point to note is the differences in price reversal in small and large firm samples. In the smaller firms, the price reversal was not found to be as significant as in the larger firms. The large firm sample experiences a statistically significant price reversal on day +2 and +3 with a magnitude of −0.40 per cent, and −0.49 per cent respectively.

The comparison of small and large firms' AARs and CARs in sell recommendations are reported in Table 18.8. The findings do not show any significant differences between two groups although pre-publication returns are mostly negative for large firms and mostly positive for small firms.

Summary and Conclusions

The question of whether trading based on a particular set of information can lead investors to obtain abnormal returns continues to receive attention from researchers and investors. There are several studies investigating the effect of analysts' recommendations or rumours on stock prices. A vast majority of these studies report statistically significant stock price reaction to the publication of information and conclude that such information has value.

The purpose of this study is to investigate the second-hand effects of analysts' recommendations on the prices of stocks traded at the Istanbul Stock Exchange. Additionally, the paper investigates the issues of whether an investor can gain by using analysts' recommendation after their publication. The sample consists of 535 buy and 67 sell recommendations reported in *Para* weekly magazine. The empirical findings suggest that there are statistically significant abnormal returns around the publication date. While positive, significant abnormal returns are observed in each of the four days prior to the publication date for all recommendations and buy recommendations, insignificant negative reaction is noted for sell recommendations. Furthermore, statistically significant price reversals are detected for whole sample and buy recommendations. This possibly suggests that investors making investment decisions based on the publication of a recommendation may not benefit from it.

TABLE 18.7: *Buy recommendations and firm size*

	Small Firms (n=107)		Large Firms (n=161)	
Panel A: Daily Average Abnormal Returns (AARs)				
Event days	AARs (%)	t-value	AARs (%)	t-value
−10	−0.06	−0.05	0.62	2.14**
−9	0.26	0.67	0.24	1.19
−8	−0.49	−0.69	−0.14	−0.63
−7	1.08	2.85***	0.25	1.04
−6	0.26	0.18	0.34	1.45
−5	0.92	2.26**	−0.28	−0.90
−4	0.92	2.54**	0.43	1.94**
−3	−0.31	−0.67	0.52	2.56**
−2	1.26	3.14***	0.40	1.17
−1	1.56	3.74***	0.80	3.37***
0	−	−	−	−
+1	−0.22	−0.53	0.63	2.18**
+2	0.44	1.12	−0.40	−1.75*
+3	−0.43	−1.25	−0.49	−1.92*
+4	−0.22	−0.55	−0.06	−0.06
+5	−0.14	−0.06	0.07	0.30
+6	−0.14	−0.96	−0.03	−0.01
+7	0.11	0.53	−0.25	−0.69
+8	−0.42	−1.30	0.04	0.07
+9	0.25	0.88	−0.06	−0.15
+10	−0.63	−1.47	−0.19	−0.13
Panel B: Cumulative Abnormal Returns (CARs)				
Windows	CARs (%)	t-value	CARs (%)	t-value
Combined periods				
(−1,+1)	1.33	2.27**	1.42	3.92***
(−2,+2)	3.04	3.73***	1.43	2.49**
(−5,+5)	3.76	3.07***	1.61	2.17**
(−10,+10)	2.99	1.88**	2.43	2.56**
(−20,+20)	1.94	1.23	1.04	1.31
(−30,+30)	−1.94	−0.17	−0.53	−0.30
Prior to publication date				
(−5,−1)	4.33	4.93***	1.87	3.64***
(−10,−1)	5.39	4.43***	3.17	4.22***
(−20,−1)	5.98	3.71***	2.57	2.76***
After publication date				
(+1,+5)	−0.58	−0.57	−0.25	−0.56
(+1,+10)	−1.39	−0.77	−0.74	−0.59

***, **, and * are statistically significant at 1%, 5% and 10% respectively.

TABLE 18.8: *Sell recommendations and firm size*

	Small Firms (n=15)		Large Firms (n=29)	
Panel A: Daily Average Abnormal Returns (AARs)				
Event days	AARs (%)	t-value	AARs (%)	t-value
−10	2.11	1.86*	0.53	0.28
−9	0.39	0.13	−0.49	−0.84
−8	1.33	1.02	−0.18	−0.29
−7	0.75	0.60	1.06	1.52
−6	−0.66	−0.55	−0.49	−0.46
−5	1.17	0.80	−0.04	−0.01
−4	0.23	0.21	0.13	0.17
−3	−0.52	−0.36	−0.94	−1.40
−2	−0.86	−0.59	−0.51	−0.60
−1	0.66	1.07	0.15	−0.24
0	–	–	–	–
+1	−0.23	−0.11	0.77	1.14
+2	1.97	1.72*	−1.10	−1.59
+3	−2.26	−1.99**	1.06	1.56
+4	−0.26	−0.14	−1.12	−2.08**
+5	1.80	1.16	0.37	0.64
+6	1.10	0.75	0.29	0.51
+7	−0.54	−0.51	−0.89	−1.47
+8	−0.45	−0.30	−0.73	−1.12
+9	−1.40	−0.95	0.59	0.39
+10	0.54	0.43	−0.89	−1.45
Panel B: Cumulative Abnormal Returns (CARs)				
Windows	CARs (%)	t-value	CARs (%)	t-value
Combined periods				
(−1,+1)	0.43	0.79	0.61	0.63
(−2,+2)	1.54	1.12	−0.99	−0.65
(−5,+5)	1.70	0.60	−1.52	−0.73
(−10,+10)	4.86	0.98	−2.71	−1.17
(−20,+20)	5.37	0.56	−7.08	−1.78*
(−30,+30)	2.94	0.16	−6.69	−1.37
Prior to publication date				
(−5,−1)	0.68	0.47	−1.51	−0.93
(−10,−1)	4.60	1.30	−1.07	−0.59
(−20,−1)	5.59	0.95	−4.23	−1.41
After publication date				
(+1,+5)	1.01	0.38	−0.02	−0.10
(+1,+10)	0.26	0.09	−1.64	−1.06

***, **, and * are statistically significant at 1%, 5% and 10% respectively.

However, the significant stock price reaction in pre-publication days may indicate that information has value for clients of the analyst's firm. The issue that analysts usually recommend firms which perform well recently is investigated by re-analysing the stock price reaction around the publication date utilizing post-estimation period data. By using post-estimation data potential bias introduced by upward alpha is avoided. The findings indicate that there are still statistically positive price reactions around the publication period, indicating that information provided by analysts is valuable and is not a publicity stunt per se. Finally, the relationship between price reaction and firm size is investigated. The results show that the stocks of smaller firms are more responsive to the release of the analysts' recommendations to their firm's clients than are the prices of larger firms, while the price reversal appears to be more pronounced in larger firms than smaller firms.

References

BARBER, B. M. and LOEFFLER, D. (1993) The Dartboard column: Second-hand information and price pressure, *Journal of Financial and Quantitative Analysis*, Vol. 28, pp. 273–283.

BENEISH, M. D. (1991) Stock prices and the dissemination of analysts' recommendations, *Journal of Business*, Vol. 64, pp. 393–416.

BROWN, S. J. and WARNER, J. B. (1985) Using daily stock returns: The case of event studies, *Journal of Financial Economics*, Vol. 14, pp. 3–31.

DIEFENBACK, R. (1972) How good is institutional brokerage research? *Financial Analysts Journal*, Vol. 28, pp. 54–60.

DIMSON, E. and MARSH, P. (1986) Event study methodologies and the size effect: The case of UK press recommendations, *Journal of Financial Economics*, Vol. 17, pp. 113–142.

HUTH, W. L. and MARIS, B. A. (1992) Large and small firm stock price responses to Heard On The Street recommendations, *Journal of Accounting and Auditing*, Vol. 7, pp. 27–47.

LIU, P., SMITH, D. and SYED, A. (1990) Stock reaction to the Wall Street Journal's securities recommendations, *Journal of Financial and Quantitative Analysis*, Vol. 25, pp. 399–410.

LLOYD-DAVIES, P. and CANES, M. (1978) Stock prices and publication of second-hand information, *Journal of Business*, Vol. 51, pp. 43–56.

LOGUE, D. and TUTTLE, D. (1973) Brokerage houses investment advice, *The Financial Review*, Vol. 8, pp. 38–54.

MATHUR, I. and WAHEED, A. (1995) Stock price reactions to securities recommended in Business Week's Inside Wall Street, *The Financial Review*, Vol. 30, pp. 583–604.

STICKEL, S. E. (1985) The effect of value line investment survey rank changes on common stock prices, *Journal of Financial Economics*, Vol. 14, pp. 121–143.

Notes

I would like to thank Fernanda M. Garcia for her excellent research assistance.

1. The following reasons are commonly cited for the shortages of sell recommendations: 1) the availability of fewer target clients for sell recommendations than buy recommendations. To sell a stock, investor must own the stock or be willing to short sell stock, indicating smaller potential commissions for broker; 2) analysts are unwilling to alienate managers, who are sources of information.
2. *Para* weekly magazine is published and distributed on Sundays. Hence, there is no trading on the day of publication.
3. The purpose of selection of one and five trillion TL as a benchmark in determining small and large firms was to maximize the differences in size of small and large firms and at the same time still have groups large enough to allow meaningful analysis.

19

Banking, Economic Development and Integration

EDGAR ORTIZ and JEAN-PIERRE GUEYIE

Introduction

The importance of financial markets and financial institutions in economic development has been clearly established by numerous authors. A common denominator of these studies has been to recommend financial liberalization to enhance the role of financial markets and institutions, which are frequently 'repressed' in the developing economies by excessive regulation and high direct intervention of the state in the financial sector, by developing banking and direct controls on interest and credit allocations.

This policy has been followed by developing nations during the last two decades, in the aftermath of the debt crisis and induced by economic and financial globalization. Among other 'modernization' changes, these countries have implemented profound reforms in their financial sector to be able to open up their economies advantageously to the world markets and achieve high and sustained rates of economic development. An alternative strategy, for responding to the challenges of global competitive markets and enhancing development, has been to promote economic integration which, on a worldwide basis, has led to the formation of strong economic blocs. Both economic development and economic integration depend significantly on the soundness of local financial markets and institutions and their capacity to respond to those two challenges. At the end of the of the twentieth century, the world's global economic and political scenario changed substantially due to the fall of the Berlin Wall and the re-unification of Germany, the fall of State-led (totalitarian) socialism, and above all, the end of the 'cold war'. The world is therefore undergoing a true transition towards a new economic order led by free markets and their institutions.

Banking institutions are accordingly called to play an important role in the new developing processes of both emerging and transition economies[1]. Financial literature has studied banking institutions in these countries extensively during the last few years. However, those studies have been limited to examining the nature of banking crisis, neglecting to assess the role of the banking sector on economic development and economic integration.

This chapter aims to overcome such limitation by building up a conceptual framework to analyse the role of banking institutions in developing nations in the context of economic development tempered by economic liberalization and economic integration schemes. This is a necessary step in the path to strengthen, in the forthcoming decades of the new millennium, deregulation and liberalization policies that can prevent re-occurrences of twin currency and banking crisis in the developing and transition economies, and similarly prevent costly banking rescue programmes[2].

Financial Intermediation and Economic Development

Financial Assets and Institutions and Growth

Economic theory presents astonishingly different views concerning the importance of the financial system for economic development. In deep contrast to the dominant theories, which express either skepticism or lack of interest about the role of financial markets and institutions in development, the theories on financial development pioneered by Gurley and Shaw (1960), Goldsmith (1968, 1969), McKinnon (1973), Bennet (1965), Patrick (1966), Shaw (1973) and later further elaborated by Fry (1988, 1989), Galbis (1977), Gupta (1984), Ortiz (1993; 1995) and others[3] maintain that the financial sector is important in development. The rate of growth and the quality of economic development of an economy depends not only on real variables and their technological parameters, but also on financial variables and their functional relationships with real variables. Equilibrium conditions for an economy can, therefore, be defined in terms of financial variables and financial markets (Gurley and Shaw, 1960, p. 3).

Furthermore, financial development theories also define the role of financial institutions in development. Financial institutions can promote economic development by assuming, in the provision of their services and lending power, an innovative supply-leading role rather than a demand-following approach to development. Certain financial intermediation techniques can be developed to enhance the process of economic growth. To this category belong financial techniques such as efficient credit management, improved communications, lower transaction costs, innovations, and especially the development of various types of securities and their markets, and the development of financial intermediation institutions (Ibid, pp. 125–126).

Concretely, an economic system is an aggregate of spending units and financial intermediaries. Spending units engage primarily in the transaction of goods and services. Financial intermediaries specialize in financial transactions. Spending units include three sectors: (1) consumer households, which sell their labour services in exchange for wage income; (2) business firms, which own physical capital and combine it with labour services to produce national output; and (3) government spending units (independent of the government financial sector) (Ibid, pp. 13–14). Spending units are also divided into deficit spending units, and surplus spending units depending on whether their disposable income is less than or greater than their expenditure. Generally, households are surplus units and business firm are deficit units. This specialization by households in savings and by business enterprises in investment is the basis for debt, financial assets, and financial institutions, i.e., financial intermediation. The function of financial intermediaries is to promote the transfer of funds from savers to investors (Bennet, 1965, pp. 6–7).

The financial intermediation sector is composed of monetary intermediaries and non-monetary intermediaries, including government financial intermediaries. Monetary intermediaries, i.e., banking institutions, are those which have money as part of their liabilities. In the case of non-monetary financial intermediaries (mutual savings banks, savings and loan associations, insurance companies, etc.), none of their liabilities are part of the medium of exchange (Ibid, pp. 6–7).

Financial intermediaries specialize in the transaction of financial assets. The term 'financial assets' refers to both primary and indirect securities. Primary securities are all the liabilities and outstanding equities of non-financial units; they are assumed to be issued only by the business sector. Indirect securities are the liabilities and equities of financial intermediaries, and can be further classified as money and non-monetary indirect securities. Money is a medium of exchange and it can be a liability of monetary intermediaries. Non-monetary indirect securities are all other liabilities of financial intermediaries, i.e., claims issued against themselves (Ibid, p.7).

Business firms finance their investment opportunities in three ways: (1) internal resources or self-financing through retained earnings; (2) direct financing by issuing direct securities which are purchased by households; and (3) indirect financing. Primary securities issued by business firms are purchased by financial intermediaries; the latter issue their own liabilities – indirect securities – to surplus spending units (Goldsmith, 1968).

Indirect debt is the most advantageous to the economic growth of a nation. Self-financing would limit investment to the amounts of internal resources available. Similarly, direct financing can limit the size of investments made because the issues of business firms may not accommodate the portfolio needs and preferences of surplus spending units in terms of risk, liquidity, maturity, legal size, currency redeemability, transaction costs, or any combination of these factors (Ibid, pp. 26–28).

To fully exploit the ability of a society to accumulate productive capital, it is therefore important to bridge the gap in needs and preferences between savers and investors. Financial intermediaries help to bridge this gap by issuing indirect debt in the form of financial assets tailored to the needs and preferences of households (Ibid, pp. 27–28). Thus, financial intermediaries develop when it is necessary or preferable to substitute indirect for direct external financing.

The existence of surplus and deficit units as well as financial assets to promote the transfer of funds is a necessary but insufficient condition for the development of financial intermediaries; funds could be transferred directly between surplus units and deficit units. However, no transfer of funds would take place if the financial instruments available could not meet the preferences of surplus units (Ibid, p. 25).

The existence of a channel of communication between savers and investors is, therefore, as important to economic expansion as savings themselves, for it permits access for needed funds (Gurley and Shaw, pp. 196–197). The capacity of growth in an economy could be limited by its financial system and its structure. With no financial assets other than money and direct debt, there are impediments to savings and capital formation. The inefficient allocation of savings to investment results in decreases in output and income. In contrast to an economy where there are developed markets and institutions for financial claims, a rudimentary economy would tend to attain lower levels of savings and investment at each level of income, and hence lower rates of economic growth (Ibid, p. 13).

Financial Intermediation and Efficiency in Savings and Investment

Savings has been identified as the main factor determining investments and economic growth. Financial intermediation enhances them by specializing in the transaction of financial assets. Indeed, the raison d'être of economic specialization is efficiency. Financial intermediaries promote efficiency in the savings–investment process by (1) creating various and attractive financial assets and using efficient financial intermediation techniques; (2) exploiting economies of scale in lending and borrowing so that the marginal value of investments increases; and (3) regulating capital flows to make feasible at certain locations interdependent or large-scale indivisible projects.

Furthermore, financial intermediaries contribute to enhance the savings and investment processes in various ways:

1. As pointed out earlier, financial intermediation allows the mobilization of funds from surplus units to deficit units. In the absence of indirect debt, investment would be limited to the internal resources of an organization and, at most, by direct financing.
2. Intermediation techniques turn primary securities into indirect securities for the portfolio of ultimate lenders. By creating a wide variety of financial assets suited to the needs of ultimate lenders, financial intermediaries help ease the need of borrowers to issue securities which may not be appropriate for their type of business, for example, contractual insurance plans (Ibid, p.197). Specialization in financial intermediation allows investing units to concentrate on the efficient production of goods and services.
3. Intermediation techniques increase the level of savings. By creating assets suited to the needs of households, financial intermediaries help eliminate excess and/or surplus consumption. Consumers can purchase from financial intermediaries' financial assets to suit their needs and preferences, such as savings deposits, certificates of deposit, pension plans, insurance contracts, etc. In turn, financial intermediaries can purchase direct securities from business firms and finance their investments. As a general rule, the short-term securities issued by financial

intermediaries are more liquid, more easily divisible, easier and less costly to transact, and less risky than direct securities. Long-term securities issued by financial intermediaries also share those characteristics, with the exception of transferability. In addition, long-term securities are tailored to fit households' needs, such as in the case of insurance and pension contracts (Ibid, p. 194).

4. Financial intermediaries bear risk and illiquidity. The reward for their operations comes from the difference between the rate of return between primary securities and indirect securities. Intermediaries can attain such economic gain by using economies of scale in borrowing and lending, and especially by efficient management of their portfolios.

5. Resource allocation becomes more efficient. Financial intermediaries and their techniques help to establish an efficient ordering of investments. By classifying investments more extensively by their own characteristics, financial intermediaries help to exclude the allocation of funds to inferior investments. Financial intermediaries are themselves selective in the process of fund allocation; in addition, direct financing also becomes more efficient since the operations of financial intermediaries affect supply and demand for direct securities.

6. The creation of indirect securities to fund investments is not limited to cash balances of individual households. All financial intermediaries create financial assets. Monetary intermediaries create money when they purchase primary securities; non-monetary intermediaries create various forums of non-monetary indirect assets when they purchase money. The difference between monetary and non-monetary intermediaries is not that one creates and the other does not, but rather that each creates its own form of debt. Credit creation of this manner, with or without reserve requirements, is important to an economy. It allows it to increase its capacity to invest without simultaneous increases in goods and services, but rather in relation to the present value of existing investment opportunities.

7. Financial assets issued by financial intermediaries simplify and enhance portfolio selection from surplus units. In the first place, savers do not have to search through all types of securities to choose those which fit their needs. Second, indirect assets have, and introduce, a degree of differentiation themselves. Savers can choose not only between the assets offered by monetary and non-monetary financial intermediaries, but also some direct

securities too. Thus, the portfolio of households can become more diversified.

8. Financial intermediaries also strengthen and enhance the efficiency and benefits of the savings–investment process by attaining economies of scale in lending and borrowing so that the utility of money increases. As Gurley and Shaw (1960) point out, on the lending side financial intermediaries can invest and manage investment on primary securities at unit costs well below the standards achieved by individual lenders. Also, large-size portfolios allow financial intermediaries to achieve a significant reduction in risk through financial asset diversification.

9. Finally, financial intermediaries can minimize liquidity crises by proper scheduling of the purchase of direct securities of different maturities, including long-term securities (Ibid). Similarly, on the borrowing side, financial intermediaries can attract a large number of depositors and rely fairly well on a schedule of claims for repayments; hence, they can operate with relatively illiquid portfolios (Ibid). In turn, financial intermediaries can distribute the advantages of their economies of scale in borrowing and lending to their debtors in the form of favourable terms of lending, to their creditors in the form of stable returns and other services, and to their stockholders in the form of adequate dividend payments, which may also help to attract additional capital funds (Ibid).

Thus, acting independently, individual investors cannot optimize their portfolio by diversification due to the limited amount of their savings as well as to the indivisibility of many direct financial assets; in addition, individual savers cannot usually support long-term investments due to their particular liquidity needs. The pooling of savings resources allows financial intermediaries to purchase different types of securities and minimize risk due to diversification. Hence, consistent with current portfolio theory, at certain levels of risk financial intermediaries can attain higher rates of return than would be feasible to individual savers; conversely, for a level of interest returns, financial intermediaries can attain lower levels of risk. The pooling of funds and the channeling of investments through financial intermediaries are therefore advantageous to society. As pointed out earlier, the benefits of resource pooling are shared by financial intermediaries with savers and investors. In addition, the allocation of resources is more efficient through the selectivity of financial intermediaries; this means that, for equal levels of savings, a nation can achieve greater levels of output.

By controlling financial flows, financial intermediaries can improve the savings–investment process. First, financial intermediaries must choose direct securities to insure profitability. Thus the flow of funds from savers to investors is improved by an intermediate step to assess investment opportunities. Second, financial intermediaries can pool savings to support long-term, interdependent and indivisible projects, as previously observed in context with the use of economies of scale in borrowing and lending. Third, by establishing adequate channels of communication and transaction in various regions, financial intermediaries can help the free flow of financial assets in an economy. This is an important process in an economy, for it promotes factor price equalization. Finally, as a corollary, financial intermediaries can increase the size of savings available at certain locations. Surpluses from certain regions can be pooled to support attractive high-return investments in other locations.

Financial Liberalization and Development

The ideas previously put forth assume liberated markets and fully-fledged competition. This is consistent with economic integration which demands some degree of financial opening. However, following World War II, most developing economies enforced significant financial controls to promote economic development. In order to overcome low savings rates, traditional and lean investments carried out by an embryonic entrepreneurial sector, and to promote growth of some priority sectors, governments from developing countries placed ceilings on lending interest rates, marked savings rates, set credit allocations selectively, placing strict shares to each sector, favouring those considered important, and enforced controls on capital movements. Additionally, the state intervened directly in the economy by means of state-owned and -managed developing banks. These policies sent distorted signals to the market, promoted inefficiency among banks, and inhibited the growth of non-monetary intermediaries. Financial development theory always recommended financial liberalization and deregulation to enhance the role of financial markets and institutions that were frequently 'repressed' in the developing economies (Studart, 1998).

Nevertheless, developing countries resisted financial liberalization for many years. However several factors, among them the debt crisis of the 1980s, diminished returns derived from import substitution, and the accelerated growth and importance of economic and financial globalization induced those nations to adopt economic liberalism. Consequently, governments have enforced ambitious modernization programmes which mainly include opening up to foreign trade and investments, and financial liberalization and deregulation. The aim is increasing economic growth by taking full advantage of globalization. In addition, an alternative strategy for responding to the challenges of global competitive markets, and enhancing development has been to promote economic integration, which, on a worldwide basis, has led to the formation of strong economic blocs.

Thus, although the functions of financial intermediaries remain the same, they must currently be carried out in a more complex environment than the one existing before the end of the cold war. It involves benefits and risks derived from economic and financial liberalization in a globalized economy, and the benefits and risks derived from regional economic integration. In this respect, both economic development and economic integration depend significantly on the soundness of local financial markets and institutions and their capacity to respond rapidly and efficiently to contemporary economic challenges.

Banks as Intermediaries and their Role in Development

Banks are one of the most important financial intermediaries. In most developing countries they are the main component of the financial sector, since full-arms securities markets are still in the process of formation[4]. Essentially, their liabilities are primarily short-term deposits which compose part of a nation's money supply (they are monetary intermediaries), while their assets are short- and long-term loans to business firms, governments, and consumers.

In addition to all those financial intermediation practices previously identified, which promote economic development, for the specific case of banking institutions it should be first acknowledged that they constitute the payments system of a nation. In this respect, Tobin (1965) emphasized their role as instruments of monetary policy. They create money, and contribute to the country's money management. They mobilize savings through deposits, and make loans to agents in need of liquidity to realize their productive investments. They offer various financial products and services to their customers, and set up a wide system of payments.

Several authors point out that bank's loans are 'special' (Fama, 1984; James, 1987). They provide investors with valuable information about borrowers which is not available at financial markets. In this vein, Diamond (1984) presents banks as "delegated monitors". When the acquisition of information about a firm is costly, finance can be provided to firms in a more efficient manner if savers delegate the collection of information about firms to a financial intermediary, provided that the intermediary has appropriate incentives to act in the savers' interests. Even in the absence of such delegation, however, banks' actions, such as a new loan to a firm, can provide valuable information to the market, since they have access to a firm's privileged information.

Banks are also important participants in capital markets, and a useful complement to cover their insufficiencies. Because not all firms can meet the listing standards of securities markets, banking credit becomes the most important source of funds for small and medium-sized firms. Similarly, because many financial assets offered in these markets are highly standardized, banks remain the only means of providing specific products to customers, in relation to their particular savings and investment needs.

Banks also support the development of capital markets. They often initiate many kinds of financial services which, once standardized, are provided to all agents in the financial markets. Recent developments, such as securitization of their assets, have reinforced their presence and role in capital markets. Banks' loans, instead of being held in their original form until maturity, are securitized and sold in financial markets.

Banks, therefore, participate in the national flow of funds process, either as main actors or as brokers. Their role in the economy is fundamental. A crisis in the banking sector can therefore affect the economy in general. According to Bernanke (1983), such a crisis yields a financial intermediation disruption, and affects the money and claims supply in the economy. He argues that the difficulties in the banking sector during the great depression of 1928 greatly affected the real sector.

In this respect, it is worth noting that an excessive predominance of the banking sector in an economy can be harmful to its development. Due to the lack of development of other forms of intermediation, savings and investment levels would remain restricted. Furthermore, this phenomenon might be accompanied by monopolistic practices which in turn would lead to high costs of capital in the economy, inhibiting even more the growth of the economy.

Similarly, the lack of arms-length financial markets leads to closed patterns of corporate governance and strong links between firms and banks. Corporations are owned and managed by family groups which show limited interest in expanding the operations of the firm in line with the innovative technological developments and competitiveness prevailing in international markets. Firms therefore remain small and non-competitive, inhibiting national growth. Strong ties between banks and corporations restrain growth of other forms of financial non-banking intermediation, which in turn leads to rigidity and inefficiencies in corporate decision-making.

Banking and Economic Integration

Benefits of Economic Integration

Economic globalization has led to greater interdependence among nations. Moreover, countries throughout the world are not only closer to each other, but many have also committed themselves to enforce economic integration schemes with their main economic partners, which has led to the formation of large economic blocs such as the European Union, the North American Free Trade Agreement, and informally the Far Eastern economic bloc, headed by Germany and France, the United States, and Japan, respectively. Economic integration has been promoted because it offers important benefits which promote economic development. Among these benefits, the following must be mentioned:

1. Integration increases economic activity. First, it increases investment levels. Economic integration promotes the mobilization of international savings, which in turn overcomes limited local levels of savings, increasing investments and national output to higher levels. In short, corporations have greater access to international financing, and to international credits which support export activity. Empirical evidence shows that capital inflows amounting to 3–4 per cent in relation to GNP would increase it by 0.5 per cent (Reisen, 1996).

   Development is also enhanced because economic integration increases returns on investments and savings. This is because there is a change towards more profitable economic activity at the international level. Similarly, foreign direct investments also increase, which in turn boosts employment, output, exports and economic activity in general.

   Finally, economic integration favours the adoption of new technologies. This increases productivity and makes firms from the participating members more competitive at the international level.

2. Economic integration strengthens entrepreneurship and advances new (open) patterns of corporate ownership and control, and improved corporate management. In order to become competitive at the international level, large family firms from developing countries seek external financing which widens ownership and enrol professional managers to the firm.

3. Concerning the financial sector, economic integration entails financial opening, which promotes competitiveness and efficiency of local financial markets and institutions. Integration leads to significant transfers of know-how and financial intermediation technologies; application of better forms of regulation; growth and efficiency of the securities markets. Economic integration brings about important financial innovations which lower the cost of capital and increase the level of investments. Finally, financial integration leads to better banking administration through the adoption of international norms and practices (World Bank, 1997).

In short, economic integration can be seen as an important engine for achieving high economic growth. Because banks play an important part in the allocation of resources in a developing economy, and because they play the most important role in cross-border financial operations, the banking system will undoubtedly constitute a leading actor in all processes of economic integration. In other words, economic integration cannot be achieved with a weak banking system.

Similarly, economic integration cannot be fully achieved unless the concerning parties harmonize their economic and financial policies in order to secure large mobilizations of labour, goods and capital to support investments throughout the bloc. Under such circumstances, financial institutions, and especially banking institutions, become the centre of economic integration. Under ordinary conditions, the majority of payments and international transfers are made through the banking system. Hence, under an economic integration scheme, the role of these institutions becomes even more important for the success of the economic bloc.

International economic transactions depend highly on the capacity from the economic agents to regulate them, regardless of existing barriers among nations. Moreover, direct investment projects and international financing are not feasible in the absence of mechanisms that assist international capital movements.

In their long-established role as financial intermediaries, banks expedite the mobilization of funds among partners of an economic bloc, and promote fluid and effective operations. They assist in this objective and facilitate an effective regulation of trade and financial operations among economic agents from the bloc.

Banks can be justly considered as the most important link in the realization of international commercial and trade transactions. Since only in the long run is a monetary union possible, member countries must maintain their own currencies. In this context, financial institutions become even more important since economic exchange among the member countries includes constant exchange rate operations.

Banks contribute to financial integration within a bloc through their traditional activities as borrowers and lenders. They continuously create, to the benefit of their clients, new techniques and instruments to increase their competitiveness at the local markets, as well as to achieve an international competitive edge.

Finally, it is worth mentioning that an analysis of the role of financial institutions in a process of economic integration involves three important issues, taking into account that financial activity should contribute to enhance economic growth of the bloc.

One concerns the efficiency and competitiveness of financial institutions of each country member of the bloc. Indeed, this is an important motivation for economic integration. It is for this reason that various international economic agreements include important chapters about their financial institutions.Founded on clear financial provisions, it is expected that economic integration would ideally open up free spaces where financial institutions of the member countries can have access to the financial markets from other members of the group, i.e., entry without undue restrictions. In this context, the possibility of greater efficiency from financial institutions is obvious, considering the fact that there are conditions for greater competition in the new financially-integrated market. Financial institutions must therefore prepare themselves for the challenges brought about by economic integration, training their employees, strengthening their financial position, and matching the competitive standards of their neighbours.

A second issue deals with the response of banking institutions to financial liberalization and deregulation, and economic integration. Due to the fact that banks can increase lending more easily, solvency problems could take place. In this respect, it is imperative to identify problems of bank solvency and offer alternatives to regulate bank operations and avoid bank runs.

Finally, a third issue pertains to the costs of deposit insurance programs. Full implicit or explicit government guarantees are the extreme negative case that promote poor bank management. It is therefore important to study risks associated with a bank and its value in the context of financial liberalization and integration.

Risks of Financial Integration and Globalization

Although economic integration should have positive impacts on the economies of the participating countries, it also involves risks that must be correctly identified to control them effectively and prevent ill effects. The most important risk associated with financial integration concerns increments in the volatility of financial operations, which in turn could lead to insolvency problems and even bankruptcy of financial institutions, as well as severe financial shocks that lead to a fully-fledged economic crisis. Greater volatility can result from both local and international causes.

On the domestic side, volatility in financial operations can increase due to unattended economic disequilibria or changes in the political scenario. Since integration policies are frequently implemented along with financial deregulation and liberalization policies, the roots of financial volatility would be associated with the lack of appropriate responses from financial institutions and entrepreneurs to the new economic environment characterized by competition and expanded economic activity covering the space of the bloc. Higher competitiveness could lead to greater uncertainty in prices, profits, and payments of liabilities. Similarly, economic integration can lead to excessive corporate and bank financing with foreign resources. In turn, expanded economic activity can create over-optimistic attitudes towards future levels of trade and investments. These attitudes might overshadow the breadth of existing disequilibria, overheat the economy, and lead to abrupt changes in financial prices when expectations adjust to more realistic levels.

On the international level, volatility in financial operations in the developing nations can increase as a result of downfalls in economic activity of major economic partners, or industrialized countries in general, or as a result of profound international portfolio adjustments and capital reversals made by large institutional investors in response to financial cracks at some developed or developing financial markets. In the first case, the impacts of a downturn in economic activity in a developed partner would lead to extreme volatility in financial operations of developing partners. The impact could be magnified if integration has been built on an asymmetric basis. Moreover, as a result of financial integration, smaller nations would be less capable of implementing adjusting policies on their own. In the second case, the transmission effects of financial crisis, local or from a group of countries, has been identified as the contagion effect. They result from worldwide portfolio adjustments made by international institutional investors to overcome downfalls in a market.

In the case of nations with soft currencies, volatility in financial operations can also increase due to unstable exchange rates, expectations of a local devaluation of an overvalued local currency, and ultimately from sharp devaluations which affect the local financial markets and institutions. Moreover, recent studies confirm that currency crisis and banking crisis go hand in hand. The usual sequence is: 1) weak policy-making, which undermines the external sector and the value of the local currency coupled with a marked fragility of the financial system, particularly large levels of non-performing loans and excessive banking liabilities in hard currencies[5]; 2) currency crisis, which fuels the insolvency problems of the banking system, which could even lead to bank runs and a systemic crisis. A twin financial crisis (currency and banking crisis) then ensues and leads to a fully-fledged crisis of the economy (Kaminsky and Reinhart, 1999). In developing and transition economies with emerging capital markets, a triple crisis might take place: the currency crisis leads to massive capital withdrawals by foreign investors leading to a securities market crash. Each of the crises of these triple phenomena feed on each other and might even become contagion mechanisms to initiate crisis in other countries or regions.

Government Guarantees, Development and Integration

To protect all participants in the banking system, governments often offer full guarantee to all banks. This shifts private risk associated with bank liabilities to the government (World Bank, 1997), specifically to all taxpayers. These guarantees protect the payments system, prevent bank runs, and protect depositors against losses. However, empirical evidence shows that these guarantees promote poor and ambitious bank management. Strained by increased competition, resulting from financial liberalization and deregulation policies, and distressed by the entry of foreign intermediaries to the local market which lowers the franchise value of banks, local bank managers are induced to lend haphazardly, to clients willing to pay high interest rates, but pursuing very risky projects which undermines their capacity to pay. In short, these type of bank managers gamble on future economic growth. This phenomenon, rooted in asymmetric information problems and known as 'adverse selection' and 'moral hazard,' is made possible by the guarantee which operates in a similar way to a put option (King, 1992). If the value of the bank's assets falls below the value of its liabilities, the guarantee makes up the difference. An increase in the riskiness of the asset portfolio increases the value of the guarantee to bank owners and executives, for greater risks increase the potential for large up-side profits, while the government guarantee insures depositors against downside losses (Ibid). Banks can therefore bear greater risks, searching for big gains, without worrying about possible losses. This situation is summarized in Figure 19.1.

This becomes a source of financial instability since banks try to increase profits without proper measuring of risk undertaken. Indeed, credit practices weaken. Credit analysis is incomplete and poor since banks rather attempt to maximize the value of the guarantees.

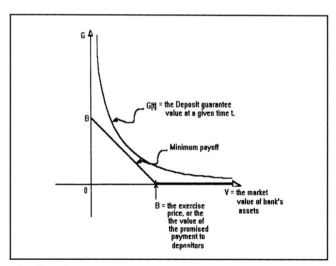

G = Deposit guarantee
t = Time
B = Exercise price, or the value of the promised payment to
     depositors
Y = Market value of bank's assets

FIGURE 19.1: *Deposit Insurance as a Put Option*

Moral hazard also becomes a source of financial fragility because banks use their access to international credits to acquire debt at lower interest rates than those prevailing in the local markets, and lend locally at very high rates. This circuit leads to continuous capital outflows which weaken the nation's international reserves and become a mechanism to trigger and transmit local crisis to other countries.

As a corollary of the previous point, it must be stressed that adverse selection and moral hazard induce large increments in lending rates, repressing savings rates leading to large interest rate spreads, enforced to achieve quick gains. However, these policies lead to large increases in bad loans. As a result, the balance sheet statement and the income statement show sharp weaknesses; financial performance ratios derived from those statements show a clear trend to deterioration. If this situation is sustained for too long, banks will try to solve their problems by falling into a vicious circle of further increases in lending rates and repression of savings rates.

Moral hazard also leads banks to deviate large amounts of resources to speculative investments at the secondary money and capital markets, in lieu of supporting lending activities related to real investments. Finally, moral hazard can also lead to illegal actions by some managers and executives. They access their bank's financial resources to purchase property registered in their name, transfer money to personal accounts at offshore banks, etc.

Implementing governmental guarantees usually enforce large rescue programmes which, although created to protect users of the payments system, reward poor bank management and socialize costs. It also means that strengthening the banking system capital and improving its efficiency to a great extent depends on wide and complex mergers, as well as on increased participation of foreign capital, even to a 100 per cent level, in the local insolvent institutions. This could lead, in some countries, to an undesirable de-nationalization of the payments system and some loss of autonomous monetary policy-making. This is particularly the case with developing countries.

In short, financial liberalization, deregulation, and economic integration could encourage banks toward excessive risk-taking, weakening significantly the banking system. As a result, governments might be forced to implement large long-range rescue programmes. Consequently, economic and financial integration will be slowed down, while development would be restrained for many years.

It is therefore important to enforce policies and regulations that diminish moral hazard. An important part of these policies and regulations must include establishing a system of non-governmental deposit guarantees.

Conclusion

Financial assets and financial institutions are important factors in the allocation of scarce resources. Financial intermediaries promote efficient mobilization of surplus funds from saving units to deficit spending investing units. The essential fact is that financial structure and hence financial intermediation do matter in economic growth. Financial intermediaries have an important role in output because they help to: (1) increase savings and optimize the portfolio holdings of ultimate lenders; (2) optimize their own portfolio holdings by proper risk–return management; and, (3) make funds available to efficient deficit spending investing units. In short, financial intermediation involves a transformation of the funds process – a process which, as Goldsmith (1969) puts it, is economically though not technically equivalent to the transformation taking place in the production of commodities and services (Goldsmith, 1968, p. 26).

Economic integration leads to considerable benefits for each member country and the integrated unit as a whole. Benefits arise from increased investments, open and more efficient patterns of corporate governance and management, and greater competition and efficiency of the financial system, particularly banking institutions. All these benefits accelerate economic growth.

In short, economic integration can be seen as an important engine for achieving high economic growth. Because banks play an important part in the allocation of resources in developing economies, and because they play the most important role in cross-border financial operations, the banking system constitutes a leading actor in economic integration.

However, economic integration, like any other economic activity, involves risk. The most important risk associated with financial integration concerns increments in the volatility of financial operations, which could lead to severe insolvency problems and even bankruptcy of financial institutions, as well as severe financial shocks that lead to fully-fledged economic crisis. Greater volatility can result from both local and international causes. In this respect, an important source of increased instability in the local financial markets is poor banking practices due to moral hazard. Because liberalization eases credit granting by banks, and particularly because government guarantees to deposits are ample, and because economic integration creates over-optimistic expectations, credit practices weaken. Hence, bank assets tend to increase more than liabilities. Furthermore, bad loans increase beyond sustainable levels. As a result the government must intervene with massive rescue plans which slow down integration and restrain economic growth for long periods.

In conclusion, to promote economic development, taking full advantage of the benefits brought about by economic integration, it is important to strengthen the banking system.

References

ALLEN, F. and GALE, D. (2000) Optimal currency crisis, *Carnegie–Rochester Series in Public Policy*, forthcoming.

BENNET, R. L. (1965) *The Financial Sector and Economic Development: The Mexican Case*, Johns Hopkins, Baltimore.

BERNANKE, B. S. (1983) Non-monetary effects of the financial crisis in the propagation of the Great Depression, *American Economic Review*, Vol. 73 (June), pp. 257–276.

BLEJER, M. I. and SKREB, M. (eds.) (1999) *Financial Sector Transformation. Lessons from Economics in Transition*, Cambridge University Press, New York.

CABELLO, A. (1999) *Globalización y Liberalización Financieras y Bolsa Mexican de Valores. Del Auge a la Crisis*, Plaza y Valdés, Mexico, DF.

DIAMOND, D. (1984) Financial intermediation and delegated monitoring, *Review of Economic Studies*, Vol. 51 (Autumn), pp. 393–414.

FAMA, E. (1984) The information in the term structure, *Journal of Financial Economics*, Vol. 13 (December), pp. 509–528.

FRY, M. (1988) *Money, Interest and Banking in Economic Development*, Johns Hopkins, Baltimore.

FRY, M. (1989) Financial development: Theories and recent experience, *Oxford Review of Economic Policy*, Vol. 5, No. 4, pp. 13–28.

GALBIS, V. (1977) Financial intermediation and economic growth in less developed countries: A theoretical approach, in P.C. AYRE (ed.), *Finance in Developing Countries*, Frank Cass, London.

GOLDSMITH, R. W. (1968) *Financial Institutions*, Randa House, New York.

GOLDSMITH, R. W. (1969) *Financial Structure and Development*, Yale University Press, New York.

GUPTA, K. (1984) *Finance and Growth in Developing Countries*, Croom Helm, London.

GURLEY, J. G. and SHAW, E. S. (1960) *Money in a Theory of Finance*, Brookings Institution, Washington DC.

IVANOVA, A. (1998) *Los Intermediarios Financieros no Bancarios y el Crecimiento Económico. El Caso de México*, Doctoral Thesis, Universidad Nacional Autónoma de México.

JAMES, C. (1987) Some evidence on the uniqueness of bank loans, *Journal of Financial Economics*, Vol. 19, No. 2, pp. 217–236.

KAMINSKY, G. L. and REINHART, C. M. (1999) The twin crisis: The causes of banking and balance of payments crisis, *American Economic Review*, June, pp. 473–500.

KING, K. K. (1992) Deposit insurance as a put option: Alternative approaches to modeling regulatory forbearance, *Board of Governors of the Federal Reserve System*.

LEVINE, R. (1997) Financial development and economic growth, *Journal of Economic Literature*, Vol. XXXV, No. 2, pp. 688–726.

LOPEZ OBRADOR, A. M. (1999) *Fobaproa: Expediente Abierto*, Grijalbo, Mexico, DF.

MCKINNON, R. I. (1973) *Money and Capital in Economic Development*, Brookings Institution, Washington DC.

MOSKOW, M. H. (2000) *Disruption in Global Financial Markets: The Role of Public Policy*, Paper presented at the Global Finance Conference, April 21.

ORTIZ, E. (1993) Emerging markets and economic development, in K. FATEMI and D. SALVATORE (eds.), *Foreign Exchange Issues, Capital Markets and International Banking in the 1990s*, Taylor and Francis, Washington DC.

ORTIZ, E. (1995) Take-off into development and emerging capital markets: Stages of financial development and equity financing, in H. P. GRAY and S. C. RICHARD (eds.), *International Finance in the New World Order*, Pergamon, New York.

PATRICK, H. T. (1966) Financial development and economic growth in underdeveloped countries, *Development and Cultural Change*, Vol. 14, No. 2, pp. 77–97.

REISEN, H. (1996) Managing volatile capital inflows: The experience of the 1990s, *Asian Development Review*, Vol. 14, pp. 72–96.

SHAW, E. S. (1973) *Financial Deepening in Economic Development*, Oxford University Press, New York.

STUDART, R. (1998) Politicas financieras y crecimiento en el contexto de desarrollo: Lecciones derivadas de América Latina y del Sudoeste Asíatico en los Años Ochenta, *Investigación Económica*, Vol. LVII, No. 1, pp. 15–42.

TOBIN, J. (1965) Money and economic growth, *Econometrica*, Vol. 33, No. 4, pp. 671–684.

WORLD BANK, The (1997) *Private Capital Flows to Developing Countries, the Road to Financial Integration*, Oxford University Press, Oxford.

Notes

The authors acknowledge research support from the Research Fund for Studies of the North American Region, created by El Colegio de México, Universidad Nacional Autonoma de México, Centro de Investigacion y Docencia Economicas and El Colegio de la Frontera Norte.

1. This work stresses the case of developing nations. See Blejer and Skreb (1999) for recent and excellent coverage of financial reforms issues in transition economies.

2. Costs of the 1995 Mexican banking crisis have been recently estimated as 20–25 per cent of GDP (Lopez Obrador, 1999); costs of the 1997 Asian countries crisis vary between 20 and 65 per cent of GDP (Moskow, 2000).

3. Levine's (1997) paper lists, in the References section, the most important thinkers of development financing. Other useful bibliographies can be found in Ortiz (1995), Cabello (1999), and Ivanova (1998).
4. Equity markets correspond to the last stage of financial development. See: Ortiz (1995).
5. Central bank and commercial bank borrowing impacts on currency crises are modeled in Allen and Gale (2000).

20

Bank Risk Management Practices in Emerging Markets

KURT R. JESSWEIN

Introduction

Two of the more significant developments in the international financial markets over the past couple of decades can be summarized by the buzzwords 'risk management' and 'emerging markets'. Risk management has become a focal point of both financial institutions and those charged with regulating and supervising those institutions. Institutions large and small have seen risk management become both a requirement of operating in an increasingly volatile global financial marketplace and for some, as a core competency or strength upon which to develop their competitive or strategic advantages. Likewise, market regulators charged with domestic market surveillance, such as the Securities and Exchange Commission (SEC) and Board of Governors of the Federal Reserve System in the United States (Fed), and those responsible for the efficient functioning of the international markets, such as the Bank for International Settlements (BIS) and International Organization of Securities Commissions (IOSCO), have focused their activities on ensuring that financial institutions adequately manage their exposures to financial risks.

Likewise, due to market liberalization efforts, new emerging financial markets are under development worldwide. In Central and Eastern Europe, Asia, Africa and Latin America, financial services industries are being created in scores of nations in conjunction with the development and growth of their local domestic economies. Unfortunately, accompanying the economic opportunities available to the newly-created institutions and markets are the risks that have confounded the more mature markets and institutions of North America and Western Europe. This paper examines the possibilities of extending the risk management techniques developed and advocated by the major multinational financial institutions and regulatory agencies for use by institutions operating in these emerging markets.

Advances in Risk Measurement and Management

Risk management has become a focal point of bank management as the world moves into the twenty-first century. However, effective risk management requires a significant commitment. To support the process fully, a bank must make substantial investments in both information technology and human capital.

The fundamental risks facing modern financial institutions are many. Among the most critical are market risk and credit risk[1]. Market risk refers to changing interest rates, exchange rates, and other asset prices adversely affecting the value of assets and liabilities (and derivatives) being traded by financial institutions. Interest rate risk can also refer to the cost of rolling over or reborrowing funds rising above the returns earned on asset investments (i.e., refinancing risk), or to the returns on funds invested falling below the cost of funds (i.e., reinvestment risk). Currency risk occurs when exchange rate changes affect the value of assets and liabilities held abroad or denominated in foreign currencies. Credit risk refers to situations where the promised cash flows from loans, securities, and derivatives are not paid in full on a timely basis.

Market Risk Measurement

The measurement of market risk focuses on an assessment of the size of the exposures, the sensitivity of the exposures to changes in risk variables, and the likelihood of those changes occurring. Market risk is typically measured (and managed) using a value-at-risk (VaR) model[2]. The methodology allows one to measure or define exposures to risk in absolute dollar terms or as relative amounts against a benchmark. VaR models provide information on how much risk is associated with various activities or positions. Consequently, they allow a bank to set position guidelines and limits. They also can be used for capital allocation decisions and for the analysis of performance on a risk-adjusted basis.

A VaR is calculated using the distribution of daily changes in the market value of individual positions (daily earnings at risk) usually using historical data. The risk measure calculated is a function of the size of the standard-deviation change assumed for the model (i.e., based on how critical potential losses are assumed to be). For example, if one needs assurance of exceeding a loss limit only five per cent of the time (and recalling that 90 per cent of a normal curve lies within ± 1.65 standard deviations from the mean), one can use an estimate of 1.65 standard deviations. Extending the analysis over several days requires an adjustment so that total VaR is the daily earnings at risk multiplied by the square root of the number of days. Adjustments for liquidity constraints associated with trading the particular asset are often also needed.

The VaR for an individual financial instrument is dependent on several factors. It is based on the size and sign (long or short) of the position, the sensitivity or elasticity of its market value to changes in market factors (duration for fixed-income assets), and the volatility of the markets or corresponding market factors.

The VaR for a portfolio of assets is calculated using a time series of daily changes in the market value of that portfolio. The market risk of the portfolio is determined by the exposures of its components and by the correlations between movements in the underlying asset prices of each component. As a result, the risk for a portfolio is generally smaller than the sum of the risks for the individual positions. Similarly, the risk added to a portfolio by adding a new position is generally less than the risk for the new position on a stand-alone basis.

VaR models are based on some critical assumptions. First, the relevant time horizon for measuring the potential loss must be set; this is typically one day but can be extended. Second, the estimation period (i.e., how much past data is to be used and how it will be used) must be determined. RiskMetrics generally uses at least one year of historical data weighted exponentially, meaning recent data has more weight than past data. Third, the distribution of the historical data must be assumed. VaR models often assume asset returns are normally distributed, which can cause problems since some asset returns (e.g., foreign exchange) are not normally distributed and others (e.g., options) differ significantly from normal. Fourth, the risk level of the estimate must be chosen (i.e., the allowable frequency of crossing the risk threshold). Fifth, correlations among the variables (the different components of the bank's asset portfolio) must be calculated.

The VaR methodology can be applied in different ways. One application often referred to as risk-adjusted return on capital (RAROC) is used to allocate capital to those banking activities producing the highest returns. In this regard it is used both as a performance measurement tool and for determining capital adequacy, since it can be designed to assess the market risks, credit risks and operational risks a bank undertakes in each activity.

With the refinement of VaR modeling, the BIS and domestic regulators have adjusted their risk-based capital standards to include market risk. Banks with accurate models of market risk can qualify for lower amounts of required risk capital (as much as their models would require them to hold). To qualify for such treatment, the specific model employed by a bank must meet certain criteria[3].

Credit Risk Measurement

Historically, the core of banking activity has revolved around credit. Yet, credit risk has always been an extremely difficult risk to measure. Given the explosive growth in emerging market credits, junk bonds and derivatives in recent years, the analysis of credit exposures has become even more complex.

The changing credit markets have led to improvements in measuring credit risks and the creation of derivatives contracts to manage the risks. As with market risk, credit risk is analysed at the individual and portfolio levels. At the individual level, default risk is assessed qualitatively or quantitatively. Qualitative models focus either on borrower-specific factors (e.g., the five Cs of credit – character, capital, capacity, conditions, collateral) or market-specific factors (e.g., the position of the economy in the business cycle or general level of interest rates), or on both. Quantitative models such as credit-scoring models try to calculate the probability of default based on an analysis of financial data (e.g., accounting ratios) or by sorting borrowers into different risk classes (e.g., discriminant functions). Other quantitative techniques attempt to extract expected credit risk from the term structure of interest rates for securities with different levels of default risk or analyse historic default rates, using mortality rates of bonds and loans of similar quality.

Another set of models is based on RAROC techniques. Rather than evaluating the default risk of future cash flows, RAROC models focus on the returns expected against the risk taken in a particular credit. In equation terms, RAROC can be defined as the ratio of one year's expected income on a credit exposure to the credit risk accepted or risk capital invested.

The expected risk of the credit is estimated by adapting duration analysis to credit risk[4]. The expected return is estimated using the expected net proceeds from the credit. The RAROC calculation is then compared against a predetermined threshold (typically the bank's cost of funds). Based on this comparison, the credit application is accepted (continued) or rejected (canceled). If rejected, the bank must either demand a higher return (raise the loan rate or increase the fees) or reduce the risk (shorten the duration or the size of the loan) to justify granting or continuing the credit.

The RiskMetrics methodology has also been extended to examine credit risk. CreditMetrics[TM5] is based largely on an application of option-pricing techniques first proposed by Robert Merton (1974) and put into practice by the KMV Corporation. The model measures the market value of a risky loan based on its time to maturity, the borrower's leverage ratio and the riskiness of the asset (e.g., variance in the rate of change in the value of the borrower's assets). The critical adaptation by KMV involves extracting the asset risk as the implied volatility from the option valuation equation given the observable values for the other variables in the equation[6].

The CreditMetrics methodology follows the RiskMetrics framework. A bank establishes its credit exposure profile, incorporating all activities that lead to credit risk (e.g., bonds and drawn loans, undrawn instruments like loan commitments, letters of credit and trade credits, and swaps and other derivatives, all adjusted to credit equivalent amounts). These credit exposures are remapped to fit the CreditMetrics framework. The model then incorporates the volatility in the credit markets computed from or associated with upgrades, downgrades, and defaults, collectively known as credit events. This calculation evaluates (is the product of) the probability of a shift in the credit market and the estimated change in value from a shift. The correlations among credit events are also incorporated. Thus, if a bank can model its potential credit exposures into the framework and incorporate the volatility and correlation data provided by the RiskMetrics Group, it arrives at a single number representing the bank's overall credit risk exposure just as RiskMetrics provides a single number representing market risk.

Risk Management and Derivative Securities

Having examined some of the sophisticated methodologies for measuring financial risks, attention is next drawn to the management of those risks. And although risk management encompasses a wide variety of operational and strategic activities, the focus here will be on the use of derivative securities as part of the overall risk management operation.

Most, if not all, global banking institutions are involved in the derivative securities markets. In the normal course of business, banks become a party to a variety of derivative and off-balance sheet financial instruments to meet the needs of their customers, to manage their exposures to market risk and other risks, and to take trading positions. These financial instruments consist of derivative securities such as forward contracts, futures, swaps and options that all involve varying degrees of credit risk and market risk.

Banks generally manage the credit risk of their derivative portfolios by limiting the total amount of arrangements outstanding with individual customers, by monitoring the size and maturity structure of the portfolios, by obtaining collateral based on management's credit assessment of the customer, and by applying a uniform credit process for all credit exposures. In addition, banks evaluate their portfolios periodically to determine whether the allowance for credit losses is adequate to absorb potential losses in such portfolios. Thus, the risks of engaging in derivative security transactions is generally managed in similar fashion to the management of the bank's investment and loan portfolios.

Banks, as end users, use various types of derivative products to manage the interest rate, currency and credit risks associated with their various liabilities (interest-bearing deposits, short-term borrowings and long-term debt) and assets (credit obligations and investments in debt and equity instruments). For example, when banks purchase assets and issue liabilities at fixed interest rates they subject themselves to fair value fluctuations as market interest rates change. These fluctuations in fair value can be managed by entering into interest rate contracts that change the fixed-rate instrument into a variable-rate instrument. If banks purchase foreign currency denominated assets, issue foreign currency denominated debt or have foreign net investments, they subject themselves to changes in value as exchange rates move. These fluctuations can be managed by entering into currency contracts.

A more recent introduction to the global financial marketplace has been a variety of credit derivatives. While earlier risk management products focused on financial (interest rate, currency or commodity) price risk, these newer products deal with the more complex issue of managing credit risk. One example is the total return swap in which one party pays the total return (coupon or interest payments plus capital gains or losses) on an underlying credit instrument (i.e., bond or loan) either individually or in a portfolio, and receives a funding payment. The spread on the funding payment depends on the creditworthiness of the counter-parties, the type of underlying asset and its quality, its maturity and any associated collateral. Other examples include default swaps, in which one party pays a default premium and receives a payment if the underlying credit or asset experiences a default event, and spread options that allow one to take a position on a changing credit spread. For example, purchasing a put option pays off when the spread becomes smaller, while a call option pays off when the spread widens.

Applicability of Advanced Risk Management Techniques to Emerging Markets

Given the recent advances in risk measurement and management, one may wonder whether the advanced techniques developed by the major global financial institutions are applicable to smaller banks or to those operating in emerging markets. For example, how can one use CreditMetrics in a market where explicit credit ratings do not exist? Or how can one use futures contracts to manage risks where no futures markets exist?

Honohan (1997) and Goldstein and Turner (1996) have examined past problems in emerging markets with a view to future improvements. Both discuss the necessity of adequate regulation and supervision to ensure individual bank and market solvency. The wider use of market-based hedging instruments to help reduce market volatility and its potential damaging consequences for banking systems in emerging markets is also advocated.

Unfortunately, there are often many impediments for financial institutions in emerging markets to enter into more sophisticated risk management contracts (Claessens, 1993). Creditworthiness is typically a big hurdle. Because of the low credit ratings of the banks, not to mention the countries in which they reside, investors typically shy away from dealing with developing countries' governments and financial institutions. A related issue is cost. Risk management products typically involve either the use of a line of credit (often difficult to obtain) or the payment of upfront premiums that can deter institutions already having difficulties raising foreign funds.

Domestic institutional barriers can also be a hindrance. Domestic legal and regulatory constraints can affect an institution's ability to hedge abroad. Likewise, there may be considerable basis risk in that the element of risk in question cannot easily be hedged since the global market for risk management products is incomplete. There is often no perfectly matched hedging tool for some risks or a mismatch (e.g., maturity) between the characteristics of the variable to be hedged and those of the hedging tool. In addition, there may be infrastructure issues (insufficient communications, computing, and information systems) that act as barriers to implementing effective risk management strategies.

Finally, there are the simple issues of awareness and expertise. Not only is there often a lack of familiarity with the market instruments and their strategic use, but also misunderstandings of the role of hedging and a likening of it to speculation. Beyond this, many institutions (not to mention the countries in which they operate) have deficient institutional frameworks necessary to adequately report, record, monitor, and evaluate risk management transactions, or do not have the regulations necessary to avoid (and protect against) undue speculation.

How then can advanced risk management techniques be introduced to the emerging markets? First, it must be noted that many of the problems facing emerging markets are the same as those facing the more developed markets; it is only a matter of degree. The high cost of information technology, the lack of technical knowledge and trained personnel, the difficulty in calculating risk measurement parameters (correlations and volatilities) and the lack of liquidity of many assets all make risk management a difficult operation to undertake. These only become more acute given the greater volatilities and lower levels of market liquidity associated with most emerging markets (IOSCO, 1997).

Creditworthy financial institutions in developed countries have always had easy access to the many derivative financial instruments available for hedging risks. The acceptance of these techniques has grown remarkably during the past decade. With current outstanding amounts in the privately negotiated (over-the-counter) derivatives market of over US$81 trillion, and another US$17 trillion in exchange-traded contracts, there is now a US$100 trillion market in these types of products (BIS, 1999). This compares to a market of only US$800 billion in outstanding contracts only ten years ago. Given the overwhelming acceptance of derivative securities in the predominantly developed financial markets, it is only a matter of time before similar usage occurs in the emerging markets.

But the barriers to use must be overcome. The International Finance Corporation (1998) reports that country risk consider-ations and the strict credit requirements of the derivative financial markets can prevent even the strongest of credits in emerging markets from gaining sufficient access to financial risk management products. To the limited extent that derivative products are avail-able to those based in developing countries, they tend to be prod-ucts with minimal credit exposure, such as short-term interest rate swaps and interest rate caps. While such risk management products provide value, they may not represent the most effective hedging strategy for many institutions.

Sometimes access to longer-term risk management services may be possible but would entail an institution posting collateral or using up credit lines that could be so costly as to negate much of the benefit of hedging. What is necessary is the need to bridge the credit gap between emerging country financial institutions and the market requirements.

The IFC, the European Bank for Reconstruction and Develop-ment and other development banks have increasingly filled this void in providing risk management services to typically non-creditworthy institutions. Using the facilities of these institutions, financial insti-tutions in emerging markets have access to derivative products to hedge their own asset–liability mismatches, to extend the types of credit products that they offer, and to provide their clients with risk management products.

To ensure that these products are used for hedging purposes only and that their potential risk is prudently monitored by the financial institutions, sales and trading controls and systems management must be in place. In addition, these products lead to credit risk, so potential exposures must be estimated by pricing and value-at-risk systems. The consequent replacement costs, or 'mark-to-market values', also must be carefully monitored over time. It is in these areas where the advances in risk management made by the major global financial institutions may offer the greatest potential benefits for emerging markets.

Although the specific examples outlined in the documentation for the RiskMetrics and CreditMetrics methodologies may have little relevance for emerging market institutions, they do provide a glimpse at the future towards which such markets can strive. What is more important, however, is that the underlying methodologies of these techniques can offer a great deal of value in providing the tools for understanding and quantifying the many risks institutions in emerging markets face (even those risks that they may not realize they face).

While the markets in which the institutions operate may not be as efficient as their developed market brethren, there may still be many insights to be gained by examining the advances in risk management theory and practice. For instance, the portfolio diversification techniques presented in RiskMetrics and CreditMetrics can be used no matter where an institution operates.

Likewise, individual aspects of these techniques can provide guidance to institutions operating in emerging markets. The concept of risk sensitivity (e.g., duration) can be applied to virtually any financial activity in which an institution is involved. In addition, the concept of credit migration by a single credit or portfolio of assets is relevant to all sorts of activities and to all sorts of markets.

What may be a more important issue than the outright applicability of a CreditMetrics or RAROC approach is the ability to train and educate those operating in emerging markets in the underlying theories and techniques. Emerging markets coping with the many uncertainties of developing their domestic economies can go a long way toward establishing stable financial markets and institutions by fully embracing the 'Brave New World' of risk management and derivatives. Adequate exposure and training in the use of advanced risk measurement and management techniques is a necessary first step.

IOSCO (1997) has offered one prescription for expanding risk management practices into the emerging financial markets. At the macroeconomic level, institutional arrangements such as adequate capital requirements, accounting disclosure rules, efficient clearing operations, and the auditing or supervision of bank operations and internal controls must first be implemented to allow risk management practices to develop. This can and should be done with the assistance of representatives from the developed markets (IOSCO, G-30, etc.) whose experiences can be used to better develop and implement the necessary changes in the country.

At the microeconomic level, training is necessary at all levels of the financial institutions. First, adequately prepared seminars and training programs are necessary to ensure both practical knowledge and technical expertise on the part of the professionals charged with measuring and managing the risks. Likewise, senior management must be made aware of and learn to better appreciate the need for adequate risk management systems. Advanced risk measurement and management tools are useless if the corporate culture does not reflect a commitment to risk management. Proper internal controls, flows of information and engagement of senior management are all prerequisites to effective risk management programs.

To summarize, although there have been many significant advances in risk management in the developed markets in recent years, both from the measurement and management perspectives, one should not overlook the benefits of such advances on the progress of banking and risk management in emerging markets. Institutions and regulators in emerging markets must not assume a lack of relevance nor the inability to capitalize on the techniques and insights produced by the more developed banking markets. There is a danger they could neglect the very things that would provide the necessary stability to their markets and the tools for increasing efficiencies and strength to the individual institutions within their markets.

Conclusions

The global financial markets have seen significant advances in risk measurement and management techniques over the past decade. From the development and refinement of sophisticated risk measurement models to the introduction and explosive growth of the derivative securities markets, participants in the global finance and banking markets have witnessed a significant shift in emphasis in financial market activities. Yet, in the end the basic structures that drive financial institutions (efficient and profitable intermediation of funds within the global economy) have changed only in their terminology and focus.

To enable stability in the global markets and strength and development of emerging markets, it is necessary for institutions in those markets to embrace the risk management techniques to better control their own situations. Given adequate regulatory oversight and supervision to allow individual emerging markets to develop their own institutional presence, successful risk management will become paramount to the eventual success of each institution. Those comprehending this early will be those who will be better able to compete in the global marketplace. And emerging nations that nurture and pursue risk management efforts within their economies will see their financial markets stabilize and strengthen.

References

BANK FOR INTERNATIONAL SETTLEMENTS (BIS) (1999) *The Global OTC Derivatives Market at end-June 1999*, Bank for International Settlements, Basle, November.

BASLE COMMITTEE ON BANKING SUPERVISION (1996) *Amendment to the General Accord to Incorporate Market Risks*, Bank for International Settlements, Basle, January.

CLAESSENS, S. (1993) *Risk Management in Developing Countries*, World Bank Technical Paper No. 235, The World Bank, Washington DC, September.

GOLDSTEIN, M. and TURNER, P. (1996) *Banking Crises in Emerging Economies: Origins and Policy Options*, BIS Economic Papers No. 46, Bank for International Settlements, Basle, October.

HONOHAN, P. (1997) *Banking System Failures in Developing and Transition Countries: Diagnosis and Prediction*, BIS Working Paper No. 97–39, Bank for International Settlements, Basle, January.

INTERNATIONAL FINANCE CORPORATION (IFC) (1998) *IFC Risk Management*, (available online at www.ifc.org/main/html/pubrisk.html).

INTERNATIONAL ORGANIZATION OF SECURITIES COMMISSIONS (IOSCO) (1997) *Financial Risk Management in Emerging Markets, Report of the Emerging Markets Committee*, IOSCO, Montreal, Quebec, November.

MERTON, R. (1974) On the pricing of corporate debt: The risk structure of interest rates, *Journal of Finance*, Vol. 29, pp. 449–470.

SAUNDERS, A. (2000) *Financial Institutions Management: A Modern Perspective*, 3rd ed., Irwin-McGraw Hill, Boston, Massachussetts.

Notes

1. Other concerns include off-balance sheet risk, technological and operational risks, country risk and liquidity risk. In addition, banks face macroeconomic risks such as volatility in inflation and unemployment rates and event risks such as tax and regulatory changes, theft and crime risk, and shocks to the global financial markets caused by wars, revolutions, or crashes in local markets. See Saunders (2000) for an introduction to risk management issues facing financial institutions today.

2. The definitive introductory reference material on Value at Risk modeling is found in the RiskMetrics™ documentation available online at www.riskmetrics.com.

3. The requirements include: a VaR model computed daily and based on more than one year's data and a 99 per cent confidence level; one that captures the non-linear price characteristics of option positions; a set of risk factors (including credit spread risk) for each currency in which a bank has a position; and a set of risk factors for exchange rates, equity prices, and commodity prices for each significant currency, equity and commodity position the bank holds. (Basle Committee on Banking Supervision, 1996).

4. Duration analysis traditionally focuses on the elasticity of a fixed income security's price to a given change in interest rates based on the security's time to maturity, its coupon rate, and the general level of market interest rates. The

adaptation focuses the analysis on credit quality changes as measured by changes in credit risk premiums rather than changes in interest rates.
5.   CreditMetrics is a trademark of the RiskMetrics Group, Inc.
6.   The definitive introductory material on CreditMetrics is also available at the RiskMetrics website (www.riskmetrics.com).

Part VI

Currency Markets

21

Impact of Currency Depreciation on the Performance of International Funds: A Comparative Study of the Asian and Mexican Currency Crises

ABRAHAM MULUGETTA, YUKO MULUGETTA and DILIP K. GHOSH

Introduction

As of January 1998, in the US alone, more than US$4 trillion is invested in mutual funds and of this amount US$2.4 trillion is invested in equity mutual funds. With the phenomenal growth of assets of equity mutual funds, the necessity for international diversification is becoming more important. Single country closed-end funds (SCCEFs) are recommended as one of the most convenient vehicles for international diversification. Despite the increasing interest in SCCEFs, the existence of deep discounts in these funds is still not satisfactorily explained. The discount or premium of closed-end funds is calculated by taking the difference between the market price and the net asset value (NAV) and dividing it by the NAV. The higher the NAV to the market price results in the closed-end fund trading at a discount; the lower the NAV to the market price results in the closed-end fund trading at a premium. Whether the closed-end fund is a SCCEF or US equity closed-end fund, most trade at discounts, but the discounts of SCCEFs are, in general, greater than that of US equity closed-end funds. Interest by academia in tackling the puzzle and clarifying the enigma surrounding closed-end funds has been on the rise. Our study is one such attempt with a focus on the periods of the Mexican and recent Asian currency crises by testing the 'differential information holding' hypothesis.

The recent study by Mulugetta et al. (1998) has closely examined the movements of discounts/premiums of 34 SCCEFs during the Asian currency crisis period (July 1 1997 – December 5 1997) in comparison to the pre-crisis period (January 1 1996 – June 30 1997). The study identified two distinctive patterns: the Southeast Asian pattern unique to the funds in crisis and the Latin American pattern unique to the funds least affected by the crisis. The present study uses quasi-experimental design and investigates whether these patterns could also be found during the pre-, crisis, and post-Mexican currency crisis periods.

Background and Research Questions of the Study

Several studies, including Barclay et al. (1993); Mulugetta and Mulugetta (1997a and 1997b); Lee et al. (1991); Eun et al. (1991); Kim (1994): and Droms and Walker (1994), attempted to identify the reasons for discounts or premiums in closed-end funds and the performance of these funds. Portfolio theory states, all other things being equal, that diversification reduces risk and leads to price appreciation. SCCEFs are mainly composed of different securities within a specific single country. They are portfolios of securities where each of the securities is traded in the issuing country while the SCCEF itself is traded as a fund in another country such as Hong Kong, UK, US, etc. Therefore, the market price of the SCCEF must be greater than the weighted average price of securities that make up the SCCEF as a result of the diversification embedded in the fund. However, similar to most other studies, more than 80 per cent of the samples registered persistent discounts according to the Mulugetta and Mulugetta (1997b) study from June 19 1995 to June 16 1997. Some of the major reasons for the persistent discount in SCCEFs are attributed to lack of awareness of closed-end funds by the investing public in general, inferior management compared to open-end funds, agency costs, unrealized capital gain liabilities not included in the computation of NAV and illiquidity of some securities included in closed-end funds in particular.

In their 1990 article, Lee et al. explored the role of investors' sentiment in explaining closed-end fund discounts and the small-firm effects by analysing data from July 1965 to December 1985. They have expanded the previous study conducted by De Long et al. (1990). They explain that there are two types of investors: rational and noise investors. Unlike rational investors, noise traders' expectations about asset returns are partly influenced by their sentiments, which cause overestimation on asset return at some times and underestimation at other times. It is reasoned that noise traders' overestimation and underestimation on returns are unpredictable by rational investors and that the ill-estimations tend to be correlated across noise traders and therefore cannot be diversified. As a result, the funds, such as closed-end funds, which are largely comprised of individual investors, are subject to the systematic risk of such noise traders' sentiments. When this risk is priced at equilibrium, the funds are expected to earn higher returns in comparison to their fundamental values and therefore the funds tend to be under-priced. This is one of the reasons forwarded as to why closed-end funds are usually discounted in comparison to NAV of the funds.

Lee et al.'s work was challenged by Chen et al. (1993a, 1993b) in terms of statistical significance of the model. The revised model by Chen et al. attempted to associate the return on closed-end fund market price to: 1) the return on net asset value and 2) the return on each of the Center for Research in Security Price's size-decile portfolios. Chopra et al. (1993a, 1993b) improved their original model by acknowledging the contributions by Chen et al. in subtracting the return on the net asset value from the return on the share price of closed-end funds, and revealed that investors' sentiment still played a significant role in explaining anomaly.

Mulugetta and Mulugetta (1997a, 1997b) attempted to examine the anomaly of SCCEF discounts from a similar but slightly different angle. Although the 'investor sentiment' argument is convincing, this argument still fails to explain the existence of persistent premiums of some funds. Such funds were represented by several Asian SCCEFs. The question that arises is how to explain the existence of persistent premium if the anomaly of closed-end funds' share price is caused by the resale price risk attributed to individual investors' sentiment. Mulugetta and Mulugetta turned to the 'differential information holding' explanation. They argue that, in contrast to individual investors, closed-end fund (CEF) managers and institutional investors are likely to hold more accurate information (i.e., change in exchange rate) affecting the prices of securities that make up the SCCEFs. SCCEF market prices, being largely determined by individual investors, might not adjust to information as quickly and accurately as the NAVs, which are traditionally computed by fund management professionals. Individual investors' inability to incorporate information into price accurately (overestimate or underestimate) determines the magnitude/direction of fluctuations of discounts/premiums of SCCEFs after their initial public offerings.

In their 1997b study, Mulugetta and Mulugetta expected that market prices of SCCEFs funds were partly driven by the sentiment of individual investors to a particular country. The majority of individual investors who do not have access to up-to-date exchange rate information may underestimate dollar appreciation (or overestimate local currency). Then, this investor sentiment will lead SCCEF prices to depreciate slower than NAV and, therefore, cause SCCEFs' discounts to decrease or premiums to increase. The majority of Far East SCCEFs supported this expectation, indicating that widening premiums of Asian SCCEFs seem to be caused by overestimation of regional economic growth and underestimation of dollar appreciation. This pattern, however, did not emerge among the European SCCEFs.

The recent study by Mulugetta et al. (1998) has closely examined the movements of discounts/premiums of 34 SCCEFs during the Asian currency crisis period (July 1 1997 – December 5 1997) in comparison to the pre-crisis period (January 1, 1996 to June 30 1997). The study identified two distinctive patterns: the Southeast Asian pattern unique to the funds in crisis and the Latin American pattern unique to the funds least affected by the crisis. The SCCEFs of Indonesia, Malaysia, Singapore, Thailand and Japan represented the first pattern, where the discounts significantly shrank (or the premiums grew) due to the faster depreciation of the NAV in comparison to the reduction in price. From the differential information holding perspective, it is reasoned that during the currency crisis most individual investors faced difficulty in accurately understanding the speed and the magnitude of the depreciation of the currency and the values of the securities that made up the SCCEFs. As a result, the reduction of the SCCEFs' price may not have occurred as quickly as the NAV, which led to the shrinking discounts and widening premiums.

In contrast, the discounts of the Latin American funds widened during the crisis period due to faster growth of the NAVs in comparison to the market prices. In Latin America as well as in Taiwan, the securities that made up the SCCEFs remained strong and increased in value over the period studied despite the temporary depreciation of the local currencies. The depreciation appeared to be a sympathetic reaction rather than one driven by fundamental economic forces. This reaction had been discerned more clearly by managers than by investors in SCCEFs. In this intriguing investment environment, it seemed difficult for individual investors to understand the speed and the magnitude of the appreciation or depreciation of the underlying securities. Thus, the increase in the SCCEFs' price was smaller than the NAV, which widened the discounts. These macro-level analysis results were also supported by the regression analysis at the micro level. The movements of discounts/premiums of European SCCEFs were similar to those in Latin America, but were less distinctive than the Latin American funds.

Research Questions

The present study further explores the 'differential information holding' explanation. The study examines the behaviour of major SCCEFs during the Mexican currency crisis in comparison to the pre-crisis as well as the post-crisis period in order to examine the following research questions:

1. Would any significant changes in SCCEFs' prices and NAVs be observed during the crisis period in comparison to the pre-crisis as well as the post-crisis period? An SCCEF is a portfolio comprised mainly of securities of a specific country traded in another national market. Since a SCCEF is a portfolio of securities, for example from Mexico, traded in the US, and the number of shares outstanding is fixed, the appreciation of the dollar against the Mexican peso will reduce the market price of the SCCEF. The appreciation of the dollar will now have more purchasing power in Mexico for goods, services, or securities, whereas Mexican securities bundled as a portfolio, traded in the US will command a lower price than the pre-dollar appreciation era. If SCCEF investors are reasonably rational, then we expect that as currency depreciates against the dollar, the market price of SCCEF and NAV will also depreciate by the same magnitude. Thus, significant reductions in SCCEFs' prices and NAVs are expected to occur between the pre-crisis and the crisis periods, and appreciation in SECCEF prices and NAVs are expected when the crisis is over.

2. Would the change in SCCEFs' prices differ from the changes in NAVs during the crisis period in comparison to the pre-crisis as well as the post-crisis period? If SCCEF investors are rational investors, then we should expect that as currency depreciates against the dollar, the market price of SCCEF and NAV will also depreciate by the same magnitude. However, if a significant number of SCCEF investors are noise traders who have less

access to accurate information and tend to be driven by sentiment, the market price of SCCEF may not be influenced by fundamental economic factors, including exchange rate, in the way
described above. In the currency crisis, individual investors tend
to underestimate the magnitude of the change in the local currency rate against the dollar as our recent study indicates. If this
is the case, we may expect that the market price of Mexican
SCCEFs may not depreciate as fast as the NAVs during the Mexican currency crisis. Similarly, the market price of Mexican
SCCEFs may not appreciate as fast as the NAVs during the post-
Mexican currency crisis.

3. Would there be any significant change in the magnitude and
   direction of SCCEFs' discounts/premiums during the crisis
   period in comparison to the pre-crisis period as well as the post-
   crisis period? According to the 'differential information holding' explanation, the majority of individual investors may not
   have access to accurate information in the change in exchange
   rate and other key variables. If these noise traders tend to underestimate the magnitude of the change because of lack of accurate   information,   then   investors   underestimate   dollar
   appreciation (or overestimate local currency as well as local
   economy strength), which will result in slower depreciation of
   SCCEF prices than NAVs. In such instances, the existing discounts are likely to shrink or the premiums are likely to widen.
   In the post-currency crisis period on the other hand, individual
   investors underestimate the magnitude and the speed of the
   local currency recovery, which will lead to slower appreciation of
   SCCEF prices than NAVs. In this case, the existing discounts will
   widen or the premiums will shrink.

Types of Data for the Study and Statistical Models

Types of Data for the Study

To answer the above questions a sample of 15 SCCEFs were investigated from January 1 1994 to November 30 1994 (the pre-Mexican
crisis period), from December 1 1994 to December 31 1995 (the
crisis period) and from January 1 1996 to December 31 1996. Similarly, 34 SCCEFs were also examined from January 1 1996 to June 30
1997 (the pre-Asian crisis period) and from July 1 1997 to
December 5 1997 (the Asian crisis period). For each, the daily price
and volume of shares traded were collected. Corresponding to each
SCCEF nation, exchange rates and regional representative five

SCCEFs' prices (one each from Central and South America and Europe, and two from Asia), were also retrieved from the Center for Trading and Analysis of Financial Instruments at Ithaca College. The daily S&P index was retrieved for the same period, as well as the net asset value (NAV) of the 15 SCCEFs from *Wall Street Journal*, and the Wiesenberger Fund Edge data base.

Model and Statistical Method

To examine the research expectations, four statistical models are used:

$$Y_1 = B_0 + D + B_1X_{11} + B_2X_{12} + B_3X_{13} + B_4X_{14} + B_5D^*X_{11} + B_6D^*X_{12} + B_7D^*X_{13} + B_8D^*X_{14} + e \qquad (1)$$

Where:

Y_1	= Ln SCCEF prices
D	= Dichotomous variable to distinguish the crisis period from the pre-crisis (post-crisis) period
X_{11}	= Ln S&P500 index
X_{12}	= Ln Regional CEF price index
X_{13}	= Ln volume of share traded
X_{14}	= Ln exchange rate (currency/$)
$D^*X_{11} \ldots D^*X_{14}$	= Interaction terms between D and $X_{11} \ldots X_{14}$
$B_0 \ldots B_8$	= Regression coefficients

$$Y_2 = B_0 + D + B_1X_{21} + B_2X_{22} + B_3X_{23} + B_4X_{24} + B_5D^*X_{21} + B_6D^*X_{22} + B_7D^*X_{23} + B_8D^*X_{24} + e \qquad (2)$$

Where:

Y_2 = Ln NAV

Independent variables are the same as above

Models (1) and (2) examine the impact of four independent variables on SCCEF price and NAV separately, and also examine the statistical difference in the coefficients of the independent variables in study periods 1 and 2 using interaction terms.

$$Y_3 = B_0 + D + B_1X_{31} + B_2X_{32} + B_3X_{33} + B_4X_{34} + B_5X_{35} + B_6D^*X_{31} + B_7D^*X_{32} + B_8D^*X_{33} + B_9D^*X_{34} + B_{10}D^*X_{35} + e \qquad (3)$$

Where:

Y_3	= Ln SCCEF prices
D	= Dichotomous variable to distinguish the crisis period from the pre-crisis (post-crisis) period

X_{31} = Ln NAV
X_{32} = Ln S&P 500 index
X_{33} = Ln Regional CEF price index
X_{34} = Ln volume of share traded
X_{35} = Ln exchange rate (currency/$)
$D*X_{31} \ldots D*X_{35}$ = Interaction terms between D and $X_{31} \ldots X_{35}$
$B_0 \ldots B_{10}$ = Regression coefficients

By using NAV as an independent variable and SCCEF price as a dependent variable, Model (3) examines how much S&P, Region Index, Volume and Exchange rates can explain SCCEF price variance which are not explained by NAV. If the coefficient associated with exchange rate change is positive, for example, it indicates that depreciation of the SCCEF price is slower in comparison to the depreciation of NAV. This implies that as the dollar appreciates, SCCEFs' discount shrinks or SCCEFs' premium enlarges.

$$Y_4 = B_0 + D + B_1X_{41} + B_2X_{42} + B_3X_{43} + B_4X_{44} +$$
$$B_5D*X_{41} + B_6D*X_{42} + B_7D*X_{43} + B_8D*X_{44} + e \qquad (4)$$

Where:

Y_4 = Discounts/premiums ((SCCEF prices -NAV)/NAV);
D   = Dichotomous variable to distinguish study period 1 (Jan 1996 – June 1997) and study period 2 (July 1997 – Dec 1997);
X_{41} = Ln S&P500 Index;
X_{42} = Ln Regional CEF price index;
X_{43} = Ln volume of share traded;
X_{44} = Ln exchange rate (regional currency/$);
$D*X_{41} \ldots D*X_{44}$ = Interaction terms between D and $X_{41} \ldots X_{44}$;
$B_0 \ldots B_8$ = Regression coefficients

Model (4) uses discounts/premiums as a dependent variable and examines the impact of the four independent variables more directly than Model (3).

Results

Descriptive Analysis Results

Tables 21.1(a) and 21.1(b) indicate the descriptive statistics of the change in exchange rates during the Asian crisis and the Mexican currency crisis respectively. The volatility and the magnitude of the

TABLE 21.1(a): Currency Rate Change: Pre vs. Asian Currency Crisis Period)

	Pre-Crisis Mean	Crisis Mean	% Change	T-test	Pre-Crisis Minimum	Crisis Minimum	Pre-Crisis Maximum	Crisis Maximum	Pre-Crisis STD	Crisis STD
Japanese Yen	112.54	118.99	5.73%	***	103.92	111.42	127.03	127.74	6.66	3.93
Korean Won	824.36	919.59	11.55%	***	768.90	884.70	893.70	1169.00	38.16	53.83
Taiwan Dollars	27.43	28.91	5.38%	***	26.90	27.77	27.85	32.64	0.20	1.27
Indonesian Rupiah	2350.22	2940.20	25.10%	***	2293.33	2419.03	2447.31	3716.76	36.16	448.31
Malaysian Ringgit	2.51	2.92	16.22%	***	2.47	2.49	2.56	3.53	0.02	0.34
Singapore Dollars	1.42	1.50	6.29%	***	1.39	1.42	1.45	1.60	0.01	0.06
Thai Baht	25.51	32.88	28.91%	***	24.90	22.60	26.20	40.60	0.28	4.96
Indian Rupees	35.61	36.25	1.77%	***	34.10	35.71	38.05	39.10	0.61	0.62
Australian Dollars	0.78	0.73	-6.53%	***	0.73	0.68	0.82	0.76	0.02	0.02
Brazilian Reals	1.04	1.09	4.81%	***	1.01	1.07	1.07	1.11	0.02	0.01
Chilean Pesos	413.89	416.77	0.70%	***	402.20	411.40	428.00	436.50	5.12	4.36
Mexican Pesos	7.68	7.91	2.98%	***	7.33	7.72	8.05	8.41	0.19	0.19
German Marks	1.56	1.77	14.02%	***	1.44	1.71	1.73	1.88	0.09	0.04
Irish Punt	1.59	1.48	-6.73%	***	1.49	1.43	1.69	1.53	0.04	0.03
Italian Lira	1576.47	1734.03	9.99%	***	1496.00	1675.50	1718.61	1840.75	63.30	40.65
Spanish Pesetas	131.08	149.78	14.27%	***	120.95	144.35	146.10	158.80	7.46	3.74
Swiss Francs	1.30	1.46	12.81%	***	1.16	1.39	1.49	1.54	0.10	0.04
British Pounds	0.46	0.44	-5.39%	***	0.43	0.42	0.49	0.46	0.02	0.01
South African Rand	4.36	4.66	7.05%	***	3.63	4.47	4.75	4.86	0.30	0.11

*** Significant at the .0001 level

Pre-Asian Currency Crisis Period – January 1, 1996 to June 30, 1997

Asian Currency Crisis Period – July 1, 1997 to December 5, 1997

TABLE 21.1(b): Currency Rate Change: Pre vs. Mexican Currency Crisis vs. Post Period

	Pre-Crisis Mean	Crisis Mean	Pre vs. Crisis % change	T-test	Post-Crisis Mean	Crisis vs. Post % change	T-test	Pre-Crisis Minimum	Crisis Minimum	Post-Crisis Minimum	Pre-Crisis Maximum	Crisis Maximum	Post-Crisis Maximum	Pre-Crisis STD	Crisis STD	Post-Crisis STD
Japanese Yen	102.36	94.45	-7.74%	***	108.78	15.18%	***	96.77	81.12	103.92	113.10	104.20	116.13	4.16	7.12	2.89
Korean Won	807.91	774.35	-4.15%	***	803.64	3.78%	***	797.32	758.39	768.90	817.17	797.61	844.90	4.49	12.00	21.47
Malaysian Ringgit	2.63	2.51	-4.45%	***	2.52	0.12%	ns	2.55	2.39	2.48	2.79	2.57	2.56	0.08	0.04	0.02
Singapore Dollars	1.53	1.42	-7.31%	***	1.41	-0.77%	***	1.46	1.39	1.39	1.61	1.47	1.43	0.05	0.02	0.01
Thai Baht	25.16	24.93	-0.92%	***	25.36	1.71%	***	1511.50	1569.00	1496.00	1706.75	1736.25	1602.00	52.03	38.00	24.32
Mexican Pesos	3.33	6.26	87.73%	***	7.60	21.50%	***	3.11	3.44	7.33	3.45	8.05	8.05	0.11	0.95	0.16
German Marks	1.63	1.44	-11.25%	***	1.50	4.23%	***	1.49	1.36	1.44	1.76	1.58	1.57	0.08	0.06	0.03
Irish Punt	1.49	1.60	6.96%	***	1.60	0.13%	ns	1.40	1.52	1.55	1.62	1.66	1.69	0.06	0.03	0.03
Italian Lira	1609.57	1629.78	1.26%	***	1542.66	-5.35%	***	1511.50	1569.00	1496.00	1706.75	1736.25	1602.00	52.03	38.00	24.32
Spanish Pesetas	133.99	125.25	-6.52%	***	126.69	1.15%	***	124.54	118.54	120.95	145.47	133.93	131.55	5.70	4.32	2.33

*** Significant at the .0001 level

Pre- Mexican Currency Crisis Period – January 1, 1994 to November 30, 1994

Mexican Currency Crisis Period – December 1, 1994 to December 31, 1995

Post- Mexican Currency Crisis Period – January 1, 1996 to December 31, 1996

depreciation of the Korean Won, Indonesian Rupiah, Malaysian Ringgit and Thai Baht were large in the recent Asian Crisis, but not as much as the depreciation of the Mexican Peso in the 1994 crisis. Although it became less volatile, the depreciation of the Mexican Peso continued in 1996. Interestingly, the majority of the currencies examined showed some depreciation reacting to the Asian currency crisis, whereas 70 per cent of the currencies appreciated during the Mexican crisis. The differential reaction to the currency crises may be partly attributed to the accelerated pace of global integration of the financial markets as well as the economic influence of Mexico in comparison to Southeast Asia on global financial markets.

Tables 21.2(a) and 21.2(b) as well as Table 21.3(a) and 21.3(b) represent the change in SCCEF market prices and NAVs. Under the Asian crisis, the decreases in both market values and NAVs of SCCEFs in South Korea, Indonesia, Malaysia, Singapore, Thailand and Japan were large, ranging from -16 per cent to -38 per cent change in market price, and from -16.5 per cent to -57 per cent change in NAV. Under the Mexican crisis, the reduction of Mexican SCCEFs ranged from -46 per cent to -57 per cent in price and from -49 per cent to -61 per cent in NAV.

As indicated in Tables 21.2(a) and 21.3(a), under the Asian crisis, the non-Asian SCCEFs remained solid, and the prices and the NAVs of the SCCEFs significantly increased. The South American and European funds were particularly bullish. Interestingly, the behaviour of the Taiwanese funds was remarkably similar to the South American funds, with significant increase in both the market price and the NAV. Taiwan was, in a sense, the 'oasis' amid the region in crisis. In contrast, under the Mexican crisis, almost all non-Mexican SCCEFs declined in prices and NAVs, but the declines were less dramatic in comparison to the depreciation of the Mexican SCCEFs.

Table 21.4(a) indicates the change in discounts or premiums of SCCEFs in the Asian crisis. Two distinctive patterns were identified in this table: the Southeast Asian pattern unique to the funds in crisis and the Latin American pattern unique to the funds least affected by the crisis. The SCCEFs of Indonesia, Malaysia, Singapore, Thailand and Japan represent the first pattern, where the discounts significantly shrank (or the premiums grew) due to the faster depreciation of the NAV in comparison to the reduction of the price. This phenomenon can be interpreted from the 'differential information holding' perspective. Closed-end fund (CEF) managers and institutional investors are likely to hold more

TABLE 21.2(a): SCCEF Price Change: Pre vs. Asian Currency Crisis Period

	Pre-Crisis Mean	Crisis Mean	% Change	T-test	Pre-Crisis Minimum	Crisis Minimum	Pre-Crisis Maximum	Crisis Maximum	Pre-Crisis STD	Crisis STD
Japan OTC Equity	7.77	6.39	-17.69%	***	5.88	4.88	9.75	7.38	1.02	0.63
Japan Equity	11.42	9.05	-20.73%	***	9.00	6.63	14.75	10.75	1.60	1.11
Korea Equity	7.64	5.41	-29.19%	***	5.88	3.00	9.50	7.13	1.13	1.17
Korea Fund	18.53	12.28	-33.74%	***	11.75	6.44	24.00	16.25	3.42	2.73
Fidelity Advisor Korea	10.33	7.30	-29.31%	***	7.38	4.00	12.50	9.63	1.44	1.65
Taiwan Fund	23.04	24.00	4.18%	***	19.88	17.69	26.50	28.44	1.34	2.68
Taiwan Equity	10.56	13.55	28.28%	***	8.88	9.88	12.38	16.50	0.70	1.97
ROC Taiwan	10.83	11.72	8.18%	***	8.63	8.06	13.63	14.19	1.03	1.52
Indonesia Fund	10.75	8.81	-18.07%	***	8.75	5.5	13.25	12.38	1.20	1.73
Indonesian Jakalta Grwoth	8.87	7.45	-16.04%	***	7.50	4.13	10.50	10.38	0.71	1.91
Malaysia Fund	18.53	11.74*	-36.67%	***	14.25	6.63	21.25	15.25	1.50	2.64
Singapore Fund	12.69	10.62	-16.29%	***	10.75	7.63	15.50	12.00	1.17	1.30
Thai Fund	20.54	12.68	-38.28%	***	14.00	7.63	27.50	18.25	3.76	2.46
Thai Capital	12.14	7.75	-36.18%	***	8.00	4.63	16.75	11.38	2.38	1.40
Morgan Stanley India Inv	10.24	11.49	12.20%	***	8.00	7.69	12.63	14.25	0.96	1.55
India Fund	8.59	9.34	8.78%	***	6.63	7.94	11.13	10.75	1.07	0.50
Australia Fund	8.91	8.38	-5.95%	***	8.13	7.00	9.56	9.00	0.29	0.57
Brazil Fund	23.14	27.20	17.57%	***	20.63	18.63	27.25	31.88	1.72	3.20
Brazil Equity	13.97	15.27	9.26%	***	11.88	10.13	17.00	17.88	1.26	1.95
Chile Fund	23.53	24.54	4.27%	***	20.50	19.88	26.63	27.38	1.16	2.04
Mexico Fund	15.55	20.51	31.84%	***	13.25	17.00	17.25	23.25	0.88	1.79
Mexico Equity	10.14	13.02	28.37%	***	9.00	10.75	11.25	14.81	0.47	1.04
Emerging Mexico Fund	7.28	10.01	37.52%	***	6.13	8.13	8.38	11.81	0.47	0.97
New Germany	13.16	15.24	15.76%	***	11.75	12.94	15.50	16.69	0.91	0.85
Germany Fund	12.39	14.85	19.87%	***	11.13	12.00	14.38	16.38	0.81	0.97
Emerging Germany Fund	7.86	10.55	34.26%	***	7.00	9.63	9.75	11.56	0.61	0.43
Irish Fund	13.84	16.44	18.77%	***	12.00	15.50	16.50	17.38	0.88	0.45
Italy Fund	8.71	9.78	12.30%	***	7.75	9.00	10.25	10.75	0.52	0.44
Spain Fund	10.28	14.16	37.73%	***	8.75	13.13	13.75	15.88	1.12	0.63
Spain Growth	11.94	15.10	26.40%	***	10.75	13.81	14.50	16.88	0.77	0.68
Swiss Helvetia	21.10	24.88	17.89%	***	19.50	23.38	24.00	26.50	0.78	0.79
UK Fund	13.18	13.54	2.67%	***	11.75	12.50	14.75	15.13	0.83	0.59
South Africa New Fund	14.13	14.85	5.04%	***	12.25	12.50	18.00	16.50	1.26	1.13
Southern Africa Fund	16.55	17.38	5.02%	***	14.13	15.31	19.88	18.44	1.00	0.82

*** Significant at the .001 level

Table 21.2(b): SCCEF Price Change: Pre vs. Mexican Currency Crisis vs. Post Period

	Pre-Crisis Mean	Crisis Mean	Pre vs. Crisis % change	T-test	Post-Crisis Mean	Crisis vs. Post % change	T-test	Pre-Crisis Minimum	Crisis Minimum	Post-Crisis Minimum	Pre-Crisis Maximum	Crisis Maximum	Post-Crisis Maximum	Pre-Crisis STD	Crisis STD	Post-Crisis STD
Japan OTC Equity	12.20	8.98	−26.40%	***	8.27	−7.90%	***	9.75	7.88	6.63	14.50	10.00	9.75	1.09	0.52	0.72
Japan Equity	15.63	13.14	−15.96%	***	12.16	−7.45%	***	13.50	10.63	9.25	17.88	16.00	14.75	0.86	0.99	1.29
Korea Equity	11.29	8.47	−24.97%	***	8.12	−4.09%	***	9.13	7.38	6.13	14.88	9.63	9.50	1.22	0.48	0.97
Korea Fund	23.44	21.27	−9.26%	***	20.14	−5.32%	***	18.88	18.75	14.50	27.63	23.38	24.00	1.96	0.96	2.53
Malaysia Fund	22.65	18.20	−19.63%	***	19.26	5.84%	***	17.75	15.38	17.00	29.63	21.50	21.25	1.81	1.44	0.74
Singapore Fund	18.09	14.52	−19.74%	***	13.08	−9.92%	***	15.00	12.63	11.38	23.13	17.25	15.50	1.43	1.18	1.13
Thai Fund	29.65	24.00	−19.05%	***	22.34	−6.92%	***	24.25	19.50	16.00	37.13	28.38	27.50	2.52	1.66	2.88
Thai Capital	18.25	15.72	−13.87%	***	13.32	−15.25%	***	15.00	13.50	9.63	24.00	19.00	16.75	1.53	1.17	1.74
Mexico Fund	32.36	16.64	−48.58%	***	15.21	−8.60%	***	25.13	10.75	13.25	39.50	31.13	17.00	3.23	4.01	0.78
Mexico Equity	21.77	11.68	−46.34%	***	10.03	−14.14%	***	17.75	8.38	9.00	25.13	23.50	11.25	1.54	2.97	0.48
Emerging Mexico Fund	19.81	8.57	−56.76%	***	7.06	−17.55%	***	15.13	5.25	6.13	26.63	18.50	7.88	2.40	2.58	0.35
Emerging Germany Fund	8.20	7.32	−10.77%	***	7.56	3.28%	***	7.25	6.75	7.00	9.25	8.00	8.25	0.40	0.24	0.32
Irish Fund	9.56	10.56	10.51%	***	13.41	26.98%	***	8.38	8.50	12.00	11.00	12.50	14.75	0.62	1.14	0.56
Italy Fund	10.23	8.04	−21.44%	***	8.48	5.46%	***	8.13	7.25	7.75	12.38	9.25	9.13	1.02	0.40	0.33
Spain Fund	9.94	8.49	−14.55%	***	9.65	13.68%	***	8.63	7.38	8.75	12.75	9.25	11.38	0.85	0.39	0.47

*** Significant at the .001 level

TABLE 21.3(a): Net Asset Value Change: Pre vs. Asian Currency Crisis Period

	Pre-Crisis Mean	Crisis Mean	% Change	T-test	Pre-Crisis Minimum	Crisis Minimum	Pre-Crisis Maximum	Crisis Maximum	Pre-Crisis STD	Crisis STD
Japan OTC Equity	7.67	6.23	-18.71%	***	5.77	4.48	9.14	7.46	0.97	0.85
Japan Equity	10.39	7.99	-23.06%	***	7.61	6.22	12.58	9.38	1.49	1.00
Korea Equity	7.72	5.49	-28.89%	***	5.67	2.86	10.01	6.52	1.30	0.94
Korea Fund	17.03	11.85	-30.42%	***	11.92	6.57	22.18	13.82	3.10	1.95
Fidelity Advisor Korea	10.57	7.66	-27.47%	***	7.73	3.92	13.66	9.14	1.80	1.45
Taiwan Fund	23.61	31.03	31.46%	***	17.41	23.44	31.72	36.37	4.28	3.73
Taiwan Equity	11.53	17.76	54.09%	***	8.84	12.17	15.59	21.97	1.95	2.79
ROC Taiwan	11.21	14.67	30.86%	***	8.49	10.65	15.78	17.63	2.03	2.03
Indonesia Fund	10.22	8.54	-16.45%	***	8.6	4.7	11.97	12.51	0.83	2.70
Indonesian Jakalta Growth	9.45	7.72	-18.30%	***	8.26	3.87	10.82	11.37	0.64	2.67
Malaysia Fund	20.36	11.21	-44.97%	***	16.25	4.99	22.26	17.30	1.48	3.93
Singapore Fund	13.07	10.61	-18.77%	***	11.96	7.88	14.08	12.59	0.53	1.60
Thai Fund	20.49	8.79	-57.12%	***	11.60	4.86	27.81	12.13	5.22	2.17
Thai Capital	12.29	5.53	-55.03%	***	6.86	3.52	17.52	7.52	3.08	1.10
Morgan Stanley India Inv	9.75	10.96	12.46%	***	7.86	8.97	11.61	12.50	0.98	0.81
India Fund	8.63	9.66	12.02%	***	6.95	8.65	10.16	10.42	0.83	0.44
Australia Fund	10.70	10.58	-1.11%	*	9.98	9.14	11.39	11.16	0.32	0.60
Brazil Fund	26.33	33.72	28.09%	***	20.69	23.89	32.64	38.09	2.87	3.40
Brazil Equity	15.95	18.96	18.86%	***	12.85	13.03	19.50	21.26	1.68	2.06
Chile Fund	26.02	29.08	11.79%	***	22.59	24.95	28.89	30.68	1.08	1.61
Mexico Fund	18.55	25.67	38.38%	***	15.09	21.09	21.51	29.52	1.44	2.35
Mexico Equity	12.25	16.28	32.97%	***	10.19	13.46	13.68	18.70	0.79	1.42
Emerging Mexico Fund	8.72	12.55	43.97%	***	6.75	9.92	10.13	14.55	0.75	1.28
New Germany	17.11	19.33	12.98%	***	15.28	16.32	19.72	20.80	1.07	0.99
Germany Fund	15.22	18.28	20.12%	***	13.52	14.61	17.82	20.07	1.00	1.24
Emerging Germany Fund	10.15	12.84	26.54%	***	9.11	11.62	11.99	13.73	0.69	0.51
Irish Fund	15.99	19.46	21.72%	***	13.69	17.92	17.92	20.54	1.13	0.67
Italy Fund	10.37	11.97	15.41%	***	8.91	10.56	12.12	13.14	0.71	0.63
Spain Fund	12.82	17.54	36.84%	***	10.79	16.38	16.98	18.91	1.53	0.65
Spain Growth	14.67	18.43	25.64%	***	13.00	17.14	18.40	19.84	1.11	0.63
Swiss Helvetia	25.15	30.86	22.70%	***	22.99	28.49	29.73	32.88	1.13	1.00
UK Fund	15.91	16.17	1.69%	***	14.40	15.11	17.35	17.27	0.84	0.61
South Africa New Fund	17.59	18.20	3.47%	***	15.20	15.83	21.49	19.37	1.51	1.01
Southern Africa Fund	20.34	21.19	4.17%	***	17.11	18.35	23.41	22.28	1.27	0.89

*** Significant at the .001 level
** Significant at the .01 level
* Significant at the .05 level

TABLE 21.3(b): Net Asset Value Change: Pre vs. Mexican Currency Crisis vs. Post Period

	Pre-Crisis Mean	Crisis Mean	Pre vs. Crisis % change	T-test	Post-Crisis Mean	Crisis vs. Post % change	T-test	Pre-Crisis Minimum	Crisis Minimum	Post-Crisis Minimum	Pre-Crisis Maximum	Crisis Maximum	Post-Crisis Maximum	Pre-Crisis STD	Crisis STD	Post-Crisis STD
Japan OTC Equity	11.00	8.51	−22.63%	***	8.20	−3.66%	***	8.95	7.47	6.96	12.35	10.40	9.14	0.74	0.78	0.56
Japan Equity	14.49	12.31	−15.04%	***	11.26	−8.51%	***	11.39	11.06	8.98	15.93	13.97	12.58	0.95	0.60	0.65
Korea Equity	10.63	9.49	−10.74%	***	8.38	−11.72%	***	9.96	8.52	6.07	11.51	11.19	10.01	0.41	0.57	0.93
Korea Fund	19.79	20.52	3.67%	***	18.54	−9.62%	***	16.64	18.95	13.22	24.41	22.69	22.18	2.02	0.88	2.32
Malaysia Fund	22.41	19.47	−13.14%	***	21.09	8.35%	***	19.43	16.48	18.58	27.46	21.99	22.26	1.82	1.45	0.78
Singapore Fund	16.82	14.03	−16.63%	***	13.08	−6.73%	***	15.14	12.57	12.12	18.50	17.12	13.88	0.95	0.88	0.47
Thai Fund	32.55	27.49	−15.54%	***	23.16	−15.78%	***	27.26	24.70	15.63	39.42	32.45	27.81	2.88	1.71	3.66
Thai Capital	19.86	17.91	−9.81%	***	13.92	−22.28%	***	17.02	16.23	9.61	23.81	20.37	17.52	1.80	1.16	2.00
Mexico Fund	33.70	16.47	−51.14%	***	17.84	8.38%	***	27.94	9.47	15.09	39.98	33.66	19.57	3.04	4.54	1.02
Mexico Equity	20.88	10.75	−48.51%	***	12.02	11.75%	***	18.05	6.61	10.19	23.23	22.29	13.25	1.37	2.97	0.79
Emerging Mexico Fund	19.97	7.72	−61.35%	***	8.37	8.43%	***	17.04	4.62	6.75	24.32	19.22	9.24	1.83	2.88	0.59
Emerging Germany Fund	9.67	9.30	−3.82%	***	9.79	5.32%	***	9.00	8.67	9.11	10.19	9.95	10.68	0.28	0.27	0.38
Irish Fund	10.52	12.44	18.22%	***	15.55	24.98%	***	9.77	9.92	13.69	11.20	14.07	17.24	0.37	1.39	1.04
Italy Fund	10.51	9.19	−12.52%	***	10.07	9.53%	***	9.49	8.12	8.91	12.06	10.04	11.15	0.71	0.49	0.54
Spain Fund	10.18	10.09	−0.92%	*	11.97	18.66%	***	9.63	8.81	10.79	10.79	11.23	14.60	0.27	0.61	0.78

*** Significant at the .001 level
* Significant at the .05 level

Table 21.4(a): Discount/Premium Change: Pre vs. Asian Currency Crisis Period

	Pre-Crisis Mean	Crisis Mean	% Change	T-test	Pre-Crisis Minimum	Crisis Minimum	Pre-Crisis Maximum	Crisis Maximum	Pre-Crisis STD	Crisis STD
Japan OTC Equity	1.56	3.19	1.63%	**	-13.08	-7.84	22.80	17.43	7.82	5.92
Japan Equity	10.39	13.38	2.99%	***	-7.73	0.38	28.60	23.78	8.46	4.95
Korea Equity	-0.61	-2.08	-1.47%	*	-12.68	-22.48	18.75	13.64	5.30	7.77
Korea Fund	8.82	2.65	-6.17%	***	-4.07	-24.70	20.06	22.46	4.67	8.82
Fidelity Advisor Korea	-1.63	-5.26	-3.63%	***	-13.28	-19.69	15.85	12.36	5.54	6.67
Taiwan Fund	0.06	-22.50	-22.56%	***	-25.25	-31.79	31.09	-13.11	14.59	3.52
Taiwan Equity	-6.62	-23.54	-16.92%	***	-26.61	-32.08	17.88	-12.70	11.74	3.19
ROC Taiwan	-1.65	-19.99	-18.34%	***	-19.20	-27.76	26.75	-11.88	11.37	3.00
Indonesia Fund	5.72	7.58	1.85%	ns	-15.03	-12.74	30.73	45.02	13.03	15.50
Indonesian Jakalta Growth	-5.93	-0.05	5.87%	***	-16.09	-16.83	16.14	26.58	6.93	11.27
Malaysia Fund	-8.93	9.88	18.81%	***	-16.23	-12.59	6.84	43.56	4.58	15.38
Singapore Fund	-3.01	0.54	3.55%	***	-13.45	-7.67	16.45	12.60	6.71	5.04
Thai Fund	2.45	46.55	44.10%	***	-14.09	20.57	26.55	88.02	9.90	13.05
Thai Capital	0.57	41.09	40.52%	***	-13.55	17.10	25.73	73.97	8.59	11.93
Morgan Stanley India Inv	5.34	4.40	-0.95%	ns	-7.69	-17.70	24.70	19.10	6.80	7.97
India Fund	-0.48	-3.23	-2.76%	***	-13.02	-16.97	18.31	5.75	7.01	4.47
Australia Fund	-16.73	-20.87	-4.14%	***	-22.77	-28.93	-9.56	-17.78	2.30	1.78
Brazil Fund	-11.53	-19.48	-7.95%	***	-20.92	-28.68	17.21	-13.53	7.90	2.60
Brazil Equity	-11.83	-19.56	-7.73%	***	-28.40	-38.06	32.30	-11.26	9.25	4.29
Chile Fund	-9.52	-15.74	-6.22%	***	-16.73	-26.19	-0.80	-8.94	3.12	3.22
Mexico Fund	-15.96	-20.03	-4.07%	***	-22.95	-27.18	-2.25	-0.01	3.73	3.15
Mexico Equity	-17.01	-19.92	-2.91%	***	-26.35	-35.54	-1.87	-12.06	3.60	3.30
Emerging Mexico Fund	-16.28	-20.14	-3.86%	***	-23.69	-34.64	3.70	-10.10	4.22	3.50
New Germany	-23.07	-21.18	1.90%	***	-28.30	-28.02	-17.20	-15.97	2.12	1.69
Germany Fund	-18.55	-18.72	-0.17%	ns	-23.70	-26.32	-11.24	-14.67	2.03	1.55
Emerging Germany Fund	-22.58	-17.81	4.76%	***	-28.64	-24.59	-17.12	-12.85	2.15	1.86
Irish Fund	-13.27	-15.46	-2.19%	***	-22.97	-23.28	0.65	-10.02	4.71	3.23
Italy Fund	-15.95	-18.23	-2.29%	***	-22.46	-23.70	0.00	-13.31	2.44	2.11
Spain Fund	-19.68	-19.30	0.38%	*	-23.80	-23.32	-12.84	-13.44	2.18	1.51
Spain Growth	-18.48	-18.08	0.40%	ns	-23.21	-21.87	-11.60	-11.46	1.91	2.20
Swiss Helvetia	-16.03	-19.36	-3.34%	***	-23.19	-25.13	-7.57	-14.62	2.59	1.84
UK Fund	-17.14	-16.30	0.84%	***	-21.62	-23.49	-12.70	-10.61	1.72	2.15
South Africa New Fund	-19.64	-18.49	1.15%	***	-25.19	-28.81	-15.42	-14.34	1.55	2.60
Southern Africa Fund	-18.62	-18.00	0.62%	***	-24.05	-22.58	-12.51	-14.40	1.90	1.31

*** Significant at the .001 level
** Significant at the .01 level
* Significant at the .05 level

Table 21.4(b): Discount/Premium Change: Pre vs. Mexican Currency Crisis vs. Post Period

	Pre-Crisis Mean	Crisis Mean	Pre vs. Crisis % change	T-test	Post-Crisis Mean	Crisis vs. Post % change	T-test	Pre-Crisis Minimum	Crisis Minimum	Post-Crisis Minimum	Pre-Crisis Maximum	Crisis Maximum	Post-Crisis Maximum	Pre-Crisis STD	Crisis STD	Post-Crisis STD
Japan OTC Equity	11.36%	6.08%	-5.28%	***	1.15%	-4.93%	***	-3.85%	-9.81%	-13.08%	45.44%	25.63%	22.80%	11.60%	7.54%	2.89%
Japan Equity	8.31%	6.89%	-1.42%	ns	7.87%	0.98%	ns	-5.33%	-13.32%	-7.73%	33.20%	31.80%	28.60%	8.53%	8.44%	8.40%
Korea Equity	6.15%	-10.68%	-16.84%	***	-3.07%	7.61%	***	-17.27%	-18.70%	-12.68%	31.87%	-1.16%	5.47%	10.35%	3.33%	3.46%
Korea Fund	19.01%	3.74%	-15.27%	***	8.63%	4.89%	***	-0.76%	-6.90%	0.55%	44.98%	14.17%	17.84%	9.69%	3.96%	3.27%
Malaysia Fund	1.26%	-6.45%	-7.71%	***	-8.53%	-2.07%	***	-12.57%	-18.13%	-14.19%	17.41%	5.94%	6.84%	6.34%	3.73%	5.23%
Singapore Fund	7.64%	3.55%	-4.09%	***	-0.16%	-3.71%	***	-6.08%	-15.50%	-10.37%	38.89%	16.84%	16.45%	7.94%	6.14%	5.86%
Thai Fund	-8.74%	-12.64%	-3.89%	***	-2.92%	9.72%	***	-24.99%	-28.16%	-14.09%	4.13%	-0.43%	8.29%	5.24%	4.42%	5.19%
Thai Capital	-7.87%	-12.20%	-4.34%	***	-3.95%	8.26%	***	-24.26%	-21.84%	-13.55%	4.60%	0.22%	11.04%	5.35%	3.58%	4.92%
Mexico Fund	-3.96%	2.32%	6.28%	***	-14.66%	-16.97%	***	-14.16%	-26.93%	-22.26%	7.92%	42.56%	-2.25%	4.16%	12.38%	3.59%
Mexico Equity	4.31%	10.13%	5.82%	***	-16.37%	-26.50%	***	-10.67%	-15.36%	-26.35%	16.92%	55.07%	-1.87%	4.59%	16.12%	3.92%
Emerging Mexico Fund	-0.95%	13.39%	14.34%	***	-15.40%	-28.80%	***	-14.45%	-15.29%	-23.69%	18.12%	67.75%	3.70%	5.31%	17.39%	4.53%
Emerging Germany Fund	-15.11%	-21.26%	-6.15%	***	-22.78%	-1.52%	***	-23.20%	-25.57%	-28.64%	-3.34%	-16.93%	-17.12%	4.03%	1.79%	2.13%
Irish Fund	-9.27%	-15.04%	-5.77%	***	-13.48%	1.56%	***	-15.72%	-23.24%	-22.97%	1.00%	-6.83%	0.65%	3.69%	2.69%	5.39%
Italy Fund	-2.50%	-12.47%	-9.96%	***	-15.70%	-3.23%	***	-18.67%	-18.42%	-19.84%	22.65%	0.22%	-7.05%	8.77%	3.36%	2.41%
Spain Fund	-2.42%	-15.70%	-13.28%	***	-19.24%	-3.54%	***	-14.56%	-22.78%	-23.15%	18.69%	-8.38%	-12.84%	7.65%	2.92%	2.28%

*** Significant at the .001 level

accurate information on the change in exchange rate or the forecasting of the country's future economic prospects, which affect the prices of securities that make up the SCCEFs. SCCEF market prices, being largely determined by individual investors, might not adjust to information as quickly and accurately as the NAVs. Particularly, during the economic crisis such as the one being observed in these countries, it is probably most difficult for individual investors to comprehend accurately the speed and the magnitude of the depreciation of the currency and the securities that make up the SCCEFs. As a result, the reduction in the SCCEFs' price may not occur as quickly as the NAV, which led to the shrinking discounts and the widening premiums.

During the Asian currency crisis, the Latin American pattern is an intriguing contrast to the Southeast Asian pattern. SCCEFs in Brazil, Chile, Mexico and Taiwan represented the Latin American pattern, whereas SCCEFs in India, Ireland, Italy and Switzerland also formed a similar pattern but to a limited extent. All of these funds were sold at a discount and the discounts widened during the crisis period, due to faster growth of the NAVs in comparison to the market prices. According to the 'differential information holding' explanation, this is indeed a mirror image of the Southeast Asian pattern. Despite the temporary depreciation of the local currencies of South American countries, the securities that make up the SCCEFs remained strong and increased in value over the period studied. In this confusing investment environment, SCCEF market prices, being largely determined by individual investors, were not adjusted as quickly and accurately as the NAVs. Particularly, when underlying securities are appreciating rapidly, it is rather difficult for individual investors to adjust with equal speed and magnitude to the appreciation of the securities that make up the SCCEFs. As a result, the increase in the SCCEFs' price was smaller than the NAV, which widened the discounts.

As presented in Table 21.4(b), the analysis of the Mexican SCCEFs during the Mexican currency crisis in comparison to the pre- as well as the post-crisis period also revealed a pattern quite similar to the Southeast Asian pattern described above. During the crisis, the discounts shrank (or the premiums grew) due to the faster depreciation of NAV than the reduction in price. Furthermore, during the post-crisis period, the discounts grew due to the faster growth of the NAV than the price as expected. In contrast to the Mexican SCCEFs, other non-Mexican SCCEFs demonstrated a pattern similar to the Latin American pattern observed in the Asian crisis, where the discounts widened and the premiums shrank as we had anticipated.

Regression Analysis Results

The results of the four regression models under the Mexican currency crisis are presented in Tables 21.5 to 21.8. They attempt to answer how exchange rates affected SCCEFs' prices and NAVs and how exchange rates impacted on the magnitude and direction of the SCCEFs' discounts/premiums.

If the depreciation of the currencies is rationally incorporated in the reduction of the SCCEFs' prices and NAVs as predicted, we should observe significant beta coefficients in the negative direction in the results of Model (1) and Model (2) tests. During the pre-Mexican crisis period, seven out of 15 funds' prices and 12 out of 15 funds' NAVs were significantly affected by change in exchange rates in the expected direction. During the Mexican crisis, however, only six funds' market prices and nine NAVs were explained as expected by the change in exchange rates. During the post-crisis period, 12 out of 15 funds' prices and 13 out of 15 NAVs were similarly explained. An important question, then, is why a substantial number of SCCEFs, nearly 50 per cent of the fund prices during the Mexican crisis period, were not explained by exchange rates in the expected direction. Although the data are not presented here, nearly 40 per cent of the fund prices during the Asian crisis period were not accounted for by exchange rates. These findings suggest that the change in the non-Asian currencies was most likely a sympathetic reaction to the currency crisis and thus an insignificant reflection of their economic fundamentals. Consequently, the currency change did not significantly affect the movements of the SCCEFs market prices or NAVs during the crisis.

Model (4) directly tests how much the change in exchange rate accounted for the movement of the discounts/premiums. It is of interest to examine whether the 'differential information holding' reasoning that was previously provided for the macro-level analysis still holds valid to explain the influence of the exchange rate on discounts/premiums for the micro-level analysis.

As mentioned earlier, the significant shrinkage of discounts (or widening of premiums) was observed among the Mexican SCCEFs in crisis. We have reasoned that it is difficult for individual investors to comprehend accurately the speed and magnitude of the depreciation of the currency and the securities that make up the SCCEFs.

TABLE 21.5. Pre vs. Mexican Currency Crisis vs. Post Periods

| | Japan Equity Fund | | | | | | | | Japan OTC Fund | | | | | | | |
| | Pre-Crisis Period | | Crisis Period | | Pre. vs Crisis | Post-Crisis Period | | Crisis vs. Post | Pre-Crisis Period | | Crisis Period | | Pre. vs Crisis | Post-Crisis Period | | Crisis vs. Post |
	Beta	Sig.	Beta	Sig.	Beta Change	Beta	Sig.	Beta Change	Beta	Sig.	Beta	Sig.	Beta Change	Beta	Sig.	Beta Change
Model 1																
Intercept	3.637	0.02	-0.191	0.70		9.531	0.00		7.050	0.00	2.773	0.00		10.940	0.00	
X1: SP500	-0.307	0.16	0.090	0.06	ns	-0.471	0.00	***	-1.382	0.00	-0.343	0.00	***	-0.574	0.00	**
X2: Region	0.051	0.49	0.420	0.00	***	0.634	0.00	**	0.276	0.01	0.341	0.00	ns	0.272	0.00	ns
X3: Volume	-0.004	0.52	-0.025	0.00	**	-0.022	0.00	ns	-0.006	0.47	-0.001	0.73	ns	0.003	0.47	ns
X4: Currency	0.187	0.24	0.271	0.00	ns	-1.169	0.00	***	0.681	0.00	0.149	0.00	**	-1.240	0.00	***
Model 2																
Intercept	14.918	0.00	4.820	0.00		10.835	0.00		17.263	0.00	7.159	0.00		12.780	0.00	
X1: SP500	-0.974	0.00	-0.306	0.00	***	-0.271	0.00	ns	-1.535	0.00	-0.874	0.00	***	-0.605	0.00	**
X2: Region	0.086	0.09	0.090	0.00	ns	-0.105	0.01	***	0.270	0.00	0.076	0.01	**	-0.571	0.00	***
X3: Volume	-0.001	0.84	-0.005	0.07	ns	-0.020	0.00	**	-0.007	0.15	-0.004	0.26	ns	-0.005	0.31	ns
X4: Currency	-1.409	0.00	-0.132	0.00	***	-1.336	0.00	***	-1.340	0.00	0.062	0.10	***	-1.116	0.00	***
Model 3																
Intercept	-11.020	0.00	-3.901	0.00		0.239	0.70		-12.377	0.00	0.313	0.59		3.308	0.00	
X1: NAV	0.983	0.00	0.770	0.00	ns	0.858	0.00	ns	1.125	0.00	0.344	0.00	***	0.597	0.00	**
X2: SP500	0.651	0.00	0.325	0.00	ns	-0.239	0.00	***	0.345	0.20	-0.043	0.52	ns	-0.212	0.00	ns
X3: Region	-0.034	0.55	0.351	0.00	***	0.724	0.00	***	-0.028	0.74	0.315	0.00	***	0.613	0.00	***
X4: Volume	-0.003	0.49	-0.021	0.00	*	-0.005	0.11	*	0.002	0.77	0.000	0.98	ns	0.006	0.04	ns
X5: Currency	1.571	0.00	0.373	0.00	***	-0.023	0.87	ns	2.189	0.00	0.128	0.00	***	-0.574	0.00	***
Model 4																
Intercept	-1284.889	0.00	-550.813	0.00		-143.393	0.00		-1226.60	0.00	-472.684	0.00		-180.933	0.00	
X1: SP500	80.230	0.00	42.412	0.00	ns	-25.399	0.00	***	30.819	0.26	55.071	0.00	ns	-1.830	0.80	***
X2: Region	-4.472	0.47	36.424	0.00	***	80.680	0.00	***	0.384	0.97	29.460	0.00	**	86.442	0.00	***
X3: Volume	-0.181	0.72	-1.969	0.00	*	-0.046	0.88	**	0.288	0.71	0.361	0.44	ns	0.870	0.01	ns
X4: Currency	176.217	0.00	45.479	0.00	***	23.110	0.10	ns	226.067	0.00	11.553	0.03	***	-7.344	0.66	ns

TABLE 21.5: *Continued*

| | Korea Equity | | | | | | | | Korea Fund | | | | | | | |
| | Pre-Crisis Period | | Crisis Period | | Pre. vs Crisis | Post-Crisis Period | | Crisis vs. Post | Pre-Crisis Period | | Crisis Period | | Pre. vs Crisis | Post-Crisis Period | | Crisis vs. Post |
	Beta	Sig.	Beta	Sig.	Beta Change	Beta	Sig.	Beta Change	Beta	Sig.	Beta	Sig.	Beta Change	Beta	Sig.	Beta Change
Model 1																
Intercept	-40.510	0.00	-9.879	0.00		28.595	0.00	***	72.153	0.00	-0.225	0.93	**	34.049	0.00	***
X1: SP500	1.031	0.00	0.411	0.00	**	-0.657	0.00	***	0.843	0.00	0.143	0.01		-0.942	0.00	***
X2: Region	0.647	0.00	0.091	0.05	***	-0.023	0.55	ns	0.486	0.00	0.083	0.04	***	-0.236	0.00	***
X3: Volume	-0.005	0.09	-0.001	0.75	ns	-0.007	0.00	ns	-0.013	0.04	-0.009	0.03	ns	-0.017	0.00	ns
X4: Currency	5.187	0.00	1.383	0.00	***	-3.309	0.00	***	-11.280	0.00	0.334	0.35	***	-3.618	0.00	***
Model 2																
Intercept	21.872	0.00	3.424	0.32		33.454	0.00	***	102.455	0.00	9.200	0.00	***	38.145	0.00	***
X1: SP500	0.140	0.30	0.116	0.08	ns	-0.461	0.00	***	0.801	0.00	0.000	1.00	***	-0.656	0.00	***
X2: Region	0.243	0.00	-0.152	0.00	***	-0.328	0.00	**	0.057	0.27	-0.198	0.00	***	-0.408	0.00	***
X3: Volume	0.006	0.00	0.000	0.91	ns	-0.005	0.04	ns	-0.008	0.07	0.001	0.76	ns	-0.017	0.00	***
X4: Currency	-3.155	0.00	-0.225	0.62	**	-4.106	0.00	***	-15.610	0.00	-0.851	0.01	***	-4.454	0.00	***
Model 3																
Intercept	-43.297	0.00	-12.421	0.00		5.968	0.00	ns	17.522	0.13	-7.443	0.00	**	3.780	0.03	ns
X1: NAV	0.127	0.21	0.742	0.00	***	0.676	0.00	ns	0.533	0.00	0.784	0.00	ns	0.793	0.00	***
X2: SP500	1.013	0.00	0.325	0.00	***	-0.345	0.00	***	0.415	0.11	0.144	0.00	**	-0.421	0.00	***
X3: Region	0.616	0.00	0.204	0.00	***	0.199	0.00	ns	0.456	0.00	0.238	0.00	ns	0.088	0.00	***
X4: Volume	-0.006	0.06	-0.001	0.70	ns	-0.004	0.01	ns	-0.008	0.15	-0.009	0.00	ns	-0.004	0.14	ns
X5: Currency	5.589	0.00	1.550	0.00	***	-0.532	0.02	***	-2.956	0.07	1.001	0.00	**	-0.083	0.69	***
Model 4																
Intercept	-6336.737	0.00	-1176.533	0.00		-480.613	0.00	***	-3399.09	0.00	-976.762	0.00	ns	-445.451	0.00	***
X1: SP500	100.088	0.00	26.162	0.00	***	-19.044	0.00	***	9.791	0.75	14.783	0.00	**	-31.067	0.00	***
X2: Region	44.754	0.00	21.595	0.00	***	29.814	0.00	ns	52.434	0.00	29.353	0.00	**	18.787	0.00	**
X3: Volume	-1.090	0.00	-0.054	0.80	**	-0.255	0.15	ns	-0.468	0.51	-0.968	0.00	ns	-0.041	0.89	*
X4: Currency	836.967	0.00	141.984	0.00	***	78.601	0.00	***	479.020	0.00	122.709	0.00	***	90.885	0.00	ns

Note: Differences in beta coefficients between the pre-crisis (post-crisis) and the crisis periods are tested by interaction terms. Only significance levels are reported here.

*** Significant at the .001 level
** Significant at the .01 level
* Significant at the .05 level

TABLE 21.6: *Pre vs. Mexican Currency Crisis vs. Post Periods*

Malaysia Fund

	Pre-Crisis Period		Crisis Period		Pre. vs Crisis	Post-Crisis Period		Crisis vs. Post
	Beta	Sig.	Beta	Sig.	Beta Change	Beta	Sig.	Beta Change
Model 1								
Intercept	-5.101	0.00	-0.200	0.62	***	1.201	0.00	ns
X1: SP500	1.281	0.00	0.209	0.00	***	0.121	0.00	ns
X2: Region	0.556	0.00	0.710	0.00	**	0.317	0.00	***
X3: Volume	0.004	0.42	-0.002	0.55	ns	0.000	0.99	ns
X4: Currency	-1.348	0.00	-0.098	0.67	***	0.164	0.58	ns
Model 2								
Intercept	-7.438	0.00	1.280	0.01	***	3.096	0.00	***
X1: SP500	1.940	0.00	0.171	0.00	***	0.402	0.00	***
X2: Region	0.168	0.00	0.506	0.00	***	0.157	0.00	***
X3: Volume	0.014	0.01	-0.002	0.73	*	0.004	0.15	ns
X4: Currency	-2.002	0.00	-0.787	0.01	***	-3.349	0.00	***
Model 3								
Intercept	-0.780	0.42	-0.773	0.02	*	-0.749	0.01	**
X1: NAV	0.581	0.00	0.447	0.00	ns	0.630	0.00	***
X2: SP500	0.154	0.39	0.132	0.00	ns	-0.132	0.00	***
X3: Region	0.458	0.00	0.484	0.00	ns	0.217	0.00	***
X4: Volume	-0.004	0.34	-0.001	0.63	ns	-0.002	0.26	ns
X5: Currency	-0.185	0.24	0.255	0.19	ns	2.274	0.00	***
Model 4								
Intercept	221.790	0.03	-134.009	0.00	***	-177.920	0.00	***
X1: SP500	-64.317	0.00	3.093	0.25	**	-26.696	0.00	ns
X2: Region	39.083	0.00	18.813	0.00	ns	15.146	0.00	ns
X3: Volume	-0.952	0.05	-0.028	0.94	ns	-0.350	0.10	ns
X4: Currency	66.469	0.00	63.257	0.01	ns	331.578	0.00	***

Singapore Fund

	Pre-Crisis Period		Crisis Period		Pre. vs Crisis	Post-Crisis Period		Crisis vs. Post
	Beta	Sig.	Beta	Sig.	Beta Change	Beta	Sig.	Beta Change
Model 1								
Intercept	-5.760	0.00	3.358	0.00	***	3.618	0.00	ns
X1: SP500	1.189	0.00	-0.319	0.00	ns	-0.323	0.00	ns
X2: Region	0.599	0.00	0.600	0.00	ns	0.804	0.00	***
X3: Volume	0.014	0.00	-0.016	0.00	***	-0.005	0.05	**
X4: Currency	-1.132	0.00	-0.550	0.02	*	-2.907	0.00	***
Model 2								
Intercept	-4.077	0.00	1.627	0.00	***	2.173	0.00	ns
X1: SP500	1.146	0.00	-0.063	0.12	***	0.058	0.03	*
X2: Region	0.167	0.00	0.465	0.00	***	0.377	0.00	ns
X3: Volume	0.012	0.00	0.003	0.37	ns	0.001	0.43	ns
X4: Currency	-1.614	0.00	0.439	0.09	***	-2.792	0.00	***
Model 3								
Intercept	-4.630	0.00	2.839	0.00	ns	1.598	0.00	***
X1: NAV	0.277	0.00	0.319	0.00	***	0.929	0.00	ns
X2: SP500	0.872	0.00	-0.299	0.00	ns	-0.377	0.00	ns
X3: Region	0.553	0.00	0.452	0.00	***	0.454	0.00	**
X4: Volume	0.010	0.01	-0.017	0.00	ns	-0.006	0.01	ns
X5: Currency	-0.685	0.00	-0.690	0.00	ns	-0.312	0.55	ns
Model 4								
Intercept	-203.59	0.09	175.981	0.00	ns	133.852	0.00	ns
X1: SP500	7.729	0.71	-26.547	0.00	ns	-37.094	0.00	***
X2: Region	47.773	0.00	14.727	0.00	***	43.500	0.00	***
X3: Volume	0.343	0.47	-1.972	0.00	***	-0.602	0.01	**
X4: Currency	49.173	0.01	-97.918	0.00	***	-5.380	0.90	ns

TABLE 21.6: *Continued*

	Thai Fund									Thai Capital								
	Pre-Crisis Period		Crisis Period		Pre. vs Crisis	Post-Crisis Period		Crisis vs. Post		Pre-Crisis Period		Crisis Period		Pre. vs Crisis	Post-Crisis Period		Crisis vs. Post
	Beta	Sig.	Beta	Sig.	Beta Change	Beta	Sig.	Beta Change		Beta	Sig.	Beta	Sig.	Beta Change	Beta	Sig.	Beta Change
Model 1																	
Intercept	17.624	0.00	−5.547	0.00	***	20.184	0.00	***		10.717	0.00	−7.849	0.00	***	24.752	0.00	***
X1: SP500	1.535	0.00	0.232	0.00	***	−0.976	0.00	***		1.758	0.00	−0.005	0.87	**	−0.851	0.00	ns
X2: Region	0.672	0.00	0.631	0.00	ns	0.687	0.00	ns		0.560	0.00	0.736	0.00	ns	0.729	0.00	*
X3: Volume	0.009	0.07	0.004	0.31	ns	−0.033	0.00	***		0.008	0.08	0.002	0.62	ns	−0.011	0.01	*
X4: Currency	−7.965	0.00	1.732	0.00	***	−3.808	0.00	***		−6.292	0.00	2.695	0.00	***	−5.712	0.00	***
Model 2																	
Intercept	15.557	0.00	−7.602	0.00	***	38.469	0.00	***		8.876	0.01	−11.481	0.00	***	31.578	0.00	***
X1: SP500	2.175	0.00	−0.112	0.00	***	−1.417	0.00	***		2.611	0.00	−0.168	0.00	***	−1.258	0.00	ns
X2: Region	0.178	0.01	0.535	0.00	***	0.598	0.00	ns		0.039	0.57	0.623	0.00	***	0.597	0.00	ns
X3: Volume	0.021	0.00	0.011	0.00	ns	−0.037	0.00	***		0.022	0.00	−0.004	0.24	***	−0.012	0.01	ns
X4: Currency	−8.080	0.00	3.152	0.00	***	−8.489	0.00	***		−6.863	0.00	4.286	0.00	***	−6.883	0.00	***
Model 3																	
Intercept	8.230	0.00	−0.946	0.35	ns	−4.876	0.02	ns		5.442	0.00	1.095	0.28	**	6.223	0.02	**
X1: NAV	0.604	0.00	0.605	0.00	ns	0.651	0.00	***		0.594	0.00	0.779	0.00	ns	0.587	0.00	**
X2: SP500	0.222	0.17	0.300	0.00	ns	−0.054	0.42	ns		0.206	0.21	0.126	0.00	***	−0.113	0.18	*
X3: Region	0.565	0.00	0.308	0.00	***	0.298	0.00	ns		0.537	0.00	0.251	0.00	***	0.379	0.00	*
X4: Volume	−0.004	0.33	−0.003	0.29	ns	−0.009	0.01	ns		−0.004	0.19	0.005	0.05	*	−0.003	0.30	*
X5: Currency	−3.086	0.00	−0.176	0.59	***	1.722	0.01	**		−2.213	0.00	−0.644	0.05	**	−1.673	0.05	ns
Model 4																	
Intercept	161.126	0.42	162.548	0.07	***	−1781.741	0.00	*		160.54	0.44	313.716	0.00	***	−681.648	0.02	***
X1: SP500	−55.915	0.00	29.092	0.00	***	42.940	0.00	ns		−75.826	0.00	13.989	0.00	***	38.522	0.00	ns
X2: Region	44.243	0.00	8.837	0.00	***	8.413	0.00	**		47.089	0.00	10.363	0.00	***	11.884	0.00	ns
X3: Volume	−1.022	0.01	−0.548	0.04	ns	0.476	0.17	***		−1.126	0.00	0.545	0.02	***	0.210	0.57	ns
X4: Currency	14.997	0.76	−117.476	0.00	**	456.179	0.00	***		50.760	0.32	−138.004	0.00	***	122.245	0.20	**

Note: Differences in beta coefficients between the pre–crisis (post–crisis) and the crisis periods are tested by interaction terms.
Only significance levels are reported here.

*** Significant at the .001 level
** Significant at the .01 level
* Significant at the .05 level

TABLE 21.7: *Pre vs. Mexican Currency Crisis vs. Post Periods*

	Mexico Fund				Pre. vs Crisis			Crisis vs. Post	Mexico Equity Fund				Pre. vs Crisis			Crisis vs. Post
	Pre-Crisis Period		Crisis Period		Beta	Post-Crisis Period		Beta	Pre-Crisis Period		Crisis Period		Beta	Post-Crisis Period		Beta
	Beta	Sig.	Beta	Sig.	Change	Beta	Sig.	Change	Beta	Sig.	Beta	Sig.	Change	Beta	Sig.	Change
Model 1																
Intercept	-5.933	0.00	0.079	0.86		2.026	0.00		-2.796	0.00	2.536	0.00		0.085	0.88	
X1: SP500	1.360	0.00	0.077	0.33	***	0.884	0.00	***	0.688	0.00	-0.320	0.00	***	0.799	0.00	***
X2: Region	0.452	0.00	1.113	0.00	***	0.054	0.46	***	0.443	0.00	0.921	0.00	***	0.087	0.28	***
X3: Volume	0.008	0.01	-0.018	0.00	***	0.012	0.00	***	-0.001	0.84	0.008	0.04	ns	0.005	0.15	ns
X4: Currency	-0.402	0.00	-0.397	0.00	ns	-2.614	0.00	***	0.167	0.04	-0.386	0.00	***	-1.604	0.00	***
Model 2																
Intercept	-3.490	0.01	-7.984	0.00		0.992	0.08		-5.124	0.00	-7.309	0.00		-0.005	0.99	
X1: SP500	0.894	0.00	1.789	0.00	*	1.177	0.00	***	0.956	0.00	1.684	0.00	*	1.123	0.00	***
X2: Region	0.493	0.00	0.646	0.00	ns	-0.192	0.02	***	0.402	0.00	0.432	0.00	ns	-0.348	0.00	***
X3: Volume	0.000	1.00	0.022	0.00	**	-0.010	0.02	***	0.001	0.80	0.055	0.00	***	-0.011	0.02	***
X4: Currency	-0.082	0.46	-1.346	0.00	***	-2.544	0.00	***	0.804	0.00	-1.352	0.00	***	-1.860	0.00	ns
Model 3																
Intercept	-5.071	0.00	3.207	0.00		1.384	0.00		-1.891	0.04	3.432	0.00		0.088	0.83	
X1: NAV	0.247	0.00	0.392	0.00	ns	0.647	0.00	**	0.177	0.00	0.123	0.00	ns	0.541	0.00	***
X2: SP500	1.139	0.00	-0.624	0.00	***	0.123	0.06	***	0.519	0.00	-0.526	0.00	***	0.192	0.00	***
X3: Region	0.330	0.00	0.860	0.00	***	0.178	0.00	***	0.372	0.00	0.868	0.00	***	0.275	0.00	***
X4: Volume	0.008	0.01	-0.026	0.00	***	0.019	0.00	***	-0.001	0.79	0.001	0.77	ns	0.011	0.00	*
X5: Currency	-0.382	0.00	0.130	0.15	***	-0.969	0.00	***	0.025	0.78	-0.221	0.00	ns	-0.598	0.00	ns
Model 4																
Intercept	-234.204	0.07	825.811	0.00		85.382	0.02		224.89	0.09	1109.083	0.00		6.992	0.87	
X1: SP500	44.787	0.05	-173.355	0.00	***	-25.698	0.00	***	-24.622	0.29	-224.450	0.00	***	-28.807	0.00	***
X2: Region	-4.056	0.36	44.081	0.00	***	21.285	0.00	ns	3.474	0.44	51.924	0.00	***	37.036	0.00	ns
X3: Volume	0.876	0.04	-3.546	0.00	***	1.947	0.00	***	-0.111	0.80	-4.999	0.00	***	1.427	0.00	***
X4: Currency	-31.371	0.00	94.119	0.00	***	-3.743	0.78	**	-66.771	0.00	108.326	0.00	***	25.423	0.12	*

TABLE 21.7: *Continued*

| | Emerging Mexico | | | | Pre. vs Crisis | | Crisis vs. Post |
| | Pre–Crisis Period | | Crisis Period | | | Post–Crisis Period | | |
Model 1	Beta	Sig.	Beta	Sig.	Beta Change	Beta	Sig.	Beta Change
Intercept	-6.434	0.00	1.992	0.00		-1.423	0.01	
X1: SP500	1.589	0.00	-0.199	0.00	***	0.928	0.00	***
X2: Region	0.368	0.00	0.930	0.00	***	0.226	0.00	***
X3: Volume	0.002	0.54	0.001	0.86	ns	0.017	0.00	**
X4: Currency	-1.293	0.00	-0.669	0.00	***	-1.678	0.00	***
Model 2								
Intercept	-2.011	0.03	-7.350	0.00		-1.650	0.02	
X1: SP500	0.688	0.00	1.762	0.00	ns	1.343	0.00	**
X2: Region	0.453	0.00	0.409	0.00	ns	-0.304	0.00	***
X3: Volume	0.002	0.52	0.059	0.00	***	-0.003	0.54	***
X4: Currency	-0.596	0.00	-1.777	0.00	***	-2.020	0.00	ns
Model 3								
Intercept	-6.090	0.00	3.296	0.00		-0.661	0.11	
X1: NAV	0.171	0.06	0.177	0.00	ns	0.462	0.00	***
X2: SP500	1.471	0.00	-0.512	0.00	***	0.308	0.00	***
X3: Region	0.290	0.00	0.858	0.00	***	0.367	0.00	***
X4: Volume	0.002	0.59	-0.010	0.07	ns	0.019	0.00	***
X5: Currency	-1.191	0.00	-0.354	0.00	***	-0.746	0.00	ns
Model 4								
Intercept	-434.704	0.00	1064.782	0.00		16.017	0.73	
X1: SP500	89.590	0.00	-224.140	0.00	***	-37.111	0.00	***
X2: Region	-8.605	0.09	59.120	0.00	***	45.954	0.00	ns
X3: Volume	0.065	0.88	-6.064	0.00	***	1.794	0.00	***
X4: Currency	-72.912	0.00	126.875	0.00	***	34.562	0.05	ns

Note: Differences in beta coefficients between the pre–crisis (post–crisis) and the crisis periods are tested by interaction terms. Only significance levels are reported here.

*** Significant at the .001 level

** Significant at the .01 level

* Significant at the .05 level

TABLE 21.8: Pre vs. Mexican Currency Crisis vs. Post Periods

	Emerging Germany										Irish Fund									
	Pre-Crisis Period		Crisis Period		Pre. vs Crisis	Post-Crisis Period		Crisis vs. Post	Pre-Crisis Period		Crisis Period		Pre. vs Crisis	Post-Crisis Period		Crisis vs. Post				
	Beta	Sig.	Beta	Sig.	Beta Change	Beta	Sig.	Beta Change	Beta	Sig.	Beta	Sig.	Beta Change	Beta	Sig.	Beta Change				
Model 1																				
Intercept	1.150	0.16	2.225	0.00		0.311	0.42		-10.103	0.00	-4.139	0.00		-2.465	0.00					
X1: SP500	-0.049	0.75	-0.251	0.00	ns	0.130	0.10	***	1.842	0.00	0.906	0.00	***	0.856	0.00	***				
X2: Region	0.433	0.00	0.517	0.00	ns	0.462	0.00	ns	0.352	0.05	0.197	0.01	ns	-0.095	0.15	**				
X3: Volume	-0.008	0.02	0.003	0.13	***	-0.001	0.78	ns	0.007	0.00	0.000	0.98	ns	0.003	0.11	ns				
X4: Currency	0.454	0.00	0.081	0.10	ns	-0.892	0.00	***	0.362	0.00	0.656	0.00	ns	-0.588	0.00	***				
Model 2																				
Intercept	7.228	0.00	2.304	0.00		-0.380	0.14		-2.609	0.00	-4.096	0.00		0.038	0.93					
X1: SP500	-0.959	0.00	-0.138	0.00	***	0.321	0.00	***	0.657	0.00	0.834	0.00	ns	0.204	0.03	***				
X2: Region	0.419	0.00	0.341	0.00	ns	0.334	0.00	ns	0.276	0.00	0.421	0.00	ns	0.576	0.00	ns				
X3: Volume	-0.003	0.25	0.001	0.55	ns	0.000	0.97	ns	0.007	0.00	-0.001	0.74	**	-0.018	0.00	***				
X4: Currency	-0.226	0.00	-0.188	0.00	ns	-0.769	0.00	***	0.514	0.00	0.688	0.00	ns	-0.147	0.36	***				
Model 3																				
Intercept	-4.802	0.00	0.231	0.15		0.397	0.30		-6.964	0.00	-0.454	0.16		-2.454	0.00					
X1: NAV	0.823	0.00	0.865	0.00	ns	0.227	0.02	***	1.203	0.00	0.900	0.00	**	-0.295	0.00	***				
X2: SP500	0.740	0.00	-0.132	0.00	***	0.058	0.50	*	1.051	0.00	0.156	0.03	***	0.916	0.00	***				
X3: Region	0.087	0.20	0.222	0.00	ns	0.386	0.00	*	0.020	0.82	-0.182	0.00	ns	0.075	0.28	**				
X4: Volume	-0.006	0.04	0.002	0.11	**	-0.001	0.79	ns	-0.002	0.49	0.001	0.76	ns	-0.002	0.38	ns				
X5: Currency	0.640	0.00	0.244	0.00	***	-0.718	0.00	***	-0.256	0.01	0.037	0.74	*	-0.632	0.00	***				
Model 4																				
Intercept	-543.030	0.00	-8.386	0.36		53.582	0.11		-676.98	0.00	-5.257	0.69		-225.320	0.00					
X1: SP500	81.758	0.00	-8.998	0.00	***	-15.218	0.03	ns	106.667	0.00	6.229	0.09	***	58.659	0.00	***				
X2: Region	0.076	0.99	13.946	0.00	**	10.088	0.03	ns	7.621	0.34	-19.224	0.00	**	-61.044	0.00	***				
X3: Volume	-0.400	0.09	0.174	0.15	*	-0.028	0.87	ns	-0.019	0.93	0.074	0.70	ns	1.886	0.00	***				
X4: Currency	59.141	0.00	21.142	0.00	***	-9.832	0.29	***	-13.745	0.08	-2.403	0.78	ns	-35.161	0.11	ns				

TABLE 21.8: *Continued*

	Italy Fund								Spain Fund							
	Pre–Crisis Period		Crisis Period		Pre. vs Crisis	Post–Crisis Period		Crisis vs. Post	Pre–Crisis Period		Crisis Period		Pre. vs Crisis	Post–Crisis Period		Crisis vs. Post
	Beta	Sig.	Beta	Sig.	Beta Change	Beta	Sig.	Beta Change	Beta	Sig.	Beta	Sig.	Beta Change	Beta	Sig.	Beta Change
Model 1																
Intercept	20.034	0.00	9.305	0.00	***	-4.147	0.00	***	-11.435	0.00	3.853	0.00	***	-2.162	0.00	***
X1: SP500	-3.604	0.00	-0.491	0.00	***	0.367	0.00	ns	1.682	0.00	-0.371	0.00	*	0.351	0.00	***
X2: Region	1.433	0.00	0.233	0.00	***	0.105	0.13	ns	0.513	0.00	0.781	0.00	ns	0.216	0.00	***
X3: Volume	0.026	0.66	-0.001	0.66	***	0.004	0.02	ns	0.022	0.00	0.003	0.00	***	-0.002	0.35	ns
X4: Currency	0.088	0.70	-0.638	0.00	**	0.489	0.00	***	0.409	0.00	-0.280	0.00	***	0.325	0.01	***
Model 2																
Intercept	25.647	0.00	15.427	0.00	***	4.576	0.00	***	4.170	0.00	3.144	0.00	ns	-5.048	0.00	***
X1: SP500	-2.704	0.00	-0.539	0.00	**	0.527	0.00	***	-0.315	0.00	-0.056	0.28	ns	0.562	0.00	***
X2: Region	0.800	0.00	0.411	0.00	**	0.057	0.45	***	0.478	0.00	0.640	0.00	ns	0.222	0.00	***
X3: Volume	0.006	0.13	-0.006	0.03	ns	0.003	0.12	**	0.004	0.06	0.007	0.04	ns	-0.006	0.01	**
X4: Currency	-1.186	0.00	-1.464	0.00	ns	-0.799	0.00	**	-0.233	0.00	-0.438	0.00	ns	0.685	0.00	***
Model 3																
Intercept	-4.977	0.10	-1.984	0.03	**	-7.794	0.00	ns	-12.064	0.00	1.443	0.00	***	0.912	0.07	**
X1: NAV	0.975	0.00	0.732	0.00	***	0.797	0.00	ns	0.151	0.25	0.766	0.00	***	0.609	0.00	***
X2: SP500	-0.967	0.01	-0.097	0.03	***	-0.053	0.26	ns	1.729	0.00	-0.328	0.00	ns	0.009	0.89	**
X3: Region	0.653	0.00	-0.068	0.23	***	0.060	0.07	ns	0.441	0.00	0.290	0.00	ns	0.081	0.06	**
X4: Volume	0.020	0.00	0.003	0.10	***	0.002	0.05	ns	0.022	0.43	-0.002	0.00	***	0.002	0.34	ns
X5: Currency	1.245	0.00	0.434	0.00	***	1.126	0.00	***	0.444	0.39	0.056	0.00	**	-0.091	0.36	ns
Model 4																
Intercept	-613.758	0.00	-544.192	0.00	***	-743.863	0.00	**	-1620.74	0.00	56.323	0.14	***	237.353	0.00	ns
X1: SP500	-78.776	0.24	4.147	0.00	***	-14.052	0.00	**	206.594	0.00	-26.693	0.00	***	-17.755	0.00	ns
X2: Region	59.136	0.00	-15.755	0.00	***	4.550	0.14	***	-1.267	0.91	11.984	0.00	ns	0.028	0.99	*
X3: Volume	2.102	0.01	0.463	0.00	***	0.096	0.26	ns	1.808	0.00	-0.272	0.18	***	0.341	0.03	**
X4: Currency	126.552	0.00	73.388	0.00	**	109.927	0.00	**	70.288	0.00	13.884	0.01	***	-29.536	0.00	***

Note: Differences in beta coefficients between the pre–crisis (post–crisis) and the crisis periods are tested by interaction terms.
Only significance levels are reported here.

*** Significant at the .001 level
** Significant at the .01 level
* Significant at the .05 level

This may be especially true during the currency crisis. As a result, the reduction of the SCCEFs' price may not occur as quickly as the NAV, which causes the discount to shrink or the premium to widen. In the regression models, this reasoning is translated as a significant, positive coefficient associated with the exchange rate in accounting for the movement of the discount/premium. All coefficients obtained from the analyses on Mexican SCCEFs were positive and statistically significant during the Mexican crisis period.

Conclusion

The study has attempted to examine the impact of currency crisis on the performance of international funds with a focus on the periods of the Mexican and the recent Asian currency crisis by testing the 'differential information holding' hypothesis.

The study has once again found evidence supporting the hypothesis. The macro-level analysis of the Asian currency crisis period in comparison to the pre-crisis period identified two distinctive fund performance patterns: the Southeast Asian pattern unique to the funds in crisis and the Latin American pattern unique to the funds least affected by the crisis. The SCCEFs of Indonesia, Malaysia, Singapore, Thailand and Japan represented the first pattern, where the discounts significantly shrank (or the premiums grew) due to the faster depreciation of the NAV in comparison to the reduction in price. From the 'differential information holding' perspective, it is reasoned that during the currency crisis, most individual investors faced difficulty in accurately understanding the speed and the magnitude of the depreciation of the currency and the values of the securities that made up the SCCEFs. As a result, the reduction of the SCCEFs' price may not have occurred as quickly as the NAV, which led to the shrinking discounts and widening premiums. In contrast, the discounts of the Latin American funds widened during the crisis period due to faster growth of the NAVs in comparison to the market prices. In Latin America, the securities that made up the SCCEFs remained strong and increased in value over the period studied despite the temporary depreciation of the local currencies. In this bullish but confusing investment environment, it seemed difficult for individual investors to understand the speed and the magnitude of the appreciation or depreciation of the underlying securities. Thus, the increase in the SCCEFs' price was smaller than the NAV, which widened the discounts. These macro level analysis results were also supported by the regression analysis at the micro level.

The analysis of the Mexican SCCEFs during the Mexican currency crisis in comparison to the pre- as well as the post-crisis period also revealed a pattern quite similar to the Southeast Asian pattern described above. During the crisis, the discounts shrank (or the premiums grew) due to the faster depreciation of NAV than the reduction in price. In contrast, the discounts grew during the post-crisis period due to the faster growth of the NAV than the price, as expected.

In summary, the present study, based on the quasi-experimental design, has revealed several interesting patterns of international funds in crisis. Remarkably similar patterns found during the Asian and the Mexican currency crisis may provide basis to help develop useful trading strategies for the post-Asian currency crisis period.

References

BARCLAY, M. J., HOLDERNESS, C. G. and PONTIFF, J. (1993) Private benefits from block ownership and discounts on closed-end funds, *Journal of Financial Economics*, June, pp. 263–291.

CHEN, N., KAN, R. and MILLER, M. H. (1993a) Are discounts on closed-end funds a sentiment index? *Journal of Finance*, Vol. 48, pp. 795–800.

CHEN, N., KAN, R. and MILLER, M. H. (1993b) A Rejoinder, *Journal of Finance*, Vol. 48, pp. 809–810.

CHOPRA, N., LEE, C., SHLEIFER, A. and THALER, R. H. (1993a) Yes, discounts on closed-end funds are a sentiment index, *Journal of Finance*, Vol. 48, pp. 801–808.

CHOPRA, N., LEE, C., SHLEIFER, A. and THALER, R. H. (1993b) Summing up, *Journal of Finance*, Vol. 48, pp. 811–812.

DE LONG, J. B., SHLEIFER, A., SUMMERS, L. H. and WALDMANN, R. J. (1990) Noise trader risk in financial markets, *Journal of Political Economics*, Vol. 98, pp. 703–738.

DROMS, W. G. and WALKER, D. A. (1994) Investment performance of international mutual funds, *Journal of Financial Research*, Vol. 17, pp. 1–14.

EUN, C. S., KOLODNY, R. and RESNICK, B. G. (1991) US-based international mutual funds: A performance evaluation, *Journal of Portfolio Management*, Vol. 17, pp. 88–94.

KIM, C. (1994) Investor tax trading opportunities and discounts on closed-end mutual funds, *Journal of Financial Research*, Vol. 17, pp. 65–75.

LEE, C. F., SHLEIFER, A. and THALER, R. H. (1991) Investor sentiment and the closed-end fund puzzle, *Journal of Finance*, Vol. 46, pp. 75–109.

MULUGETTA, A. and MULUGETTA, Y. (1997a) The influence of exchange rates, institutional holdings, volume of shares traded and indices on discount or premium of single-country closed-end funds, *Journal of International Finance*, Vol. 9, pp. 607–624.

MULUGETTA, A. and MULUGETTA, Y. (1997b) Inter-temporal relationship between the movements of prices of closed-endfunds and currencies, in the *Proceedings of the 1997 Association for Global Business*, Washington DC.

MULUGETTA, A., GHOSH, D. K. and MULUGETTA, Y. (1998) *Regional and Country Closed-End Funds in Currencies Crisis*, Paper presented at the 1998 Association for Global Finance, Mexico City.

22

Measuring Extreme Movements in Foreign Exchange Markets: Application of Extreme Value Theory to Stress Testing

FRANÇOIS M. LONGIN

Introduction

Since regulators have allowed financial institutions to use internal models (Basle Committee, 1995 and 1996), Value at Risk (VaR) has become a standard measure of market risks. The VaR of a position is a single number measuring and summarizing the risk of this position; it is defined as the maximal loss for a given probability over a given period[1]. A major problem with existing VaR methods is the modeling of distribution tails. In most cases, the weight of the tail is underestimated and this leads to low VaR especially at very high probability levels. For this reason, VaR models are complemented with a stress testing analysis based on catastrophe scenarios.

VaR: The Classical Approach

Different VaR methods have been developed and tested by banks since regulators allowed the use of internal models. The classical approach consists in modeling the entire distribution of asset price changes. The main methods of the classical approach can be classified in three categories: the historical simulation method, the Monte Carlo simulation method, and the method of variance–covariance.

The historical simulation method uses the past realizations of portfolio value or risk factors. This non-parametric method evaluates the impact of the past evolution of prices on the value of the position. The historical method allows the real characteristics of the statistical distribution of risk factors to be taken into account. By going back far in the past, different market conditions can be taken into consideration. In practice, however, a short period of time is considered sufficient to take into account the recent market conditions.

The Monte Carlo simulation method uses an econometric model to determine the time-evolution of risk factors, the parameters of the model being fixed by the user or estimated using past data. The method of Monte Carlo simulation uses a multitude of scenarios, generated randomly, as defined by the econometric model, while the method of historical simulation relies on the unique scenario based on the past behaviour of financial markets. Like the historical method, it evaluates the impact of the randomly simulated evolution of prices on the value of the position (full valuation). The Monte Carlo simulation method is flexible in terms of modeling and allows all types of market position to be considered once the behaviour of the market prices of the products has been described.

The method of variance–covariance, also called the correlation method or the delta-normal method, assumes that the returns on risk factors are distributed as a multivariate normal distribution and that the sensitivity of the position to the factors measured by the deltas is also constant (local valuation). The variance–covariance matrix or correlation matrix is computed from past observations using a statistical model. The hypotheses of normality and linearity of the position as a function of the risk factors allow an analytical computation of the VaR.

Stress Testing: A Complement to VaR Models of the Classical Approach

As extreme events are a central issue in finance and particularly in risk management, the methods given above have been completed by stress testing methods. As explained in Jorion (1997, chapter 10), stress testing methods examine the impact of simulated large movements in risk factors on the value of the portfolio. The first step is to define stress values for the risk factors considered in the analysis. As given in Jorion (1997, p. 196), the Derivative Policy Group suggests the following guidelines: parallel yield curve shifting by ±100bp, yield curve twisting by ±25bp, equity index values changing by ±10 per cent and currencies moving by ±6 per cent, volatilities changing by ±20 per cent of current values.

The second step is to compute for each scenario the change in the value of the portfolio based on the changes in the risk factors values previously defined. Two main criticisms have been addressed to stress testing methods: first, it is difficult to quantify the probability attached to catastrophe scenarios, and second, it is difficult to handle correlation among risk factors during extremely volatile periods.

VaR: The Extreme Value Approach

Longin (1997) introduces the extreme value approach to compute the VaR of a market position. Instead of considering the entire distribution of changes in risk factors, it focuses on the distribution of extreme changes in risk factors. A VaR model using extreme values covers both types of market conditions (ordinary and extraordinary) as extreme asset price changes defined by the theory are associated both with little tremors, like market adjustments or corrections during ordinary periods, and with earthquake-like stock market crashes or foreign exchange crises observed during extraordinary periods. With the extreme value approach, a stress testing method is not really necessary as extreme asset price movements are already taken into account.

Goal and Organization of this Paper

The goal of this paper is then to develop a rigorous method to compute a coherent set of the stress values for risk factors. Such stress values can then be used in a stress testing method to complement VaR models of the classical approach. Such a method is indeed very useful for financial institutions that have already invested in VaR models of the classical approach and still need to consider catastrophe scenarios missing in their models.

First, extreme value theory is briefly presented. Then it is applied to the computation of stress values. An empirical study using foreign exchange data is provided to illustrate the method.

Extreme Value Theory

A detailed presentation of extreme value theory can be found in Gumbel (1958), Galambos (1978) and Embrechts et al. (1997). The

extreme value distribution allows one to model the behaviour of extremes of a random process. Extremes are defined as the highest observation (the maximum denoted by Y) and the lowest (the minimum denoted by Z) over a given period. As the limiting distribution of extremes is degenerate, it is necessary to consider the asymptotic distribution of standardized extremes $(Y\text{-}b_n)/a_n$. The extreme value theorem (Gnedenko, 1943) gives the form of this distribution as n goes to infinity. Three possible types of limiting extreme value distribution F_Y can be reached:
the Gumbel distribution (type I):

$$F_Y(y) = \exp{-e^y}) \quad \text{for } y \in R,1 \tag{1}$$

the Fréchet distribution (type II):

$$F_Y(y) = < \begin{array}{ll} 0 & \text{for } y \le 0 \\ \exp(-y^{-k}) & \text{for } y > 0 (k > 0), \end{array} \tag{2}$$

and the Weibull distribution (type III):

$$F_Y(y) = < \begin{array}{ll} \exp(-(-y)^{-k}) & \text{for } y < 0 \ (k < 0) \\ 1 & \text{for } y \ge 0. \end{array} \tag{3}$$

The tail of the distribution of returns is either declining exponentially (type I), or by a power (type II) or remains finite (type III). For the first and third cases all moments of the distribution are well-defined. For the second case the shape parameter k reflects the weight of the tail of the distribution of returns: the lower k, the fatter the distribution. The shape parameter corresponds to the maximal order moment: the moments of order greater than k are infinite and the moments of order less than k are finite: the distribution is fat-tailed (Gumbel 1958, p. 266). For example, if k is greater than unity, then the mean of the distribution exists; if k is greater than two, then the variance is finite; if k is greater than three, then the skewness is well-defined, and so forth. The shape parameter is an intrinsic parameter of the process of returns and does not depend on the length of the selection period of extremes.

Jenkinson (1955) proposes a generalized formula, which groups the three types of extreme value distribution:

$$F_Y(y) = \exp\left(-\left(1 - \tau \cdot y\right)^{\frac{1}{\tau}}\right) \tag{4}$$

for $y>\tau^{-1}$ if t<0 and for $y<\tau^{-1}$ if t>0. The parameter τ, called the tail index, is related to the shape parameter k by the relation $\tau=-1/k$. The tail index determines the type of distribution: $\tau<0$ corresponds to a Fréchet distribution (type II), $\tau>0$ to a Weibull distribution (type III), and the intermediate case ($\tau=0$) corresponds to a Gumbel distribution (type I). The Gumbel distribution can be regarded as a transitional limiting form between the Fréchet and the Weibull distributions as $(1-\tau\times y)^{1/\tau}$ is interpreted as e^{-y}. For small values of τ (or large values of k) the type II and type III distributions are very close to the type I distribution.

Gnedenko (1943) gives necessary and sufficient conditions for a particular distribution to belong to the domain of attraction of one of the three types. For example, the normal and log-normal distributions commonly used in finance lead to the Gumbel distribution for the extremes. The Student-t distribution considered by Praetz (1972) obeys the Fréchet distribution with a shape parameter k equal to its degree of freedom ($k>2$). Stable Paretian laws introduced by Mandelbrot (1963) also lead to a Fréchet distribution with a shape parameter k equal to their characteristic exponent ($0<k<2$). The uniform distribution belongs to the domain of attraction of the Weibull distribution. These theoretical results show the generality of the extreme value theorem: all mentioned distributions of returns lead to the same form of distribution for extreme returns, the extreme value distributions obtained from different distributions of returns being differentiated only by the value of the tail index and scale and location parameters.

The extreme value theorem has been extended to time-series: Berman (1964) shows that the same result stands if the variables are correlated (the sum of squared correlation coefficients remaining finite); Leadbetter et al. (1983) consider various processes based on the normal distribution: auto-regressive processes with normal disturbances, discrete mixtures of normal distributions as studied in Kon (1984) and mixed diffusion jump processes as advanced by Press (1967) all have thin tails so that they lead to a Gumbel distribution for the extremes; as explained in Longin (1997), the volatility of the process of returns (modelled by the class of ARCH processes) is influenced by the extremes; if r follows the GARCH process introduced by Engle (1982) and Bollerslev (1986), then the maximum has a Fréchet distribution. For an ARCH(1) model defined by $r_t = e_t \times (a_0 + a_1 \times r_{t-1}^2)^{1/2}$ where innovations e_t are independent and identically distributed as a $N(0,1)$, the shape parameter k is greater than two and is obtained from the equation $G(k+0.5) = p^{1/2} \times (2 \times a_1)^{-k}$.

Application of Extreme Value Theory to Stress Values

Equation (4) is used to link the stress value (expressed as a percentage change and denoted by SV) to a chosen level of probability. I call this probability an extreme probability (denoted by p^{ext}) as it pertains to the distribution of extreme changes in risk factors. Using equation (4), the two variables SV and p^{ext} are linked by:

$$ p^{\text{ext}} = \exp\left(-\left(1 - \tau \cdot \frac{(SV - \beta_n)}{\alpha_n} \right)^{\frac{1}{\tau}} \right), \tag{5} $$

where the values of the three parameters a_n, b_n and τ have to be estimated (see Gumbel, 1958 for a description of different methods of statistical estimation).

Application of the Method to Foreign Exchange Markets

The method previously described is now applied to define stress values for foreign currencies. Four currencies are chosen: the German mark, the French franc, the Japanese yen and the British pound[2]. Foreign exchange rates are expressed in US dollars. Results are also given for the stock index Standard & Poor's 500 (S&P500) to compare with another class of assets. Table 22.1 gives the estimates of the parameters of the asymptotic distribution of extreme daily changes in foreign exchange rates. Extremes are selected over non-overlapping quarters containing 63 days on average. The regression method (see Gumbel, 1958, pp. 226, 260 and 296, for a presentation) is used here[3]. Estimates for the scale and location parameters are similar for all time-series. For example, for minimal daily changes, the scale parameter ranges from 0.432 for the Japanese yen to 0.569 for the French franc and the location parameter ranges from −1.212 for the Japanese yen to −1.538 for the British pound. Similar results are obtained for the stock index (0.673 and -1.576). Estimates of the tail index differ from one series to another. Tail index values are sometimes positive and sometimes negative and in some cases not significantly different from zero. There is no particular type (Fréchet, Gumbel or Weibull) for the distribution of extreme changes in foreign currencies. For example, for the Japanese yen, it is equal to -0.084 for minimal daily changes, implying a Fréchet distribution, and 0.065 for maximal changes, implying a Weibull distribution[4]. Tail index values for the S&P500 are always negative, implying a Fréchet distribution, for extreme daily stock

TABLE 22.1: *Estimation of the parameters of the asymptotic distribution of extreme daily changes in foreign exchange rates*

Foreign currency	Scale parameter α	Location parameter ß	Tail index β
Panel A: Minimal daily changes in foreign exchange rates			
German mark	0.537	−1.462	0.071
	(0.014)	(0.010)	(0.021)
French franc	0.569	−1.421	0.186
	(0.026)	(0.018)	(0.042)
Japanese yen	0.432	−1.212	−0.084
	(0.012)	(0.010)	(0.021)
British pound	0.535	−1.564	0.122
	(0.013)	(0.011)	(0.020)
S&P500 index	0.673	−1.576	−0.758
	(0.027)	(0.022)	(0.037)
Panel B: Maximal daily changes in foreign exchange rates			
German mark	0.527	1.499	−0.050
	(0.013)	(0.012)	(0.020)
French franc	0.566	1.431	−0.021
	(0.010)	(0.008)	(0.014)
Japanese yen	0.594	1.509	0.065
	(0.017)	(0.013)	(0.024)
British pound	0.448	1.326	−0.270
	(0.013)	(0.011)	(0.024)
S&P500 index	0.605	1.833	−0.368
	(0.033)	(0.032)	(0.048)

Note: This table gives the estimates of the parameters of the asymptotic distribution of extreme daily changes in foreign exchange rates (minimal daily changes in Panel A and maximal daily changes in Panel B). Extreme daily changes are selected over non-overlapping quarters containing 63 trading days on average. Estimates are obtained by the regression method. Standard errors are given in parentheses. The database contains the following currencies: the German mark, the French franc, the Japanese yen and the British pound. Foreign exchange rates are expressed in US dollars. The database covers the period from December 30 1983 to December 31 1993. Results for the S&P500 index are also given for comparison.

market returns[5]. As tail index values for the S&P500 index are much more negative than any values obtained for exchange rates of foreign currencies, it can be concluded that the distribution of the S&P500 index presents fatter tails.

These estimation results are now used to compute stress values that can be used for stress testing methods. A stress value is computed for a given level of extreme probability p^{ext} or equivalently for a given value of mean return period T. The extreme probability represents the probability to observe an extreme over a given period (here a quarter). The return period represents the average period

TABLE 22.2: *Definition of catastrophe scenarios for stress testing (stress values)*

Foreign currency	Level of extreme probability		
	$p^{ext} = 0.90$ $T = 2.5$ years	$p^{ext} = 0.99$ $T = 25$ years	$p^{ext} = 0.999$ $T = 250$ years
Panel A: Long position in foreign currencies			
German mark	−2.58	−3.57	−4.40
	(0.20)	(0.54)	(1.44)
French franc	−2.47	−3.18	−3.63
	(0.16)	(0.33)	(0.69)
Japanese yen	−2.28	−3.64	−5.26
	(0.23)	(0.88)	(3.38)
British pound	−2.62	−3.45	−4.06
	(0.18)	(0.42)	(1.01)
S&P500 index	−4.89	−20.12	−86.97
	(1.38)	(19.89)	(278.34)
Panel B: Short position in foreign currencies			
German mark	2.75	4.23	5.85
	(0.26)	(0.92)	(3.27)
French franc	2.73	4.16	5.63
	(0.26)	(0.86)	(2.86)
Japanese yen	2.75	3.87	4.81
	(0.22)	(0.61)	(1.66)
British pound	2.71	5.41	10.36
	(0.36)	(2.15)	(12.64)
S&P500 index	3.95	9.13	21.11
	(0.69)	(5.21)	(38.54)

Note: This table gives stress values for foreign exchange risk factors for different levels of extreme probability p^{ext} (or equivalently different levels of mean return period T). Panel A deals with a long position for a US investor in the foreign currency, for which the catastrophe scenario is related to the minimal daily change in the foreign exchange rate observed over one quarter. Similarly, Panel B deals with a short position for a US investor. Results for long and short positions in the S&P500 index are also given for comparison. The link between the extreme change in risk factors and the extreme probability is obtained with the extreme value distribution (equation (5) in the text). Estimates of the parameters of the asymptotic distribution of extreme changes in risk factors are given in Table 22.1.

to wait to observe an extreme of a given level. Empirical results are given in Table 22.2 (Panel A for a long position in the foreign currency and Panel B for a short position). For an extreme probability of 99 per cent, the stress value is around −3 per cent for a long position in the foreign currency (it ranges from −3.18 per cent for the French franc to −3.64 per cent for the Japanese yen) and around 4 per cent for a short position (it ranges from 3.87 per cent for the Japanese yen to 5.41 per cent for the British pound). As the distribution of S&P500 index returns presents fatter tails than the distributions of foreign exchange rates, stress values for the stock index are much higher: −20.12 per cent for a long position in the index and 9.13 per cent for a short position. Such empirical results obtained for the same probability level are in line with the guidelines of the Derivative Policy Group, which suggested lower values for currencies (±6 per cent) than for equity indexes (±10 per cent).

Note that stress values given by extreme value theory are based on a rigorous treatment of the data. The modeling of the data is quite general as the asymptotic extreme value distribution is obtained for many unconditional distributions and conditional processes. The method also allows one to distinguish between long and short positions. This is important as the weight of the left and right tails of the distribution may be different.

Conclusion

In this paper, I develop a rigorous method to define stress values for risk factors that can then be used in stress testing methods. The method is based on extreme value theory, which models the tails of statistical distribution.

In most applications, a portfolio is decomposed over several risk factors. It is then important to consider the correlation of the risk factors during extremely volatile periods. Longin and Solnik (1997) use multivariate extreme value theory to study the extreme correlation in international equity markets. Such a method may be used to compute stress values of different factors in a multivariate setting.

References

BASLE COMMITTEE ON BANKING SUPERVISION (1995) *An Internal Model-Based Approach to Market Risk Capital Requirements*, Bank for International Settlements, Basle.

BASLE COMMITTEE ON BANKING SUPERVISION (1996) *Amendment to the Capital Accord to Incorporate Market Risks*, Bank for International Settlements, Basle, January.

BERMAN, S. M. (1964) Limiting theorems for the maximum term in stationary sequences, *Annals of Mathematical Statistics*, Vol. 35, pp. 502–516.

BOLLERSLEV, T. (1986) Generalized autoregressive conditional heteroskedastcity, *Journal of Econometrics*, Vol. 31, pp. 307–327.

BOOTHE, P. and GLASMANN, D. (1987) The statistical distribution of exchange rates: Empirical evidence and economic implications, *Journal of International Economics*, Vol. 22, pp. 297–320.

DACOROGNA, M. M., MÜLLER, U. A., PICTET, O. V. and DE VRIES, C. G. (1995) *The Distribution of Extremal Foreign Exchange Rate Returns in Extremely Large Data Sets*, Working Paper, Olsen and Associates.

EMBRECHTS, P., KLÜPPELBERG, C. and MIKOSCH, T. (1997) *Modeling Extremal Events for Insurance and Finance*, Springer, Berlin Heidelberg.

ENGLE, R. F. (1982) Auto-regressive conditional heteroskedasticity with estimates of the variance of United Kingdom inflation, *Econometrica*, Vol. 50, pp. 987–1007.

GALAMBOS, J. (1978) *The Asymptotic Theory of Extreme Order Statistics*, John Wiley and Sons, Inc., New York.

GNEDENKO, B. V. (1943) Sur la distribution limite du terme maximum d'une série aléatoire, *Annals of Mathematics*, Vol. 44, pp. 423–453.

GUMBEL, E. J. (1958) *Statistics of Extremes*, Columbia University Press, New York.

HOLS, M. C. A. and DE VRIES, C. G. (1991) The limiting distribution of exchange rate returns, *Journal of Applied Econometrics*, Vol. 6, pp. 287–302.

JANSEN, D. W. and DE VRIES, C. G. (1991) on the frequency of large stock returns: Putting booms and busts into perspective, *Review and Economics and Statistics*, Vol. 78, pp. 18–24.

JENKINSON, A. F. (1955) The frequency distribution of the annual maximum (or minimum) values of meteorological elements, *Quarterly Journal of the Royal Meteorology Society*, Vol. 87, pp. 145–158.

JORION, P. (1997) *Value at Risk: The New Benchmark for Controlling Market Risk*, The McGraw-Hill Company, Chicago.

KON, S. (1984) Models of stock returns. A comparison, *Journal of Finance*, Vol. 39, pp. 147–165.

LEADBETTER, M. R., LINDGREN, G. and ROOTZÈN, H. (1983) *Extremes and Related Properties of Random Sequences and Processes*, Springer Verlag, New York.

LONGIN, F. M. (1996) The asymptotic distribution of extreme stock market returns, *Journal of Business*, Vol. 63, pp. 383–408.

LONGIN, F. M. (1997) *From VaR to Stress Testing: The Extreme Value Approach*, CERESSEC Working Paper 97–004, ESSEC, Cergy-Pontoise, France.

LONGIN, F. M. and SOLNIK, B. (1997) *Dependence Structure of International Equity Markets During Extremely Volatile Periods*, Working Paper, ESSEC, Cergy-Pontoise, France.

LORETAN, M. and PHILLIPS, P. C. B. (1994) Testing covariance stationarity of heavy-tailed series, *Journal of Empirical Finance*, Vol. 1, pp. 211–248.

MANDELBROT, B. (1963) The variation of certain speculative prices, *Journal of Business*, Vol. 36, pp. 394–419.

PRAETZ, P. D. (1972) The distribution of share price changes, *Journal of Business*, Vol. 45, pp. 49–55.

PRESS, S. J. (1967) A compound events model for security prices, *Journal of Business*, Vol. 40, pp. 317–335.

WILSON, T. C. (1996) Calculating risk capital, in C. ALEXANDER (ed.) *The Handbook of Risk Management and Analysis*, John Wiley and Sons, Chichester.

Notes

This research has benefited from the financial support of the CERESSEC research fund.

1. An exposition of the subject can be found in Wilson (1996) and Jorion (1997).

2. See Boothe and Glasmann (1987) for a study of the statistical distribution of exchange rates.
3. The maximum likelihood procedure did not converge for some series. When convergence was obtained, estimates given by the regression method were close to those given by the maximum likelihood method. For example, the tail index estimate for S&P500 index minimal returns was equal to -0.758 for the regression method and to -0.645 for the maximum likelihood method.
4. Such results differ from previous studies (e.g. Hols and De Vries, 1991 and Dacorogna et al. 1995) which most of times conclude to a Fréchet distribution for extreme changes in foreign exchange rates.
5. Such a result is similar to previous studies (e.g. Jansen and De Vries (1991), Loretan and Phillips (1994) and Longin (1996)).

References

ADAMS, C., MATHIESON, D. J. and SCHINASI, G. (1999) *International Capital Markets: Developments, Prospects and Key Policy Issues*, The International Monetary Fund, Washington DC, September.

AGGARWAL, R. (1981) International differences in capital structure norms: An empirical study of large European companies, *Management International Review*, Vol. 1, pp. 75–88.

AGGARWAL, R., INCLÀN, C. and LEAL, R. (1999) Volatility in emerging stock markets, *Journal of Financial and Quantitative Analysis*, Vol. 34, No. 1, pp. 33–35.

AIGNER, D. J., LOVELL, C. A. and SCHMIDT, P. (1977) Formulation and estimation of stochastic frontier production function models, *Journal of Econometrics*, December, pp. 21–37.

AKDOGAN, H. (1996) A suggested approach to country selection in international portfolio diversification, *Journal of Portfolio Management*, (Fall), pp. 33–39.

ALLEN, F. and GALE, D. (2000) *Comparing Financial Systems*, MIT Press, Boston, Massachusetts.

ALLEN, F. and GALE, D. (2000) Optimal currency crisis, *Carnegie–Rochester Series in Public Policy*, forthcoming.

ALLEN, L. and RAI, A (1996) Operational efficiency in banking: An international comparison, *Journal of Banking and Finance*, Vol. 20, pp. 655–672.

ALTMAN, E. I. (1968) Financial ratios, discriminant analysis, and the prediction of corporate bankruptcy, *Journal of Finance*, Vol. 23, No. 4, pp. 589–609.

AMMER, J. (1996) Macroeconomic state variables as determinants of asset price co-movements, *International Finance Discussion Paper 553*, Board of Governors of the Federal Reserve.

AMMER, J. and MEI, J. (1996) Measuring international economic linkages with stock market data, *Journal of Finance*, Vol. 51, No. 5, pp. 1743–1763.

ARDITTI, F. D. (1967) Risk and the required return on equity, *Journal of Finance*, Vol. 22, pp. 19–36.

ARDITTI, F. D. and LEVY, H. (1975) Portfolio efficiency analysis in three moments: The multi-period case, *Journal of Finance*, Vol. 30, pp. 797–809.

ARMENDARIZ, P. and MIJANGOS, M. (1995) Retos de la liberalización en el tratado de libre comercio: El caso de los servicios bancarios, in A. GIRÓN, E. ORTIZ and E. Correa (eds.), *Integración Financiera y TLC. Retos y Perspectivas*, Siglo XXI, Mexico, DF.

ARMSTRONG, H. W., BALASUBRAMANYAM, V. N. and SALISU, M. A. (1996) Domestic savings, intra-national and intra-European capital flows, *European Economic Review*, Vol. 40. pp. 1229–1235.

ARSHANAPALLI, B. and DOUKAS, J. (1993) International stock market linkages: Evidence from the pre- and post-October 1987 period, *Journal of Banking and Finance*, Vol. 17, No. 1, pp. 193–208.

ARTUS, P. (1995) *La Politique budgétaire en union monétaire et les critères de Maastricht*, Document de travail de la CDC, No.16/T.

ASHEGHIAN, P. and FOOTE, W. (1985) The productivities of US multinationals in the industrial sector of the Canadian economy, *Eastern Economic Journal*, April/June, pp. 123–133.

AVGOUSTINOS, P., LONIE, A. A., POWER, D. M. and SINCLAIR, C. D. (1994) An examination of the argument for increased investment in emerging equity markets, *Dundee Discussion Papers in Accountancy and Business Finance*, FIN/9402, pp. 1–19.

BAIG, T. and GOLDFAJN, I. (2000) *The Russian Default and the Contagion to Brazil*, PUC-Rio, Department of Economics Working Paper #420, Brazil (obtained from www.puc-rio.br/economia).

BAILEY, W. and STULTZ, R. (1990) Benefits of international diversification: The case of Pacific Basin stock markets, *Journal of Portfolio Management*, Vol. 16, No. 4 (Summer), pp. 57–61.

BANK FOR INTERNATIONAL SETTLEMENTS (BIS) (1996) *Central Bank Survey of Foreign Exchange and Derivatives Market Activity 1995*, Bank for International Settlements, Basle, May.

BANK FOR INTERNATIONAL SETTLEMENTS (BIS) (1999) *69th Annual Report*, Bank for International Settlements, Basle, June.

BANK FOR INTERNATIONAL SETTLEMENTS (BIS) (1999) *The Global OTC Derivatives Market at end-June 1999*, Bank for International Settlements, Basle, November.

BANKING FEDERATION OF THE EUROPEAN UNION (1995) *Survey*, March.

BARBER, B. M. and LOEFFLER, D. (1993) The Dartboard column: Second-hand information and price pressure, *Journal of Financial and Quantitative Analysis*, Vol. 28, pp. 273–283.

BARCLAY, M. J., HOLDERNESS, C. G. and PONTIFF, J. (1993) Private benefits from block ownership and discounts on closed-end funds, *Journal of Financial Economics*, (June), pp. 263–291.

BASLE COMMITTEE ON BANKING SUPERVISION (1995) *An Internal Model-Based Approach to Market Risk Capital Requirements*, Bank for International Settlements, Basle.

BASLE COMMITTEE ON BANKING SUPERVISION (1996) *Amendment to the General Accord to Incorporate Market Risks*, Bank for International Settlements, Basle, January.

BASLE COMMITTEE ON BANKING SUPERVISION (1996) *Amendment to the Capital Accord to Incorporate Market Risks*, Bank for International Settlements, Basle, January.

BECKERS, S., GRINOLD, R., RUDD, A. and STEFEK, D. (1992) The relative importance of common factors across the European equity markets, *Journal of Banking and Finance*, Vol. 16, No. 1, pp. 75–95.

BEKAERT, G. (1993) Market integration and investment barriers in emerging equity markets, in S. CLAESSENS and S. GOOPTU, *Portfolio Investment in Developing Countries*, World Bank Discussion Paper 228, (September), pp. 221–251.

BEKAERT, G. (1995) Market integration and investment barriers in emerging equity markets, *World Bank Economic Review*, Vol. 9, No. 1 (January), pp. 75–107.

BEKAERT, G. and HARVEY, C. R. (1995) Time varying world market integration, *Journal of Finance*, Vol. 50, No. 2, pp. 403–444.

BEKAERT, G. and HARVEY, C. R. (1997) Emerging equity market volatility, *Journal of Financial Economics*, Vol. 43, pp. 29–77.

BELKAOUI, A. (1978) Financial raios as predictors of Canadian takeovers, *Journal of Business Finance and Accounting*, Vol. 5, No. 1, pp. 93–108.

BENEISH, M. D. (1991) Stock prices and the dissemination of analysts' recommendations, *Journal of Business*, Vol. 64, pp. 393–416.

BENNET, R. L. (1965) *The Financial Sector and Economic Development: The Mexican Case*, Johns Hopkins, Baltimore.

BERG, S. A., BUKH, P. N. D. and FORSUND, F. R. (1995) *Banking Efficiency in the Nordic Countries: A Four-Country Malmquist Index Analysis*, Working Paper, University of Aarhus, Denmark.

BERGER, A. N. and DEYOUNG, R. (1997) Problem loans and cost-efficiency in commercial banks, *Journal of Banking and Finance*, Vol. 21, pp. 849–870.

BERGER, A. N., DEYOUNG, R., GENAY, H. and UDELL, G. (2000) The globalization of financial institutions: Evidence from cross-border banking performance, *Brookings–Rochester Economic Series*, forthcoming.

BERGER, A. N. HUNTER, W. C. and TIMME, S. G. (1993) The efficiency of financial institutions: A review and preview of research past, present and future, *Journal of Banking and Finance*, Nos. 2–3, pp. 221–249.

BERMAN, S. M. (1964) Limiting theorems for the maximum term in stationary sequences, *Annals of Mathematical Statistics*, Vol. 35, pp. 502–516.

BERNANKE, B. S. (1983) Non-monetary effects of the financial crisis in the propagation of the Great Depression, *American Economic Review*, Vol. 73 (June), pp. 257–276.

BERNDT, E. K., HALL, H. B., HALL, R. E. and HAUSMAN, J. A. (1974) Estimation and inference in nonlinear structual models, *Annals of Economic and Social Measurement*, Vol. 4, pp. 653–666.

BIKKER, J. A. (1999) *Efficiency in the European Banking Industry: An Explanatory Analysis to Rank Countries*, De Nederlandsche Bank, Amsterdam, The Netherlands.

BIRDSALL, N., ROSS, D. and SABOT, R. (1995) Inequality and growth reconsidered: Lessons from East Asia, *The World Bank Economic Review*, Vol. 9, No. 3 (September), pp. 477–508.

BLACK, F. (1976) Studies of stock market volatility changes, *Proceedings of the American Statistical Association, Business and Economic Studies Section*, pp. 177–181.

BLANCO, G. H. and VERMA, S. (1996) *The Mexican Financial System*, Captus Press, North York, Ontario.

BLANDEN, M. (1996) Visions of Europe, *Banker*, December.

BLEJER, M. I. and SKREB, M. (eds.) (1999) *Financial Sector Transformation. Lessons from Economics in Transition*, Cambridge University Press, New York.

BMS Bossard (1996) *Euro Survey*, BMS Bossard, Paris.

BOLLERSLEV, T. (1986) Generalized autoregressive conditional heteroskedastcity, *Journal of Econometrics*, Vol. 31, pp. 307–327.

BOLLERSLEV, T., CHOU, R. Y. and KRONER, K. F. (1992) ARCH modeling in finance: A review of the theory and empirical evidence, *Journal of Econometrics*, Vol. 52, pp. 5–59.

BOLLERSLEV, T., ENGLE, R. and NELSON, D. (1994) ARCH models, in R. F. ENGLE and D. L. McFADDEN (eds.), *Handbook of Econometrics*, Elsevier Science, B.V., pp. 2959–3038.

BONSER-NEAL, C., BRAUER, G., NEAL, R. and WHEATLEY, S. (1990) International investment restrictions and closed-end country funds, *Journal of Finance*, Vol. 45, No. 2, pp. 523–547.

BOOTH, D. G. and FAMA, E. F. (1992) Diversification returns and asset contributions, *Financial Analysts Journal*, (May/June), pp. 26–32.

BOOTH, G. G., MARTIKAINEN, T. and TSE, Y. (1997) Price and volatility spillovers in Scandinavian stock markets, *Journal of Business Finance and Accounting*, Vol. 21, pp. 811–823.

BOOTHE, P. and GLASMANN, D. (1987) The statistical distribution of exchange rates: Empirical evidence and economic implications, *Journal of International Economics*, Vol. 22, pp. 297–320.

BRANDER, J. A. and LEWIS, T. R. (1986) Oligopoly and financial structure: The limited liability effect, *American Economic Review*, Vol. 76, pp. 956–970.

BRITISH BANKERS ASSOCIATION and THE ASSOCIATION OF PAYMENT CLEARING SERVICES (1995) *Joint 1995 Survey on Euro Changeover Costs*, British Bankers Association, London, and the Association of Payment Clearing Services, London.

BROWN. G. W. (1999) Volatility, sentiment and noise traders, *Financial Analysts Journal*, Vol. 55, No. 2, pp. 82–90.

BROWN, S. J. and WARNER, J. B. (1985) Using daily stock returns: The case of event studies, *Journal of Financial Economics*, Vol. 14, pp. 3–31.

BRULL, S. V. and LEE, C. K. (1997) South Korea: Why Seoul is seething, *Business Week*, January 27, pp. 44–48.

BRYSON, J. H. (1994) Fiscal policy coordination and flexibility under European monetary union: Implications for macroeconomic stabilization, *Journal of Policy Modelling*, Vol. 16, No. 6, pp. 541–557.

BUCKLEY, P., DUNNING, J. H. and PEARCE, R. D. (1978) The influence of firm size, nationality and degree of multinationality on the growth and profitability of the world's largest firms, *Welwirtschaftliches Archiv*, Vol. 114, No. 2, pp. 243–257.

CABELLO, A. (1997) Liberalization and deregulation of the Mexican stock market, in D. K. GHOSH and E. ORTIZ (eds.), *The Global Structure of Financial Markets*, Routledge, London.

CABELLO, A. (1999) *Globalización y Liberalización Financieras y Bolsa Mexican de Valores. Del Auge a la Crisis*, Plaza y Valdés, Mexico, DF.

CALOMIRIS, C. and CAREY, M. (1994) Loan market competition between foreign and US banks: Some facts about loans and borrowers, *Bank Structure and Competition*, Federal Reserve Bank of Chicago.

CAMPBELL, J. Y. and AMMER, J. (1993) What moves the stock and bond markets? A variance decomposition for long-term asset returns, *Journal of Finance*, Vol. 48, pp. 3–37.

CASSON, M. (1990) Evolution of multinational banks: A theoretical perspective, in G. JONES (ed.) *Banks As Multinationals*, Routledge, London, pp. 14–29.

CHANG, C. E., HASAN, I. and HUNTER, W. C. (1998) Efficiency of multinational banks: An empirical investigation, *Applied Financial Economics*, December, pp. 689–696.

CHANG, R. and VELASCO, A. (1998) The Asian liquidity crisis, *Federal Reserve Bank of Atlanta, Working Paper Series*, No. 98–11 (July).

CHEN, N., KAN, R. and MILLER, M. H. (1993a) Are discounts on closed-end funds a sentiment index? *Journal of Finance*, Vol. 48, pp. 795–800.

CHEN, N., KAN, R. and MILLER, M. H. (1993b) A Rejoinder, *Journal of Finance*, Vol. 48, pp. 809–810.

CHEUNG, Y. W. and HO, Y. (1991) The intertemporal stability of the relationships between the Asian emerging equity markets and the developed equity markets, *Journal of Business Finance and Accounting*, Vol. 18, No. 2 (January), pp. 235–254.

CHEUNG, Y. W. and NG, L. K. (1992) Stock price dynamics and firm size: An empirical investigation, *Journal of Finance*, Vol. 47, pp. 1985–1997.

CHOPRA, N., LEE, C., SHLEIFER, A. and THALER, R. H. (1993a) Yes, discounts on closed-end funds are a sentiment index, *Journal of Finance*, Vol. 48, pp. 801–808.

CHOPRA, N., LEE, C., SHLEIFER, A. and THALER, R. H. (1993b) Summing up, *Journal of Finance*, Vol. 48, pp. 811–812.

CHRISTIE, A. A. (1982) The stochastic behaviour of common stock variances: Value, leverage and interest rate effects, *Journal of Financial Economics*, Vol. 10, pp. 407–432.

CHRISTOFFERSEN, P. and ERRUNZA, V. (2000) Towards a global financial architecture: Capital mobility and risk management issues, *Emerging Markets Review*, Vol. 1, No. 1, pp. 3–20.

CHRISTOFI, A. and PERICLI, A. (1999) Correlation in price changes and volatility of major Latin American stock markets, *Journal of Multinational Financial Management*, Vol. 9, pp. 79–93.

CHUGH, L. C., KOUNDINYA, R. and PURI, Y. R. (1996) Financial leverage: A cross-country analysis, *The International Journal of Finance*, Vol. 8, No. 4, pp. 411–424.

CHUNHACHINDA, P., DANDAPANI, K., HAMID, S. and PRAKASH, A. J. (1997) Portfolio selection and skewness: Evidence from international stock markets, *Journal of Banking and Finance*, Vol. 21, pp. 143–167.

CLAESSENS, S. (1993) *Risk Management in Developing Countries*, World Bank Technical Paper No.235, The World Bank, Washington DC, September.

CLARK, J. A. (1986a) Market structure, risk and profitability: The quiet life hypothesis revisited, *Quarterly Review of Economics and Business*, Spring, pp. 45–56.

CLARK, J. A. (1986b) Single-equation, multiple-regression methodology: Is it an appropriate methodology for the estimation of the structure–performance relationship in banking? *Journal of Monetary Economics*, November, pp. 295–312.

COLLINS, J. M. and SEKELY, W. S. (1983) The relationship of headquarters, country and industry classification to financial structure, *Financial Management*, Autumn, pp. 45–51.

COOPER, S., FRASER, D., ROSE, P. and WOLKEN, L. (1989) US activities of Pacific-Rim and European banks: Evidence for a global integrated market for bank credit? *The Review of Research in Banking and Finance*, (Fall), pp. 1–25.

COOPERS and LYBRAND (International) (1993) *International Accounting Summaries: A Guide for Interpretation and Comparison*, 2nd ed., John Wiley and Sons Inc., New York.

DACOROGNA, M. M., MÜLLER, U. A., PICTET, O. V. and DE VRIES, C. G. (1995) *The Distribution of Extremal Foreign Exchange Rate Returns in Extremely Large Data Sets*, Working Paper, Olsen and Associates.

DAMANPOUR, F. (1990) *The Evolution of Foreign Banking Institutions in the United States*, Quorum Books, New York.

DE ALBA MONROY, J. DE J. A. (2000) *El Mercado de Dinero y Capitales y El Sistema Financiero Mexicano*, Editorial Pac, Mexico, DF.

DE LONG, J. B., SHLEIFER, A., SUMMERS, L. H. and WALDMANN, R. J. (1990) Noise trader risk in financial markets, *Journal of Political Economics*, Vol. 98, pp. 703–738.

DENTON, N. (1997) European monetary union: Impact on IT systems, *Financial Times*, February 5.

DE SANTIS, G. (1993) Asset pricing and portfolio diversification: Evidence from emerging financial markets, in S. CLAESSENS and S. GOOPTU, *Portfolio Investment in Developing Countries*, World Bank Discussion Paper 228, (September), pp. 145–168.

DEYOUNG, R. and HASAN, I. (1998) The performance of De Novo commercial banks: A profit efficiency approach, *Journal of Banking and Finance*, (May), pp. 565–587.

DEYOUNG, R. and NOLLE, D. E. (1996) Foreign-owned banks in the United States: Earning market share or buying it, *Journal of Money, Credit and Banking*, (May), pp. 622–636.

DIAMOND, D. (1984) Financial intermediation and delegated monitoring, *Review of Economic Studies*, Vol. 51 (Autumn), pp. 393–414.

DIEFENBACK, R. (1972) How good is institutional brokerage research? *Financial Analysts Journal*, Vol. 28, pp. 54–60.

DIMSON, E. and MARSH, P. (1986) Event study methodologies and the size effect: The case of UK press recommendations, *Journal of Financial Economics*, Vol. 17, pp. 113–142.

DIVECHA, A. B. (1994) Emerging markets and risk reduction, in J. LEDERMAN and R. A. KLEIN (eds.), *Global Asset Allocation*, John Wiley and Sons, Inc., New York, pp. 340–348.

DIVECHA, A. B., DRACH, J. and STEFEK, D. (1992) Emerging markets: A quantitative perspective, *Journal of Portfolio Management*, Vol. 18, No. 1 (Fall), pp. 41–50.

DIWAN, I., ERRUNZA, V. R. and SENBET, L. W. (1993) Country funds for emerging economies, in S. CLAESSENS and S. GOOPTU, *Portfolio Investment in Developing Countries*, World Bank Discussion Paper 228, (September), pp. 252–286.

DOMOWITZ, I., GLEN, J. and MADHAVAN, A. (1997) Market segmentation and stock prices: Evidence from an emerging market, *Journal of Finance*, Vol. 52, pp. 1059–1085.

DUNNING, J. H. (1970) *Studies in International Investment*, George Allen and Unwin, London.

DROMS, W. G. and WALKER, D. A. (1994) Investment performance of international mutual funds, *Journal of Financial Research*, Vol. 17, pp. 1–14.

DUNNING, J. H. (1970) *Studies in International Investment*, George Allen and Unwin, London.

ECONOMIST, THE (1995) Those lovely *chaebols* and their little local difficulty, *The Economist*, November 11, pp. 61–62.

ECONOMIST, THE (1997a) A survey of Indonesia, *The Economist*, July 26.

ECONOMIST, THE (1997b) And South-East Asia thinks it's all over, *The Economist*, November 8, pp. 41–42.

ECONOMIST, THE (1998a) Banking in Korea: No exit, *The Economist*, April 4, pp. 81–82.

ECONOMIST, THE (1998b) South-East Asia: Fusion confusion, *The Economist*, April 4, p. 81.

ECONOMIST, THE (1998c) Asian financial reform: Listen closely for the bang, April 4, pp. 80–81.

ECONOMIST, THE (1998d) A survey of East Asian economies, *The Economist*, March 7, Table 3, p. 5 and charts 5 and 7, pp. 6 and 14.

ECONOMIST, THE (2000) Survey of South-East Asia, *The Economist*, February 12, p. 6.

EDMINSTER, R. O. (1972) An empirical test of financial ratio analysis for small business failure prediction, *Journal of Financial and Quantitative Analysis*, Vol. 7, No. 2, pp. 1477–1493.

EICHENGREEN, B. (1993) European monetary unification, *Journal of Economic Literature*, Vol. 31. pp. 1321–1357.

EICHENGREEN, B. and PORTES, R. (2000) A short-sighted vision for IMF reform, *Financial Times*, March 9, p. 13.

EL-ERIAN, M. A. and KUMAR, M. S. (1995) Emerging equity markets in Middle Eastern countries, *IMF Staff Papers*, Vol. 42, No. 2 (June), pp. 313–343.

ELLIOT, K. A. (1997) (ed.) *Corruption and The Global Economy*, Institute for International Economics, Washington DC, June.

ELTON, E. J. and GRUBER, M. J. (1973) Estimating the dependence structure of share prices – implications for portfolio selection, *Journal of Finance*, Vol. 28, No. 5 (December), pp. 1203–1232.

ELTON, E. J., GRUBER, M. J. and URICH, T. (1978) Are betas best? *Journal of Finance*, Vol. 33, No. 5 (December), pp. 1375–1384.

ELYASIANI, E. and MEHDIAN, S. M. (1990) A nonparametric approach to measurement of efficiency and technological change: The case of large US commercial banks, *Journal of Financial Services Research*, August, pp. 157–168.

ELYASIANI, E. and MEHDIAN, S. M. (1992) *A Nonparametric Frontier Model of Internationally-Owned and Domestically-Owned Bank Cost Structures*, Paper presented at the Financial Management Association Meetings.

EMBRECHTS, P., KLÜPPELBERG, C. and MIKOSCH, T. (1997) *Modeling Extremal Events for Insurance and Finance*, Springer, Berlin Heidelberg.

ENDERS, W. (1995) *Applied Econometric Time Series*, John Wiley and Sons, Inc., New York.

ENGLE, R. F. (1982) Auto-regressive conditional heteroskedasticity with estimates of the variance of United Kingdom inflation, *Econometrica*, Vol. 50, pp. 987–1007.

ENGLE, R. F. and KRONER, K. (1995) Multivariate simultaneous GARCH, *Econometric Theory*, Vol. 11, 122–150.

ENGLE, R. F. and NG, V. K. (1993) Measuring and testing the impact of news on volatility, *Journal of Finance*, Vol. 48, pp. 1749–1778.

ERB, C. B., HARVEY, C. R. and VISKANTA, T. E. (1994) Forecasting international equity correlations, *Financial Analysts Journal*, November/December, pp. 32–45.

ERB, C. B., HARVEY, C. R. and VISKANTA, T. E. (1995) Country risk and global equity selection, *Journal of Portfolio Management*, (Winter), pp. 74–83.

ERRUNZA, V. R. (1977) Gains from portfolio diversification into less developed countries' securities, *Journal of International Business Studies*, (Fall), pp. 83–99.

ERRUNZA, V. R. (1979), Determinants of financial structure in the Central American common market, *Financial Management*, (Autumn), pp. 72–77.

ERRUNZA, V. R. (1994) Emerging markets: Some new concepts, *Journal of Portfolio Management*, Vol. 20, No. 3 (Spring), pp. 82–87.

EUN, C. S., KOLODNY, R. and RESNICK, B. G. (1991) US-based international mutual funds: A performance evaluation, *Journal of Portfolio Management*, Vol. 17, pp/ 88–94.

EUN, C. S. and RESNICK, B. F. (1989) Estimating the correlation structure of international share prices, *Journal of Finance*, Vol. 41, pp. 313–330.

EUN, C. S. and RESNICK, B. F. (1994) International diversification of investment portfolios: US and Japanese perspectives, *Management Science*, (January), pp. 140–161.

EUN, C. S. and SHIM, S. (1989) International transmission of stock market movements, *Journal of Financial and Quantitative Analysis*, Vol. 24, No. 2, pp. 241–256.

EUROPEAN CENTRAL BANK (ECB) (1999) *Annual Report*.

EUROPEAN CENTRAL BANK (ECB) (2000) *Monthly Bulletin*, January, March and April.

EUROPEAN COMMISSION (1997) *Report from the Euro Working Group for the Consumer Committee*, September 15.

EUROPEAN COMMISSION (1997) Economic Policy in EMU, *Economic Papers*, part B, section II–8, No. 125, November.

FAMA, E. (1984) The information in the term structure, *Journal of Financial Economics*, Vol. 13 (December), pp. 509–528.

FECHER, F. and PESTIEAU, P. (1993) Efficiency and competition in OECD financial services, in H. O. FRIED, C. A. K. LOVELL and S. S. SCHMIDT (eds.), *The Measurement of Productive Efficiency Techniques and Applications*, Oxford University Press, Oxford, pp. 374–385.

FINANCIAL TECHNOLOGY INTERNATIONAL BULLETIN (1995) Europe's bank faces Ecu8–10 billion bill in run-up to EMU, *Financial Technology International Bulletin*, April 1995 and April 1996.

FINANCIAL TIMES (1996) Anxiety over EMU starts to creep in, *Financial Times*, December 3.

FISCHER, K. and PALASVIRTA, A. P. (1990) High road to a global marketplace: The international transmission of stock market fluctuations, *Financial Review*, Vol. 25, No. 3, pp. 371–394.

FRASER, K. (1993) The odd ways of closed-end funds, *Euromoney*, July, pp. 88–89.

FRIEDMAN, J. and SHACHMUROVE, Y. (1997) Co-movements of major European Community stock markets: A vector autoregression analysis, *Global Finance Journal*, Vol. 8, No. 2, pp. 257–277.

FRY, M. (1988) *Money, Interest and Banking in Economic Development*, Johns Hopkins, Baltimore.

FRY, M. (1989) Financial development: Theories and recent experience, *Oxford Review of Economic Policy*, Vol. 5, No. 4, pp. 13–28.

GALAMBOS, J. (1978) *The Asymptotic Theory of Extreme Order Statistics*, John Wiley and Sons, Inc., New York.

GALBIS, V. (1977) Financial intermediation and economic growth in less developed countries: A theoretical approach, in P. C. AYRE (ed.), *Finance in Developing Countries*, Frank Cass, London.

GASTINEAU, G. L. (1995) The currency hedging decision: A search for synthesis in asset allocation, *Financial Analysts Journal*, May/June, pp. 8–16.

GNEDENKO, B. V. (1943) Sur la distribution limite du terme maximum d'une série aléatoire, *Annals of Mathematics*, Vol. 44, pp. 423–453.

GOLDBERG, E. (1981) Analysis of current operations of foreign-owned US banks in US, in US Comptroller of the Currency, *Foreign Acquisition of US Banks*, Robert.R. Dame, Richmond, Virginia, pp. 343–368.

GOLDBERG, E. (1982) Comparative cost analysis of foreign-owned US banks, *Journal of Bank Research*, Vol. 13, pp. 144–159.

GOLDBERG, L. and SAUNDERS, A. (1981a) The determinants of foreign banking activities in the United States, *Journal of Banking and Finance*, March, pp. 17–32.

GOLDBERG, L. and SAUNDERS, A. (1981b) The growth of organizational forms of foreign banks in the US, *Journal of Money, Credit and Banking*, Vol. 13, pp. 365–374.

GOLDSMITH, R. W. (1968) *Financial Institutions*, Randa House, New York.

GOLDSMITH, R. W. (1969) *Financial Structure and Development*, Yale University Press, New York.

GOLDSTEIN, M. and TURNER, P. (1996) *Banking Crises in Emerging Economies: Origins and Policy Options*, BIS Economic Papers No. 46, Bank for International Settlements, Basle, October.

GRADDY, D. B. and KYLE, R. III (1979) The simultaneity of bank decision-making, market structure, and bank performance, *Journal of Finance*, Vol. 34, pp. 1–18.

GRANGER, C. W. (1969) Investigating causal relations by econometric models and cross-spectral models, *Econometrica*, Vol. 37, pp. 424–438.

GRAY, P. and GRAY, J. (1981) The multinational bank: A financial MNC? *Journal of Banking and Finance*, March, pp. 33–63.

GREENWOOD, J. G. (1993) Portfolio investment in Asian and Pacific economies: Trends and Prospects, *Asian Development Review*, Vol. 11, No. 1, pp. 120–150.

GRINOLD, R., RUDD, A. and STEFEK, D. (1989) Global factors: Fact or fiction? *Journal of Portfolio Management*, Vol. 16, No. 1 (Fall), pp. 79–88.

GROSSE, R. and GOLDBERG, L. (1991) Foreign banking activity in the United States: An analysis of country of origin, *Journal of Banking and Finance*, December, pp. 1093–1112.

GRUBEL, H. G. (1968) International diversified portfolios: Welfare gains and capital flows, *American Economic Review*, Vol. 58, pp. 1299–1314.

GUITIAN, M. (1998) The challenge of managing global capital flows, *Finance and Development*, June, pp. 14–17.

GULTEKIN, M. N., GULTEKIN, N. B. and PENATI, A. (1989) Capital controls and international capital market segmentation: The evidence from the Japanese and American stock markets, *Journal of Finance*, Vol. 44, No. 4, pp. 849–870.

GUMBEL, E. J. (1958) *Statistics of Extremes*, Columbia University Press, New York.

GUP, B. E., LINDLEY, J. T., McNULTY, J. E. and VERBRUGGE, J. A. (1992) Investment policy, financing policy and performance characteristics of De Novo Savings and Loan Association, *Journal of Banking and Finance*, (April), pp. 313–330.

GUPTA, K. (1984) *Finance and Growth in Developing Countries*, Croom Helm, London.

GURLEY, J. G. and SHAW, E. S. (1960) *Money in a Theory of Finance*, Brookings Institution, Washington DC.

HALE, D. D. (1994) Stock markets in the new world order, *Columbia Journal of World Business, Focus Issue: Emerging Capital Markets*, Vol. 29, No. 2 (Summer), pp. 14–28.

HAMAO, Y. R., MASULIS, R. W. and NG, V. K. (1990) Correlation in price changes and volatility across international stock markets, *The Review of Financial Studies*, Vol. 3, pp. 281–307.

HARRIS, M. and RAVIV, A. (1991) The theory of capital structure, *Journal of Finance*, (March), pp. 297–355.

HARTMANN, M. A. and KHAMBATA, D. (1993) Emerging stock markets: Investment strategies of the future, *Columbia Journal of World Business*, (Summer), pp. 82–104.

HARVEY, C. R. (1993) Portfolio enhancement using emerging markets and conditioning information, in S. Claessens and S. Gooptu, *Portfolio Investment in Developing Countries*, World Bank Discussion Paper 228, (September), pp. 110–144.

HARVEY, C. R. (1994) Conditional asset allocation in emerging markets, *NBER Working Paper 4623*, (January), pp. 1–45.

HARVEY, C. R. (1995) Predictable risk and returns in emerging markets, *Review of Financial Studies*, Vol. 8, No. 3 (Fall), pp. 773–816.

HASAN, I., HASAN, T. and PICKERAL, R. (1995) Are mortgage specialized thrifts viable? An empirical analysis, *International Review of Economics and Finance*, Vol. 4, No. 2, pp. 189–204.

HASAN, I. and HUNTER, T. W. (1996) Efficiency of Japanese multinational banks in the United States, *Research in Finance*, Vol. 14, pp. 157–173.

HASAN, I. and LOZANO-VIVAS, A. (1998) *Foreign Banks, Production Technology, and Efficiency: Spanish Experience*, Working Paper presented at the Georgia Productivity Workshop III, Athens, Georgia.

HASAN, I., LOZANO-VIVAS, A. and PASTOR, J. (2000) *Cross-border Performance in European Banking*, Paper presented at the Wharton School and Frankfurt Finance Centre Conference.

HENRY, P. B. (2000) Stock market liberalization, economic reform and emerging market equity prices, *Journal of Finance*, Vol. 55, No. 2, pp. 529–564.

HOLS, M. C. A. and DE VRIES, C. G. (1991) The limiting distribution of exchange rate returns, *Journal of Applied Econometrics*, Vol. 6, pp. 287–302.

HONOHAN, P. (1997) *Banking System Failures in Developing and Transition Countries: Diagnosis and Prediction*, BIS Working Paper No. 97–39, Bank for International Settlements, Basle, January.

HOUPT, J. (1983) Foreign ownership of US banks: Trends and effects, *Journal of Bank Research*, Vol. 14, pp. 144–156.

HSIEH, D. (1989) Modeling heteroskedasticity in daily foreign exchange rates, *Journal of Business and Economic Statistics*, Vol. 7, pp. 307–317.

HUERTA, A. (1997) *Carteras Vencidas, Inestabilidad Financiera. Propuestas de Solucion*, Diana, Mexico, DF.

HULTMANN, C. and McGEE, L. (1989) Factors affecting the foreign banking presence in the US, *Journal of Banking and Finance*, October, pp. 383–396.

HUTCHINSON, P., MERIC, I. and MERIC, G. (1988) The financial characteristics of small firms which achieve quotation on the UK securities markets, *Journal of Business Finance and Accounting*, (Spring), pp. 9–19.

HUTH, W. L. and MARIS, B. A. (1992) Large and small firm stock price responses to Heard On The Street recommendations, *Journal of Accounting and Auditing*, Vol. 7, pp. 27–47.

INCLÀN, C. and TIAO, G. C. (1994) Use of cumulative sum of squares for retrospective detection of changes in variance, *Journal of American Statistical Association*, Vol. 89, pp. 913–923.

INTERNATIONAL FINANCE CORPORATION (IFC) (1998) *IFC Risk Management*, (available online at www.ifc.org/main/html/pubrisk.html).

INTERNATIONAL MONETARY FUND (IMF) (1999) *World Economic Outlook, October 1999*, The International Monetary Fund, Washington DC.

INTERNATIONAL ORGANIZATION OF SECURITIES COMMISSIONS (IOSCO) (1997) *Financial Risk Management in Emerging Markets, Report of the Emerging Markets Committee*, IOSCO, Montreal, Quebec, November.

ISLAM, M. M. and RODRIGUEZ, A. J. (1998) Evidence on the benefits of portfolio investment in emerging capital markets in Latin America, in J. C. BAKER (ed.), *Selected International Investment Portfolios*, Elsevier Science B.V., pp. 75–89.

IVANOVA, A. (1998) *Los Intermediarios Financieros no Bancarios y el Crecimiento Económico. El Caso de México*, Doctoral Thesis, Universidad Nacional Autónoma de México.

JAMES, C. (1987) Some evidence on the uniqueness of bank loans, *Journal of Financial Economics*, Vol. 19, No. 2, pp. 217–236.

JANSEN, D. W. and DE VRIES, C. G. (1991) on the frequency of large stock returns: Putting booms and busts into perspective, *Review and Economics and Statistics*, Vol. 78, pp. 18–24.

JENKINSON, A. F. (1955) The frequency distribution of the annual maximum (or minimum) values of meteorological elements, *Quarterly Journal of the Royal Meteorology Society*, Vol. 87, pp. 145–158.

JENSEN, G. R. and JOHNSON, R. R. (1995) Discount rate changes and security returns in the US, 1962–1991, *Journal of Banking and Finance*, Vol. 19, No. 1, pp. 79–95.

JENSEN, G. R., MERCER, J. M. and JOHNSON, R. R. (1996) Business conditions, monetary policy, and expected security returns, *Journal of Financial Economics*, Vol. 40, pp. 213–237.

JENSEN, M. and MECKLING, W. H. (1976) Theory of the firm: Managerial behaviour, agency costs and ownership structure, *Journal of Financial Economics*, October, pp. 305–360.

JEON, B. N. and VON FURSTENBERG, G. M. (1990) Growing international co-movement in stock price indexes, *Quarterly Review of Economics and Business*, Vol. 30, No. 3, pp. 15–30.

JOHNSON, G., SCHNEEWEIS, T. and DINNING, W. (1993) Closed-end country funds: exchange rate and investment risk, *Financial Analysts Journal*, Vol. 49, No. 6, pp. 74–82.

JOHNSTON, M. (1997) Public officials, private interests, and sustainable democracy: When politics and corruption meet, in K. A. ELLIOT (ed.), *Corruption and The Global Economy*, Institute for International Economics, Washington DC, (June), chapter 3.

JORION, P. (1997) *Value at Risk: The New Benchmark for Controlling Market Risk*, The McGraw-Hill Company, Chicago.

KAMINSKY, G. L. and REINHART, C. M. (1999) The twin crisis: The causes of banking and balance of payments crisis, *American Economic Review*, (June), pp. 473–500.

KARMIN, C. (1999) More efficient WEBS provide alternative closed-end funds, *Wall Street Journal*, July 6.

KARP, R. (2000) Doomed dinosaurs, *Barron's*, Vol. 80, No. 9 (February), pp. 27–28.

KESSLER, T. P. (1999) *Global Capital and National Politics. Reforming Mexico's Financial System*, Praeger, London.

KESTER, C. W. (1986) Capital and ownership structure: Comparison of United States and Japanese manufacturing corporations, *Financial Management*, (Spring), pp. 5–16.

KIM, C. (1994) Investor tax trading opportunities and discounts on closed-end mutual funds, *Journal of Financial Research*, Vol. 17, pp. 65–75.

KING, K. K. (1992) Deposit insurance as a put option: Alternative approaches to modeling regulatory forbearance, *Board of Governors of the Federal Reserve System*.

KING, M. A., SENTANA, E. and WADHWANI, S. (1994) Volatility and the links between national stock markets, *Econometrica*, Vol. 62, pp. 901–934.

KING, M. A. and WADHWANI, S. (1990) Transmission of volatility between stock markets, *The Review of Financial Studies*, Vol. 3, pp. 281–307.

KLIBANOFF, P., LAMANT, O. and WIZMAN, T. (1998) Investor reaction to salient news in closed-end country funds, *Journal of Finance*, Vol. 53, No. 2, pp. 673–699.

KOCH, P. D. and KOCH, T. W. (1991) Evolution in dynamic linkages across daily national stock indices, *Journal of International Money and Finance*, Vol. 10, No. 2, pp. 231–251.

KON, S. (1984) Models of stock returns. A comparison, *Journal of Finance*, Vol. 39, pp. 147–165.

KOUTMOS, G. (1992) Asymmetric volatility and risk return tradeoff in foreign stock markets, *Journal of Multinational Financial Management*, Vol. 2, pp. 27–43.

KOUTMOS, G. (1996) Modeling the dynamic interdependence of major European stock markets, *Journal of Banking, Finance and Accounting*, Vol. 23, pp. 975–988.

KOUTMOS, G. and BOOTH, G. G. (1995) Asymmetric volatility transmission in international stock markets, *Journal of International Money and Finance*, Vol. 14, No. 5, pp. 747–762.

KRAUSS, A. L. and LIZENBERGER, R. H. (1976) Skewness preference and the valuation of risk assets, *Journal of Finance*, Vol. 31, No. 4, pp. 1085–1100.

KRUEGER, A. O. (1997) Trade policy and economic development: How we learn, *American Economic Review*, Vol. 87, No. 1 (March), pp. 1–22.

KUCZYNSKI, P. (1994) Why emerging markets? *Columbia Journal of World Business, Focus Issue: Emerging Capital Markets*, Vol. 29, No. 2 (Summer), pp. 8–13.

KUMAR, P. C., PHILIPPATOS, G. C. and EZZELL, J. R. (1978) Goal programming and the selection of portfolios by dual-purpose funds, *Journal of Finance*, Vol. 33, pp. 303–310.

LACHICA, E. (2000) Asian capital controls were no panacea: IMF financial crisis study finds such interventions brought mixed blessings, *Wall Street Journal*, January 12, p.A18.

LAI, T. Y. (1991) Portfolio selection with skewness: A multiple-objective approach, *Review of Quantitative Finance and Accounting*, Vol. 1, pp. 293–305.

LEADBETTER, M. R., LINDGREN, G. and ROOTZÈN, H. (1983) *Extremes and Related Properties of Random Sequences and Processes*, Springer Verlag, New York.

LEE, S. B. and KIM, K. J. (1992) Causal relations among stock returns, interest rates, real activity and inflation, *Journal of Finance*, Vol. 47, No. 4, pp. 1591–1603.

LEE, B. S. (1993) Does the October 1987 crash strengthen the co-movements among national stock markets? *Review of Financial Economics*, Vol. 3, No. 1, pp. 89–104.

LEE, C. F., FINNERTY, J. E. and NORTON, E. A. (1997) *Foundations of Financial Management*, West Publishing Company, New York.

LEE, C. F., SHLEIFER, A. and THALER, R. H. (1991) Investor sentiment and the closed-end fund puzzle, *Journal of Finance*, Vol. 46, pp. 75–109.

LEIBOWITZ, M. L., KOGELMAN, S., BADER, L. N. and DRAVID, A. R. (1994) Interest rate sensitive asset allocation, *Journal of Portfolio Management*, (Spring), pp. 8–15.

LESSARD, D. (1973) International portfolio diversification: A multivariate analysis for a group of Latin American countries, *Journal of Finance*, Vol. 28, No. 3 (June), pp. 619–633.

LESSARD, D. (1974) World, national and industry factors in equity return, *Journal of Finance*, Vol. 26, pp. 379–391.

LEVINE, R. (1997) Financial development and economic growth, *Journal of Economic Literature*, Vol. XXXV, No. 2, pp. 688–726.

LEVY, H. and SARNAT, M. (1970) International diversification of investment portfolios, *American Economic Review*, Vol. 60, No. 4 (September), pp. 668–675.

LEWIS, M. and DAVIS, K. (1987) *Domestic and International Banking*, MIT Press, Cambridge, Massachusetts.

LITTERMAN, R. and WINKELMANN, K. (1996) Managing market exposure, *Risk Management Series*, Goldman Sachs.

LIU, P., SMITH, D. and SYED, A. (1990) Stock reaction to the Wall Street Journal's securities recommendations, *Journal of Financial and Quantitative Analysis*, Vol. 25, pp. 399–410.

LLOYD-DAVIES, P. and CANES, M. (1978) Stock prices and publication of second-hand information, *Journal of Business*, Vol. 51, pp. 43–56.

LOGUE, D. and TUTTLE, D. (1973) Brokerage houses investment advice, *The Financial Review*, Vol. 8, pp. 38–54.

LONGIN, F. M. (1996) The asymptotic distribution of extreme stock market returns, *Journal of Business*, Vol. 63, pp. 383–408.

LONGIN, F. M. (1997) *From VaR to Stress Testing: The Extreme Value Approach*, CERESSEC Working Paper 97–004, ESSEC, Cergy-Pontoise, France.

LONGIN, F. M. and SOLNIK, B. (1995) Is the correlation in international equity returns constant: 1960–1990? *Journal of International Money and Finance*, Vol. 14, pp. 3–26.

LONGIN, F. M. and SOLNIK, B. (1997) *Dependence Structure of International Equity Markets During Extremely Volatile Periods,* Working Paper, ESSEC, Cergy-Pontoise, France.

LOPEZ OBRADOR, A. M. (1999) *Fobaproa: Expediente Abierto,* Grijalbo, Mexico, DF.

LORETAN, M. and PHILLIPS, P. C. B. (1994) Testing covariance stationarity of heavy-tailed series, *Journal of Empirical Finance,* Vol. 1, pp. 211–248.

MACDOUGALL, D. (1977) *Report of the study group on the role of public finance in European integration,* Chaired by Sir Donald MacDougall, Economic and Finance Series, No. A13, Commission of the European Community, Brussels, April.

MCCAULEY, R. N. and WHITE, W. R. (1997) *The Euro and European Financial Markets* Working Paper No. 41, Monetary and Economics Depart, BIS, Basle, May.

MCCLURE, K., GARY, K. and ATKINSON, S. M. (1994) International capital structures: Are there differences among G7 nations, *Journal of Business and Economic Perspectives,* Vol. 21, p. 2.

MCINISH, T. H. and LAU, S. T. (1993) Co-movements of international equity returns: A comparison of the pre- and post-October 19, 1987 periods, *Global Finance Journal,* Vol. 4, No. 1, pp. 1–19.

MCKINNON, R. I. (1973) *Money and Capital in Economic Development,* Brookings Institution, Washington DC.

MACEDO, R. (1995) Value, relative strength and volatility in global equity country selection, *Financial Analysts Journal,* (March/April), pp. 70–78.

MAHAJAN, A., RANGAN, N. and ZARDKOOHI, A. (1996) Cost structures in multinational and domestic banking, *Journal of Banking and Finance,* Vol. 20, pp. 238–306.

MALHOTRA, D. K. and MCLEOD, R. W. (2000) Closed-end fund expenses and investment selection, *Financial Review,* Vol. 35, No. 1, pp. 85–104.

MALLIARIS, A. G. and URRUTIA, J. L. (1992) The international crash of October 1987: Causality tests, *Journal of Financial and Quantitative Analysis,* Vol. 27, No. 3, pp. 353–364.

MANDELBROT, B. (1963) The variation of certain speculative prices, *Journal of Business,* Vol. 36, pp. 394–419.

MARKOWITZ, H. (1991) *Portfolio Selection: Efficient Diversification of Investments,* Blackwell, Oxford.

MASSON, P. R. (1996) Fiscal dimensions of EMU, *Economic Journal,* Vol. 106, pp. 996–1004.

MATHUR, I. and SUBRAHMANYAM, V. (1990) Interdependencies among the Nordic and US stock markets, *Scandinavian Journal of Economics,* Vol. 92, pp. 587–597.

MATHUR, I. and WAHEED, A. (1995) Stock price reactions to securities recommended in Business Week's Inside Wall Street, *The Financial Review,* Vol. 30, pp. 583–604.

MAYER, C. (1989) Financial systems, corporate finance and economic development, in G. R. G. Hubbard (ed.) *Asymmetric Information, Corporate Finance and Investment,* University of Chicago, Chicago, Illinois.

MENCHACA TREJO, M. (1998) *El Mercado de Dinero en Mexico,* Trillas, Mexico, DF.

MENDENHALL, W., MCCLAVE, J. T. and RAMMEY, M. (1977) *Statistics for Psychology,* 2nd edition, Dubury Press, Massachusetts, pp. 143–154.

MERIC, G., LEVEEN, S. S. and MERIC, I. (1991) The financial characteristics of commercial banks involved in interstate acquisitions, *Financial Review*, (Spring), pp. 75–90.

MERIC, I. and MERIC, G. (1989) Potential gains from international portfolio diversification and inter-temporal stability of international stock market relationships, *Journal of Banking and Finance*, Vol. 13, pp. 627–640.

MERIC, I. and MERIC, G. (1994) A comparison of the financial characteristics of US and Japanese manufacturing firms, *Global Finance Journal*, Vol. 5, No. 1, pp. 205–218.

MERIC, I. and MERIC, G. (1997) Co-movements of European equity markets before and after the 1987 crash, *Multinational Finance Journal*, Vol. 1, No. 2, pp. 137–152.

MERIC, I. and MERIC, G. (1998) Correlation between the world's stock markets before and after the 1987 crash, *Journal of Investing*, Vol. 7, No. 3, pp. 67–70.

MERIC, I., RATNER, M., LEAL, R. and MERIC, G. (1998) Co-movements of Latin American equity markets, *International Journal of Finance*, Vol. 10, No. 3, pp. 1163–1178.

MERIC, I., ROSS, L. W., WEIDMAN, S. M. and MERIC, G. (1997) A comparison of the financial characteristics of US and Japanese chemical firms, *Multinational Business Review*, (Fall), pp. 23–27.

MERTON, R. (1974) On the pricing of corporate debt: The risk structure of interest rates, *Journal of Finance*, Vol. 29, pp. 449–470.

MESTER, L. (1993) Efficiency in the savings and loan industry, *Journal of Banking and Finance*, (April), pp. 267–286.

MEEUSEN, W. and BROECK, J. (1977) Efficiency estimation from Cobb–Douglas production function with composed error, *International Economic Review*, (June), pp. 435–444.

MICHAUD, R. O., BERGSTROM, G. M., FRASHURE, R. D. and WOLAHAN, B. K. (1996) Twenty years of international equity investing, *Journal of Portfolio Management*, (Fall), pp. 9–22.

MISHKIN, F. S. (1998) The Mexican financial crisis of 1994–95: An asymmetric information analysis, in S. S. Rehman (ed.), *Financial Crisis Management in Regional Blocs*, Kluwer Academic Publishers, Boston.

MODIGLIANI, F. and MILLER, M. H. (1958) The cost of capital, corporation finance, and the theory of investment, *American Economic Review*, Vol. 48, pp. 261–297.

MODIGLIANI, F. and MILLER, M. H. (1963) Corporate income taxes and the cost of capital: A correction, *American Economic Review*, Vol. 53, pp. 433–443.

MONTAGNON, P. (1998) Recovery hangs on reform and refinancing, *Financial Times*, January 16, p. 8.

MOSKOW, M. H. (2000) *Disruption in Global Financial Markets: The Role of Public Policy*, Paper presented at the Global Finance Conference, April 21.

MULUGETTA, A. and MULUGETTA, Y. (1997a) The influence of exchange rates, institutional holdings, volume of shares traded and indices on discount or premium of single-country closed-end funds, *Journal of International Finance*, Vol. 9, pp. 607–624.

MULUGETTA, A. and MULUGETTA, Y. (1997b) Inter-temporal relationship between the movements of prices of closed-endfunds and currencies, in the *Proceedings of the 1997 Association for Global Business*, Washington DC.

MULUGETTA, A., GHOSH, D. K. and MULUGETTA, Y. (1998) *Regional and Country Closed-End Funds in Currencies Crisis*, Paper presented at the 1998 Association for Global Finance, Mexico City.

MYERS, S. C. and MAJLUF, N. (1984) Corporate financing and investment decisions when firms have information that investors do not have, *Journal of Financial Economics*, Vol. 13, pp. 187–221.

NELSON, D. B. (1991) Conditional heteroskedasticity in asset returns: A new approach, *Econometrica*, Vol. 59, pp. 347–370.

O'BRIEN, T. J. (1996) *Global Financial Management*, John Wiley and Sons Inc., New York.

OJAH, K. and KAREMERA, D. (1999) Random walks and market efficiency tests of Latin American equity markets: A revisit, *Financial Review*, Vol. 34, No. 2, pp. 57–72.

ORTIZ, E. (1993) Emerging markets and economic development, in K. FATEMI and D. SALVATORE (eds.), *Foreign Exchange Issues, Capital Markets and International Banking in the 1990s*, Taylor and Francis, Washington DC.

ORTIZ, E. (1995) Take-off into development and emerging capital markets: Stages of financial development and equity financing, in H. P. GRAY and S. C. RICHARD (eds.), *International Finance in the New World Order*, Pergamon, New York.

ORTIZ, E. (2000a) La inversión extranjera de portafolios en los mercados de dinero y capital de Mexico y su impacto en la crisis Mexicana, in I. MANRIQUE-CAMPOS (ed.), *Arquitectura de la Crisis Financiera*, Miguel Angel Porrua, Mexico, DF.

ORTIZ, E. (2000b) *Crisis and the Future of the Mexican Banking System*, Working Paper, Universidad Nacional Autónoma de México.

OUDIZ, G. and SACHS, J. D. (1984) Macroeconomic policy coordination among the industrial economies, *Brookings Papers on Economic Activity*, Vol. 1, pp. 1–64.

PARK, K. and RATTI, R. A. (2000) Real activity, inflation, stock returns and monetary policy, *Financial Review*, Vol. 35, No. 2, pp. 59–78.

PASTOR, J. M., PÉREZ, F. and QUESADA, J. (1997) Efficiency analysis in banking firms: An international comparison, *European Journal of Operational Research*, pp. 119–223.

PATELIS, A. D. (1997) Stock return predictability and the role of monetary policy, *Journal of Finance*, Vol. 52, pp. 1951–1972.

PATRICK, H. T. (1966) Financial development and economic growth in underdeveloped countries, *Development and Cultural Change*, Vol. 14, No. 2, pp. 77–97.

PEEK, J., ROSENGREN, E. S. and KASIRYE, F. (1999) The poor performance of foreign bank subsidiaries: Were the problems acquired or created? *Journal of Banking and Finance*, Vol. 22, No. 6, pp. 799–819.

POON, S-H. and TAYLOR, S. J. (1992) Stock returns and volatility: An empirical study of the UK stock market, *Journal of Banking and Finance*, Vol. 16, pp. 37–59.

POSHAKWALE, S. (1996) Emerging markets as new channels for international diversification, *Manchester Business School*, pp. 6–7.

PRAETZ, P. D. (1972) The distribution of share price changes, *Journal of Business*, Vol. 45, pp. 49–55.

PRESS, S. J. (1967) A compound events model for security prices, *Journal of Business*, Vol. 40, pp. 317–335.

RAGUNATHAN, V., FAFF, R. W. and BROOKS, R. D. (1999) Correlations, business cycles and integration, *Journal of International Financial Markets, Institutions and Money*, Vol. 9, pp. 75–95.

RAJAN, P. and ZINGALES, L. (1995) What do we know about capital structure? Some evidence from international data, *Journal of Finance*, (December), pp. 1421–1460.

RANIS, G. (1995) Another look at the East Asian miracle, *The World Bank Economic Review*, Vol. 9, No. 3 (September), pp. 509–537.

RATNER, M. and LEAL, R. (1996) Causality tests for the emerging markets of Latin America, *Journal of Emerging Markets*, Vol. 1, No. 1, pp. 29–40.

RATNER, M. and LEAL, R. (1999) Tests of technical trading strategies in the emerging markets of Latin America and Asia, *Journal of Banking and Finance*, Vol. 23, No. 12, pp. 1887–1905.

REGE, U. P. (1984) Accounting ratios to locate takeover tagets, *Journal of Business Finance and Accounting*, Vol. 11, No. 3, pp. 301–311.

REHMAN, S. S. (1997) *The Path to European Economic and Monetary Union*, Kluwer Academic Publishers, Boston.

REISEN, H. (1996) Managing volatile capital inflows: The experience of the 1990s, *Asian Development Review*, Vol. 14, pp. 72–96.

REMMERS, L., STONEHILL, A., WRIGHT, R. and BEEKHUISEN, T. (1974) Industry and size as debt ratio determinants in manufacturing internationally, *Financial Management*, (Summer), pp. 23–32.

RICHTER, F-J. (1999) (ed.) *Business Networks in Asia: Promises, Doubts, and Perspectives*, Quorum Books, Westport, Connecticut, and London.

ROLL, R. (1988) The international crash of October 1987, *Financial Analysts Journal*, Vol. 44, No. 5, pp. 19–35.

RUBINSTEIN, M. (1973) The fundamental theorem of parameter preference security valuation, *Journal of Financial and Quantitative Analysis*, Vol. 8, pp. 61–69.

RUTHENBERG, D. and ELIAS, R. (1996) Cost economies and interest rate margins in a unified European banking market, *Journal of Economics and Business*, Vol. 48, pp. 231–249.

RUTHERFORD, J. (1988) An international perspective on the capital structure puzzle, *Midland Corporate Finance Journal*, (Fall), pp. 60–72.

SALA-I-MARTIN, X. and SACHS, J. (1992) Fiscal federalism and optimal currency areas: evidence for Europe from the United States, in CANZONIERI, M. B., GRILLI, V. and MASSON, P. R. (eds.) *Establishing a Central Bank: Issues in Europe and Lessons from the US*, Cambridge University Press, Cambridge, pp. 195–219.

SALOMON BROTHERS (1996) What EMU might mean for European banks, *European Equity Research*, October 29.

SAMUELSON, P. (1970) The fundamental approximation of theorem of portfolio analysis in terms of means, variances and higher moments, *Review of Economic Studies*, Vol. 37, pp. 537–542.

SAUNDERS, A. (2000) *Financial Institutions Management: A Modern Perspective*, 3rd ed., Irwin-McGraw Hill, Boston, Massachussetts.

SCHOLLHAMMER, H. and SAND, O. (1985) The interdependence among the stock markets of major European countries and the United States: An empirical investigation of interrelationships among national stock market movements, *Management International Review*, Vol. 25, No. 1, pp. 17–26.

SCHWARZ, E. and ARONSON, J. R. (1967) Some surrogate evidence in support of the concept of optimal capital structure, *Journal of Finance*, (March), pp. 10–18.

SCOTT, D. (1972) Evidence on the importance of financial structure, *Financial Management,* (Summer), pp. 45–50.

SHAKED, I. (1985) International equity markets and the investment horizon, *Journal of Portfolio Management,* Winter, pp. 80–84.

SHAPIRO, A. C. (1983) *Multinational Financial Management,* Allyn and Bacon, London.

SHARPE, W. F., ALEXANDER, G. J. and BAILEY, J. V. (1998) *Investments,* 6th ed., Prentice Hall, Upper Saddle River, New Jersey.

SHAW, E. S. (1973) *Financial Deepening in Economic Development,* Oxford University Press, New York.

SIEGEL, S. (1956) *Nonparametric Statistics for the Behavioral Sciences,* McGraw Hill, New York.

SIMS, C. (1980) Macroeconomics and reality, *Econometrica,* Vol. 48, No. 1, pp. 1–49.

SINCLAIR, C. D., POWER, D. M., LONIE, A. A. and AVGOUSTINOS, P. (1994) An investigation of the stability of relationships between returns from emerging stock markets, *Dundee Discussion Papers in Accountancy and Business Finance,* FIN/9406, pp. 3–35.

SMITH, R. C. and WALTER, I. (1996) Rethinking emerging markets, *Washington Quarterly,* Vol. 19, No. 1, pp. 45–64.

SOLNIK, B. H. (1974) Why not diversify internationally rather than domestically? *Financial Analysts Journal,* Vol. 30, pp. 48–54.

SOLNIK, B. H. (1995) Why not diversify internationally rather than domestically? *Financial Analysts Journal,* January/February, pp. 89–93.

SOLNIK, B. H., BOUCRELLE, C. and LE FUR, Y. (1996) International market correlation and volatility, *Financial Analysts Journal,* Vol. 52, No. 5, September/October, pp. 17–34.

SPEIDELL, L. S. and SAPPENFIELD, R. (1992) Global diversification in a shrinking world, *Journal of Portfolio Management,* Vol. 19, No. 1 (Fall), pp. 57–67.

STANDARD and POOR'S (2000) *Emerging Stock Markets Factbook 2000.*

STEHLE, R. (1977) An empirical test of the alternative hypothesis of national and international pricing of risky assets, *Journal of Finance,* Vol. 32, No. 2, pp. 493–502.

STEPHENS, A. and PROFFITT, D. (1991) Performance measurement when return distributions are nonsymmetric, *Quarterly Journal of Business and Economics,* Vol. 30, pp. 23–41.

STICKEL, S. E. (1985) The effect of value line investment survey rank changes on common stock prices, *Journal of Financial Economics,* Vol. 14, pp. 121–143.

STIGLITZ, J. E. (1998) What caused Asia's crash?... Bad private sector decisions, *Wall Street Journal,* February 4, p. A22.

STIGLITZ, J. E. (1999) Reforming the global economic architecture: Lessons from recent crises, *Journal of Finance,* Vol. 54, No. 4, pp. 1508–1521.

STUDART, R. (1998) Politicas financieras y crecimiento en el contexto de desarrollo: Lecciones derivadas de América Latina y del Sudoeste Asíatico en los Años Ochenta, *Investigación Económica,* Vol. LVII, No. 1, pp. 15–42.

STULZ, R. (1981) On the effects of barriers to international investment, *Journal of Finance,* Vol. 36, No. 4, pp. 923–934.

SZEKELY, G. (1999) *Fobaproa e IPAB: El Acuerdo que no Debio Ser,* Oceano, Mexico, DF.

TAYI, G and LEONARD, P. (1988) Bank balance-sheet management: An alternative multi-objective model, *Journal of the Operational Research Society*, Vol. 39, pp. 401–410.

THEODOSSIOU, P. (1994) The stochastic properties of major Canadian exchange rates, *Financial Review*, Vol. 29, pp. 193–221.

THEODOSSIOU, P. and LEE, U. (1993) Mean and volatility slipovers across major national stock markets: Further empirical evidence, *Journal of Financial Research*, Vol. 16, pp. 337–350.

THEODOSSIOU, P. and LEE, U. (1995) Relationships between volatility and expected returns across international stock markets, *Journal of Business Finance and Accounting*, Vol. 22, pp. 289–300.

THEODOSSIOU, P., KAHYA, E., KOUTMOS, G. and CHRISTOFI, A. (1997) Volatility reversion and correlation structure of returns in major international stock markets, *Financial Review*, Vol. 32, pp. 205–224.

THOENES, S. (1998) Suharto family benefits in peril from spirit of reforms, *Financial Times*, January 16, p. 6.

THORBECKE, W. (1997) On stock market returns and monetary policy, *Journal of Finance*, Vol. 52, pp. 635–654.

TOBIN, J. (1958) Liquidity preference as behavior towards risk, *Review of Economic Studies*, No. 1, pp. 65–86.

TOBIN, J. (1965) Money and economic growth, *Econometrica*, Vol. 33, No. 4, pp. 671–684.

UNITED NATIONS (1998) *World Investment Report*, United Nations Organization.

UNITED NATIONS (1999) *World Investment Report*, United Nations Organization.

URRUTIA, J. L. (1995) Test of random walk and market efficiency for Latin American equity markets, *Journal of Financial Research*, Vol. 18, pp. 299–309.

VANDER VENNET, R. (1996) The effects of mergers and acquisitions on the efficiency and profitability of EC credit institutions, *Journal of Banking and Finance*, Vol. 20, No. 9, pp. 1531–1558.

VAZIRI, M. T. and SHALCHI, H. (1992) Are the US firms inferior to Japanese firms in profitability and management, in K. FATEMI, ed., *International Trade and Finance in a Rapidly Changing Environment*, International Trade and Finance Association, Loredo, Texas.

VON HAGEN, J. and EICHENGREEN, B. (1996) Federalism, fiscal restraints and European monetary union, *American Economic Review*, Vol. 86, No. 2, pp. 134–138.

WALTER, A. (1981) Supervisory performance of foreign-controlled US banking organization, in US Comptroller of the Currency, *Foreign Acquisition of US Banks*, Robert. R. Dame, Richmond, Virginia, pp. 329–342.

WHEATLEY, S. (1988) Some tests of international equity integration, *Journal of Financial Economics*, Vol. 21, No. 2, pp. 177–212.

WHITE, D. (1997) Costs to banks for Euro switch 'overestimated' *Financial Times*, June 10.

WILLOUGHBY, J. (1998) Caught in the WEBS, *Institutional Investor*, Vol. 32, No. 12, p. 164.

WILSON, T. C. (1996) Calculating risk capital, in C. Alexander (ed.) *The Handbook of Risk Management and Analysis*, John Wiley and Sons, Chichester.

WOLF, JR., C. (1998) What caused Asia's crash?...Too much government control, *Wall Street Journal*, February 4, p.A22.

WORLD BANK, THE (1993) *The East Asian Miracle: Economic Growth and Public Policy*, Oxford University Press, New York.

WORLD BANK, THE (1996) *Global Economic Prospects and the Developing Countries*, The World Bank, Washington DC.

WORLD BANK, THE (1997) *The World Development Report 1997*, The World Bank, Washington DC.

WORLD BANK, THE (1997) *Private Capital Flows to Developing Countries, the Road to Financial Integration*, Oxford University Press, Oxford.

WORLD BANK, THE (1998) *Global Economic Prospects and the Developing Countries. Beyond Financial Crisis*, The World Bank, Washington DC.

WORLD BANK, THE (1998a) *East Asia: The Road to Recovery*, The World Bank, Washington DC.

WORLD BANK, THE (1998b) *The World Development Report 1998/99*, The World Bank, Washington DC.

WORLD BANK, THE (1999) *The World Development Report 1999/2000*, The World Bank, Washington DC.

WORTHY, F. S. (1989) When somebody wants a payoff, *Fortune*, Vol. 120, No. 13 (Autumn), p. 117(4).

ZERVOS, S. J. (1996) Industry and Country Components in emerging market stock returns, *Discussion Paper 96-02*, Centre for Empirical Research in Finance, Brunel University.

Author Index

The location of contributors' chapters in this book are shown in *italic*. (n) after some page numbers refers to one or more notes cited on that page; the notes appear at the end of the chapter.

Subject Index